# Creative Fidelity

# American Catholic Identities
## A Documentary History
*Christopher J. Kauffman, General Editor*

American Catholic Identities is a nine-volume series that makes available to the general reader, the student, and the scholar seminal documents in the history of American Catholicism. Subjects are wide-ranging and topically ordered within periods to encounter the richly textured experiences of American Catholics from the earliest years to the present day. The twenty-six editors of these volumes reveal a command of trends in historiography since the publication of John Tracy Ellis's three-volume work, *Documents of American Catholic History.* Hence the American Catholic Identities series shows developments in our understanding of social history — the significance of gender, race, regionalism, ethnicity, and spirituality, as well as Catholic thought and practice before and since the Second Vatican Council.

The series elucidates myriad meanings of the American Catholic experience by working with the marker of religious identity. It brings into relief the historical formations of religious self-understandings of a wide variety of Catholics in a society characterized by the principles of religious liberty, separation of church and state, religious pluralism, and voluntarism.

American Catholic Identities is united by such dominant factors in American history as waves of immigration, nativism, anti-Catholicism, racism, sexism, and several other social and ideological trends. Other aspects of unity are derived from American Catholic history: styles of episcopal leadership, multiple and various types of Catholic institutions, and the dynamic intellectual interaction between the United States and various national centers of Catholic thought. Woven into the themes of this documentary history are the protean meanings of what constitutes being American and Catholic in relation to the formations of religious identities.

Titles of books in the series are:

*Public Voices: Catholics in the American Context,* Steven M. Avella and Elizabeth McKeown

*The Frontiers and Catholic Identities,* Anne M. Butler, Michael E. Engh, S.J., and Thomas W. Spalding, C.F.X.

*Creative Fidelity: American Catholic Intellectual Traditions,* R. Scott Appleby, Patricia Byrne, C.S.J., and William L. Portier

*Keeping Faith: European and Asian Catholic Immigrants,* Jeffrey M. Burns, Ellen Skerrett, and Joseph M. White

*Prayer and Practice in the American Catholic Community,* Joseph P. Chinnici, O.F.M., and Angelyn Dries, O.S.F.

*Gender Identities in American Catholicism,* Paula Kane, James Kenneally, and Karen Kennelly, C.S.J.

*"Stamped with the Image of God": African-Americans as God's Image in Black,* Cyprian Davis, O.S.B., and Jamie Phelps, O.P.

*¡Presente! U.S. Latino Catholics from Colonial Origins to the Present,* Timothy Matovina and Gerald E. Poyo, in collaboration with Cecilia González-Andrieu, Steven P. Rodríguez, and Jaime R. Vidal

*The Crossing of Two Roads: Being Catholic and Native in the United States,* Marie Therese Archambault, O.S.F., Mark G. Thiel, and Christopher Vecsey

A workshop for the editors of these books was entirely funded by a generous grant from the Louisville Institute.

**American Catholic Identities**
**A Documentary History**
*Christopher J. Kauffman, General Editor*

# Creative Fidelity

## *American Catholic Intellectual Traditions*

R. Scott Appleby

Patricia Byrne, C.S.J.

William L. Portier

Editors

ORBIS BOOKS

Maryknoll, New York 10545

Founded in 1970, Orbis Books endeavors to publish works that enlighten the mind, nourish the spirit, and challenge the conscience. The publishing arm of the Maryknoll Fathers and Brothers, Orbis seeks to explore the global dimensions of the Christian faith and mission, to invite dialogue with diverse cultures and religious traditions, and to serve the cause of reconciliation and peace. The books published reflect the opinions of their authors and are not meant to represent the official position of the Maryknoll Society. To obtain more information about Maryknoll and Orbis Books, please visit our website at www.maryknoll.org.

**Library of Congress Cataloging-in-Publication Data**

Creative fidelity : American Catholic intellectual traditions / R. Scott Appleby, Patricia Byrne, William L. Portier, editors.
    p. cm. — (American Catholic identities)
  Includes bibliographical references and index.
  ISBN 1-57075-454-3 – ISBN 1-57075-349-0 (pbk.)
    1. Catholics – United States – Intellectual life. I. Appleby, R. Scott, 1956- II. Byrne, Patricia. III. Portier, William L. IV. Series.
BX1407.I5 C74 2004
282′.73 – dc22

                      2003018675

*To*
*James Hennesey, S.J.*
*1926–2001*
*who died as this volume was being produced,*
*leaving a profound legacy of humanity and scholarship*

# CONTENTS

## Part 1
## INTELLECTUAL LIFE

## Part 2
## SCHOLASTICISMS AND THOMISMS

## Part 3
## CATHOLIC EDUCATION
## IN THE UNITED STATES:
## FOUNDATIONS

## Part 4
## CATHOLIC EDUCATION:
## TWENTIETH-CENTURY DEVELOPMENTS

# Part 5
# CHURCH AND STATE

# Part 6
# MORAL THEOLOGY AND SOCIAL THOUGHT

# Part 7
# SPIRITUALITY AND ART

# Part 8
# THEOLOGY AND SCIENCE

# Part 9
# THE PATH TO VATICAN II

# Part 10
# THE CONTESTED LEGACY OF VATICAN II

# FOREWORD

## *Christopher J. Kauffman*

It is appropriate that this book is dedicated to the historian James Hennesey, S.J., whose book on the American Catholic bishops at Vatican I initiated a new era in historiography, one that led to a fresh understanding of Americanism. The editors of this volume are indebted to Hennesey's theological interpretation of the period. His scholarship was complemented by an artful style of teaching and lecturing laced with wit, humor, and candor. Father Hennesey inspired a generation of historians, as is evident in the festschrift published by the *U.S. Catholic Historian* (Fall 1996), in which his former student Patricia Bryne, C.S.J., published a piece on Hennesey's many publications. William L. Portier also published an article in that special issue, while R. Scott Appleby's book on the relationship between Americanism and Modernism begins with Hennesey's ideas. He was known for his commitment to elucidate the relationships between theology and history, and the dedication is a fitting tribute by three editors who dwell in the interstices of that relationship. Like Hennesey, they would tend to identify themselves as historians of American Catholicism but also teach and publish in areas informed by theology and religious history.

In his Introduction to this engaging documentary history of American Catholic intellectual traditions R. Scott Appleby elaborates on the meanings of its title and on its basic themes. The reader will note the significance of the philosopher Alasdair MacIntyre in expanding the understanding of the relationships between tradition, knowledge, and wisdom, as well as the programs and activities that support these relationships. Rather than reiterate the philosopher's thoughts, I prefer to underscore a salient feature of this book: this and each of the ten introductions have organizing principles and conceptual frameworks that integrate the documents according to ideas and trends. In a very real sense the reader is treated with introductory essays that together form a contribution to Catholic intellectual life.

Catholic education cultivated separatism, driven by the need to provide a protective canopy in a society given to fits of nativism and anti-Catholicism. Though most historians refer to this separatism in terms of the Catholic subculture, Appleby prefers the term "Christian subculture," which he defines as a "set of shared symbols and practices [that] powerfully shaped the personal identity of church members, including their perceptions of and attitudes toward society." Patricia Byrne notes that Catholic education was influenced by trends in the public schools and was shaped "by a tension between the options of separation from and assimilation to the predominant (Protestant, then secular) culture."

Appleby explains that "this tension between resistance and accommodation to mainstream social norms and practices shapes the traditional American Catholic 'argument' over church and state, science, literature, politics, and theology, as well as education; it therefore constitutes a major theme of this volume." The last two parts on the movement toward Vatican II and the conflicting legacy of the council cannot be explained by the resistance-accommodation model but rather by the "tradition of Catholic pluralism." Each part is therefore thematically integrated; they are also in chronological sequence culminating in the period from the 1960s to the 1990s (except for the first part on Catholic education). It is significant to note that nearly 33 percent of the documents in this volume fall into the contemporary period of the 1960s through the 1990s.

A thorny problem for the editors of each of the nine volumes in this series is the principle of selectivity and the topical arrangement of the material. The editors of this volume on Catholic intellectual traditions could have designed the book with fewer than ten topics but its coherence would have been fragmented by the stretching of the relationships among the documents. The choice of topics appears to have determined the types of material suitable for some parts such as "Catholic Education" and "Spirituality and Art." Because of the many documents that need to be included, it was a matter of placing them in congenial and discrete relationships, resulting in precise titles of parts of a book characterized by clarity, intelligence, and commitment.

The inclusive character of the book is an obvious mark of its identity. Besides reflecting the historical trends in theology and philosophy, its documents also illuminate the several spheres of education, science, and the American Catholic imagination. Though Appleby's reflection on the meanings of the title will engage the readers, it is important to note that the structure of the book is both creative and faithful to it purpose. Without a comprehensive text steeped in the primary sources there was no model for this book. The editors creatively designed a book that reveals the complexities of faith as articulated in the academy, in the church, and in society. After the readers encounter ninety-five documents divided into ten topical parts introduced by experts who weave patterns of relationships between American and Catholic dimensions of intellectual traditions broadly considered, they will conclude that this book is appropriate for undergraduate and graduate courses, as well as for professors engaged in research for scholarly articles.

# ACKNOWLEDGMENTS

Many talented historians and archivists made this volume of primary sources possible. We thank Barbara Baer, C.S.J., Sisters of St. Joseph, Wichita; Mark Harvey, State Archives of Michigan; David Poremba, Burton Historical Collection, Detroit Public Library; Shawn Weldon, Philadelphia Archdiocesan Historical Research Center; Tricia Pynne and Janine M. Bruce, Sulpician Archives, St. Mary's Seminary and University, Baltimore; Charline Sullivan, C.S.J., Archives of Sisters of St. Joseph of Carondelet, St. Louis Province; Msgr. Roman Nir and Chris Tyburski, Archives of the Orchard Lake Schools; Luke Salm, F.S.C., Archives of the De La Salle Christian Brothers, Manhattan College, New York; Barbara Keebler, Director of Communications, NCEA, Washington, D.C.; Patricia Lynch, S.B.S., Archives, Xavier University, New Orleans; Dr. Stephanie Morris, Archives, Sisters of the Blessed Sacrament, Bensalem, Pennsylvania; Phil Runkel, Marquette University Archives, Milwaukee; Sue Miller, S.C.L., Sisters of Charity of Leavenworth; Ann Leonard, R.S.C.J., General Archives of the Society of the Sacred Heart, Villa Lante, Rome; Aidan Kavanaugh, O.S.B., Yale University Divinity School; David Holeton, Societas Liturgica; Paul F. Bradshaw, *Studia Liturgica;* Mary Elizabeth Sperry, USCCB Publishing, Washington, D.C.; Patricia J. Bunker, Mary Curry, and Jennifer van Sickle, Trinity College Library; and Katherine A. McCloskey, '03, Trinity College, Hartford.

We are grateful to Professor Maureen Tilley of the University of Dayton for her fine translation of the selection from Francis Kenrick's *Theologia Moralis.* Thanks are also due to Timothy Dillon, Jane Leukart, and Vernon Meyer, doctoral students at the University of Dayton and stalwart researchers in helping to assemble the selections in Parts 1, 5, and 6. Thanks as well to the staff at Phillips Library, Mount Saint Mary's College, Emmitsburg, Md.

Two talented historians of American religion and culture — Christopher Shannon and James McCartin — deserve a share of editorial credit for helping to select some of the sources. They also tracked down documents, entered them into the manuscript, and acquired reprint permissions. Chris and Jim were typically meticulous and shrewd in their work for this volume, and we stand in their debt.

The staff of the Cushwa Center for the Study of American Catholicism, especially the omnicompetent Barbara Lockwood, contributed dozens of hours of careful secretarial work.

This series and volume is the brainchild of our esteemed friend and colleague Christopher J. Kauffman. Chris continues to inspire us with his prodigious service to church and academy, reflected in the energy and devotion he gives to the fostering of research and scholarly writing in American Catholic history.

Typically in a project one person stands out in the mind of the author or editors as indispensable to its success. In this case that person is William R. Burrows, managing editor of Orbis Books. From start to finish Bill provided sage advice, encouragement, and consolation. We salute the intellectual tradition of excellence in Catholic and religious publishing, editing, and mentoring personified by Bill Burrows.

# GENERAL INTRODUCTION

## R. Scott Appleby

Virtually any title for a volume of this kind would be an exercise in hyperbole. No single edited and annotated collection of primary source documents could begin to encompass the range of achievements by American Catholics in the realm of ideas and imagination over the course of more than two centuries. Nor can one volume settle the contested question of what constitutes a noteworthy contribution to "intellectual life," broadly defined. *Creative Fidelity: American Catholic Intellectual Traditions* is, we suppose, no more or less misleading than various alternatives. But misleading it is. And possibly presumptuous, for good measure.

## Definition of Terms

Let's begin with the subtitle. The phrase "American Catholic Intellectual Traditions" is, on the face of it, imprecise and ambiguous. "American" is a slippery and controversial term, especially when used, as it is here, to refer to "citizens of the United States of America." Peoples living in the western hemisphere north and south of the United States also lay claim to the term "American," as do the descendants of the native tribes that inhabited the precolonial continents of north and south "America." In addition, many Roman Catholics themselves object heatedly to the term "American Catholic," insofar as it implies a church or religious body set apart and separate from the Church of Rome. We are Roman Catholics who happen to live in the United States, they insist.

"Catholic" is itself an inherently imprecise term, whose ambiguity lies in its open-ended referent: virtually any enduring idea or practice associated with Christianity registers as "catholic," if that term is defined, in the original Greek, as "that which permeates the whole" (*kath holous*). Doctrinaire Roman Catholics worry that the use of the term "Catholic" without the modifier "Roman" opens the door to every variety of belief and practice, however loosely connected to orthodox faith and morals as defined by the *magisterium* (the teaching office of the Roman Catholic Church, composed of the pope and the other bishops in full communion with him). The underlying anxiety, in the case of Catholicism in the United States, is that "American," understood as bearing a quite specific political, social, and ethical content, plays an inappropriately important and perhaps decisive role in determining the content of "Catholic."

Finally, to speak of an American Catholic or U.S. Catholic Church implies that Roman Catholicism is a body of affiliated national churches, each with its own constitution or mode of governance unregulated by the Vatican; this is clearly not the case.

Why, then, do we editors employ the term "American Catholic"? Notwithstanding the important concerns mentioned above, we believe that, while the Roman Catholic Church in the United States is not a "national church" in the sense of a self-governing or autonomous entity, it is a culturally and socially distinct body, a reality conveyed by the term "American Catholic." The church in the United States, that is, has evolved in interaction with the distinctive cultural, social, and political environment of the nation. It has therefore been shaped not only by a universal Catholic religious identity mediated by the ecclesial oversight of the Vatican, but also by the specific historical experience of the United States. (The same is true, *mutatis mutandis*, of the Roman Catholic Church in France, Germany, Brazil, etc. Thus we speak of "the French church," "the church of Germany," etc.) In this sense it is accurate and appropriate to speak of an American Catholic experience, and even of American Catholic "traditions" — Catholic ideas and practices that are uniquely American, forged in response to the unique challenges and opportunities that the church has faced in the United States.

The history of church-state relations in this country is a case in point. The constitutional prohibition of an established religion, reinforced by the guarantee of the free exercise of religion and by the freedoms of speech, press, and assembly enshrined in the Bill of Rights, made religion a voluntary pursuit, created a "free marketplace of ideas," and promoted a spirit of competition among religious communities in the United States. Inevitably, Catholicism in its intellectual as well as its institutional life was shaped by these religious and political circumstances. Accordingly, part 5 is devoted to an exploration of the Catholic intellectual tradition that evolved in response to the unique American experience of "church and state."

Which brings us to the final potentially misleading term in our volume subtitle. What is meant by an "intellectual tradition"? When speaking of Catholicism, what counts? Should theology and philosophy take precedence among intellectual disciplines? Do ruminations and writings on church and state — or on Catholic education, spirituality, or art — enjoy equal status?

# Criteria for Selection

In formulating answers to these questions, the philosopher Alasdair MacIntyre provides guidance by explaining the relationship between a tradition of wisdom and knowledge, on the one hand, and the practices that sustain it, on the other. MacIntyre defines a living tradition as "an historically extended, socially embodied argument, and an argument precisely in part about the goods which constitute that tradition."[1] The ongoing discernment of the good occurs through virtuous practices which aim to embody or achieve the good in question.

By "practices," MacIntyre means "any coherent and complex form of socially established cooperative human activity through which the goods internal to that form of activity are realized in the course of trying to achieve those standards of excellence which are appropriate to, and partially definitive of, that form of activity, with the result that human powers to achieve excellence, and human conceptions of the ends and goods involved, are systematically extended."[2] A practice, in other words, enriches the community by enacting the tradition, by living its wisdom and way of life in a particular sphere of activity. Traditions, in turn, being arguments extended across generations, provide the context for contemporary practices.

Finally, MacIntyre argues that a tradition is sustained and strengthened by practices marked by the virtues relevant to that tradition. Such virtues include the intellectual virtues of truthfulness, justice, meticulous attention to detail, rigorous logic, careful use of sources, etc.[3]

Before applying MacIntyre's definitions and insights to the traditions of U.S. Catholicism, a word on the meaning of "intellectual" is necessary. Lest we overlook major achievements of the American Catholic intellect and imagination, we cannot restrict the meaning of "intellectual life" to philosophy and theology. This is true for at least two reasons. First, while the American Catholic community has certainly produced original thinkers in these disciplines, such as Orestes Brownson, John Courtney Murray, David Tracy, Walter Ong, and Mary Daly, all of whom are represented in this volume, many of the most influential philosophers and theologians have been non-U.S. citizens, such as the Europeans Jacques Maritain, Yves Congar, Henri de Lubac, Bernhard Häring, and Karl Rahner, the Peruvian Gustavo Gutiérrez, and the Canadian Bernard Lonergan. Indeed, the genius of the specifically American contribution to modern Catholic theology and philosophy lies less in establishing new traditions than in the elaboration of seminal concepts embedded in the Thomistic tradition. One thinks, for example, of Murray's application of natural law philosophy to American political philosophy, or Tracy's exploration of the analogical imagination.

Second, the unique contribution of Catholicism to the intellectual life of the United States has been the living out of the Catholic communitarian vision of society — a vision rooted in natural law, revealed truth, and the principle of hierarchical authority — in several sectors of U.S. society, including the academy, but also in science, politics and law, the arts, and primary and secondary education. The great contribution of the church in America to the universal church, in turn, has been the development of the Roman Catholic understanding of freedom, the role of the state, and natural rights. This development was

---

1. Alasdair MacIntyre, *After Virtue: A Study in Moral Theory,* 2nd ed. (Notre Dame, Ind.: University of Notre Dame Press, 1984), 222.
2. Ibid., 187.
3. Ibid., 223.

stimulated by U.S. Catholics' encounter with the insights and truths about the human person that are enshrined in the American social contract as codified in the U.S. Constitution. This striking dual legacy of the American Catholic experience has not and could not have been confined to theology and philosophy per se; it had to be, and has been, worked out and given expression, albeit with varying degrees of influence and success, in literature, cinema, art, science, higher education, political philosophy, social ethics, and cultural studies.

Applying MacIntyre's insights to the historical narrative of American Catholicism, then, we understand "intellectual traditions" as multigenerational arguments among U.S. Catholics, and between Catholics and non-Catholics, about the nature of "the good" — that is, about what constitutes "excellence" in the practice of education, art, the sciences, theology, literature, cinema, philosophy, history, ecclesial life, and so on. These arguments, moreover, form the context for evaluating the current practices designed to achieve those ends.

Accordingly, we prepared chapters spanning a range of disciplines and sectors of U.S. society. Finding material for these chapters was not difficult, for Catholics have been deeply involved in each of these areas, as one would expect from a people given over to seeing God's presence in virtually everything — "permeating the whole," as it were.

Selecting the material to include was the difficult task. What drove our selection process, in addition to limitations of space and availability of sources for reprinting? In retrospect, looking back over this completed volume, it seems that we editors were drawn to passages that addressed the following MacIntyrean questions: Which virtues are appropriate to these traditions? What practices were best suited to help American Catholics realize the internal, or inherent, goods carried by these traditions? That is to say: we were drawn to authors and excerpts that reflected insightfully and consequentially on questions of meaning and method, on the why and the how of the "intellectual" activity in which each author was engaged.

# Common Themes

American Catholics have been engaged, first and foremost, in educating and forming children, teens, and young adults. Catholic education in the United States, as Patricia Byrne notes in her introduction to part 3, "is the largest private educational enterprise known to history." The two sections on Catholic education compiled and edited by Professor Byrne constitute a significant contribution to the historical record on the subject, in that they provide annotated primary sources, covering both the nineteenth and twentieth centuries, that are critical to an understanding of the topic but have not been previously anthologized.

Intentional, organized efforts to educate children, teens, and young adults hold a central place in the history of Christian pedagogy. In certain settings religious education has occurred within the context of formal schooling in a variety of subjects. Elsewhere, Catholic educators have embraced a more expansive approach, working with a notion similar to Lawrence Cremin's sense of education as "the deliberate, systematic, and sustained effort to transmit, evoke, or acquire attitudes, values, skills, or sensibilities, as well as any outcomes of that effort."[4] This concept of education preserves the intentional character of education while focusing attention not only on the school and professional teachers, but on other settings, individuals, and institutions — e.g., the family, the workplace, the congregation — which participated powerfully in the educative process.

Whatever the setting, Catholic education was conducted by and for the community of believers; it strove to strengthen and perpetuate a Christian subculture, or set of shared symbols and practices, in the United States; and it powerfully shaped the personal identity of church members, including their perceptions of and attitudes toward society.

Byrne brings these generalities to life by making available documentary evidence of their concrete historical expression. In fine MacIntyrean form she focuses on the why and how, the meaning and methods, of Catholic educational practices over the centuries. Regarding the former, she notes that Catholic education, in the United States as in Europe (whence came most of the religious orders that built and staffed the American Catholic schools), has always been distinguished by the mission of *formation* that stands at its heart.

What, precisely, is meant by formation, and how did the goal of forming Catholics (and, eventually, non-Catholics) both reflect and shape the historical situation in which Catholic educators pursued their mission?

The language of formation is prominent in Pope Pius XI's 1929 encyclical, *The Christian Education of Youth*, which teaches that the "end of Christian education is to cooperate with divine grace in forming the true and perfect Christian, that is, to form Christ Himself in those regenerated by baptism."[5] Mary Boys has described the subsequent Catholic understanding of formation as "a paradoxical process through which one becomes increasingly attentive to one's interiority, and thereby learns ways of transcending self-absorption." In the specific language of Christianity, formation teaches persons to live their baptismal commitments. "It is the process that helps to fashion and sustain a way of life congruent with 'putting on Christ' (Rom. 13:14) or, as the Orthodox put it, with *theosis* (divinization)," she explains. "But, paradoxically, formation does not necessarily *result in* or *cause* transformation, because conversion of life is far more elusive and mysterious than any process of formation can 'produce.'"[6]

The distinctive qualities associated with Catholic education flow from the church's commitment to formation. They include emphasis on the mastery of the basic facts and skills in a variety of subjects; an insistence on order and personal discipline; and the priority given to normative, that is, ethical questions. Such qualities are intended to promote, among other virtues, self-discipline,

---

4. Lawrence Cremin, *Public Education* (New York: Basic Books, 1976).

5. Pope Pius XI, "Divini illius magistri," in Henry Denzinger, *The Sources of Catholic Dogma*, trans. Roy J. Deferrari (St. Louis: B. Herder Book Co., 1957), 581.

6. Mary C. Boys, "Formation in Faith," unpublished paper, March 1, 1993.

studiousness, and dedication to justice and truth. (Recently this educational philosophy has attracted to the U.S. Catholic school system a significant number of non-Catholic, inner-city families hoping to give their children the best possible preparation for economic achievement and social mobility.)[7]

At its peak operating efficiency, U.S. Catholicism provided education and formation in multiple venues, both inside and outside the classroom. Catholics developed what MacIntyre calls practices — including *programs* (e.g., guided retreats and spiritual direction for religious), *disciplines* (e.g., fasting at prescribed times of the week), and *devotions* (e.g., the recitation of the prayers of the Rosary, or daily attendance at mass).[8] Catholic educators of the eighteenth and nineteenth centuries, however, were convinced that such practices would not survive in the cultural and social environment of the United States, which they experienced as unsympathetic and frequently hostile to Roman Catholic values and practices.[9] Such practices, they concluded, must be secured and nurtured within a Catholic educational system.

Inevitably, however, the Catholic educational system took some of its bearings from, even as it competed against, the U.S. common or public school system. The practices of Catholic education, Byrne notes, were shaped in part by a tension between the options of separation from and assimilation to the predominant (Protestant, then secular) culture. This tension between resistance and accommodation to mainstream social norms and practices shapes the traditional American Catholic "argument" over church and state, science, literature, politics, and theology, as well as education; it therefore constitutes a major theme of our volume.

Part 3 charts the balancing of autonomy and adaptation in the educational sphere; and the steps Catholics took to ensure both. An early exemplar was John Carroll, who, shortly before he was elected (by his fellow clergy) the first Roman Catholic bishop of the new nation, developed his vision of Georgetown Academy as a "private" (i.e., nonpublic, non-Protestant) educational institution that, while initially dependent on teachers from Europe, would be staffed eventually by American seminarians and priests drawn from the pool of American "youths [who] will be called to the service of the Church" (document 20a). Carroll, in short, sought a measure of autonomy from Rome as well as from the mainstream Protestant society of the United States. Yet his adaptation to America was almost modest in comparison to that of the incredible Gabriel Richard,

---

7. See Anthony S. Bryk, Valerie E. Lee, and Peter B. Holland, *Catholic Schools and the Common Good* (Cambridge, Mass.: Harvard University Press, 1993).

8. Over the course of the twentieth century, some of these programs, disciplines, and devotions faded, were replaced by others, or were adapted to reflect changed circumstances and understandings of the Christian tradition. After the 1930s, for example, the development of "the lay apostolate" in connection with the Catholic Action movement enabled Catholics to adopt a more inclusive sense of formation, with spiritual direction increasingly seen as necessary for laity as well as priests and religious. Thus, innovative programs of formation, such as the Christian Family Movement, emerged in the 1940s in response to the new understanding of the lay Catholic's role in the world. See Jeffrey M. Burns, *Disturbing the Peace: A History of the Christian Family Movement, 1949–1974* (Notre Dame, Ind.: University of Notre Dame Press, 1999).

9. John T. McGreevy, *Catholics and American Freedom: A History* (New York: W. W. Norton, 2003), 7–42.

who combined in one person a U.S. Congressman's political savvy, an American educator's dedication to the building up of public institutions of higher learning (such as the University of Michigan, which he cofounded), a French Sulpician missionary's zeal for formation, and an American Catholic pastor's concern for the provision of instruction to a diverse populace (doc. 21).

The agents of the drive toward a separate Catholic school system also included the Sisters of the Visitation (doc. 24), whose petition for a monastery and academy for "young females" at Georgetown presaged a wave of academies and schools for women, run by women religious such as the Sisters of St. Joseph (doc. 25); Orestes Brownson, who urged Catholic colleges to upgrade their operations by adopting some of the principles and procedures of well-established public institutions (doc. 27); and John Hughes, archbishop of New York, who resisted assimilation and opted for separation, in part on the grounds that, in the public schools, "religious exercises were used which we did not recognize, and our children were compelled to take part in them" (doc. 26).

Part 4 takes the story into the twentieth century, by which point the separation-or-assimilation dynamic had been subsumed under the banner of "Americanization." As Philip Gleason points out, however, the more encompassing and accurate term for the trend toward rationalization, system, bureaucracy, standardization, and urban sprawl is "modernization."[10] The struggle with modernity is evident on virtually every page of the section. It colors Father Francis Gigot's rationale, formulated in 1900, for his attempt to incorporate the higher criticism of the Bible into the curriculum at St. Joseph's Seminary (a.k.a. Dunwoodie) in Yonkers, New York — an attempt that ultimately failed because it was tarred with the charge of "Modernism" (doc. 32). It looms as the background to the Land O'Lakes statement signed by representatives of nine American Catholic universities in 1967. The statement, which constitutes the charter of the modern Catholic university in the United States, unambiguously embraced the American university tradition of academic freedom (doc. 40). Nineteenth- and early twentieth-century educational methods and practices are on trial — and found wanting by the standards of "modern" pedagogy — in Mary Perkins Ryan's polemic against parochial schools in 1964 (doc. 39), no less than in Sister Madeleva Wolff's vision, articulated in 1949, of the (vital, enthusiastic, quick-minded) teacher-sister of the future (doc. 37). Discontent with the status quo, aggravated by awareness and envy of secular standards of excellence, are the threads of continuity binding together these diverse reformers in their disparate settings.

If, as the documents on education suggest, American Catholic intellectual traditions were shaped by continuous negotiation with modernity, then one can appreciate the near-inevitability of the countermodernist role played by Thomism — another major theme of this volume. American Catholic intellectuals' enthusiastic reception of the nineteenth-century revival of the thought of St. Thomas Aquinas (1224–74) reflected their eagerness to chart a course

---

10. Philip Gleason, *Contending with Modernity: Catholic Higher Education in the Twentieth Century* (New York and Oxford: Oxford University Press, 1995), 21–80 passim.

between the alternatives of the unsatisfying separatism associated with the immigrant ghetto, on the one hand, and uncritical assimilation into the host society, on the other. The choice of Aquinas must have seemed divinely inspired. (Leo XIII, papal patron of the revival, implied as much.) Here at hand was a comprehensive, encompassing system of thought that yielded nothing to secular modernity in its celebration of the wonders of human reason, but which anticipated the limitations of reason with a sense of realism that post–world war American intellectuals would come to share. With their commitment to taking into account the workings of divine grace in human affairs now fortified by the priority Thomism gives to the supernatural order, American Catholics could compete — intellectually, culturally, psychologically — on terms they found acceptable. Thus armed, they built a viable, indeed vibrant, subculture that produced the most sustained flowering of intellectual and artistic creativity prior to the ferment surrounding the Second Vatican Council.

Part 2 charts the American history of Scholasticism, neo-Scholasticism, Thomism, neo-Thomism — terms that are used interchangeably to refer to the neo-Thomist revival — that is, to the "updated" medieval intellectual system that undergirded American Catholicism from the 1880s to the 1950s. Something of the intensity, vitality, and dramatic, conversion-inspiring character of Thomism, as it was popularized among Catholics during the first half of the twentieth century, is on display in Thomas Merton's account of his intellectual and spiritual awakening — stimulated, naturally, by his reading of the great Thomist philosopher, Étienne Gilson (doc. 17). The intellect and the spirit, reason and faith, were intertwined and inseparable in the self-understanding of the famous American Trappist monk and author; and millions of American Catholics shared his conviction that the Catholic worldview — as presented in the Baltimore Catechism, ritualized and celebrated in the Latin Mass, and embedded in Catholic education, art, spirituality, and social action — was a trustworthy guide to reality, a spur to decisive action for the common good, and a path to personal wholeness through the integration of mind, will, and spirit.

Indeed, Thomism was nothing if not integrative, unifying, and pervasive. It was truly "catholic" in every sense of the word. Thomists perceived — and confessed — a divinely ordained integrity of design and purpose binding faith and reason, intellect and will, nature and supernature; they embraced an epistemological realism that located the foundations for knowledge and unity in the order of being itself; and, most consequentially for the American Catholic intellect and imagination, they presented Thomism as an interpretive lens through which virtually every intellectual and imaginative human endeavor could be assessed and, as necessary, transformed.

Thus construed, Thomism did indeed "permeate the whole" of Catholic intellectual life. In the realms of art, literature, and cinema it shaped MacIntyrean "practices" such as critical discernment and craftsmanship (docs. 68–70, 72), and produced skilled practitioners such as Flannery O'Connor and Mary Gordon (docs. 71–73). In the intraecclesial battles over how far Catholics should accommodate or incorporate U.S. church and state, religious freedom, and related points of law and politics, Thomism, when not explicitly invoked, was the taken-for-granted deep background, the uncontested template, informing and shaping every exchange of views (docs. 52–54). Thomistic ethics was the canopy beneath which the particulars of Catholic moral theology and social ethics were refined, tested, and inculcated in generations of schoolchildren, seminarians, and priest-confessors (docs. 56, 58, 60). American Catholic engagement with modern science, most notably in the encounter with the theory of evolution and its offspring in the realm of social engineering (genetic screening, eugenics, artificial birth control, and abortion), was cast, by church officials and their opponents alike, as the application (or misconstrual) of Thomistic natural law teleology (docs. 74–77).

So dominant was Thomism during the formative century of American Catholicism (1850–1950) that its intellectual competitors within the church were defined negatively, that is, in terms of the degree of their departure from the Thomist paradigm. At the turn of the twentieth century a company of priests and bishops opposed to every intellectual trend that threatened the official Catholic/Thomistic philosophy lobbied for the condemnation of "Americanism" and "Modernism." Pope Leo XIII obliged, condemning Americanism in 1899; his successor, Pope Pius X, solemnly condemned Modernism in 1907. The countermodernist Thomists, who are called "integralists" or "neo-Scholastics" in the scholarly literature, included certain Jesuit theologians and philosophers who held influential positions in the Vatican, and their allies in the United States. These men believed that Modernism in the intellectual order manifested itself as Americanism in the political order, and that the bitter root of both heresies was their repudiation of central tenets of Thomism. In their view, Modernists were unduly enamored of critical scientific methods that could reduce the gospel and church to the end products of purely natural and mundane historical processes, and they preferred to think of the divine presence as immanent — indwelling in individuals and historical events, rather than as transcendent, requiring mediation by the established church authorities. In their view, Americanists were unduly enamored of democracy and empirical science ungoverned by overarching metaphysical truths, and they preferred natural virtues and pragmatic action to the supernatural virtues and the life of contemplation and prayer.[11]

It is true that some Catholic intellectuals, such as Isaac Hecker (doc. 14), John Hogan (doc. 57), John Zahm (doc. 74), Dorothy Day (doc. 59), and Pierre Teilhard de Chardin (doc. 78), attempted to balance or complement Thomism with other intellectual traditions because they found it partly or wholly inadequate to meet the specific challenges posed to religious belief and to the church by modern warfare, skepticism, agnosticism, and materialism. Prior to the 1960s, however, few, if any, American Catholic intellectuals fulfilled the integralist stereotype by wholly rejecting the Thomistic worldview in favor of an empiricist, unduly pragmatic Americanism.

---

11. For the classic account of the Americanist episode, see Thomas T. McAvoy, C.S.C., *The Great Crisis in American Catholic History, 1895–1900* (Chicago: H. Regnery, 1957).

By the mid-sixties, however, Thomism had assumed the odor of a stale orthodoxy and fragmented into competing schools whose existence undermined
the illusion of unity. Even Thomas Merton, he of the Thomist-inspired conversion, came to doubt the continuing relevance of the system as it "closed
[St. Thomas] in upon himself in a little triumphalist universe of airtight correctness" (doc. 18). American Catholic intellectuals took up the search for a
successor in earnest.

No one successor was to be found. Theologians and philosophers, historians and sociologists were forced to confront a reality that had characterized
other American Catholic intellectual traditions from the days of John Carroll — namely, the reality of internal pluralism, a third major theme that runs
throughout this volume. In education, health care, and the social justice apostolate in particular, the fact of racial, ethnic, and class diversity was undeniable:
The Catholic Church, perhaps more than any other U.S. denomination, contained within its ranks the vast range of peoples that compose the United States
of America.

We have made much of MacIntyre's notion of practices — activities through
which the goods internal to that form of activity are realized. Perhaps it is inaccurate to speak of the "practice of diversity," but it is surely correct to identify
practices or activities that honored the fact of diversity by making provision
for the particular needs of each ethnic, racial, or socioeconomic group. Accordingly, in keeping with our criteria of selection that features distinctive Catholic
practices and virtues, we have included testimonials to the multigenerational
efforts of American Catholics to serve the common good by transforming
mere diversity into genuine pluralism. Thus, the sections on Catholic education give attention to black Catholics' struggle for educational equality within
the Catholic system (docs. 22, 33); to poor and marginalized youth who were
educated by the Christian Brothers, among other religious orders (doc. 31); to
Polish immigrants seeking to enter the seminary (doc. 28); and to the special
instructional needs of Native American tribes (doc. 41). Although hardly a minority, women assumed prominent roles in education (docs. 33–34, 37–39) and
established a Catholic feminist tradition in theology (docs. 79, 89). Catholic
moral theology and social action, from slavery to civil rights, struggled, with
mixed results, to address the fact of racial diversity in a manner consistent with
the gospel and the Christian tradition (docs. 56, 85).

Despite the effort of neo-Scholastic conservatives to deny the reality of internal pluralism in Roman Catholic theology and philosophy, alternatives to the
Thomistic synthesis could not be suppressed. They burst forth in the 1960s,
triggered not only by the Second Vatican Council (1962–65) but by the historical researches promoted by Thomism itself. As I mention in the introduction to
part 9, neo-Thomism took history seriously. The retrieval of Aquinas's writings
in their original historical context inspired the scholarly exploration of other
Christian traditions, most significantly those established in the apostolic era.
Eventually the models for theology and ecclesiology multiplied, a process that
was further stimulated by the turn to subjective historical experience as a privileged source of theological reflection. Practically, for the purposes of intellectual

inquiry and constructive work in philosophy and theology, the people of God, Vatican II's biblically resonant image of the church, was rendered as the *peoples* of God. The inculturation of the gospel naturally led to the inculturation of theologies, triggering a dizzying and wonderfully creative explosion of world theologies, liberation theologies, ecumenical theologies, feminist theologies, mujerista theologies, and so on.

American Catholics embraced and helped to develop this "tradition of Catholic pluralism." Parts 9 and 10 provide the documentation. Excerpts provide elements of the argument in favor of pluralism (and religious freedom) articulated by Catholic intellectuals such as John Courtney Murray (doc. 82) and David Tracy (doc. 93). Joseph C. Fenton (doc. 81), David L. Greenstock (doc. 83) and others represent the dissenting side of this tradition.

# Faithfully Creative?

So much for our imprecise and misleading subtitle. In the opening paragraph of this essay, I suggested that the main title of our volume, *Creative Fidelity*, might be considered presumptuous. The presumption seems clear: who are we to judge the quality of the intellectual traditions represented here, in terms either of creativity or faithfulness to Roman Catholic Christianity?

As for "creativity," indeed, one could reasonably argue that mediocrity rather than excellence characterizes several of the ideas and arguments anthologized here, as well as the larger projects they represent. The mediocrity has at least two, perhaps interrelated sources: the quality of the individual intellect itself, and the tendency of some American Catholic thinkers in each generation to place their intellectual talents exclusively in the service of institutional needs, which tend to be inherently conservative and unimaginative.[12] "Thinking with the church" does not mean "thinking only what the church tells you to think," but it has frequently been interpreted that way. Indeed, genuine "fidelity" to the church may require the believer to refuse to be uncritically receptive to the received teaching of the magisterium, and to test the teaching — with the intent of bringing it alive rather than undermining it — by subjecting it to the challenges and questions thrown up against it by Catholics and non-Catholics in each society in which the church exists as a living tradition. This is the argument, at least, put forward by Father Charles Curran, the American Catholic theologian and social ethicist who was dismissed from his faculty position at the Catholic University of America for contesting aspects of the ordinary (i.e., non-infallible) magisterium's moral teaching on human sexuality (doc. 90).

In short, "creativity" and "fidelity" have existed in tension within the Roman Catholic community in the United States, but history shows that they are not mutually exclusive. Within each of the intellectual traditions featured in

---

12. On this point, see Avery Dulles, S.J., *Models of the Church* (New York: Image/Doubleday, 1987 [1974]), 10.

this volume, one encounters faith-filled arguments and faithful adaptations to contemporary horizons of understanding, precisely for the sake of realizing the goods of the tradition in that historical moment. One thinks of Flannery O'Connor's revelatory fictive explorations of the dynamics of sin and grace in narratives set in the American South (doc. 71); John Courtney Murray's adroit development of the Roman Catholic natural law tradition in light of the American experiment in pluralism and ordered liberty (doc. 54); and Daniel Patrick Moynihan's impassioned defense of the social goods produced by Catholic schools in the United States (doc. 43). This excellence born of disciplined reflection on the Christian heritage and the American experience is our definition of "creative fidelity." It has characterized the Great Tradition of Catholic thought and practice extending back to the time of Christ.

Part 1, compiled and annotated by William Portier (who also edited and introduced the documents on church and state, and those treating moral theology and social thought), provides a rich variety of historic views on this aspiration to remain faithful to the past while moving forward. The section explores the meaning of "the intellectual life" for American Catholics during the period when the leading bishops, priests, and intellectuals of the church were grappling with what it might mean to be a church living its own life in a culturally and religiously plural modern nation. The struggle to establish an identity independent of European Catholicism but loyal to Rome is almost palpable in these excerpts. The rhythm of the section, and of the historical movement itself, seems to be two steps forward — toward a measure of intellectual autonomy through the integration of modern scholarship into American Catholic self-understanding, or through the quest for alternatives to neo-Scholasticism (docs. 1–2) — followed by one step back, as evidenced in the chilling effect on American Catholic intellectual life caused by the condemnation of Modernism (doc. 10).

Consistent throughout the section, and indeed throughout the history of American Catholicism, is the historical actors' recognition of and repentance for the failures of the American Catholic intellect and imagination. On the occasions when it inspired a wave of self-criticism leading to reform and renewed efforts, that recognition counted as a major step forward.

# Part 1

# INTELLECTUAL LIFE

## Introduction

Since the days of the early republic, intellectual life broadly understood has been a serious concern of American Catholics. They have associated intellectual life with access to higher education and, more specifically, with clergy formation. In 1789 Bishop John Carroll began the institution that would eventually become Georgetown University. In 1808 John Dubois, French *emigré* and future bishop of New York, founded Mount Saint Mary's College in Emmitsburg, Maryland. At Carroll's death in 1815 these two schools, along with St. Mary's Seminary in Baltimore, offered Catholic young men — young women would have to wait until the end of the century — their only opportunities for higher education.

At the time, even Protestant New England suffered anxiety attacks about intellectual inferiority and literary dependence. By 1837 Ralph Waldo Emerson envisioned the day when "the sluggard intellect of this continent will look from under its iron lids, and fill the postponed expectation of the world with something better than the exertions of mechanical skill." In Emerson's quirky vision, the American scholar would be a one-man "university of knowledges."[1] Emerson's former transcendentalist colleague Orestes Brownson was not convinced. He wanted a real university.

Brownson had converted to Catholicism in 1844 and soon became, through *Brownson's Quarterly Review,* something of a public Catholic. In June 1853, he traveled from New York to Emmitsburg to address the graduates of Mount Saint Mary's. As if in response to Emerson, Brownson regaled the Philomathian Society with an oration on "Liberal Studies" as a calling for the few that can only be answered with the help of university resources. In all the country, he lamented, "we have not a single institution deserving the name of University." "There is not a single branch of literature or science which demands erudition for its treatment, that can be treated by the American scholar without going abroad to consult foreign libraries."[2]

Among nineteenth-century American bishops, none had a better claim to the title of "intellectual" than the "Catholic Emerson," Bishop John Lancaster

---

1. "The American Scholar," in *Selected Writings of Ralph Waldo Emerson,* ed. and with a foreword by William H. Gilman (New York: New American Library, 1965), 223–24, 239.

2. "Liberal Studies," in *The Works of Orestes A. Brownson,* ed. Henry F. Brownson (Detroit: Thorndike Nourse, Publisher, 1885), vol. 19, 443–44.

Spalding of Peoria. He carried on a lifelong campaign for a Catholic research university such as the one he had attended at Louvain, Belgium. Reminding them that "the best culture of the intellect has for three centuries been made impossible to Catholics who speak English," he urged American Catholics to take advantage of their providential opportunities. Ireland, England, and Canada have their universities. American Catholics have "nothing but the old Latin school, founded nearly a century ago." He chided their self-complacency. "If Americans in general are justly chargeable with lack of culture, may not this charge be brought home with even greater force to American Catholics?"[3] In 1884 Spalding made his plea for a "real university" to the assembled American bishops at the third Plenary Council of Baltimore.

> But if we are to be intellectually the equals of others, we must have with them equal advantages of education; and so long as we look rather to the multiplying of schools and seminaries than to the creation of a real university, our progress will be slow and uncertain, because a university is the great ordinary means to the best cultivation of the mind.[4]

Within five years, and amid considerable controversy, Spalding would have his university. Conceived as a center of graduate studies, the Catholic University of America, located in Washington, D.C., opened its doors in 1889. But even before its founding, the university became entangled with the "Americanist" controversies that divided the bishops during the 1890s and ended with Pope Leo XIII's censure of "Americanism" in 1899. At the center of the Americanist controversies was Archbishop John Ireland of St. Paul. His celebration of Catholic University in document 1 marks the beginning of a modest burst of clerical intellectualism. But then in 1907 Pope Pius X condemned "Modernism." If priest professors who answered Ireland's challenge by trying to "regain the scepter of science" and be "modern . . . in curriculum and method" were discouraged by the censure of Americanism, they were crushed by the condemnation of Modernism.[5]

The negative impact of these two censures on the development of Catholic theology and biblical studies in the United States is difficult to exaggerate (doc. 10). But intellectual life did not die. Rather its energies were channeled in new directions. In 1907, the same year Pius X condemned Modernism, there appeared one of the most widely read books in American Catholic history: *The Thirteenth, Greatest of the Centuries*, by James J. Walsh. The following year came Gilbert Keith Chesterton's *Orthodoxy*. Together these two books signal the "Catholic Renaissance" that blossomed between the two great wars. But Vatican

---

3. John Lancaster Spalding, "Religion and Culture," *American Catholic Quarterly Review* 4, no. 15 (July 1879): 413–14.

4. Excerpts from Spalding's sermon appear as a "Related Document" in Clyde Crews's article on John Lancaster Spalding in *The Encyclopedia of American Catholic History*, ed. Michael Glazier and Thomas J. Shelley (Collegeville, Minn.: Liturgical Press, 1997), 1342.

5. On Americanism and Modernism and their intellectual continuity, see R. Scott Appleby, *Church and Age Unite! The Modernist Impulse in American Catholicism* (Notre Dame, Ind.: University of Notre Dame Press, 1992).

documents and books alone cannot conjure an intellectual mood. World War I and new immigrations intervened. In their aftermath, people resonated with papal calls to build an integral Catholic alternative to modern culture. This task diverted intellectual energy into the neo-Scholastic revival of St. Thomas and the literary pursuits of the Catholic Renaissance.

During this period, the Americanist project of a positive intellectual engagement with American culture metamorphosed in two surprising ways. First, American Catholics mobilized their resources for World War I through the National Catholic War Council. The organizational and intellectual activity, especially in the social sciences, that grew out of the War Council has been called "the second Americanism."[6] Second, Catholics began to argue that American constitutional government has its sources in medieval philosophy and law. Catholic Americanism transformed into a medievalism especially suited to the embattled situation of Catholics in the 1920s. This neo-Scholastic Americanism was "the earliest clear-cut manifestation of the Catholic Renaissance in the United States."[7] In George N. Shuster and George Bull, S.J. (docs. 3 and 4), we hear two voices from the Catholic Renaissance. Protestant and secular critics countered that democracy was also a culture and questioned whether Catholics with their subculture and separate schools were fully committed to it.[8]

In responding to such criticism, John Tracy Ellis would, in many respects, appropriate it. At the heart of this section is his "American Catholics and the Intellectual Life" (doc. 5) and the "spectacular eruption of cultural self-criticism" it elicited.[9] The examples of Brownson and Spalding illustrate that such self-criticism was not unprecedented. As the Catholic Renaissance was getting under way in 1925, thirty-one-year-old George Shuster, a former Notre Dame English professor working on the editorial staff at recently founded *Commonweal*, anticipated Ellis's 1955 critique. In the columns of *America*, Shuster challenged American Catholics with the question "Have We Any Scholars?":

> If we are honest, we must admit that during seventy-five years of almost feverish intellectual activity we have had no influence on the general culture of America other than what has come from a passably active endeavor to spread to the four winds knowledge accumulated either by our ancestors or by sectarian scholars.

---

6. Douglas J. Slawson, *The Foundations and First Decade of the National Catholic Welfare Council* (Washington, D.C.: Catholic University of America Press, 1992), 10. See also Elizabeth McKeown, "From *Pascendi* to *Primitive Man:* The Apologetics and Anthropology of John Montgomery Cooper," *U.S. Catholic Historian* 13, no. 2 (Winter 1995): 1–21.

7. On the "medieval-roots-of-democracy theory" and the Catholic Renaissance, see Philip Gleason, *Contending with Modernity: Catholic Higher Education in the Twentieth Century* (New York: Oxford University Press, 1995), 125–30. The quotation appears on 125.

8. John T. McGreevy, "Thinking on One's Own: Catholicism in the American Intellectual Imagination, 1928–1960," *Journal of American History* 84 (June 1997): 97–130.

9. Philip Gleason, *Keeping the Faith: American Catholicism Past and Present* (Notre Dame, Ind.: University of Notre Dame Press, 1987), 32.

Shuster decried the status of research in Catholic schools and the exploitation of overworked faculty both religious and lay. At the root of this mediocrity, he discerned one "arch evil," namely, "multiplying schools instead of multiplying teachers." "There are American Catholic colleges in places where the students, if any, would have to seek out their Alma Mater on a pack mule."[10] As a World War I veteran, Shuster hoped to address "Catholic social indifference" with "an awakening of the student's intellectual life." But instead, he lamented, nodding in the direction of South Bend, "we have superimposed upon a splendid system of elementary training little more than excellence in football."[11]

Thirty years later and at greater length, Ellis would cover much the same ground. Between Shuster and Ellis the Catholic Renaissance had intervened. The end of World War II put Ellis at a pivotal juncture. Communism had become a more serious threat to democracy than Catholicism. Will Herberg had just included Catholics in his account of the American consensus, *Protestant-Catholic-Jew* (1955). In challenging Catholics to take the chief blame for their sorry intellectual state, Ellis criticized "their frequently self-imposed ghetto mentality which prevents them from mingling as they should with their non-Catholic colleagues." "Echoing criticisms of conformity originating outside the church," Ellis had positioned himself in the mainstream of postwar historiography with its reappreciation of America, its affirmative tone of civil consensus, and its search for a pluralist past.[12] Ignoring former dreams of a Catholic alternative to modern culture, Ellis joined in the contemporary embrace of the "liberal tradition." With his monumental biography of Cardinal James Gibbons in 1952, Ellis had leapt over the Catholic Renaissance to find a usable past in the civility and patriotism of Gibbons and the Americanists.

Ellis stood in a tradition of Catholic self-criticism that went back to Brownson, Spalding, Shuster, and the rest. Subsequent generations have returned to "American Catholics and the Intellectual Life" as if to a classic. Commenting on Ellis in the manner of rabbis or Scholastics, they have continued this tradition. Shuster's blunt question epitomizes it: Have we any scholars? The "we" of this question originates in a sense of difference analogous to the one that prompted Emerson's reflections on the American scholar.

Forty-two years after Ellis's essay, David Hollinger published the third edition of his *The American Intellectual Tradition*. John Courtney Murray was the only Catholic author to find a place in it. Imagine the reactions of Shuster and Ellis. How ought Shuster's "we," now differently constituted and in different circumstances, respond? In a volume devoted to American Catholic intellectual *identities*, an appeal to difference is a tempting first avenue of response.

---

10. George N. Shuster, "Have We Any Scholars?" *America* (August 15, 1925): 418–19.

11. [George N. Shuster,] "Insulated Catholics," *Commonweal* 2 (August 19, 1925): 337–38.

12. The phrase in quotation marks is from McGreevy, "Thinking on One's Own," 128. On the mood of postwar historiography, see Richard Hofstadter, *Anti-Intellectualism in American Life* (New York: Vintage Books, 1963), 412–15; Peter Novick, *That Noble Dream: The "Objectivity Question" and the American Historical Profession* (Cambridge: Cambridge University Press, 1988), 332–36. In *Keeping the Faith,* Philip Gleason, with specific reference to Ellis's essay, describes the effects of this mood shift to an "American celebration" of American Catholic scholars. See 31–32.

The local color of intellectual back roads has a certain fitting fascination.[13] The ironic convergence of criticisms from Joseph Clifford Fenton and Paul Giles (docs. 6 and 11) also points in the direction of difference. The one from the anti-Modernist Catholic enclave of the 1950s, the other from the postmodern academic enclave of the 1990s, both fault Ellis for being insufficiently mindful of difference, for consorting with alien intellectual gods. It is quite appropriate, if insufficient, to appeal to an alternative intellectual ideal, more explicitly communal, more rabbinic or Scholastic, if you will, than the individual quest embraced in defense of Ellis by Thomas O'Dea (doc. 8).

In the warm glow of postwar American consensus, Ellis left this largely unspoken, appealed instead to a more objectivist ideal, and wrote Catholic history into the new liberal narrative. For postwar Catholic intellectuals such as Ellis, Walter Ong, O'Dea, and John Donovan, the intellectual life debate was about gaining a certain distance and freedom from the subculture created by the Catholic Renaissance. In another time, perhaps more like the one that had a Catholic Renaissance, a different "we" sees difference more clearly.

But Ellis's formalistic approach made another aspect of intellectual life especially clear to him. It was recently recalled to me at the end of a long academic conference that had more than its bombastic share of wearying appeal to the scholarship of identity. An eminent historian stood up to remind us that, when the methodological and epistemological fireworks are done, scholarship is about doing your work, sending it up the flagpole, and letting people shoot at it. Even those more sharply attuned to difference than he was can nod in agreement when Ellis speaks of the "inescapable and exacting labor of true scholarship...intelligently directed and competently expressed."

## 1. John Ireland's Call to the Intellectual Life, 1889

*The archbishop of St. Paul, Minnesota, and leader of the progressive or Americanist party among American bishops takes the occasion of the centenary of the American hierarchy to call Catholics to an intellectual engagement with the age.*

This is an intellectual age. It worships intellect. It tries all things by the touchstone of the intellect. By intellect, public opinion, the ruling power of the age, is formed. The Church herself will be judged by the standard of intellect. Catholics must excel in religious knowledge; they must be ready to give reasons for the faith that is in them, meeting objections from whatever source, abreast of the times in their method of argument. They must be in the foreground of intellectual movements of all kinds. The age will not take kindly to religious knowledge separated from secular knowledge. The Church must regain the scepter of science, which to her honor and to the benefit of the world, she wielded for ages in the past. An important work for Catholics in the coming century will be the building of schools, colleges, and seminaries;

---

13. Sandra Yocum Mize, "On the Back Roads: Searching for American Catholic Intellectual Traditions," in *American Catholic Traditions: Resources for Renewal,* ed. Sandra Yocum Mize and William Portier (Maryknoll, N.Y.: Orbis Books, 1997), 3–23.

and a work more important still will be the lifting up of present and future in-stitutions to the highest degree of intellectual excellence. Only the best schools will give the Church the men she needs. Modern, too, must they be in curriculum and method, so that pupils going forth from their halls will be men for the twentieth century and men for America.

In love, in reverence, in hope I salute thee, Catholic University of America! Thy birth — happy omen! — is coeval with the opening of the new century. The destinies of the Church in America are in thy keeping.

> John Ireland, "The Mission of Catholics in America," in *The Church and Modern Society*, vol. 1 (St. Paul, Minn.: Pioneer Press, 1905), 92–93.

## 2. John Lancaster Spalding's *"Gesù* Sermon," 1900

*A little more than a year after Pope Leo XIII's censure of "Americanism" in 1899, Bishop Spalding of Peoria travels to Rome. In the Jesuit Church of the Gesù, he pleads for support and freedom for scholars in the church.*

The most certain result of the philosophic thought of the last hundred years is that the primal cause and final end of all things is spiritual, not mechanical or material. If only we go deep enough, we never fail to find God and the soul. Shall we dread the results of historical research? In the Church as in the world, good has been mingled with evil, — the cockle with the wheat. What God has permitted to happen, man may be permitted to know; and if we are wise, we may glean, even from the least promising fields, fruits which shall nourish us in a higher wisdom and a nobler courage. A righteous cause can never be truly served either by the timid or by the insincere. And what is true of the history of the Church is also true of the history of the Bible. No facts connected with its composition can obscure the light of God's word which shines forever in its pages, to illumine the path that leads to a higher and more perfect life, and in the end to everlasting life.

The fundamental principle of the Catholic theologian and apologist is that there is harmony between revelation rightly understood, and the facts of the universe rightly known; and since this is so, the deepest thought and the most certain knowledge must furnish the most irrefragable proof of the truth of our faith. The Catholic who holds this principle with profound conviction will not shrink from any test or any adversary. If faith does not give new strength to the mind, the heart, the whole man, is it genuine faith at all? Shall we cease to desire and strive to know, because we believe? Is it not the property of vital belief to impel to thought and action? Are not faith and hope and love, if they be living, the fountain-heads of the highest energy? Does not all history prove that right human life is possible only when men are self-active in a free and noble way, when they strive bravely for more real knowledge and greater virtue? Where we strive there is indeed danger of error and mistake; but where we rest in spiritual lethargy, decay and ruin are inevitable. A faculty unused dwindles until it ceases to be. They who dare must take risks: danger can be overcome only by encountering danger. Shall the Church speak words of approval and cheer to all her children except those who labor with honest purpose and untiring zeal, for deeper and truer knowledge? Shall she permit Catholics to fall into the sleep of self-contented ignorance, while the great world moves on and leaves them in the cerements of the grave?... The truths of salvation are doubtless infinitely more important than the truths of science; but this natural knowledge so attracts the attention and awakens the interest of the men of to-day, it so transforms and improves the methods and processes by which civilization is promoted, that it has created a new world-view, not only in the minds of the few profound thinkers and original investigators, but in the general public of intelligent men and women; and if our words are to awaken a response, we must be able to place ourselves at the standpoint of our hearers. The theologian, the apologist, the orator must be able to say to the children of this generation: "We see all that you see, and beyond we see yet diviner truth." Arguments and syllogisms have little power of persuasion. We win men by showing them the facts of life; and to do this we must be able to look at things from many points. This ability is precisely what the best education confers; for it renders the mind open, luminous, fair, supple, and many-sided.

We believe that Christ is God made manifest, and that the Catholic faith is His revelation. If our belief be not vain, the more the light of the mind is thrown upon it — its origins, its doctrines and its essential tendencies — the more divinely true and good and beautiful shall it appear to be. In the depths and amidst the beginnings of things, even the most clear-seeing must grope their way; and instead of discouraging them by throwing suspicion upon their honesty of purpose, we should be quick to overlook their errors, receiving with gratitude even the feeblest ray of light they may be able to throw on the mysteries of life and being. The good and the generous easily overlook the faults and the frailties of the wise and the great.

To live in the mind, to strive ceaselessly to learn more of the infinite truth is not easy for anyone. It requires a discipline, a courage, a spirit of self-denial, which only the fewest ever acquire; and when men of this strength and excellence devote themselves to the elucidation and defence of the doctrines of religion, we must honor and trust them, or they will lose heart or turn to studies in which their labors will be appreciated. If mistrust of our ablest minds be permitted to exist, the inevitable result will be a lowering of the whole intellectual life of Catholics, and as a consequence the lowering of their moral and religious life.

John Lancaster Spalding, "Education and the Future of Religion," in *Religion, Agnosticism and Education* (Chicago: A. C. McClurg & Co., 1903), 159–64.

## 3. George N. Shuster on Catholic Letters in the United States, 1930

*A member of* Commonweal's *editorial staff reflects on why so few American writers have contributed to the revival of Catholic literature then under way in the "Catholic Renaissance."*

Manifestly, one great reason why development has proceeded at so slow a pace is the lack of what may be termed "social reference." With the exception of the

Boston Irish, no group specifically Catholic has identified itself with the history of culture in the United States. Individual writers have reflected either the milieu in which their conversion took place, or the abstract generalities of the faith which are common to all independently of human stratification.... Granted the overwhelmingly Protestant character of the scene, it is difficult to see how a writer inside the Church can identify himself with it in that spirit of affection which breeds the masterpiece.

Moreover the lot of the Catholic writer is very hard indeed. Normally he cannot afford to ignore the markedly puritanical spirit which still pervades many of his brethren in the faith, because these wield an energetic battle-ax which is all the more effective because it is swung from ambush.... Generally, for the sake of smoothing the fur of these self-constituted tigers for the defense of "standards," the author must perforce assume that innocuous and devious "perfection" which is to literature what frost is to landscape. One great need, therefore, is a powerful and competent criticism exercised by men who blend the best endowments of humanism with the fervor of belief....

American Catholics will probably continue to devote the greater portion of their intellectual effort to apologetic, first because that is so much needed, and secondly because they are in the habit of doing so. For a time, following the lead of Father Tabb, we witnessed a renaissance of poetry;... Such good verse as remains issues from the convent and the cloister — an indication that Catholic civilization in the United States is well-nigh reduced to the terms of the early centuries, when monastic walls were the only bulwarks against barbarism.

There is, however, no doubt that in the spiritual as well as in the mechanical world need engenders creative effort. The contemporary era is one which may honestly be described as especially in need of Christian vitality. I refer not so much to any collapse of morals (for the constraints imposed by an economic system based on sharp competition render flagrant indulgence impossible for very many), but rather to the profound soul-hunger which is everywhere so manifest to anyone who has an eye for such things. An unsatisfied thirst for permanence in hope, for the reliable in faith, for the unchangeable in charity, has taken possession of many whose fathers were blandly optimistic about the progress of science, or the perfectibility of the race. And precisely because the Catholic Church is the storehouse of so much light and virtue, even the world which cannot bring itself to acknowledge ecclesiastical authority or to recognize the validity of religious dogma will borrow from that Church with an ever-increasing sense of indebtedness. That a great number particularly among the intellectual have gone into debt, for truth or beauty, to the Catholic heritage during the past decades is one of the outstanding facts of recent history. Such a process cannot be halted. The animal feeds when it is hungry, however great may be the perils of the search; but the soul of man is the most persistent of hunters, spurred on as it is by a craving the intensity of which can be judged from saints on the one hand and fanatics on the other.

George N. Shuster, *The Catholic Church and Current Literature* (New York: Macmillan, 1930), 99–102.

## 4. George Bull, S.J., on "Research and the Catholic Mind," 1938

*At the height of the Catholic Renaissance, a Fordham University philosopher critiques the ideal of the research university by an appeal to Catholicism as a culture with an integral totality of vision.*

These then are the accompaniment of research as an *attitude:* a life of the mind and its counterpart in actual academic result, stamped indigenously with dehumanization and disintegration. That it is in root conflict with the Catholic life of the mind is something which at this point of the discussion should be clear. The antinomies suggested above will, I hope, have brought this out: organic unity of knowledge vs. disintegration; humanism vs. dehumanization; the sense of tradition and of wisdom achieved vs. "progress"; of principles vs. fact; of contemplation vs. "research."

Now, if out of these I were to select one antithesis as being the most palpable, the soonest discernible by the Catholic himself as he reflects upon his own life of learning, I would put it in this: that brooding over the whole Catholic life of the mind is the sense of wisdom achieved; and over the modern the sense of "progress" or truth to be pursued.... When we speak of a sense of wisdom achieved, we do not mean merely the implicit assumption that those principles are already fixed which have to do with the things that God has revealed.... We mean also that within the realm of mere reason the ultimates have been reached. I submit that part of the background of every Catholic's intellectual activity is the implication that there can be no "discovery" which will modify essentially the metaphysics of man's relation to nature and to God.... This is not merely one of our propositions explicitly held, it is part of the furniture of the mind over which we never fall, because we take it for granted.

The same assumption we also make in the realm of the humanities. For us the answer on the literary level which the classics give to the question, "What is man?" will never be disproved by anything that lies ahead awaiting the net of research....

Now if these things lie in our background, is it any wonder that contemplation and not research is the intellectual activity we most cherish? We want not "discovery"; but a deeper penetration into reality; that reality the boundaries of which, we assume, are already fixed by God revealing and by man achieving at the best moments of his speculating, and in his loftiest embodying of beauty. Does it not follow, also, that we can have no *immediate* object for the whole life of learning other than the enrichment of the person? That it is the learner and not the "sum of learning" which is our lodestone? If something other than the human person is made our objective, if some extrinsic temporal end be sought, how is the sense of tradition to function? For, as was said above, it not only receives, it fecundates to transmit. And it is a fact that whenever art has been thin and brittle, or when cultural streams have (as in our own day) lost their torrential beauty, it has always been because men, when they thought or sang, have looked elsewhere than at man, in all his essential relations.

In sum, then, research cannot be the primary object of a Catholic graduate school, because it is at war with the whole Catholic life of the mind. That life, it is the function of a Catholic university to embody, in curriculum and in organization, or there is no function at all for a Catholic seat of learning.

George Bull, S.J., "The Function of the Catholic Graduate School," *Thought* 13, no. 50 (September 1938): 376–78.

## 5. John Tracy Ellis on the Dearth of Catholic Intellectuals, 1955

*In the context of national discussion of the role of "intellectuals," a distinguished professor of church history at Catholic University touches off an enduring debate.*

Part of the reason why American Catholics have not made a notable impression on the intellectual life of their country is due, I am convinced, to what might be called a betrayal of that which is peculiarly their own. The nature of that betrayal has been highlighted during the last quarter of a century by such movements as the scholastic revival in philosophy which found its most enthusiastic and hard-working friends on the campuses of the University of Chicago, the University of Virginia, Princeton University, and St. John's College, Annapolis. Meanwhile the Catholic universities were engrossed in their mad pursuit of every passing fancy that crossed the American educational scene, and found relatively little time for distinguished contributions to scholastic philosophy. Woefully lacking in the endowment, training, and equipment to make them successful competitors of the secular universities in fields like engineering, business administration, nursing education, and the like, the Catholic universities, nonetheless, went on multiplying these units and spreading their budgets so thin — in an attempt to include everything — that the subjects in which they could, and should, make a unique contribution were sorely neglected.

That American educators expect Catholic institutions to be strong in the humanities and the liberal arts — to say nothing of theology and philosophy — is not surprising. Eighteen years ago Robert M. Hutchins, then President of the University of Chicago, in an address before the Middle West regional unit of the National Catholic Educational Association made that point in a very forceful way. Speaking of the Catholic Church as having what he called "the longest intellectual tradition of any institution in the contemporary world," Hutchins criticized the Catholic institutions for failing to emphasize that tradition in a way that would make it come alive in American intellectual circles. He thought the ideals of Catholic educators were satisfactory, but as far as actual practice was concerned, he said, "I find it necessary to level against you a scandalous accusation." He then went on:

> In my opinion...you have imitated the worst features of secular education and ignored most of the good ones. There are some good ones, relatively speaking — high academic standards, development of habits of work and research....[1]

---

1. Robert M. Hutchins, "The Integrating Principle of Catholic Higher Education," *College Newsletter, Midwest Regional Unit, N.C.E.A.* (May 1937): 1.

Hutchins listed the bad features he had in mind as athleticism, collegialism, vocationalism, and anti-intellectualism. In regard to the first two we can claim, I think, that in recent years Catholic institutions have shown improvement, just as all other educational groups have done. As for the second two, vocationalism and anti-intellectualism, I find no striking evidence of reform in the Church's colleges and universities since 1937. Regarding the three good features of secular institutions which Hutchins named, high academic standards, development of habits of work, and the ideal of research, I would say that a better showing has been made here and there on the first, but on the development of habits of work and a cherished ideal of research, I cannot personally see much by way of a fundamental change.

A second major defect in Catholic higher education that helps to account for its paucity of scholars of distinction is what I would call our betrayal of one another. By that I mean the development within the last two decades of numerous and competing graduate schools, none of which is adequately endowed, and few of which have the trained personnel, the equipment in libraries and laboratories, and the professional wage scales to warrant their ambitious undertakings. The result is a perpetuation of mediocrity and the draining away from each other of the strength that is necessary if really superior achievements are to be attained. I am speaking here, incidentally, only of the graduate schools, and not of the competition — amounting in certain places to internecine warfare — among the more than 200 Catholic colleges of the land. In both categories, however, the situation is serious, and if Benjamin Fine, writing in the New York *Times* of May 8, 1955, is to be believed, there is every prospect that it will become more serious. There is, and there has been for years, a desperate need for some kind of planning for Catholic higher education on a national scale. As to the likelihood of such in the immediate future, there would seem to be little room for optimism. One might, perhaps, illustrate the point by a parallel in international relations....

An additional point which should find place in an investigation of this kind is the absence of a love of scholarship for its own sake among American Catholics, and that even among too large a number of Catholics who are engaged in higher education. It might be described as the absence of a sense of dedication to an intellectual apostolate. This defect, in turn, tends to deprive many of those who spend their lives in the universities of the American Church of the admirable industry and unremitting labor in research and publication which characterize a far greater proportion of their colleagues on the faculties of the secular universities. I do not pretend to know precisely what the cause of this may be, but I wonder if it is not in part due to the too literal interpretation which many churchmen and superiors of seminaries and religious houses have given to St. Paul's oft-quoted statement that "Here we have no permanent city, but we seek for the city that is to come,"[2] and their emphasis on the question of the author of the *Imitation of Christ* when he asked, "What doth it avail thee

---

2. Hebrews 13:14.

to discourse profoundly on the Trinity, if thou be void of humility, and consequently displeasing to the Trinity?"[3] Too frequently, perhaps, those training
in our institutions have had the same author's famous dictum, "I had rather
feel compunction than know its definition," quoted to them without a counter-
balancing emphasis on the evils of intellectual sloth. Certainly no intellectual
who is worthy of the name Catholic would deny the fundamental importance
of humility as an indispensable virtue in the life of the follower of Christ. But
the danger of intellectual pride, grave as it is, should not be allowed to obscure
the lesson taught by our Lord in the parable of the talents. If that principle
had been pressed too far by Albertus Magnus we might never have known the
*Summa theologiae* of St. Thomas Aquinas. Many may still recall a less dignified
example of this mistaken emphasis when William Jennings Bryan gave eminent
satisfaction to a Baptist fundamentalist audience in New York in 1923 with his
declaration: "If we have come to the stage at which we must decide between geology and Christianity, I think it is better to know the Rock of Ages than the
age of rocks."[4]

Closely connected with the question of the prevailing Catholic attitudes in
education is the overemphasis which some authorities of the Church's educational system in the United States have given to the school as an agency for
moral development, with an insufficient stress on the role of the school as an
instrument for fostering intellectual excellence. That fact has at times led to a
confusion of aims and to a neglect of the school as a training ground for the
intellectual virtues. No sensible person will for a moment question that the in-
culcation of moral virtue is one of the principal reasons for having Catholic
schools in any circumstances. But that goal should never be permitted to over-
shadow the fact that the school, at whatever level one may consider it, must
maintain a strong emphasis on the cultivation of intellectual excellence. Given
superior minds, out of the striving for the intellectual virtues there will flow,
with its attendant religious instruction, the formation of a type of student who
will not only be able to withstand the strains which life will inevitably force
upon his religious faith, but one who will have been so intellectually fortified
that he will reflect distinction upon the system of which he is a product....[5]

In conclusion, then, one may say that it has been a combination of all the
major points made in this paper, along with others which I may have failed to
consider, that has produced in American Catholics generally, as well as in the
intellectuals, a pervading spirit of separatism from their fellow citizens of other
religious faiths. They have suffered from the timidity that characterizes minority groups, from the effects of a ghetto they have themselves fostered, and, too,
from a sense of inferiority induced by their consciousness of the inadequacy
of Catholic scholarship. But who, one may rightly ask, has been responsible
in the main for its inadequacy? Certainly not the Church's enemies, for if one
were to reason on that basis St. Augustine would never have written the *City of*

---

3. Thomas à Kempis, *The Imitation of Christ* (Baltimore, n.d.), 2.

4. *New York Times,* December 8, 1923.

5. On this point cf. Edward J. Power, "Orestes Brownson on Catholic Schools," *Homiletic and Pastoral Review* 55 (April 1955): 568.

*God*, St. Robert Bellarmine the *Tractatus de potestate summi pontificis*, nor would Cardinal Baronius have produced the *Annales ecclesiatici*. In fact, it has been enmity and opposition that have called forth some of the greatest monuments of Catholic scholarship. The major defect, therefore, lies elsewhere than with the unfriendly attitude of some of those outside the Church. The chief blame, I firmly believe lies with Catholics themselves. It lies in their frequently self-imposed ghetto mentality which prevents them from mingling as they should with their non-Catholic colleagues, and in their lack of industry and the habits of work, to which Hutchins alluded in 1937. It lies in their failure to have measured up to their responsibilities to the incomparable tradition of Catholic learning of which they are the direct heirs, a failure which Peter Viereck noted, and which suggested to him the caustic question, "Is the honorable adjective 'Roman Catholic' truly merited by America's middleclass-Jansenist Catholicism, puritanized, Calvinized, and dehydrated...?"[6]

There is not a man of discernment anywhere today who is unaware that the intellectual climate of the United States is undergoing a radical change from the moribund philosophy of materialism and discredited liberalism that have ruled a good portion of the American mind for the better part of a century. Clinton Rossiter spoke of this in a thoughtful article published some months ago. He foresees a new day dawning for our country when religious and moral values will again be found in the honored place they once occupied. Concerning that ray of hope upon the horizon, he concluded: "And it will rest its own strong faith in liberty and constitutional democracy on the bedrock of these traditional, indeed eternal values: religion, justice, morality."[7] If this prediction should prove true, and there is increasing support for the view that it will, to whom, one may ask, may the leaders of the coming generation turn with more rightful expectancy in their search for enlightenment and guidance in the realm of religion and morality than to the American Catholic intellectuals? For it is they who are in possession of the oldest, wisest, and most sublime tradition of learning that the world has ever known. There has, indeed, been considerable improvement among American Catholics in the realm of intellectual affairs in the last half-century, but the need for far more energetic strides is urgent if the receptive attitude of contemporary thought is to be capitalized upon as it should be. It is, therefore, a unique opportunity that lies before the Catholic scholars of the United States which, if approached and executed with the deep conviction of its vital importance for the future of the American Church, may inspire them to do great things and, at the end, to feel that they have in some

---

6. Peter Viereck, *Shame and Glory of the Intellectuals* (Boston, 1953), 49. Speaking of the fact that the contemporary world crisis has been caused by a process of continuous secularization of what was originally produced and developed under Christian auspices, Heinrich Rommen has said, "It is for this reason that Catholics cannot simply surrender what in a twofold sense is theirs as Catholics and as men, but must irradiate their faith, informed by charity, into their own beleaguered democracy," *Catholicism in American Culture* (New Rochelle, 1955), 68. Professor Rommen's essay was one of five lectures delivered at the College of New Rochelle during the academic year 1953–54 to mark the golden jubilee of the college.

7. Clinton Rossiter, "Toward an American Conservatism," *Yale Review* 44 (Spring 1955): 372.

small measure lived up to the ideal expressed by Père Sertillanges when he said
of the Catholic intellectuals:

> They, more than others, must be men consecrated by their vocation....
> The special asceticism and the heroic virtue of the intellectual worker
> must be their daily portion. But if they consent to this double self-
> offering, I tell them in the name of the God of Truth not to lose
> courage.[8]

> John Tracy Ellis, "American Catholics and the Intellectual Life," *Thought* 30,
> no. 116 (Spring 1955): 374–78, 385–86, 387–88.

## 6. Joseph Clifford Fenton Responds to Ellis, 1956

*A professor of fundamental and dogmatic theology in Catholic University's
School of Sacred Theology and editor of the* American Ecclesiastical Review
*takes his colleague to task for accepting secular norms of scholarship.*

It seems quite obvious that, in any discussion of Catholic scholarship in terms
of impoverishment or of inadequacy, there must be an appeal to some sort of
norm. Our scholarship, in this or any other country, can be rightly designated
as impoverished only if it fails to meet the standards for intellectual activity.
Thus, if it could be shown that the writings or the teachings of Catholics, in the
realm of any section of the intellectual life, were considerably below the average,
or in any way less than what is rightly to be expected from Catholic students, it
would be true that our scholarship is impoverished.

The central and the most important element of the Catholic scholarship in
any country is, of course, theological. Now the chief norm to which Monsignor
Ellis appeals as an indication of excellence for writings, even on the theological level, is acceptance and citation of these writings by some non-Catholic
intellectual. "When the inescapable and exacting labor of true scholarship is
intelligently directed and competently expressed," he tells us, "it will win its
way on its own merits into channels of influence beyond the Catholic pale."[1]
Monsignor Ellis supports his contention by assuring us that the thought and
research of two Catholic scholars on vital aspects of the current crisis have been
brought to the attention of thousands of Americans "through the use that has
been made of them by Walter Lippmann in his latest book...."[2]

There does indeed exist a separatist mentality which is unfortunate and
which certainly is not uncommon among the Catholics it has been my good
fortune to know. This mentality is the effect of a kind of inferiority feeling, and
it seeks above all other things acceptance and recognition by groups which the
possessor of this mentality holds in high esteem, and from which he believes
he is or has been rightly excluded by reason of his Catholicism. The Catholic

8. A. D. Sertillanges, O.P., *The Intellectual Life* (Westminster, Md., 1947), 16.

1. John Tracy Ellis, *American Catholics and the Intellectual Life* (Chicago: The Heritage Foundation, Inc., 1956), 57f. [Fenton is citing from the book version of Ellis's essay. —Ed.]
2. Ibid., 58.

author, particularly in the field of sacred theology, who writes primarily with a view of being accepted and praised by non-Catholic intellectuals, and of perhaps being admitted into their company, is a victim of such a separatist mentality. But we may be grateful that this mentality is in no way characteristic of the general run of Catholic life in the United States.

> Joseph Clifford Fenton, "Intellectual Standards among American Catholics," *American Ecclesiastical Review* 135 (November 1956): 328, 333.

## 7. Walter Ong, S.J., on Étienne Gilson and Jacques Maritain as Symbols, 1957

*Student of both Marshall McLuhan and Perry Miller, a polymathic St. Louis University Jesuit analyzes, with a certain impatience, the role of Gilson and Maritain as border symbols for American Catholics during the Catholic Renaissance.*

The first half of the twentieth century will doubtless go down in history as the age when American Catholics were specializing in symbols of frontier or borderline operations. Their idols (the word is hardly too strong) include not only figures such as Chesterton, Waugh, Greene, Mrs. Clare Booth Luce, and numbers of converted Communists and other converts who have appeared in England and the United States to testify to the religio-intellectual charge at the borderline between the Church and her surroundings, as well as similar figures in France — Péguy, Bloy, Ernest Psichari, and the like — but most especially two Europeans who have been first borrowed and more recently simply annexed by the English-speaking Catholics of North America, MM. Gilson and Maritain.

There can be little doubt that Professor Gilson has been sponsored by American Catholics not only out of admiration for his superb scholarship, but also out of some deep-felt emotional need. American Catholics commonly think of M. Gilson simply as a Thomist, but the author of *Thomism* himself has credited much of his interest in philosophy and inspiration to Bergson; and Bergson's sense of history, of a present which is and has always been the frontier where the past moves into the future, is undoubtedly one of the things which give M. Gilson his appeal to the contemporary American Catholic mind. For this mind, Gilson helps symbolically to endow even the reputed static qualities of the Middle Ages, and with them the similar qualities imputed (mistakenly) by Americans to Europe in general, with the sense of movement in history so congenial to American sensibility.

As a symbol, M. Gilson affects the American Catholic mind apparently well below the threshold of consciousness, for he himself appears much more explicitly aware of the necessity of establishing a dialogue between Faith and America and more inclined explicitly to view his own work as contributing to that dialogue than are his own American backers. So far as I have observed, American Catholics seem quite unaware that the title of M. Gilson's Gifford Lectures which they so widely read, *The Unity of Philosophical Experience*, is a take-off and commentary on the title of an earlier series of Gifford Lectures by one of their fellow citizens, William James, *The Varieties of Religious Experience*. It is fascinating to note that in this exchange of views — at a distance of some years — it is James whose sense of history was not very compelling and who studies the various manifestations of drives common to all, or many individuals, focusing on an a-historical diversity, whereas Gilson focuses on the unity evinced within movement or history, and thus gives comfort to the American Catholic unconscious in its own orientation toward movement.

The other favorite symbol of borderline activity, Professor Maritain, has been sponsored even more than Professor Gilson in the United States, where he is now more eminent than in his own country. Emerging from the same European-medieval context as Gilson, and thus giving American Catholics the assurance of continuity with the past that they need, Maritain puts the American Catholic ethos in contact less with the movement of history than with something else in its surroundings: the post-Newtonian scientific developments of a generation or two ago. It may fairly be said that he predigested these developments for American Catholic consumption. On the whole, his work in this field has been more widely attended to in America than his own more valuable work on Church-state relationships, which has had to compete with the parallel work of an American Jesuit, Father John Courtney Murray.

Walter Ong, S.J., *Frontiers in American Catholicism* (New York: Macmillan, 1957), 113–14.

## 8. Thomas F. O'Dea on the Intellectual Life as Quest, 1958

*Trained in sociology at Harvard University, O'Dea was an associate professor at Fordham when he entered the intellectual life debate with a book-length contribution. In this text, he criticizes the ethos of Catholic Renaissance neo-Scholasticism with appeals to the quest and to mystery.*

One may summarize the issue here briefly as follows: Unless it is possible for a Catholic youth to understand his faith, to know what faith really is, and maintain his faith, without having on the one hand to be spoon-fed when genuine difficulties are involved, and, on the other, having his head jammed with ready-made formulae memorized in religion and philosophy classes, there is really no hope for the development of an intellectual life among Catholics. For to be an intellectual means to be engaged in a quest. As Aristotle long ago noted, knowledge begins with wonder. Many Catholic students get an impression that there is really very little wonderful about their faith — that it is so close to the rationally obvious that the real wonder is that outsiders do not see it as such. Such Catholics often seem to be puzzled by the existence of a long, honorable, and honestly searching philosophical tradition outside their own semi-sectarian world. They even express impatience with it, and feel superior to the "confusions" of modern thinkers over issues which they themselves have failed to recognize and too frequently fear when they recognize them even partially.

Such a frame of mind is based upon quite erroneous implicit assumptions, and such assumptions militate against genuine and profound Catholic contact with the non-Catholic tradition. The great Protestant and secular thinkers of

America are not just men who made mistakes, like the "adversaries" of the scholastic manual. They have positive things to say to those American Catholics who have neglected the search itself. The spiritual segregation of Catholic life from that of the general community adds difficulties in that respect, but further defensiveness concealed under lethargic self-satisfaction is hardly an adequate response to the situation. We repeat: to be an intellectual means to be engaged in a quest, and if to be a Christian has come to mean to have the whole truth that matters — albeit in capsule form — in advance (to know, for example, that "Plato had an erroneous theory of human nature," that "Comte held God knows what, which is absurd") without ever having been introduced to a genuine philosophical experience, then we are hopelessly lost.

If the Christian faith cannot enable a man to face the unknown without blinding himself to the fact that the mystery is there; to follow, in the unknown, the traces of meaning accessible to his mind; to live with his face to the existential winds that blow across the great void which modern science has opened up before us in many spheres: then it cannot really be Christian faith. To attempt to substitute for such a faith a worldly human consensus of cultural attitudes is a dishonest — and an unworkable — procedure....

We must ask: Is it true that many Catholics are not moved by the intellectual challenge of the modern scientific and scholarly world because they are told — implicitly — that they already know everything important — or can know it in capsule form — and that there is nothing further to look for? Are they also allowed to infer that a genuine intellectual quest is incompatible with faith? Are they taught to accept their faith not as a stimulus to a Christian adventure but as a soporific? Does Christianity, which should act as a Socratic gadfly upon them, actually serve as a kind of intellectual Tsetse fly?

> Thomas F. O'Dea, *American Catholic Dilemma: An Inquiry into the Intellectual Life* (New York: Sheed and Ward, 1958), 111–14.

## 9. John D. Donovan on Anti-Intellectualism in American Catholic Life, 1964

*In 1964 Mary Perkins Ryan reignited the intellectual life debate with an agonizing reappraisal of Catholic education,* Are Parochial Schools the Answer? *Richard Hofstadter's* Anti-Intellectualism in American Life *had appeared two years before. The editors of* Commonweal *invited three sociologists to participate in "The New Debate": Andrew Greeley, John D. Donovan, and James W. Trent. A professor at Boston College, Donovan had recently written* Academic Man in the Catholic College.

John Tracy Ellis and Mary Perkins Ryan are uncommon American Catholics for reasons far more significant than their common usage of two family names. In 1955, Monsignor Ellis published his timely and trenchant essay, *American Catholics and the Intellectual Life.* In 1964, Mrs. Ryan published her spiritually moving and provocative book, *Are Parochial Schools the Answer?* The intervening years, it is true, were prominently marked by the related contributions of

Thomas O'Dea, Fathers Walter Ong, Gustave Weigel, Andrew Greeley, and others. But the central figures remain Monsignor Ellis and Mrs. Ryan. The critical reactions to their works encapsule and symbolize the anti-intellectual posture and dynamics of American Catholicism in the critically important area of education.

By almost any yardstick ten years is a very short period of time. The decade between Monsignor Ellis and Mrs. Ryan, however, has been magnified because it marked the dramatic coincidence of powerful evolutionary and revolutionary forces within American Catholicism. The election of John F. Kennedy as President of the United States was clearly the most conspicuous symbol of the evolutionary process, but this event, in its turn, reflected the social and economic mobility of Catholics and their more complete identification with dominant values of the American ethos. But the vital center of socio-religious change in the United States as elsewhere was the revolutionary simplicity of Pope John XXIII. His pastoral wisdom unlocked the doors of fear and obscurantism and breathed into the Church a life-giving spirit of inquiry and innovation. Popular images to the contrary, Pope John was an intellectual. His playfulness and his piety (qualities which Richard Hofstadter's brilliant study, *Anti-intellectualism in American Life*, identifies as central to the personality of the intellectual) informed the years of his pontificate and invited Catholics everywhere to think freely and creatively about the new order. In the field of American Catholic education, Monsignor Ellis' and Mrs. Ryan's works are respectively a foreword and an afterword to his *aggiornamento*.

The anti-intellectualism of American Catholics to which these evolutionary and revolutionary forces pertain must, of course, be seen in proper perspective. This is not an easy task. For one thing, the historical dimensions are deep and complex. For another, the meaning of anti-intellectualism (and, correspondingly, of intellectualism) has defied a facile and acceptable definition. On the whole, it has been taken to describe a syndrome of fear, hostility, resentment, suspicion, and ambivalence directed against persons or ideas perceived as dangerous or imprudent because they challenge the moral and/or practical underpinnings of the *status quo*. For American Catholics, ironically, this syndrome has been fed not only by the aggressive egalitarianism of American life but by the defensive, clerical authoritarianism of their religious system. They have not been uniquely anti-intellectual, only more so and especially when the threat of radical criticism and innovation, whether from without or within the Catholic community, seemed to be directed at moral or religious institutions. In politics, in business, in education, and within the Church the critic and the innovator have generally been suspect and, not infrequently, subject to sanctions.

Despite these pervasive cultural and religious pressures of anti-intellectualism, no person is likely to be absolutely either intellectual or anti-intellectual in his total orientation. The person who is intellectually open and creative in one area may be ambivalent or hostile to equally critical or innovative persons and ideas in one or more other areas. Similarly, the temper and the targets of anti-intellectualism in the various social institutions (the family, the school, the church, etc.) are relative to the perceived threats which the new ideas and radical criticisms pose for each institution and for those persons having significant roles in them. And, as I shall point out, the source of the threat makes a substantial difference in the character of the intellectual or anti-intellectual reaction to criticism and innovation.

Within this context any evaluation of contemporary anti-intellectualism in Catholic education is necessarily partial and incomplete. The sub-system of Catholic education is part of the larger system of American Catholicism. It cannot be forgotten that this sub-system is at once subordinate to the official structure of the Church and inextricably linked to the other sub-systems of the family, parish, ethnic group, social class, etc. As a measure of Catholic intellectualism, therefore, the educational system is more significant in formal and symbolic than in strategic terms. The authority and the responsibility for the educational venture reside in the extra-academic hands of bishops, religious superiors, and pastors functioning within the bureaucratic structure of the Church. They authorize the establishment of the school, set or confirm its goals and policies, and represent the final sources of judgment and appeal. Historically, their schools have been essentially conserving and integrating rather than creative institutions. Spiritual and moral objectives have had primacy, and they have not usually been permitted or encouraged to initiate and lead the criticisms and innovations which the *aggiornamento* of Pope John now seeks. Their failures in this respect are, in fact, the core of the debate which has marked the years between Monsignor Ellis and Mrs. Ryan.

Predictably, the reactions of American Catholics to the indictments of non-intellectualism and anti-intellectualism are a mixed bag. The significant point is that in many respects the reactions provide more insight into the problem than do their critical stimuli. Whether spontaneous and visceral or calculated and cerebral, they reflect the anti-intellectual temper and range which still prominently marks the posture and dynamics of Catholic education.

Initially, it is important to note that Catholic reactions to the charges of anti-intellectualism (explicitly by Monsignor Ellis, and implicitly by Mrs. Ryan) and others have not been uniformly hostile. Indeed, Monsignor Ellis's essay won more praise than disapproval, partly because of its tone and professional sponsorship, and partly because the relevant public of scholars to whom it was directed was more open and receptive to "hard" criticism. Nor is it proper to infer that the nay-sayers were uniformly anti-intellectuals who were embittered or blind defenders of the establishment. On the contrary, many were persons of high intelligence whose minds were not closed to the many needs for change within the Church and within the educational system. More often, as their criticisms show, they were academic professionals who were proud of the achievements and the promise of Catholic education. Suddenly, the values and institutions of their own socialization were under attack and the latent anti-intellectualism nurtured in these worlds exposed their trained incapacity to evaluate criticisms and innovations in open and constructive terms. The patterns of their defensive reactions to Monsignor Ellis and Mrs. Ryan are clearcut evidences of the range and spirit of their common defensive posture.

No attempt will be made here to order either quantitatively or qualitatively the varieties of these reactions. In many quarters the charges of anti-intellectualism were met by a loud and eloquent silence. In other quarters, and with reference to Monsignor Ellis' and Professor O'Dea's works particularly, the reactions ranged from ambivalence to hostility. Some anti-critics were only disturbed by the public washing of Catholic linens; others felt that the criticisms were obsolescent in the light of recent professional institutional growth and development; others resented the invidious comparisons with non-Catholic American education which, they felt, was no better; still others sought to derail the indictments by reaffirming the primacy of spiritual and moral over intellectual goals in Catholic education or by denying the validity of criticisms with the Scotch verdict of not scientifically proved. Thus, in indirect rather than direct fashion, the defenders of Catholic education against the charges of anti-intellectualism reassured themselves and their constituencies but with a lack of conviction that betrayed their own ambiguity and the vulnerability of their positions.

More recently the debate was re-opened and more directly joined with the emergence, to his own expressed surprise, of a highly intelligent and articulate defender of Catholic education in the person of Father Andrew Greeley. For the entrenched opponents of the critical and innovative interpretations of Monsignor Ellis and Mrs. Ryan, Father Greeley's scholarly credentials and persuasive publications were life-lines eagerly grasped and effectively used. As a parish priest and a professional sociologist his was a double-barrelled voice of authority. Moreover, it was a voice which was widely heard because in the past five or six years he has published four books and about one hundred articles on topical Catholic issues.

In debating terms, Father Greeley's role has been that of rebuttal spokesman for the defenders of Catholic education. The irony is that, given the traditionally low estate of sociology in Catholic education, the once-maligned empiricism of the sociologist was now called upon to "prove" the worth of Catholic education. And to the undisguised joy of all those shaken by the charges of anti-intellectualism, Father Greeley's empiric data purported to do just that. Very directly expressed, he found in his research data virtually no evidence "to support the notion that American Catholics or American Catholic schools are anti-intellectual or anti-scientific." More than that, in his much-quoted *Religion and Career,* Father Greeley added icing to the cake. His comparative analysis of the aspirations, values, and attitudes of Catholic and non-Catholic college graduates showed the Catholic graduate as more promisingly intellectual, if only in slight degree, than his Protestant fellow graduates. The "self-critics," he seemed to be saying, were wrong and the future was rosy-tinged.

The technical problems of sampling, research design, and data interpretation aside, at least three basic considerations seem to deflate the optimism which Father Greeley's study has generated. First, it must be acknowledged that his research shifted the grounds of the debate from the intellectuals we *now* have to the intellectuals we *might* have in the years ahead. Even if his data, therefore, are accepted as valid, they do not directly reply to or discredit the criticisms which were central to the works of Monsignor Ellis and Professor O'Dea. The impoverishment of Catholic intellectual life today cannot be disproved by the yet-to-be-tested optimistic predictions about tomorrow.

Secondly, there is strong reason to suspect that the research materials of Father Greeley's study focus not on identifiable "intellectuals" but on "intelligent" graduates of the collegiate population. This distinction between "intelligence" and "intellect" is, as Hofstadter has pointed out, a critical one. Minds of penetrating intelligence provide the society with its experts and professionals in many fields, but these minds tend to be employed in living *off* rather than *for* ideas. They do not have the free-wheeling, critical, creative, and speculative bent of mind that marks the intellectual. It is here suggested that the measures of graduate aspirations and work values, particularly in the American cultural setting, are shaky grounds for optimistically projecting an intellectual resurgence in Catholic education. We most certainly do have more intelligent graduates but it is extremely doubtful that we have produced many more intellectuals.

Next, it must be noted that Father Greeley's empiricist concern with the hard facts of computer sociology barely conceals its own modest anti-intellectualism. This criticism becomes relevant not only because he feels that he disproved the "self-critics" who like Monsignor Ellis and Professor O'Dea were "unencumbered with data," but because he has dismissed Mrs. Ryan's book as "armchair research...interesting as a curiosity." It must be pointed out that by his non-speculative measure his own ambivalent but insightful "impressions" about "the new breed" among Catholic youth could be (but should not be) peremptorily devalued. In sum, Father Greeley's work on this impressionistic level as well as his research-based studies have contributed considerably to the debate but they have far from disproved the persistence of much anti-intellectualism in Catholic education.

Finally, and more briefly, the contemporary *cause célèbre* of Mrs. Ryan's book deserves special mention. Its predominantly clerical and religious reviewers during the past few months seem to have been shocked to their toenails by the daring of her criticisms and proposals. For them the parochial school system appears to be as sacred as the public school system is to the American non-Catholic public. Her recommendation, therefore, that serious considerations be given to setting it aside because it is no longer exclusively or even best suited to the spiritual and practical needs of Christian education today has provoked a massive emotional hemorrhage. Indeed, at this point in time, the issues she raises have hardly been confronted. Instead an *a priori* promise that her criticisms will be empirically disproved was wildly cheered by Catholic school educators.

The significant point is that her success in sparking a violently critical, even personally abusive and unjust, reaction is *prima facie* evidence that anti-intellectual values and sentiments are still conspicuous in Catholic education. What made her even more vulnerable to this reaction, it should be further noted, was the fact that she was not a clerical expert within the educational establishment, but a lay, female ideologue whose criticisms and proposals for a truly Christian education wore the mantle of the Council. In the classic anti-intellectual tradition she seems to be feared in some quarters as a subversive whose ideas threaten to destroy the system of Catholic education. And much more is yet to be heard along these lines.

All in all, the decade of debate which extends between Monsignor Ellis and Mrs. Ryan has not so much seen an "orgy of self-criticism" as a process of intellectual fermentation. The discomfort it may have caused is the least acceptable reason for any discontinuance or moratorium on it. The positive fact is that Catholic education has made substantial progress at all levels and that Catholic schools are increasingly producing graduates who are men and women of high intelligence as well as strong religious convictions. It is equally clear, however, that they are not yet producing the dedicated intellectuals of Monsignor Ellis' cast nor the truly Christian person of Mrs. Ryan's prayer. Their indictments of the American Catholic impoverishment in these respects have been a valuable service and have been welcomed as a spur to reform in some quarters. In other sectors, unfortunately, their criticisms have deepened the suspicion and fear of the intellect and intellectuals. They have also provoked renewed efforts at moral rather than intellectual rearmament; or they have led to the submission of the part-way house of intelligence for that of the intellect. The door is ajar but it is not really open.

> John D. Donovan, "Creating Anti-Intellectuals?" *Commonweal* 81 (October 2, 1964): 37–39.

## 10. Michael V. Gannon on *Pascendi*'s Intellectual Impact, 1971

*In a long and often cited essay, a church historian and student of John Tracy Ellis links the present state of American Catholic intellectual life to the effects of Pope Pius X's condemnation of Modernism in 1907.*

There was never any question that the American Church would comply with the Roman directives. The encyclical was accepted quietly, obediently, and, for the reasons advanced above, with no marked trauma. For all that one could see, nothing special had happened. Seminaries continued classes as before, bishops and priests continued on their accustomed rounds, and the poor had the gospel preached to them. The face that the Church presented to the nation at large remained the same. Still, something, indeed, occurred, something unperceived at the moment, something whose long-range impact on American Catholic thinking would be hard to exaggerate. The Church of the United States was overcome by a *grande peur.* As 1908 proceeded on its course a gradually enveloping dread of heresy settled over episcopal residences, chanceries, seminaries, and Catholic institutions of higher learning. Security, safety, conservatism became national imperatives. Free intellectual inquiry in ecclesiastical circles came to a virtual standstill. The nascent intellectual movement went underground or died. Contacts with Protestant and secular thinkers were broken off. It was as though someone had pulled a switch and the lights failed all across the American Catholic landscape....

There was little doubt by 1910 that a decisive pall had fallen over intellectual activity in the teaching and, *a fortiori,* the pastoral priesthood of the United States. No cleric wanted to be counted part of a subversive conspiracy against *Mater Ecclesia,* and one wanted, by writing or instruction, to lead others into temptation. Original research became original sin. The study of theology became the study of approved manuals, usually bad translations from the German. Critical studies in scripture yielded preeminence to *parti pris* history of the Church and to moral theology. The seminary faculties devoted themselves exclusively to the training of assistant pastors. The ordinary clergyman and layman lapsed into silence on matters bearing on doctrine. Bishops were selected for their orthodoxy, and almost all for the next two decades came out of Roman seminaries. The *Catholic Encyclopedia* continued to appear, but its editors paid a visit to Rome to assure Vatican authorities of the publication's orthodoxy.[1] The *Ecclesiastical Review* became strictly pastoral in character; the *Catholic University Bulletin* shed the high intellectual quality that it had exhibited for several years and became a small information bulletin; and the *Catholic World* went into the literary field. The American clerical mind turned in on itself, became romanticist, read Gilbert Keith Chesterton's new book, *Orthodoxy* (1908), with self-congratulatory fervor, and agreed with the great "G.K." that, "If there is one class of men whom history has proved especially and supremely capable of going quite wrong in all directions, it is the class of highly intellectual men."[2] In these circumstances, it goes without saying that in the years following 1907 there was exceedingly little communication between the Catholic priest and the American intellectual community. The critical mind lay at ruinous discount.

Michael V. Gannon, "Before and After Modernism: The Intellectual Isolation of the American Priest," in *The Catholic Priest in the United States: Historical Investigations,* ed. John Tracy Ellis (Collegeville, Minn.: St. John's University Press, 1971), 340–41, 350. Printed with permission.

## 11. Paul Giles on the Intellectual as Nonconformist, 1992

*Sounding like a postmodern echo of Joseph Clifford Fenton, an English literary theorist interrogates the intellectual ideal appropriated and presumed by Ellis and O'Dea.*

In American intellectual discourse of this postwar era, the term "religious" worked silently to exclude the organizing conceptual principles of Catholicism. R. P. Blackmur's 1961 essay "Religious Poetry in the United States," for instance, postulated a relationship between the privileged self and some ideal "other." ... Again the demand is that the individual mind turn back upon itself, probing for what is "numinous" within the psyche rather than what might

---

1. Francis E. Gigot, who wrote sixty-one articles for the *Catholic Encyclopedia* in the years 1907–1912, may be considered one Dunwoodie mind that did not cease activity. In the years between *Pascendi* and his death in 1920 he published three books, including one delicate study, *The Message of Moses and Modern Higher Criticism* (New York: Benziger Bros., 1915), and numerous monographs in the *Irish Theological Quarterly.*

2. *All Things Considered* (New York: John Lane Company, 1909), 213.

be "sacramental" within the external world; it is a classic American form of self-expression, with roots in the introverted musings of seventeenth-century Puritan journals.... Yet all of this seems another unwarranted cultural assumption, insofar as such a view of "otherness" could be read as an extrapolation from Karl Barth's specifically Protestant notion of God.... Whereas Catholicism stresses analogical interaction between God and man, Barth's form of Protestantism emphasizes instead this chasm or "otherness," a chasm that might be bridged only by the uncertain leap of human faith. It is not difficult to appreciate the consistency between the desire of Barth to project faith onto an unknowable God and the confidence of American prophetic writers, from John Winthrop through to Alice Walker, in some form of millennial triumph, an unknown but better future: anything rather than circumscription by the here-and-now.

It was a secularized version of this "otherness" that came to dominate the intellectual climate of the 1950s, as alienation and nonconformity became a standard intellectual response to mindless consumerism and political tranquility....

It is just at this point that self-consciousness starts to emerge in American Catholic academic circles about the lack of a reputable indigenous intellectual tradition. John Tracy Ellis's 1955 essay "The American Catholic and the Intellectual Life" sparked widespread debate about the reasons for this supposed lack of intellectual ambition. Monsignor Ellis attributed the blame partly to economic reasons — the confinement of immigrant Catholics to impoverished communities, where the acquisition of culture was naturally of secondary importance — and partly to the inculcated Catholic habit of personal humility and deference to authority....

Ellis's thesis has been enormously influential, though other possible explanations have been advanced for the kind of defensive conformity he outlined. Gustave Weigel, S.J., and Andrew Greeley suggested that as Irish-American families could never quite forget how long and difficult had been the path toward social respectability, they tended to urge their children not to take any risks with social status; as a result, members of these communities usually avoided potentially insecure areas like the arts and academia, opting instead for business, medicine, and the law.... [O]n the whole it seems likely that it was a combination of economic and psychological factors that helped to push American Catholicism toward cultural conformity in the postwar years.

It is surely a mistake, though, for Ellis to accept without question an equation between conformity and anti-intellectualism.... This reaction was understandable enough in the light of the intellectual mood of the 1950s, but it led many Catholic thinkers into erratic interpretations of their own culture. "To be an intellectual," declared Catholic scholar Thomas F. O'Dea in 1958, "means to be engaged in a quest." But this is a gross oversimplification: as we have seen, the "quest" in Kerouac and [J. F.] Powers, if it exists, is ironic and parodic, turning full circle to end up precisely where it began. It is this typical 1950s assumption that intellectualism must always coincide with nonconformity that needs rigorous interrogation: the search for the "numinous force" of "otherness" may be appropriate for Bellow and Updike, but it is by no means the only procedure available. This is not, of course, to denigrate these excellent novelists, merely to point out that the cultural assumptions implicit within their texts comprise relative, not absolute, truths.

> Paul Giles, *American Catholic Arts and Fictions: Culture, Ideology, Aesthetics* (Cambridge: Cambridge University Press, 1992), 439–42. Reprinted with the permission of Cambridge University Press.

## 12. Philip Gleason on the Appearance of "Cultural" Catholicism, 1995

*A Notre Dame historian points to a momentous change in the terms of the debate on Catholic intellectual life.*

[I]n tracing the intellectualism discussion over four decades we can discern a shift from thinking of Catholicism in doctrinal, disciplinary, and institutional terms to an emphasis on underlying cultural patterns and attitudinal dispositions.

This is, to be sure, a matter of emphasis, for the early critics were not insensitive to these matters. O'Dea and Donovan, for example, had both studied with Talcott Parsons and made much of cultural norms and socialization in "diffuse and particularistic values and attitudes," that tended to produce people who were "dependent, submissive, pietistic, and intellectually incurious."[1]

But these critics were talking about Catholics who happened to exhibit these cultural qualities, not about people who could be identified as Catholics *because* they exhibited them. What *made* people Catholics were the beliefs they held, the ritual practices they followed, and their identification with the institutional church. Those who had "lost their faith" did not count as Catholics, no matter how intellectual they might be. In fact, famous writers or thinkers who were "apostates" were regarded as telling evidence of deep-dyed anti-intellectualism in the church precisely because these "fallen away Catholics" had "left the church."

Consider, by contrast, the way Andrew Greeley and Paul Giles handle the question today. In the mid-seventies Greeley introduced "the communal Catholic": a person who identifies strongly with his or her ancestral religious tradition, "likes" being a Catholic, and intends to remain one, but follows a selective policy with respect to doctrine, adopts a more relaxed attitude toward ritual practice, and feels no great attachment to the institutional church.... When he discusses the present status of Catholic intellectual life, Greeley lists as outstanding exemplars a number of individuals. Some of them, he concedes, are said to be "fallen away Catholics." But he does not believe that undercuts his argument that Catholic intellectual life is flourishing. The reason

---

1. This language is taken from John D. Donovan, *The Academic Man in the Catholic College* (New York: Sheed and Ward, 1964), 191–92.

is that since a person cannot exorcise Catholic images from his or her creative imagination, the work produced by ex-Catholics usually "reflects Catholic vision."[2]

Paul Giles follows the same general approach in his *American Catholic Arts and Fictions,* but on a much larger scale and with intermittent bursts of bewildering post-modernist jargon. Being interested in the aesthetic results of cultural assumptions putatively absorbed by persons who were Catholics at any point in their careers, he is able to cast a net that includes persons as diverse as Orestes Brownson, Theodore Dreiser, Mary McCarthy, Alfred Hitchcock, and — perhaps most surprising of all — Robert Mapplethorpe....

These crude summaries of course oversimplify the positions of persons whose work illustrates what I am calling the cultural understanding of Catholicism. But some such thing is very definitely out there. Though I do not claim that it has become the dominant view, I do assert that its very presence constitutes a momentous change from the state of affairs that obtained when the great debate on Catholic intellectual life got under way. How are we to account for the change? A full explanation would require an entire chapter if not a book, but let me mention a couple of obvious points.

The first concerns the negative factor in the situation — that is, the collapse of the earlier understanding of what being a Catholic entailed. The historian Thomas T. McAvoy, C.S.C., who was my mentor in graduate school, used to say that American Catholics were disunited in everything except their faith. He sometimes called it "theological unity," but he meant the whole complex of doctrine, discipline, and ritual practice that was still in place in the 1950s.[3] It is hardly necessary to point out that this complex was severely shaken by the spiritual earthquake of the 1960s. To put it baldly, McAvoy's "theological unity" could no longer serve as an unambiguous litmus test of Catholicity because Catholics disagreed too much among themselves on matters of faith, morals, and practice.

This resulted in uncertainty as to what it really means to be a Catholic. And in that uncertainty other factors could, as it were, lay claim to the definitional role left ambiguous by the partial disintegration of the strictly religious criteria of Catholic identity. The first of these claimants was *ethnicity;* close upon its heels came *culture.* Both are looser, vaguer, and less ambitious in their definitional claims than McAvoy's theological unity. For what they claim (to continue speaking of them in this personified way) is not to define Catholic identity as such, but merely to be more important factors in understanding the behavior of Catholics than "religion" is.

As to ethnicity, remember how the "new ethnicity" seemed to come out of nowhere around 1970, just as the postconciliar shredding of the old theological unity was pretty well complete. And recall what a prominent role Catholics played in that so-called "ethnic revival...." Recall how often religion

---

2. Andrew Greeley, *The Catholic Myth* (New York: Scribner, 1990), 85–86.

3. See, for example, Thomas T. McAvoy, *The Great Crisis in American Catholic History, 1895–1900* (Chicago: H. Regnery, 1957), 1.

was submerged in ethnicity in the work of the new social historians. What McAvoy would have considered essential to the faith took on a distinctively ethnic coloration as "devotional Catholicism" in Jay Dolan's book. The same tendency to relativize what American Catholics of McAvoy's and Ellis's generation considered essential is also to be found in works on Italian and Hispanic Catholics....

Note, incidentally, how easily the terminology shifts here from ethnicity to culture, for there is no strict boundary between the two, ethnicity being an aspect of culture, or, if one prefers, culture a way of understanding ethnicity. But besides its overlapping with ethnicity, many other factors helped push culture to the fore. The influence of Clifford Geertz's writings, for example; the Vatican's preoccupation with "inculturation"; the revival of interest in tradition associated with Alasdair MacIntyre and other writers of "communalist" persuasion; and of course the explosion of interest in multiculturalism....

Philip Gleason, "A Look Back at the Catholic Intellectualism Issue," *U.S. Catholic Historian* 13, no. 1 (Winter 1995): 32–35. Printed with permission.

# Part 2

# SCHOLASTICISMS AND THOMISMS

## Introduction

The term *Scholasticism* refers to the methods and teaching of the "Schoolmen," that is, the philosophers and theologians who propounded their views at the medieval universities, especially the University of Paris.[1] St. Thomas Aquinas (1225–74), a Dominican friar, is considered to be the greatest of the Scholastics; he was rivaled in brilliance by a contemporary, St. Bonaventure (1217–74), a Franciscan, who also authored influential commentaries and treatises in the broad Scholastic tradition. Although Scholasticism faded for a time after the high middle ages, elements of the system were retrieved by post-Reformation commentators such as the Spanish Jesuit Francisco Suarez (d. 1617) during the sixteenth and seventeenth centuries. A case-based moral theology derived in part from Scholasticism informed the confessor's manuals that priests consulted in assigning penance for sins.

Scholasticism again faded from prominence until the 1850s, when the embattled pope, Pius IX, launched an effort to bolster papal authority and strengthen the position of the church in an increasingly threatening milieu characterized by materialism, secular nationalism, and atheism. Pius turned for assistance to the Jesuits, who had embraced Scholasticism as the basis of teaching within the order. Avid Jesuit Scholastics such as Joseph Kleutgen and Matteo Liberatore remained influential in the Vatican during the pontificate of Pius's successor, Pope Leo XIII, who, capitalizing on momentum he had helped to create, promulgated *Aeterni Patris* in 1879. The encyclical mandated a return to the thought of Aquinas himself as the authoritative Catholic response to the intellectual challenges of modernity.

In the United States during the late eighteenth and early nineteenth centuries, prior to the reemergence of Thomism, Catholic leaders such as Archbishop John Carroll and John England, the first Catholic bishop of Charleston, South Carolina, sought to demonstrate the compatibility of Catholicism and American republicanism. England has been described, aptly, as "the most articulate and dynamic Catholic representative of the Enlightenment in the

---

1. Philip Gleason, *Contending with Modernity: Catholic Higher Education in the Twentieth Century* (New York: Oxford University Press, 1995), 105.

United States."[2] But he did not take an uncritical attitude toward the Enlightenment; indeed, while Bishop England praised philosophy, he warned against the Enlightenment-era belief in human perfectibility and pointed to the vast gulf between what philosophy alone could attain and "the immensity of him who alone is perfection..." (doc. 13).

By the time Father Isaac Hecker, founder of the Congregation of the Missionary Priests of St. Paul the Apostle (Paulists), collected his major essays in a volume entitled *The Church and the Age* (1887), the neo-Thomist revival had begun. Hecker, a convert to Catholicism, was a representative of the Romantic mood in American religion, and he believed that the indwelling Spirit was at work redeeming the United States for Christ. He balanced that belief, however, within an affirmation of the necessity of "external forms of the church."[3] The former Protestant also extolled the superiority of Catholic philosophy and theology, and their compatibility with the findings of modern science. Thus, during the decade in which seminarians and priests were being newly encouraged to pursue the study of Thomism, he celebrated "the truth of the teaching of St. Thomas, who says that 'the study of creation tends to the destruction of error and the fortifying of the truths of divine faith.'" With St. Thomas, Hecker believed that "every advance in the natural sciences is a new conquest of Catholicity over heresy" (doc. 14).

Among the central tenets of Thomism are the following. Beyond the natural order there is a supernatural order, known only through God's revelation. Reason alone can neither attain to, nor disprove, the supernatural truths of Christianity (such as the doctrine of the Trinity). Yet there is no contradiction between natural reason and God-given faith, which is the perfection of reason. God's omniscience and omnipotence do not destroy human freedom; rather, those who are saved, are saved through the free gift of God by grace, but those who are damned are damned by their own free choices. The church, the mystical body of Christ, is the sole custodian of the faith and the dispenser of the sacraments, the instruments by which divine grace is ordinarily conveyed to the believer.[4]

Neo-Thomism, adhering in its basic contours to the principles of Aquinas, presented itself as the irreplaceable remedy to the several serious intellectual errors of modern epistemology (theory of knowledge). Modern thinkers, confronted by evolution, dialectical materialism, the psychology of the subconscious, and other destabilizing ideas suggested by the discoveries or theories of modern science, had become distracted and misled by the seemingly "realistic" options of skepticism and irrationalism. Boldly, neo-Thomism offered a

---

2. Patrick W. Carey, "John England: Catholic Constitutionalism," in *American Catholic Religious Thought: The Shaping of a Theological and Social Tradition,* ed. Patrick W. Carey (New York: Paulist, 1987), 73.

3. David J. O'Brien, *Isaac Hecker: An American Catholic* (New York: Paulist, 1992), 240.

4. Lawrence Cunningham, *The Catholic Heritage* (New York: Crossroad, 1986), 112–13. See also James A. Weisheipel, "Thomism," *The New Catholic Encyclopedia,* vol. 14 (Washington, D.C., 1967), 127–28.

renewed confidence in the powers of rightly ordered human reason, defiantly reaffirming its ontological reality — its participation in "being itself."

A return to Scholastic method and the concept of "the certainty of truth" upon which it was premised provided the antidote to "Modernism" in the Catholic Church as well. Largely confined to Europe, the "synthesis of all heresies," as Pius X termed Modernism in his condemnation of the "movement" (*Pascendi gregis*, 1907) was in fact an uncoordinated, disparate set of ideas and explorations mounted, at least initially, in faithful response to the challenges to Catholic tradition posed by modern biblical criticism and developmentalist thought. The so-called Modernists in Europe taught the historical "evolution" of Catholic doctrine. Pius X's neo-Scholastic advisors also charged the Modernists with promoting "vital immanence" — the immediacy of the divine presence to each individual soul — an idea that seemed to jeopardize the autonomy and necessity of the "external" revelation of scripture and tradition entrusted to the magisterium, or teaching office of the church. "Official" revelation, the Modernists taught, was complemented and even confirmed by the indwelling Spirit. The result of this teaching, the Scholastics responded, was subjectivism, an error not far removed from the disastrous Protestant insistence on the priority of the individual over the church.

Tellingly, the neo-Scholastics who published the Jesuit biweekly *Civiltà Cattolica*, the semiofficial organ of the papacy, espoused the idea that the fatal mistake of the Catholic Modernists was their disregard for, or complete abandonment of, Thomism. While few American priests toyed with Modernism, John B. Hogan, an influential priest and author teaching at the Sulpician seminary in Boston, found it difficult to summon enthusiasm for *Aeterni Patris*. A handful of priests, including three Sulpicians, teaching at St. Joseph's seminary in Dunwoodie (Yonkers), New York, published a journal, *The New York Review* (1905–8), that featured criticisms of neo-Scholasticism and promoted the thought of Bonaventure, Pascal, Cardinal Newman, Lord Acton, and other "alternatives" to the Thomist synthesis.[5]

Neo-Thomism emerged from the Modernist crisis as American Catholicism's answer to the postwar malaise affecting U.S. culture. When American Protestants, stunned by the atrocities of "world war," lost confidence in what they had believed to be enlightened humanity's inevitable progress toward an ever more just and humane society, American Catholics strode into the breach. Possessed of a unitary system of thought and assured of the civilization-building powers of human reason aided by faith, Catholics provided sorely needed legitimacy for the renewal of the American dream of a democratic, free, open, just, and rational society. The project of building a "progressive" modern civilization need not be abandoned, Catholics explained, if such a civilization is based on the proper metaphysical foundations. Thought is real, as Catholic educator James H. Ryan insists in his article on "the New Scholasticism" (doc. 15),

---

5. R. Scott Appleby, *Church and Age Unite! The Modernist Impulse in American Catholicism* (Notre Dame, Ind.: University of Notre Dame Press, 1992), 117–68.

and so are the objects in the world, which rightly ordered reason is capable of knowing — and ordering to their proper ends.

The neo-Thomist revival (also referred to, less precisely, as the neo-Scholastic revival) reached the peak of its influence in Catholic seminaries, colleges, and universities in the 1920s and 1930s. Neo-Thomism was disseminated in the United States not only by professors of the Catholic University of America and by Jesuits at Fordham and St. Louis University (home of *The Modern Schoolman,* a journal devoted to spreading the revival, first published in 1925), but also by lay philosophers such as Étienne Gilson and Jacques Maritain. Gilson, after serving as a visiting professor at Harvard, went on to direct the medieval institute at St. Michael's College, Toronto, where he oversaw the training of a whole generation of distinguished Thomists, including Gerald Phelan, Anton Pegis, Joseph Owens, and Armand Mauer. The institute's review, *Medieval Studies,* quickly became recognized as a major journal for American medievalists.[6]

In addition, *Commonweal,* a lay Catholic weekly founded in 1924; *Thought,* a Jesuit journal founded in 1926; and the American Catholic Philosophical Association (1926) were among the many vital Catholic presences that appeared on the American cultural landscape after World War I. The historian William Halsey, surveying the scene, has described the cumulative effect of the energies of Catholic intellectuals, writers, and activists under the rubric, "the survival of American innocence."[7]

Having reached its apex between the world wars, neo-Thomism continued for decades thereafter to provide the intellectual foundations of American Catholic education in general, and of the study of philosophy and theology in particular. Catholic schoolchildren learned the particulars of their faith from the Baltimore Catechism, a ubiquitous manual espousing Thomist principles and organized in a question-and-answer format not dissimilar to that preferred by Francis J. Connell, C.SS.R., who penned the widely disseminated instruction, *Father Connell Answers Moral Questions* (doc. 16). Uncannily, the popularization of neo-Thomist ideas and views extended, in the 1940s and 1950s, even beyond the walls of the so-called Catholic ghetto (which by this point were breaking down). Thomas Merton, whose spiritual autobiography was a best-seller, broke open for his readers the simple genius of St. Thomas's worldview, according to which the natural order in all its grace-filled particulars is oriented to the supernatural (docs. 17 and 18). During his improbably popular national radio and television programs Monsignor (later Bishop) Fulton J. Sheen regaled "mixed" audiences (Catholics as well as non-Catholics) with moral lessons and philosophical insights delivered with great flourish. The threat of atheistic Communism, an enemy that could only be countered by faith-filled reason, was a major theme.

---

6. Gerald A. McCool, S.J., "Thomism in America," in *The Encyclopedia of American Catholic History,* ed. Michael Glazier and Thomas J. Shelley (Collegeville, Minn.: Liturgical Press, 1997), 1385.

7. William M. Halsey, *The Survival of American Innocence: Catholicism in an Era of Disillusionment, 1920–1940* (Notre Dame, Ind.: University of Notre Dame Press, 1980).

Not least among the virtues of neo-Thomism for mid-twentieth century American Catholic philosophers and theologians was its conception of the natural law. Reflecting in its own order the truths of the eternal law of God, the natural law — the laws and structures imbedded in nature by the Creator, and accessible to human reason — also served, potentially, as a bridge between Catholics and non-Catholics. In the 1950s and 1960s Father John Courtney Murray, S.J., articulated the connections between the profound metaphysical insights of the Catholic/Thomist intellectual tradition, and the political rights and freedoms protected in the U.S. Constitution. Almost singlehandedly he forged a public philosophy that became the foundation for a generation (and more) of U.S. Catholic participation in the broader American debate about the nature of "the common good" on matters ranging from arms control to foreign policy to welfare (doc. 19).

Beset by internal fragmentation into rival schools, the neo-Thomist revival weakened considerably with the advent of the sixties and the Second Vatican Council. Radical changes in the curricula of Catholic colleges deprived Thomism of its dominant place in Catholic education. Yet Thomism continues to be a major intellectual resource for American Catholics a full generation after its heyday. The distinguished philosopher Alasdair MacIntyre, for example, has created an appealing new version of Thomistic virtue ethics that has been widely influential in philosophical discourse for decades now.[8]

The following excerpts provide glimpses into the neo-Scholastic/neo-Thomist worldview that informed the ideas and public arguments of Catholics in the United States, from the time of Bishop John England (1786–1842) to the days of John Courtney Murray, S.J. (1904–1967).

## 13. John England on the Consolations and Limitations of Philosophy, 1832

*From 1820 until his death in 1842 England, the first bishop of Charleston, South Carolina, was a national spokesman for the compatibility of Catholicism and American political and cultural institutions. He addressed the U.S. Congress in 1822 and often spoke in Protestant churches and at civic affairs. In this oration, delivered to the Literary and Philosophical Society of South Carolina, he offers a critique of the philosophical notion of human perfectibility.*

Philosophy is, properly speaking, the deduction of correct conclusions from evident principles and ascertained facts. — In order, however, to proceed safely to the results, the premises must be secured; and the mighty evil of which we have to complain is the great facility with which probablism, conjecture and speculation have been substituted for principles others have collected lest we should sink in public estimation, by turning to account what we or our colleagues had not discovered; and in decrying our predecessors, instead of profiting by their labors. It is true that the pick or the crowbar would be exceedingly

---

8. See, for example, Alasdair MacIntyre, *Three Rival Versions of Moral Inquiry* (Notre Dame, Ind.: University of Notre Dame Press, 1990).

inappropriate tools for giving the last finish of taste to a splendid golden vase; but had they never been used for excavation, the ore would not have been furnished; and what a variety of intermediate hands must be employed between that which first opened the mine and that which finally touches the vessel? The pioneer who commenced the opening of the forest should not be despised by him who subsequently occupies the mansion, and enjoys the wealth of the harvest and the luxury of the scene. Human science like human labor is progressive, and the peculiar duty of the philosopher, like that of the workman, is to exert himself for the improvement of what he received in a state of imperfection.

I am far from being an advocate for the modern theory of what is called the perfectibility and gradual progress to perfection of the human mind. My observations and reflections have led me to the conclusion, that God has given the lower world, with all its accumulated treasures and productions, as well as the firmament by which it is surrounded, and studded as it is, with so many glorious decorations, as a vast field for man's temporal occupation: to search out their several parts, to discover their relations, their properties, their uses, their affinities, their opposition, to turn them to the purposes of his own happiness here; I shall not in this place advert to their uses for hereafter.

This investigation, this application, is what I call philosophy. The astronomer, who by his patient and laborious observations and calculations enables the navigator in the midst of the waste of waters to know his place and to pursue his proper course; the mathematician and the algebraist, who give to the ship-builder, the engineer, and to so many others, the rules by whose observance they can securely attain the useful objects of their pursuit; the botanist who secures to us the benefits of our diversified vegetation; the chemist who, by analysis and composition, turns such an immense mass of varied productions to the most extensive account; the physician who applies them to the solace of the human family; the anatomist who by his almost god-like skill is able to detect and to remove the obstructions as well as to repair the defects of the animal system; the legislator, and the jurist who establish and reduce to practice, the great principles by whose operation, peace, prosperity and liberty are guarded; they who study to provide and to prepare for use the great articles of sustenance, of clothing, of shelter, of defence, of comfort and convenience for the children of Adam: all these form the vast aggregate of the several classes of philosophy. It is true that the climate, the soil, the productions, the temperament, the habits, the special wants and the peculiar tastes of nations greatly vary, and that for these variations considerable allowance should be made; yet in all cases the great principle of philosophy is the same; that is, to extend our discoveries in that range which is subject to our research and turn the discovery to beneficial account.

From this view it would seem that the duty of the philosopher, was simple, and that by his faithful attention to its discharge, man must necessarily make contrast and rapid progress to perfection; for he had only to pursue what he had received, to add his own observations to those of his predecessors, and to transmit the increased fund to those who succeed him; and since this is what really occurs, why should not man speedily arrive at perfection? The theory is plausible, but history and reflection will correct its fallacy. That the duty of the philosopher has been properly described, I readily admit; but that the specified result should be obtained, it is necessary, first, that all which has been acquired should have been preserved; and secondly, that the point of perfection should not be too remote. The advocates for what is called perfectibility perhaps never seriously examine either of these topics.

Let us try this theory of the progress of the mind, or as it is sometimes called, the march of the intellect, by the test of facts. Think you was the mind of Homer more feeble than that of Milton? Was Virgil or Horace as far below the mental grade of Pope or Dryden, or these latter below Byron or Moore as those intervened centuries between them? Had the intellect of Demosthenes less vigor than that of Patrick Henry? Or was Cicero twenty degrees upon the scale of forensic merit below William Pinckney or Daniel Webster, or even Baron Vaux and Brougham, the Lord High Chancellor of England? What shall I say of Archimedes and Euclid? Are we to find the proofs of this theory in the legislation of Greece and Rome, in the tactics of Cæsar, in the architecture of antiquity, in the statuary of the remote ages, in the minds that planned and the powers that erected the pyramids of Egypt? It is true that though the energies of the mind be unchanged, the facts upon which they operate may be extended and varied as time advances in his course. In the morning, the little speck which is scarcely perceptible upon the verge of the horizon alone breaks the serene uniformity of the vacant fields of air, but as the day advances it ascends and approximates, whilst other collections appear, accumulate and unite; the pregnant storm shrouds the meridian sun, and envelopes the ocean in its shade, until amidst the echoes of the heavens it is discharged and expires: yet the unchanged observer pre-existed and survives.

How frequently have we witnessed a noble patrimony broken up and scattered by a dissipated heir? How often has the flood or the storm swept away a splendid mansion, and reduced a rich plantation to a desert? How many times has a licentious soldiery or an unruly mob devastated a noble capital in which the wealth of nature and the decorations of art abounded? So too has the sloth or luxury of one age dissipated the mental acquisitions of those which preceded it: an incursion of barbarians has frequently swept science from its domain, and covered the land with ignorance and ruin and despair. When nations are disturbed for the purposes of ambition or the vengeance of disappointment, when the public mind is filled with discontent and indignation; when maddened hosts fly to arms and rush to mutual destruction in the rage of battle; or when the heavy yoke of robust despotism presses upon a crushed people; or when animated by the spirit of liberty, men rise to assert their rights and to overthrow their oppressors; in times like these, under circumstances of this description, especially before copies of works were multiplied by the introduction of the press; and the few that existed were destroyed by the wantonness of the victor, for the indignation of the vanquished, how frequent and how extensive was the destruction of the records and of the collections of the philosopher? Thus has the knowledge of many an ancient art been obliterated. The evidence of their

existence, like the remnants of stained glass which are still found in many ancient churches, lets in upon us a soft and mellowed light, which informs us that
if we possess knowledge which did not exist amongst men of other days, they
enjoyed some which has not reached us: like many a rich cargo that has been
lost at sea, it is covered with the waters of oblivion. Who will undertake to assert that the mass of what has been lost does not equal the bulk of what exists
to-day? I am far from inclining to the opinion that it does; but I think it would
savor of rashness, boldly to make either assertion.

But suppose all the ancient discoveries to have been faithfully preserved and
the new ones duly transmitted: when will the accumulation fill up the measure of perfection? What is its capacity? Should a myriad of men be continually
occupied in depositing grains of sand, when would they form a globe whose
axles would touch opposed points in the orbit of Herschel? Let us compare the
progress of mind with the progress of motion. If we take our observations upon
what was the perfection of the mind in the Augustian [*sic*] age and what it is
to-day, you may assume superiority to the fullest extent of your disposition;
you will at all events allow that the progress has not been with the rapidity of
light. And yet, even with this acceleration, when would you reach those fixed
stars that shew so dimly in their distance? Yet is the immensity of him who
alone is perfection spread abroad infinitely beyond where their faintest rays
terminate in an opposite direction! When do we hope to reach it? I therefore
admit that there is abundant room for the continual progress of philosophical
improvement, though I cannot subscribe to the fallacious theory of human perfectibility. I allow that there are great incentives for approaching as nearly as we
can to perfection, though we can never attain it; like the asymptotes of the hy-
perbola; he who alone is perfect continues in one changeless direction through
eternity, whilst though the created mind, like the curve, should continually
approximate as it advances, yet will they never coincide.

> Right Rev. Dr. John England, "Oration Delivered on the Anniversary of the Literary
> and Philosophical Society of South Carolina" (Baltimore: J. Myres, 1932), 33–40.

## 14. Isaac Hecker, C.S.P., "Catholicity and the Tendencies of the Age," 1887

*Hecker, sometimes called the father of Americanism in the Catholic Church,
gave considerable time and energy to evangelizing and converting non-Catholic
Americans to the truths of the Catholic faith. His essays, like this celebration of
St. Thomas Aquinas, were often cast in an apologetic and mildly polemical (i.e.,
anti-Protestant) mode.*

It is an obvious fact that a considerable number of minds in our day have been
trained in scientific studies and are devoted to intellectual pursuits. It is equally
evident that the general diffusion of education will enlarge the circle of this
class of persons and extend their influence. And it is quite natural that minds
so trained, when their attention is turned to the study of religion, should look

for its presentation under scientific forms. This expectation is not to be censured or thwarted; on the contrary, it should be met with due consideration and fairly satisfied. For the claims which Christianity lays upon man is that of a "reasonable service," and, unless it can make this demand good in the court of reason, it must lose its hold upon his intelligence, cease to exert its influence upon society, and give up the ideal of ever winning the homage of the whole human race.

And it was precisely this scientific presentation of Christianity with the aid of philosophy that was aimed at, and in great part achieved, by the Schoolmen. "For it is due to the service of philosophy that sacred theology take up and enrich itself with the nature, habit, and genius of a true science" [Leo XIII, Encyclical *Aeterni Patris*]. Before their day positive theology, which consisted in proving the divinity of Christianity by the authority of the inspired Scriptures and the words of Christ delivered to His apostles and handed down from generation to generation in His Church with the testimony of the Fathers, had received its completion. This prepared the way of the Schoolmen, who added to the arguments of positive theology those drawn from philosophy. Philosophy, as held by them, consisted in those truths which had been "discovered with the sole light of natural reason by the eminent thinkers of the past," especially by their prince, Aristotle, who reduced these truths into a system, but not unmixed with most serious, not to say appalling, errors. St. Thomas, the prince of the Schoolmen, with the aid derived from the writings of his precursors, especially of St. Dionysius the Areopagite, St. Augustine, Boëthius, St. Anselm, Blessed Albert the Great his master, and above all from the light of his own incomparable and sanctified genius, eliminated these errors, and at the same time modified, enlarged, and enriched with his own ideas the boundaries and scope of philosophy.

The aim of the Schoolmen was to produce, by the full play of the light of natural reason on the intellectual side of Christianity, aided by philosophy and consistently with positive theology, a strictly logical demonstration of Christianity. The great task which they had before them was that of the synthesis of natural and revealed truth, of science and faith. But there came a halt in the march of this intellectual progress.

In the early part of the sixteenth century earnest and zealous efforts were made by sincere churchmen to reform the evils and extirpate the abuses existing in the Church, more especially in Germany. By certain leaders whose passions swayed their judgments, combined with temporal princes who made use of these to gain despotic power, this most praiseworthy movement was turned from that of reform into one of heresy, schism, and revolution. Seized with the insane idea of destroying the Church which Christ had built, they conspired together and organized a systematic opposition, protesting defiantly against her doctrines, and rudely overturning, wherever they succeeded in gaining the power, what she had with great difficulty reared and with greater sacrifices sustained.

Consistently with the fundamental principle of their system of confining the attention exclusively to the Bible, and the interpretation of its texts by the sole light of the internal illumination of the Holy Spirit, they denied the value of human reason, contemned [*sic*] philosophy, opposed the spread of education and the study of the liberal arts and sciences, burnt up or sold as waste paper precious manuscripts, depopulated the schools and universities, and shattered to pieces, wherever they came within their reach, all works of art.

Hence Melanchthon, the learned scholar, imbued with this fanaticism, abandoned his studies, apprenticed himself to a baker in order not to distract his attention with human learning from the internal workings of the Holy Spirit. Every ignorant peasant might consistently entertain the fancy that he was called to be a preacher of the Gospel — as many did — and that he was even all the better fitted to become a preacher of the Gospel by very reason of his crass ignorance. This original characteristic trait of contempt for all human learning and culture survives here and there among Protestant sects even to our own day, more notably among the Society of Friends, the Methodists, and the Plymouth Brethren. This reaction against intellectual activity and denial of progress properly named itself Protestantism.

It has taken the greater part of three centuries for the body of those who have been infected by his contagion to throw off its effects, and to regain their intellectual and moral health sufficiently to walk again erect. This state of convalescence upon which the better part of the descendants of original Protestantism have entered has taken place by the intellect slowly assimilating those truths which the leaders of this secession from the Church denied, and in rejecting their principal errors. For the intellect, according to its own laws, as Sir Thomas teaches, seeks truth, assimilates it when found, and has a natural abhorrence of error, and, when once detected, rejects it. Thus the Protestantism of the nineteenth century, or what goes now pretty much by that name, is the reverse of the Protestantism of the sixteenth century.

The process of this transformation has been somewhat as follows: The truths of divine revelation and of human reason against which a protest was made in the beginning have been placed in such a clear light by long and frequent discussion that further controversy about them in our day is hardly possible. Where will you find an intelligent man among Protestants who could be induced to repeat Martin Luther's diatribes against human reason? or against man's free-will? or against human nature? How many Presbyterians of this generation hold and believe the five points of Calvinism pure and simple? The same might be said with equal truth of Episcopalians and the Thirty-nine Articles of Anglicanism. Very few among Protestants of this century take the pains to read their creeds, and those who do, and get an idea of their contents, either clamor for their change or would smile at the simplicity of one who seriously asked whether they believed in them. Even the human sciences appear to have had for their mission, especially since their revival in our times, to undermine the positions assumed by Protestantism in its attacks on the Catholic Church, and the drift of their real discoveries harmonizes with Catholic philosophy and theology. This confirms the truth of the teaching of St. Thomas, who says that "the study of creation tends to the destruction of error and the fortifying of the truths of divine faith." Every forward step in the sciences is a conquest of truth, and as the supernatural finds its confirmation in the natural, so every advance in the natural sciences is a new conquest of Catholicity over heresy. It is from this point of view we can fully appreciate the affirmation of Leo XIII, that *"Christ is the Restorer of the sciences...."*

The whole drift of the foregoing might be summed up in these words: If an exposition of the Catholic religion were made, following the efforts of the Schoolmen, especially St. Thomas, profiting at the same time by the knowledge, discoveries, and experience since acquired, in the light of such a presentment the prejudices against the Catholic faith would disappear, its beauty would find unbidden entrance into the hearts of men, the religious revolution of the sixteenth century would be reversed, and humanity as one man would advance with rapid strides to bring down the kingdom of heaven upon earth, and, in so doing, fit itself for its loftier ampler destiny above.

Assuming, then, the fact, which many among themselves frankly acknowledge, that Protestantism as an organized opposition to the Catholic Church has spent its main strength, and as an adequate representation of Christianity is an utter failure, is doomed to disappear, and is disappearing rapidly; assuming that in the eyes of intelligent men the efforts to invent or construct a new religion are unworthy a moment of serious thought; and granting that "the problem of problems of this hour" is, as Mr. Tyndall has put it in his Bristol address, "how to yield the religious sentiment reasonable satisfaction," the question then immediately before us is this: What prospect is there that the Catholic religion will solve this problem of problems?

This is the question with which we started out, and insisted on being frankly met and fairly answered. Religion, Christianity, the Catholic Church — which is Christianity in its unity and totality in a concrete form — has for its actual task to answer satisfactorily the intellectual demands of the age, and to perceive its opportunities in modern civilization and its onward tendencies.

The Catholic Church, so far from shrinking from this precise problem and these imperative demands, hails them with inmost delight. She is not only ready to face them fearlessly, but, conscious of the indwelling divinity and the possession of divine truth, she looks upon this problem and these demands as the very opportunities prepared by her Divine Spouse to secure, by her satisfactory solution and answers, a new and glorious triumph....

Let us now suppose, as the smoke of the successful battle with heresy vanishes from the field, that the truths brought forth so conspicuously in this conflict were properly adjusted, like the one we have taken as an illustration, and we shall perceive what is meant by the resumption and completion of the great task of the Schoolmen. If this were accomplished, and the Catholic Church were seen in the light of such a fair presentment, the false impressions and the prejudices springing from them would disappear from the minds of men as the mist yields before the light of the rising sun; their intelligence would seize hold instinctively of its divine truths, and mankind, lifted as it were by one wave of intelligence and joy, would pursue with happier zeal its great end.

Nor is this a pleasant word-picture drawn by effort of the imagination; it is the representation of the Catholic Church in her true light, and, as a proof of its truth and reality, we dare appeal to the unanimous testimony and to the consciousness of all well-informed Catholics. It was in this light St. Augustine, that lofty genius, beheld the Catholic Church when he exclaimed: "Too late have I known thee, O ancient truth! Too late have I loved thee, O beauty ancient and ever new!"

Let him, therefore, who would serve the Catholic Church in this generation, show her in her own true light, in her unity and universality, in all her beauty and majesty. It is this true vision of her divinity that will captivate man's intelligence, secure the unbidden homage of his will, and elicit his most heroic devotedness. Herein lies the mysterious force of her duration for so many centuries, the secret of the power of her sway over more than two hundred millions of souls, and the reason for the never-broken stream of her converts and the capture of the ablest minds of our century.

Very Rev. I. T. Hecker, *The Church and the Age: An Exposition of the Catholic Church in View of the Needs and Aspirations of the Present Age* (New York: Catholic World, 1887), 181–87, 189–91, 204–5.

## 15. James H. Ryan on the Contributions of the New Scholasticism, 1926

*In this excerpt from a lengthy chapter contending that "the new Scholasticism" (a.k.a. "neo-Thomism") is the antidote to the ills besetting modern philosophy, Father Ryan, a professor at the Catholic University of America in Washington, D.C., expresses the robust confidence in Thomism as a civilizational project that was shared by many Catholic thinkers during the interwar years.*

In the dark night of the intellectual anarchy which has followed upon the war, the Neo-Scholastic holds out for acceptance a systematic thought which, like a great light, penetrates the obscurities of the dungeon in which much of our thinking seems to be confined, and indicates the road to safety, sanity, and salvation. We know that the light which will penetrate this darkness is not an illusion. The eager search for it proves that mankind, too, realizes both its existence and its need. That men shall see and accept and be guided by its blessed rays depends on the energy we manifest and the skill we use in making known our belief to an age whose eyes have become unaccustomed to the strong white light of truth....

The New Scholasticism will never become acceptable if it comes to us merely as a defensive position designed to protect its adherents from the exaggerations of naturalistic philosophy. Modern thought asks of the diverse philosophies which are called before its judgment seat more than that they be strong defensive positions. It asks them, first of all, to present their credentials in the name of philosophy itself, and this Scholasticism is prepared to do. The New Scholasticism is not a protest. It is a positive doctrine and, as such, exhibits a set of principles which must be evaluated on their own merits as on their general availability for the purposes of modern science and life. We feel, too, that this philosophy has a peculiar contribution to make towards the advance of human knowledge. It is on the basis of such contributions also that both its timeliness and truth are to be judged.

The body-mind problem and the problem of knowledge are the chief questions which divide philosophers to-day. A moment's thought will cause us to realize why these questions have assumed such large proportions in present-day philosophical speculation, so as almost to exclude the consideration of all other problems. The solution, for example, given the epistemological question colors one's psychology inasfar as it is explanatory and not merely descriptive of one's metaphysics, and one's ethics. On the other hand, to profess parallelism or behaviorism or some sort of materialistic monism involves the acceptance of a group of psychological and metaphysical assumptions which cannot be squared with the postulates of the Interaction theory. In both cases the solutions offered are of immense significance for philosophy by reason of the consequences involved, as by reason of the attitude towards reality and experience which each theory necessarily implies. That the Neo-Scholastic theory of knowledge and psycho-physical relation is daily gaining ground and becoming more and more the accepted viewpoint of both science and philosophy is an indication of the construction [*sic*] possibilities for thought contained in that position.

Let us first look at the Neo-Scholastic solution of the problem of knowledge. The New Scholasticism, as far as knowledge goes, is realistic. It accepts the reality of thought; it also accepts the reality of the object known by thought. Such a position involves a dualistic reading of nature. It is by a process of mental correspondence that the real object is brought within the knowing range of the mind. Given such a correspondence, truth results from the relationship; in the absence of correspondence, we have doubt or error....

As a knowledge theory the New Scholasticism is profoundly intellectualist. It therefore approaches more closely idealistic theories than the voluntarism of Pragmatism. Yet, it sympathizes deeply with the pragmatic strictures on the "inhumanity" of the cold, narrow intellectualism which has always characterized idealists, both subjective and objective. What is more, the utility theory of truth can be accepted by us, but not in the sense in which Pragmatism propounds it. If a thing is useful, undoubtedly it is true; it is not utility, however, which makes truth, for utility presupposes truth already made. We acknowledge, too, the value of coherence theory, but cannot come to regard it as the final test of truth. Over and about the simple fact that the Real Whole, with which individual truths must cohere in order to gain truth, is for human knowledge a pure metaphysical abstraction, or, if not, then it is an unattainable acquisition. Coherence presupposes a more ultimate criterion by which we are to judge the truth or falsehood of a particular proposition presented to the mind before it is capable of being brought into relation with the whole of truth. If we are not mistaken, Realism can be presented as a higher synthesis of both Idealism and Pragmatism, for by a series of distinctions the differences between Scholasticism and these theories can be resolved into a higher and more acceptable philosophy.

Again, the New Scholasticism endeavors to steer a safe course through the exaggerations of radical empiricism, mysticism, and intuitionism. Whatever place must be accorded experience, pure, mystical, or intuitive in life and knowledge, we are convinced that these experiences in no sense exhaust the possibilities of knowledge. They do not even touch the heart of real human knowledge, which is the product of intellect alone. Nor can we accept the substitution of the will-to-believe for the intellect-which-knows. The philosophy of the place of the will in knowledge must be presented in sound and defensible terms if we are not to enmesh ourselves in a host of difficulties which will obscure rather than clarify the question at issue. The distinction between intellect and will must be maintained at any cost. It is a distinction which we present to modern philosophy, and which we consider one of the greatest contributions that the New Scholasticism has to offer to the solution of the epistemological problem....

Towards a solution of the psycho-physical problem, the New Scholasticism offers a series of ideas of vast importance, not only for this particular question, but for psychology as well. Its specific contribution to the problem at hand is the Interaction Theory. Parallelism is admittedly inadequate, and involves difficulties which are well nigh insurmountable. There has followed upon the breakdown of philosophical mechanism a decided reaction against every phase of Psychical Monism. Professor McDougall, who has done so much to make Parallelism untenable, contends that the body-mind problem can only be solved in one way, that is, by some form or other of animism. Crude animism is, of course, out of the question. However, it is animism, but a philosophical and scientific one, — what we call the Mind-Substance Theory, — that the New Scholasticism presents to the consideration of philosophy. We are quite conscious of the fact that of all the ideas which we defend, the idea of substance, and in particular mind-substance will probably be the very last that modern thought will accept. Since the days of Hume, the functional viewpoint has held undisputed sway and has acquired the prestige of being regarded almost everywhere as axiomatic. The functional idea, however, must be blasted out of the modern treatment of mind problems. In its place we must substitute a dualistic and dynamic philosophy of act and potency, substance and accident. These categories are of vital importance for metaphysical thinking to-day as they were in the days of Saint Thomas and Aristotle. That the conceptions current of these categories are scarcely better than cartoons is due perhaps as much to our lethargy as to the inadequate presentations which we have made of such necessary and far-reaching principles of thought.

Professor James H. Ryan, "The New Scholasticism and Its Contributions to Modern Thought," in *Present-Day Thinkers and the New Scholasticism: An International Symposium*, ed. John S. Zybura (St. Louis: B. Herder Book Co., 1927), 344–45, 360–66.

## 16. Francis J. Connell and the Moral Application of Neo-Thomism, 1959

*Francis J. Connell, a Redemptorist priest ordained in 1913, taught theology for twenty-five years before moving to Catholic University in 1940, where he au-thored an astounding 641 essays for the* American Ecclesiastical Review, *over 500 of which were answers to questions sent by the many priests who sub-scribed to the journal. As the excerpt below demonstrates, Father Connell was deeply formed in the Thomist worldview.*

"Interfaith" Problems

Question A: What is to be said of the use of such expressions as "inter-faith meetings," and "persons of different faiths," or of emphasizing "unity-in-diversity," when Catholics are describing their relations and attitude toward non-Catholics?

Answer A: The use by Catholics of such expressions as "interfaith meetings" and "persons of different faiths," whereby non-Catholics are said or implied to have a different *faith* from Catholics is very unfortunate. The word *faith*, as tra-ditionally used in the Catholic Church, signifies exclusively the one true faith, which is found only in the Catholic Church. Objectively, the faith is the body of truths that are proposed by the infallible magisterial of the Church as di-vinely revealed; subjectively, faith is the infused virtue whereby one accepts the truths of divine revelation on account of God's authority. It is true, the virtue of faith can reside in persons of good will separated from Catholic unity; yet, even in such the infused virtue impels them to believe only what is actually true; it does not extend to doctrines which they themselves may sincerely be-lieve but which are actually false (St. Thomas, *Sum. theol.*, II-II, q. 1, a. 3). The words of St. Paul are very explicit in this connection: "One Lord, *one faith*, one baptism" (*Ephes.* 4:5). When Catholics wish to speak of those outside the true fold, they could refer to them as persons of different denominations, different beliefs, different creeds — but the word *faith* should be retained in its traditional Catholic sense.

Similarly, to characterize the relation between Catholics and Protestants as "unity-in-diversity" is misleading, inasmuch as it implies that essentially Catho-lics are one with heretics, and that their diversities are only accidental. Actually, the very opposite is the true situation. For, however near an heretical sect may seem to be to the Catholic Church in its particular beliefs, a wide gulf separates them, inasfar as the divinely established means whereby the message of God is to be communicated to souls — the infallible magisterial of the Church — is re-jected by every heretical sect. By telling Protestants that they are one with us in certain beliefs, in such wise as to give the impression that we regard this unity as the predominant feature of our relation with them, we are actually misleading them regarding the true attitude of the Catholic Church toward those who do not acknowledge her teaching authority....

The State's Rights over Private Property

Question: Theologians tell us that if a person has damaged another's property without any formal guilt — and consequently without any obligation to make restitution, as far as the natural law is concerned — he will nevertheless be bound in strict justice to compensation if the civil authority commands him to do so (*post sententiam judicis*). Now, by what authority may the civil authority command a person to renounce a portion of his private property when he is not obliged to do so by the law of God?

Answer: It is an accepted principle of Catholic theology that in certain circumstances, for the sake of the common good, the State possesses the authority to dispose of the property of the citizens. This authoritative disposition of the State then binds the citizen in conscience, even though the natural law of itself imposes no such obligation. A concrete example would be this: Without any subjective guilt a man drives his car through his neighbor's hedge, causing considerable damage. By the natural law he is bound to no restitution because formal guilt was not present. However, if the neighbor takes the case to court — as he is perfectly entitled to do — and is accorded a certain amount of compensation, he obtains a right to this in commutative justice. Certainly, the common good demands that the State possess such a right; for, if a person whose property has been damaged could collect compensation only when the offender acknowledged subjective guilt, many acts of injustice would be perpetrated, and widespread indifference toward the property of others would prevail. It is to be noted that the principle here invoked by no means implies that the State possesses arbitrary power over the property of the citizens. It is only in certain specified cases, when otherwise the welfare of society would certainly be gravely impaired, that the civil authority is empowered to supersede the individual's right to retain his private property....

Military Activities Contrary to the Law of God

Question A: What course should be followed by a Catholic in the air corps if he is commanded to bomb a target which he knows is not a lawful military objective according to Catholic principles?

Question B: What advice should a Catholic chaplain give when such a case is submitted to him for judgment by the soldier in question?

Question C: Is it lawful for a young man to enter the air service if he realized that he may be commanded to participate in activities forbidden by the law of God?

Answer A: If a soldier is commanded to do something he knows is forbidden by the law of God as interpreted by the Catholic Church, he must refuse to obey no matter how grave the consequences. Even if he foresaw that he would be court-martialed and perhaps punished by death, he would not be justified in violating the law of God — for example, by directly bombing a group of noncombatants. It is interesting to note that the Nuremberg tribunal upheld the principle that "the fact that the defendant acted pursuant to order of his government or of a superior shall not free him from responsibility" (cf. Kenny,

*Moral Aspects of Nuremberg* [Washington, 1949], p. 55). It is to be hoped that as a correlative of this principle our government would judge a soldier deserving of praise if he disobeyed a command in war when he is convinced in conscience that what is commanded is against God's law. However, if a soldier only doubts as to the lawfulness of what is commanded, he may and should obey, since it is a general principle that a subject is bound to submit to lawful authority unless he is sure that what is being required of him is sinful. Such would be the case of the airman who is told to bomb a military objective, but is not certain whether the advantages to his side will be sufficiently great to justify the concomitant destruction of a considerable number of noncombatants.

Answer B: If a soldier explicitly proposes to a chaplain a problem as to the morality of a mission assigned to him, the chaplain should give him a correct and definite answer, as far as this is possible, according to Catholic principles. Thus, if the young man asks about the morality of a direct attack on noncombatants, it is the duty of the chaplain to inform him that this is contrary to the divine law, and cannot be justified under any circumstances. However, when the chaplain is not consulted, he is ordinarily not bound to take the initiative in condemning a measure, even though he is certain that it is unlawful, since usually such a protest would be futile.

Answer C: Since not all the activities of our air force in war are opposed to the law of God, it is not forbidden to a young man to enter this branch of the service, as long as he is determined to take no part in any particular activities that are unlawful. However, it is most desirable that Catholics who enter the air corps (in which moral problems of warfare are most likely to arise) should receive from the priests assigned to their spiritual care adequate instructions as to the laws of God concerning the means and methods of waging war, and should be told that in the event of a conflict between the law of God and a military command, they must obey the law of God....

### Bombing of Civilians

Question: Is the direct bombing of the civilian population ever permitted in war, for the purpose of breaking down their morale, so that they may the more speedily sue for peace?

Answer: The direct killing of noncombatants, even in a just war, is condemned as sinful by Catholic theologians. Even though the end may be a speedier return of peace — a most desirable objective — the use of this means is not permitted. However, when there is question of applying this principle to the bombing of the residential districts of a city, the solution is by no means simple. For, in the first place, even among the civilians of a belligerent nation today there are many who are directly engaged in war activities, such as the making of weapons and fighting planes, and accordingly they are justly regarded as combatants, even though they are not serving in the armed forces. Secondly, important military objectives are often located in the midst of civilian centres nowadays. To bomb these objectives is lawful, even though it is foreseen that death and injury will thereby be inflicted on civilians, provided that the military advantage thus gained can be justly regarded as proportionate to the harm done to noncombatants. In such a case the killing of the civilians is an indirect and unwilled, though permitted, effect of the attack on the military objectives....

## Sunday Observance

Question: If the members of a Catholic family living far away from the church are unable on this account to attend Mass on Sunday, are they bound by divine law, promulgated in the third commandment, to devote some portion of the Sunday to private worship?

Answer: The solution of this question goes back to the problem of the basis of the law prescribing the sanctification of Sunday. Under the Old Dispensation the divine law, contained in the third commandment, imposed on the chosen people the obligation to observe the Sabbath, the seventh day of the week, as the Lord's Day. However, this precept, like the other ceremonial prescriptions of the Old Law, ceased with the promulgation of the New Law (Cf. St. Thomas, *Sum. theol.*, I-II, q. 103, a. 3). In the Christian Dispensation the Lord's Day has become the first day of the week. Some theologians have held that the sanctification of Sunday is commanded by divine-positive law, but it is the more common opinion that this duty arises from ecclesiastical legislation (Cf. Damen, *Theologia moralis* [Turin, 1947], I, n. 593).

For the due observance of Sunday the Church has commanded that Christians attend Mass and abstain from servile work as well as from certain other types of activity, such as holding court. The people described by the questioner must abstain from forbidden work, as far as they are able; but, in the presumption that they are excused from hearing Mass by reason of distance from the church, they are not bound to perform any special acts of worship on Sunday — though they must pray, make acts of the theological virtues, etc., with sufficient frequency and regularity throughout the year. Needless to say, however, such persons should be strongly urged to set aside a period of time on Sunday for devotional acts, such as reading the Mass of the day in the vernacular and reciting the rosary. It should be noted also that according to some theologians there is a divine-positive precept of hearing Mass several times in the year (Cf. Damen, *op. cit.*, I, n. 529), though others deny that such a precept exists (Cf. Guiniven, *The Precept of Hearing Mass* [Washington, D.C.: C.U.A. Press, 1942], 56).

Francis J. Connell, C.SS.R., *Father Connell Answers Moral Questions* (Washington, D.C.: Catholic University of America Press, 1959), 10–11, 37, 58–60, 77–78. Printed with permission.

## 17. Thomas Merton's Intellectual Conversion to Catholicism, 1948

*Merton (1915–68), a Trappist monk, stunned the publishing world when his spiritual autobiography,* The Seven Storey Mountain, *became a best-seller. A certain kind of celebrity followed, as did numerous books and articles on topics ranging from the spirituality of the Desert Fathers, to Buddhist mysticism, to*

*the immorality of the Vietnam War and the nuclear arms race. Often, as the*
*following excerpts exemplify, he returned to one of his first intellectual loves as*
*a Catholic, the medieval synthesis of St. Thomas Aquinas.*

Now in Scribner's window, I saw a book called *The Spirit of Medieval Philosophy.*
I went inside, and took it off the shelf, and looked at the table of contents and
at the title page which was deceptive, because it said the book was made up of a
series of lectures that had been given at the University of Aberdeen. That was
no recommendation, to me especially. But it threw me off the track as to the
possible identity and character of Étienne Gilson, who wrote the book.

I bought it, then, together with one other book that I have completely
forgotten, and on my way home in the Long Island train, I unwrapped the
package to gloat over my acquisitions. It was only then that I saw, on the first
page of *The Spirit of Medieval Philosophy,* the small print which said: "Nihil
Obstat...Imprimatur."

The feeling of disgust and deception struck me like a knife in the pit of the
stomach. I felt as if I had been cheated! They should have warned me that it was
a Catholic book! Then I would never have bought it. As it was, I was tempted to
throw the thing out the window at the houses of Woodside — to get rid of it as
something dangerous and unclean. Such is the terror that is aroused in the enlightened modern mind by a little innocent Latin and the signature of a priest.
It is impossible to communicate, to a Catholic, the number and complexity of
fearful associations that a little thing like this can carry with it. It is in Latin —
a difficult, ancient and obscure tongue. That implies, to the mind that has roots
in Protestantism, all kinds of sinister secrets, which the priests are supposed to
cherish and to conceal from common men in this unknown language. Then, the
mere fact that they should pass judgement on the character of a book, and permit people to read it: that in itself is fraught with terror. It immediately conjures
up all the real and imaginary excesses of the Inquisition.

That is something of what I felt when I opened Gilson's book: for you must
understand that while I admired Catholic *culture,* I had always been afraid of the
Catholic Church. That is a rather common position in the world today. After
all, I had not bought a book on medieval philosophy without realizing that it
would be Catholic philosophy: but the imprimatur told me that what I read
would be in full conformity with that fearsome and mysterious thing, Catholic
dogma, and the fact struck me with an impact against which everything in me
reacted with repugnance and fear.

Now in the light of all this, I consider that it was surely a real grace that,
instead of getting rid of the book, I actually read it. Not all of it, it is true: but
more than I used to read of books that deep. When I think of the numbers of
books I had on my shelf in the little room at Douglaston that had once been
Pop's "den" — books which I had bought and never even read, I am more astounded than ever at the fact that I actually read this one: and what is more,
remembered it.

And the one big concept which I got out of its pages was something that was
to revolutionize my whole life. It is all contained in one of those dry, outlandish

technical compounds that the scholastic philosophers were so prone to use: the word *aseitas*. In this one word, which can be applied to God alone, and which expresses His most characteristic attribute, I discovered an entirely new concept of God — a concept which showed me at once that the belief of Catholics was by no means the vague and rather superstitious hangover from an unscientific age that I had believed it to be. On the contrary, here was a notion of God that was at the same time deep, precise, simple and accurate and, what is more, charged with implications which I could not even begin to appreciate, but which I could at least dimly estimate, even with my own lack of philosophical training.

*Aseitas* — the English equivalent is a transliteration: aseity — simply means the power of a being to exist absolutely in virtue of itself, not as caused by itself, but as requiring no cause, no other justification for its existence except that its very nature is to exist. There can be only one such Being: that is God. And to say that God exists *a se*, of and by and by reason of Himself, is merely to say that God is Being Itself. *Ego sum qui sum.* And this means that God must enjoy "complete independence not only as regards everything outside but also as regards everything within Himself."

This notion made such a profound impression on me that I made a pencil note at the top of the page: "Aseity of God — God is being *per se*." I observe it now on the page, for I brought the book to the monastery with me, and although I was not sure where it had gone, I found it on the shelves in Father Abbot's room the other day, and I have it here before me.

I marked three other passages, so perhaps the best thing would be to copy them down. Better than anything I could say, they will convey the impact of the book on my mind.

When God says that He is being [reads the first sentence so marked] and if what He says is to have any intelligible meaning to our minds, it can only mean this: that He is the pure act of existing.

Pure act: therefore excluding all imperfection in the order of existing. Therefore excluding all change, all "becoming," all beginning or end, all limitation. But from this fulness of existence, if I had been capable of considering it deeply enough, I would soon have found that the fulness of all perfection could easily be argued.

Thomas Merton, *The Seven Storey Mountain* (New York: Harcourt, 1948), 171–73. Printed with permission.

## 18. Thomas Merton on St. Thomas and the Failings of the Neo-Thomists, 1966

The current popular reaction against St. Thomas is not due to anything in Thomas himself, or even the "scholastic method." No one who takes the trouble to read St. Thomas and understand him will be surprised to find that the values people now seek elsewhere have from the first been present in him and can always be made accessible without too much difficulty. There is first of all that "turning to the world" — that awareness of the modern world, the world of poor people, of cities, of politically minded burghers and artisans, of men more interested in the authority of reason than of ecclesiastics. But there is also the Bible. And there is the turning to the non-Christian world — to Aristotle and to Islam.

The spirit and perspectives of St. Thomas are "modern" in the soundest sense of the word, although admittedly his Aristotelian physics, cosmology, biology, etc., are hardly up to date. The point is that they do not affect the worth of his thought as a whole, and where it needs to be transposed into slightly different terms, the transposition is not difficult.

The whole difficulty of St. Thomas today arises, not from Thomas himself, but (as has been said so often) from Thomists. Where Thomas was open to the world, they have closed him in upon himself in a little triumphalist universe of airtight correctness. They have unconsciously sealed off his thought in such a way that in order to embrace Thomism one has to renounce everything else. One has to undergo a full-scale conversion, thereafter becoming a militant for the cause, a militant serenely exempt from even listening to a non-Thomist argument, let alone understanding it.

Regrettable that, all of a sudden, it has become fashionable to discredit St. Thomas, to set him aside and run madly to catch up with the new philosophies (which, by the time we have caught up with them, will be themselves discredited). This unseemly haste to get off one bandwagon and find another is the most embarrassing aspect of the whole event. But it had to happen, and it is a clear judgment upon the complacency of those who thought they had "their side" forever enshrined in Canon Law, forever in a citadel of indisputable supremacy.

Now the windows are open in the *Summa* too, and there is a little peace and some fresh air!

Thomas Merton, *Conjectures of a Guilty Bystander* (Garden City, N.Y.: Doubleday, 1966), 205–6. Printed with permission.

## 19. John Courtney Murray, S.J., "The Doctrine Lives: The Eternal Return of Natural Law," 1960

*The American Jesuit John Courtney Murray (1904–67), a pioneer in formulating and defending the right to religious freedom, was the foremost U.S. Catholic public philosopher and theologian of his day. In this excerpt from an essay on the natural law, he explores the connections, in four different political-philosophical schools, between the conceptions of natural law and natural rights, on the one hand, and the "political consequences" of the conceptions, on the other.*

I shall have to be content with some brief comments on the vital resources inherent in the idea of natural law, that indicate its new vitality.

First in importance is its metaphysical character, its secure anchorage in the order of reality — the ultimate order of beings and purposes. As a metaphysical idea, the idea of natural law is timeless, and for that reason timely; for what is timeless is always timely. But it has an added timeliness. An age of order is by definition a time for metaphysical decisions. They are being made all round us. No one escapes making them; one merely escapes making this one rather than that one. Our decisions, unlike those of the eighteenth century, cannot be purely political, because our reflection on the bases of society and the problem of its freedom and its order must be much more profound. And this in turn is so because these problems stand revealed to us in their depths; one cannot any longer, like John Locke, be superficial about them. Our reflection, therefore, on the problem of freedom, human rights, and political order must inevitably carry us to a metaphysical decision in regard of the nature of man. Just as we now know that the written letter of a Bill of Rights is of little value unless there exist the institutional means whereby these rights may have, and be guaranteed, their expression in social action, so also we know — or ought to know — that it is not enough for us to be able to concoct the written letter unless we are likewise able to justify, in terms of ultimates in our own thinking about the nature of man, our assertion that the rights we list are indeed rights and therefore inviolable, and human rights and therefore inalienable. Otherwise we are writing on sand in a time of hurricanes and floods.

There are perhaps four such ultimate decisions open to our making, and each carries with it the acceptance of certain political consequences.

First, one could elect to abide by the old Liberal individualism. At bottom then one would be saying that "natural rights" are simply individual material interests (be they of individuals or social groups or nations), so furnished with an armature by positive law as to be enforceable by the power of government. In this view one would be consenting to a basically atomist concept of society, to its organization in terms of power relationships, to a concept of the state as simply an apparatus of compulsion without the moral function of realizing an order of justice; for in this view there is no order of justice antecedent to positive law or contractual agreements. In a word, one would be accepting yesterday's national and international status quo; for one would be accepting its principles.

Secondly, by an extreme reaction from individualistic Liberalism, wherein the individual as an individual is the sole bearer of rights, one could choose the Marxist concept of human rights as based solely on social function, economic productivity. One would then be saying that all rights are vested in the state, which is the sole determinant of social function. It is the state that is free, and the individual is called simply to share its freedom by pursuing its purposes, which are determined by the laws of dialectical materialism. In this view one would be consenting to the complete socialization of man (his mind and will, as well as his work) within the totalitarian state, all his energies being requisitioned for the realization of a pseudo-order of "justice," which is the triumph of collective man over nature in a classless society that will know no "exploitation of man by man." In this view, as in the foregoing one, one accepts as the ultimate reality the material fact of power — in one case the power of the individual, in the other the power of the collectivity. One bases society and the state on a metaphysic of force (if the phrase be not contradictory).

A third decision, that somehow attempts a mediation between these extreme views, is soliciting adherents today; I mean the theory that its protagonists call "modern evolutionary scientific humanism," but that I shall call "the new rationalism."

It is rationalism, because its premise is the autonomy of man, who transcends the rest of nature and is transcended by nothing and nobody (at least nothing and nobody knowable). It is new, because (unlike the old rationalism) it maintains (with Spinoza, whom Bowle has pointed to as one of its earliest forerunners) that man is something more than reason. It identifies natural law (though the term is not frequent with it) with "the drive of the whole personality," the totality of the impulses whereby men strive to "live ever more fully." It is new, too, because it abandons the old rationalist passion for deductive argument and for the construction of total patterns, in favor of the new passion for scientific method and the casting up of provisional and partial hypotheses. Finally, it is new because it does not, like eighteenth-century rationalism, conceive nature and its laws, or the rights of man, as static, given once for all, needing only to be "discovered." It adds to the old rationalistic universe the category of time; it supplements the processes of reason with the processes of history and the consequent experience of change and evolution.

Nature, therefore, is an evolving concept, and its law is emergent. It is also wholly immanent; for the new rationalism, like the old, denies to man his nature, or its law all transcendental reference. The new rationalistic universe, like the old, is anthropocentric; all human values (reason, justice, charity) are manmade, and in consequence all human "rights," which are the juridical expression of these values, look only to man for their creation, realization, and guarantee. Their ultimate metaphysical justification lies in the fact that they have been seen, by experience, to be the contemporaneously necessary "expression of life itself." And for "life itself" one does not seek a metaphysical justification; it is, when lived in its fullness, self-authenticating. In this system, therefore, the theological concept is "fullness of life." As this is the end for the individual (to be realized as best may be in his stage of the evolutionary process), so, too, it is the end for the state. The *ordo juris* is conceived, after the fashion of the modern schools of sociological jurisprudence or realistic jurisprudence, as a pure instrumentality whereby lawmakers and judges, recognizing the human desires that are seeking realization at a given moment in human society, endeavor to satisfy these desires with a minimum of social friction. The ideals of law or of human rights are "received" from the "wants" of the society of the time and place, and any particular *ordo juris* is throughout its whole texture experimental.

Much could be said further to explain, and then to criticize, this subtle and seductive system, so much a product of the contemporary secularist mentality (its basic premise is, of course, secularism, usually accepted from the surrounding climate, not reached as the term of a metaphysical journey — few secularists have ever purposefully journeyed to secularism). I shall say only two things.

First, the new rationalism is at bottom an ethical relativism pure and simple. Its immanentism, its allegiance to scientific method as the sole criterion of truth, its theory of values as emergent in an evolutionary process, alike forbid it the affirmation of any absolute values (that is, as long as its adherents stay within their own system, which, being men and therefore by intrinsic necessity of reason also natural-law jurists, they frequently do not, but rather go on to talk of right, justice, equity, liberty, rationality, etc., investing these concepts with an absoluteness they could not possibly have within the system). Second, as an ethical relativism, the new rationalism is vulnerable to all the criticisms that historically have been advanced against that ancient mode of thought, since the time when Socrates first argued against the Sophists and their dissolution of a knowable objective world of truth and value.

Chiefly, there are two objections. The first is that the new rationalism, like all the old ones, is unreasonable — surely something of a serious objection to a philosophy. "You do not," said Socrates to the Sophists, "know yourselves — your own nature, the nature of your reason." The same ignorance, though in more learned form, recurs in the modern heirs of sophistry. Secondly, the new rationalism, like all the old ones, is ruinous of sound political philosophy. "You are," said Socrates to the Sophists, "the enemies of the *polis*, who undermine its *nomoi*, especially its supreme *nomos*, the idea of justice, for whose realization all laws exist."

This objection, of course, will be vehemently repudiated by the new rationalists. They are fond of putting their system forward as the proper ideological basis of democracy; conversely, they say that democracy is the political expression of their philosophy. Its separation of church and state is the expression of their secularist humanism. Its freedom of thought and speech are the reflection of their philosophical and ethical relativism. Its respect for human rights creates the atmosphere in which science may further the evolution of man to higher dignities and fuller life. For my part, however, I should maintain that, by a curious but inevitable paradox, the relativism of the new rationalists must find its native political expression in a new and subtle form of state absolutism. The essential dialectic has already been displayed in history. The absolute autonomy of human reason, postulated by the old rationalism, had as its counterpart the juridical omnipotence of the state. And with accidental variations the dialectic will repeat itself: the autonomy of human reason (the denial of its subjection to a higher law not of its own creation) = relativism in regard of human values = absolutism in regard of the value and functions of the state. Admittedly, the new Leviathan would not be on the Hobbesian model, but it would be for all that the "Mortal God." And the outwardly humble garments that it would wear — the forms of political democracy — would hardly hide the fact that it was in effect the *divina maiestas*. It would be a long business to explain the working of this dialectic; let me state the substance in a brief paragraph.

I take it that the political substance of democracy consists in the admission of an order of rights antecedent to the state, the political form of society. These are the rights of the person, the family, the church, the associations men freely form for economic, cultural, social, and religious ends. In the admission of this prior order of rights — inviolable as well by democratic majorities as by absolute monarchs — consists the most distinctive assertion of the service-character of the democratic state. And this service-character is still further enforced by the affirmation, implicit in the admission of the order of human rights, of another order of right also antecedent to the state and regulative of its public action as a state; I mean the order of justice. In other words, the democratic state serves both the ends of the human person (in itself and in its natural forms of social life) and also the ends of justice. As the servant of these ends, it has only a relative value. Now it is precisely this service-character of the state, its relative value, that tends to be undermined by the theories of the new rationalism — by their inherent logic and by the psychology they generate.

Psychologically, it is not without significance that evolutionary scientific humanism should be the favorite creed of our contemporary social engineers, with their instrumental theories of education, law, and government. And it seems that their inevitable temptation is to hasten the process of evolution by use of the resources of government, just as it is to advance the cause of scientific humanism by a somewhat less than human application of science. The temptation is enhanced by the circumstance of the contemporary welfare state in the midst of an urbanized and industrialized mass civilization. The "sin" then takes the initial form of a desertion of their own premises. The "socially desirable objectives" are no longer "received" from society itself (as in the theory they should be); rather they are conceived in committee and imposed on society. The humanism ceases to evolve from below, and is directed from above; it remains scientific, and becomes inhuman. This is the psychological dynamism of the system: the state tends to lose its character of servant, and assume that of master. The psychological dynamism would be less destructive were it not in the service of the logic of the system. In the logic of the system is the destruction of all barriers to the expanding competence of the state. For one thing, the new rationalism is far too pale and bloodless a creed to stand against the flushed and full-blooded power of the modern state. For another, it hardly attempts to make a stand; in fact, its ethical relativism destroys the only ground on which a stand can be made — the absoluteness of the order of human rights that stands irremovably outside the sphere of state power, and the absoluteness of the order of justice that stands imperiously above the power of the state.

These then are three possible metaphysical decisions that one can make as a prelude to the construction of the new age. None of them, I think, carries a promise that the age will be one of true order.

There remains the fourth possible decision — the option of natural law in the old traditional sense. Here the decision is genuinely metaphysical; one does not opt for a rationalization of power, but for a metaphysic of right. I say "right" advisedly, not "rights." The natural law does not in the first instance furnish a philosophy of human rights in the sense of subjective immunities and powers to demand. This philosophy is consequent on the initial furnishing of a philosophy of right, justice, law, juridical order, and social order. The reason is that natural-law thinking does not set out, as Locke did, from the abstract, isolated individual, and ask what are his inalienable rights as an individual. Rather, it regards the community as "given" equally with the person. Man is regarded as a member of an order instituted by God, and subject to the laws that make the order an order — laws that derive from the nature of man, which is as essentially social as it is individual. In the natural-law climate of opinion (very different from that set by the "law of nature"), objective law has the primacy over subjective rights. Law is not simply the protection of rights but their source, because it is the foundation of duties.

John Courtney Murray, S.J., *We Hold These Truths: Catholic Reflections on the American Proposition* (Kansas City, Mo.: Sheed and Ward, 1960 [1988]), 320–27. Printed with permission.

*Part 3*

# CATHOLIC EDUCATION IN THE UNITED STATES: FOUNDATIONS

## Introduction

Catholic education in the United States is the largest private educational enterprise known to history. Religious formation, the heart of its mission, takes place through liturgy, catechesis of children and adults, seminaries, and novitiates. Numerous programs, including special education, reading groups, summer camps, open-air preaching, and the Catholic press, also inhabit its wide scope. The most visible aspect of Catholic education, however, is a formal system with schools at every level.[1] This remarkable educational phenomenon came about in response to the singular historical challenge of being simultaneously Catholic and American. American Catholics lived for long in an atmosphere openly hostile to their religious culture and beliefs. The consequent tension between integration and separatism in respect to the American environment pervades the vast and complex history of Catholic education in the United States. The documents selected for this collection therefore reflect tendencies of assimilation or separateness — sometimes both. In choosing them I generally gave preference to texts not previously anthologized.[2]

The great religious reformations of the sixteenth century gave new importance to the ability to read, to understand one's faith in a divided Christianity. The post-Tridentine Catholic Church responded through the seminaries, teaching orders, and abundant educational institutions — from catechism classes and parish schools to colleges and universities — that flourished in its domain. The Spanish, French, and English who colonized the present-day United

---

1. "American Catholicism appears to be a school system with churches attached" ("The Catholic School Crisis," *Newsweek* [October 4, 1971]: 83–84, cited in Timothy Walch, *Parish School: American Catholic Parochial Education from Colonial Times to the Present* [New York: Crossroad, 1996], 182).

2. Alice Gallin, ed., *American Catholic Higher Education: Essential Documents, 1967–1990* (Notre Dame, Ind.: University of Notre Dame Press, 1992); Neil G. McCluskey, S.J., ed., *Catholic Education in America: A Documentary History* (New York: Teachers College, Columbia University, 1964); John Tracy Ellis, ed., *Documents of American Catholic History*, 3 vols. (Wilmington, Del.: M. Glazier, 1987 [1967]); and Mary J. Oates, ed., *Higher Education for Catholic Women: An Historical Anthology* (New York: Garland, 1987).

States, Catholic or not, brought with them an educational habit of conscious Christianization tinged with defensive polemic. Although the foundations of Catholic education were laid in the colonial period, little documentation reveals the intellectual content of that education or the philosophy that guided it. Colonial schools, although they were earliest, are not represented in the following collection, which begins with John Carroll, the first Catholic bishop of the United States.

John Carroll devoted his first major pastoral letter to the diocese of Baltimore in 1792 primarily to education.[3] Long preoccupied with the importance of education to launching a fledgling church, Carroll saw it as the bedrock for success in America, and issues that persist throughout the history of Catholic education in the United States can be seen in embryonic form in Carroll's concerns. They include the formation of clergy, higher education, popular schools, and the education of women. Each without exception implies Catholic interaction with the cultural and political environment of the United States.

In the earliest days of reorganization following the American Revolution, Carroll described his plan: "The object nearest my heart is to establish a college on this continent for the education of youth, which might at the same time be a Seminary for future Clergymen. But at present I see no prospect for success."[4] The dual need for clerical and lay education prompted the establishment of Georgetown Academy in 1789, and with it the development of typically American Catholic colleges, configured on European models, primarily the Jesuit *Ratio Studiorum.*[5] Founded by bishops or religious orders, the colleges enrolled a mélange of students — from young boys learning Latin to men doing university-level work. In 1791 French Sulpicians inaugurated the first Catholic seminary in the United States at St. Mary's in Baltimore. With hardly any seminarians in sight, they added a college for laymen, Protestant as well as Catholic. It was chartered by the state of Maryland in 1805 and in 1822 became the first faculty in the country licensed to grant ecclesiastical degrees in the name of the Holy See. Catholic colleges before mid-century, however, graduated few students with degrees of any kind; the vast majority of their work remained at the secondary level.[6]

John Carroll also had the education of women in mind — so much that he arranged permission for cloistered Carmelites, then the only nuns in the United States, to teach. Every woman's congregation in the United States in the period before 1840 was involved in teaching. (Even the Carmelites, who refused Carroll in the 1790s, were later forced by poverty to operate a school.) Catholic elementary education, originally in the hands of lay men and women, quickly

---

3. Pastoral Letter, Baltimore, May 28, 1792, in *The John Carroll Papers,* ed. Thomas O'Brien Hanley, 3 vols. (Notre Dame, Ind.: University of Notre Dame Press, 1976): 2:43–52 [hereafter, *JCP*].

4. Carroll to Charles Plowden — Maryland, September 26, 1783, *JCP* 1:78.

5. Philip Gleason, "American Catholic Higher Education: A Historical Perspective," *The Shape of Catholic Higher Education,* ed. Robert Hassenger (Chicago: University of Chicago Press, 1967), 33–35.

6. *The Encyclopedia of American Catholic History,* s.v. "Catholic Education, Higher," by Philip Gleason, 250.

and immigrant population was achieved only through the financial sacrifice of disadvantaged Catholics and through the prodigious work of men and women in religious communities.

The Third Plenary Council of Baltimore in 1884 virtually identified Catholic elementary education with the parochial school, a decision that critically affected the future of the church in America. When John Lancaster Spalding preached before the Council promoting the establishment of a Catholic university, he was careful to emphasize that the liberal, humanist education he advocated for priests would invigorate, not hinder, popular education for an immigrant community.[10] Although the Baltimore Council demanded separate Catholic schools, it did not end dispute over how they should be financed, organized, or operated. That debate continued in theoretical questions about the role of the state in education and in practical issues about the use of public funds for private schools. These issues were vital in the controversies polarizing liberal and conservative Catholics during the last decades of the nineteenth century, ending in the condemnation of Americanism by Leo XIII in 1899. Whether liberal or conservative, separatist or assimilationist in philosophy, all Catholic education aimed at turning out persons who would live and function in American society, a notion that more and more shaped its development in the following century.

## 20. John Carroll and Catholic Education, 1787–1800

*John Carroll (1735–1815) was named first bishop of the newly created diocese of Baltimore on November 6, 1789. Well before then, he clearly recognized education as key in forming a stable Catholic community that could perpetuate itself in the United States. Carroll's first goal, "the object nearest my heart," was a school to prepare a native clergy. The scope of his educational vision, however, encompassed every facet of Catholic life. The following documents reveal his plans for Georgetown Academy and his first attempt to provide formal schooling for Catholic women.*

## 20a. John Carroll's Plans for Georgetown Academy, 1787

*In a lengthy letter to his friend Charles Plowden, an English ex-Jesuit, Carroll elaborated his vision for the college-cum-seminary planned at Georgetown: It would comprise the best of European Jesuit education, but adapted to American reality.*

To Charles Plowden                              Rock Creek, January 22d 1787
                                                    — Baltimore Feb. 28 — 1787

...In the beginning, the academy will not receive boarders, but they must provide lodgings in town; but all notorious deviations from the rules of morality, out, as well as in school, must be subjected to exemplary correction: every

---

10. John Lancaster Spalding, "The Higher Education," in *Means and Ends of Education* (Chicago: A. C. McClurg and Company, 1897), 218–22.

became the province of religious orders.[7] To have religious as the principal purveyors of Catholic education was consistent with the widely shared view of education as the domain of the church. It also met an acute lack of material resources, in which the gratuitous and dependable service of religious communities was indispensable. Rapid growth in Catholic population in the nineteenth century and the necessitous climate of an immigrant church reinforced this model. Catholic education in its institutional forms was so dependent on the work of religious that without them, there would be no history of Catholic education in the United States.

From the federal period through the first part of the nineteenth century, Catholic education was porous by necessity and principle, as evidenced in the 1787 broadside for Georgetown, which announced: "Agreeably to the liberal Principle of our Constitution, the SEMINARY will be open to Students of EVERY RELIGIOUS PROFESSION."[8] The Georgetown Visitation Academy, compared favorably in 1833 to the Troy Female Seminary,[9] matched the upper standards of the era for female education. Its proximity to the center of federal government made it a showplace of Catholic education, and public officials often attended end-of-term exercises. In a country where educational resources were universally scarce, Catholic institutions provided valuable service to the wider society. The small Catholic population blended rather well with its neighbors. All schools were religious, and Catholics sought government cooperation for education on the same basis as other citizens. That vision changed radically when massive immigration by the 1830s turned American Catholicism into a church of the poor and the foreign.

The momentous intervention by Bishop John Hughes in the New York City school controversy during 1840–1841 sprang from a fundamentally assimilationist idea: If Catholics enjoyed the rights of other citizens, public money should support their schools. When (due partly to the success of Hughes's political tactics) public schools became increasingly secular, Catholics withdrew, throwing their energies into separate religious institutions. Nativist aggression encouraged a culture of defensive Catholic separateness. Non-English-speaking immigrants strove to defend faith by preserving culture, particularly language. German Catholics — and later, Poles — strongly supported Catholic ethnic schools. Many English-speaking clergy, too, saw the Catholic school as the only answer to the problem of bringing up children in a society averse to their religion. The anomaly of providing private schools for large segments of a poor

---

7. The first known school in Maryland, founded in 1640, was endowed by Edward Cotton, a planter, and operated until 1659 by Ralph Crouch, a former Jesuit novice (Harold W. Buetow, *Of Singular Benefit: The Story of Catholic Education in the United States* [New York: Macmillan, 1970], 26–27); for examples of women's involvement, see George Paré, *The Catholic Church in Detroit, 1701–1888* (Detroit: Published for the Archdiocese of Detroit by Wayne State University Press, 1983 [1951]), 615–55.

8. Robert Emmett Curran, S.J., *The Bicentennial History of Georgetown University*, vol. 1: *From Academy to University, 1789–1889* (Washington, D.C.: Georgetown University Press, 1993), 26.

9. "The school in Georgetown is said not to be surpassed if equaled by Mrs. Willard's" (Governor Steven Mason to his sisters, October 13, 1833, cited in Sr. Mary Rosalita, I.H.M., Ph.D., *Education in Detroit prior to 1850* [Lansing: Michigan Historical Commission, 1928], 364).

## Part 3

# CATHOLIC EDUCATION IN THE UNITED STATES: FOUNDATIONS

## Introduction

Catholic education in the United States is the largest private educational enterprise known to history. Religious formation, the heart of its mission, takes place through liturgy, catechesis of children and adults, seminaries, and novitiates. Numerous programs, including special education, reading groups, summer camps, open-air preaching, and the Catholic press, also inhabit its wide scope. The most visible aspect of Catholic education, however, is a formal system with schools at every level.[1] This remarkable educational phenomenon came about in response to the singular historical challenge of being simultaneously Catholic and American. American Catholics lived for long in an atmosphere openly hostile to their religious culture and beliefs. The consequent tension between integration and separatism in respect to the American environment pervades the vast and complex history of Catholic education in the United States. The documents selected for this collection therefore reflect tendencies of assimilation or separateness — sometimes both. In choosing them I generally gave preference to texts not previously anthologized.[2]

The great religious reformations of the sixteenth century gave new importance to the ability to read, to understand one's faith in a divided Christianity. The post-Tridentine Catholic Church responded through the seminaries, teaching orders, and abundant educational institutions — from catechism classes and parish schools to colleges and universities — that flourished in its domain. The Spanish, French, and English who colonized the present-day United

---

1. "American Catholicism appears to be a school system with churches attached" ("The Catholic School Crisis," *Newsweek* [October 4, 1971]: 83–84, cited in Timothy Walch, *Parish School: American Catholic Parochial Education from Colonial Times to the Present* [New York: Crossroad, 1996], 182).

2. Alice Gallin, ed., *American Catholic Higher Education: Essential Documents, 1967–1990* (Notre Dame, Ind.: University of Notre Dame Press, 1992); Neil G. McCluskey, S.J., ed., *Catholic Education in America: A Documentary History* (New York: Teachers College, Columbia University, 1964); John Tracy Ellis, ed., *Documents of American Catholic History*, 3 vols. (Wilmington, Del.: M. Glazier, 1987 [1967]); and Mary J. Oates, ed., *Higher Education for Catholic Women: An Historical Anthology* (New York: Garland, 1987).

States, Catholic or not, brought with them an educational habit of conscious Christianization tinged with defensive polemic. Although the foundations of Catholic education were laid in the colonial period, little documentation reveals the intellectual content of that education or the philosophy that guided it. Colonial schools, although they were earliest, are not represented in the following collection, which begins with John Carroll, the first Catholic bishop of the United States.

John Carroll devoted his first major pastoral letter to the diocese of Baltimore in 1792 primarily to education.[3] Long preoccupied with the importance of education to launching a fledgling church, Carroll saw it as the bedrock for success in America, and issues that persist throughout the history of Catholic education in the United States can be seen in embryonic form in Carroll's concerns. They include the formation of clergy, higher education, popular schools, and the education of women. Each without exception implies Catholic interaction with the cultural and political environment of the United States.

In the earliest days of reorganization following the American Revolution, Carroll described his plan: "The object nearest my heart is to establish a college on this continent for the education of youth, which might at the same time be a Seminary for future Clergymen. But at present I see no prospect for success."[4] The dual need for clerical and lay education prompted the establishment of Georgetown Academy in 1789, and with it the development of typically American Catholic colleges, configured on European models, primarily the Jesuit *Ratio Studiorum.*[5] Founded by bishops or religious orders, the colleges enrolled a mélange of students — from young boys learning Latin to men doing university-level work. In 1791 French Sulpicians inaugurated the first Catholic seminary in the United States at St. Mary's in Baltimore. With hardly any seminarians in sight, they added a college for laymen, Protestant as well as Catholic. It was chartered by the state of Maryland in 1805 and in 1822 became the first faculty in the country licensed to grant ecclesiastical degrees in the name of the Holy See. Catholic colleges before mid-century, however, graduated few students with degrees of any kind; the vast majority of their work remained at the secondary level.[6]

John Carroll also had the education of women in mind — so much that he arranged permission for cloistered Carmelites, then the only nuns in the United States, to teach. Every woman's congregation in the United States in the period before 1840 was involved in teaching. (Even the Carmelites, who refused Carroll in the 1790s, were later forced by poverty to operate a school.) Catholic elementary education, originally in the hands of lay men and women, quickly

---

3. Pastoral Letter, Baltimore, May 28, 1792, in *The John Carroll Papers,* ed. Thomas O'Brien Hanley, 3 vols. (Notre Dame, Ind.: University of Notre Dame Press, 1976): 2:43–52 [hereafter, *JCP*].

4. Carroll to Charles Plowden — Maryland, September 26, 1783, *JCP* 1:78.

5. Philip Gleason, "American Catholic Higher Education: A Historical Perspective," *The Shape of Catholic Higher Education,* ed. Robert Hassenger (Chicago: University of Chicago Press, 1967), 33–35.

6. *The Encyclopedia of American Catholic History,* s.v. "Catholic Education, Higher," by Philip Gleason, 250.

care & precaution that can be devised, will be employed to preserve attention to the duties of Religion & good manners, in which other American schools are most notoriously deficient. One of our own Gentlemen, & the best qualified we can get, will live at the academy to have the general direction of studies; & superintendence over Scholars and masters. Four other of our Gentlemen will be nominated to visit the academy at stated times, & whenever they can make it convenient, to see that the business is properly conducted. In the beginning, we shall be obliged to employ secular Masters, under the Superintendant, of which many, & tolerably good ones, have already sollicited appointments. The great influx from Europe of men of all professions & talents has procured this opportunity of providing Teachers. But this is not intended to be the permanent system. We trust in God, that many youths will be called to the service of the Church. After finishing their academical studies, these will be sent to a seminary, which will be established in one of our own houses; & we have, thro' Gods mercy, a place & situation admirably calculated for the purpose of retirement; where these youths may be perfected in their first, & initiated into the higher studies; and at the same time formed to the virtue becoming their station. Before these young Seminarists are admitted to Orders, they will be sent to teach some years at the academy, which will improve their knowledge, & ripen their minds still more before they irrevocably engage themselves to the Church. You will observe, that the perfecting of this plan requires great exertions; and in particular, demands persons of considerable ability for the conduct of the academy; & will thereafter stand in farther need of able & interior men to take charge of the Seminary. The difficulties indeed perplex, but do not dishearten me. But I stand greatly in need of your powerful assistance to procure as soon as possible, a fit Gentleman to open, as Superintendant, the new establishment....

... You see, he must be a person old enough to carry a considerable weight of authority & respect; experienced in the detail of government for such a place of education; & capable of embracing in his mind a general & indeed universal plan of studies, of which the academical institution is only a part. He should have considerable knowledge of the world, as he will be obliged to converse with many different persons: and he should be capable of abstracting his mind from the methods used in the colleges, where he has lived, so as to adopt only as much of them as is suited to the circumstances of this country; and of substituting such others, as are better adapted to the views and inclinations of those with whom he has to deal; but all I mention, is necessary to give reputation & permanency to the plan; for you may be assured, that in the Institutions of other professions, they have procured from Europe some litterary characters of the first class: and this likewise makes me desirous of not falling behind with them....

Next to the choice of a proper Superintendant, or Principal, your assistance will be requisite, principally, in the designation of proper elementary books for our establishment. You will therefore be so kind, as to write me immediately, which are the best of every kind, for teaching English, Latin, Greek, Geometry, & the first principles of mathematics... what syntax, what prosody, what

Greek grammar and other elementary books of that language do you recommend? In these schools, established thro this country, I find they have adopted grammars, & syntaxes, both for Greek and Latin, much more concise, than our old ones of Alvarez & Gretzer:[1] whether they are equal in other respects I cannot tell excepting that they are preferable for containing the rules in English which the students understand; instead of being in Latin, which they do not.

Besides these elementary books, I wish you to recommend the best works, you know, for forming and improving the taste of students, & enlarging their minds without endangering their moral principles. I remember to have heard great commendations of the *cours de belles lettres*, by l'Abbé Batteux. I never read it, as it did not lay in my line of studies at that time. You probably have, and, I hear it is translated into English. In a word, set your mind at work; & you will, I doubt not, send us a very good system. Above all, be not afraid of tiring me by descending into too great a detail: you may see by my enquiries, how much information I want, and particularly with respect to the minutiae of the business. At the same time, inform me, where the elementary books, the classics, maps, globes &c may be had on the most reasonable terms....

Amongst other difficulties, which we shall have to overcome in the undertaking of the academy, pecuniary resources will be a great one. I expect indeed, that considerable subscriptions, considering the abilities of our people, will be obtained amongst them; but the first expence of erecting proper buildings and securing the salaries for the Masters will be very great. Notwithstanding our debilitated circumstances, by the continuance of an expensive war, yet it so happens, that all services are paid higher here than perhaps in any country. The common Grammar masters in the colleges and academies amongst us have the enormous salaries of £150 to 180, & 200. I hope indeed to get ours at an underrate; but hardly for less than £60 to £80 p ann. (*JCP* 1:241–243).

## 20b. A Maneuver to Secure the Education of Catholic Girls, 1792–1800

*The first permanent community of women religious in the thirteen original states was a Carmelite monastery, established in 1790 at Port Tobacco, Maryland. It included three American-born women from the Carmel of Hoogstraeten, Belgium, and a London-born Carmelite from Antwerp. Although Bishop Carroll respected the contemplative and strictly enclosed life of the Carmelites, he said plainly, "I wish rather for Ursulines."[1]*

*Without their knowledge, Carroll requested a dispensation from the head of the Congregation of Propaganda Fide for the cloistered nuns at Port Tobacco to teach. When permission arrived from Rome, Carroll disclosed his action to the Carmelites, and urged, without compelling them, to adapt their rule to teaching. Mother Bernadine Matthews and the sisters apparently declined.*

1. "Manoel Alvarez, S.J. (d. 1582) wrote a Latin grammar that went through 400 editions; and Jacob Gretzer S.J. (d. 1625) authored 229 books and 39 manuscripts."

1. To Charles Plowden, Rock Creek, May 26, 1788, *JCP* 1:312.

a. To Leonardo Antonelli, Prefect of the Congregation of Propaganda Fide, 1792

Baltimore, April 23, 1792

...The Carmelite nuns, who, about four [*sic*] years ago, came from Belgium, have located in Maryland. A house and a small farm was given to them by a pious Catholic man. Four came; some novices have joined them. Their example, a novelty in this country, has aroused many to serious thought on divine things. They would be far more useful if, according to their rule, and with the background of experience, they undertook the education of girls...[*JCP*] 2:32).

b. To Bernadine Matthews,[2] Superior of the Carmel at Port Tobacco, 1793

Baltimore March 1, 1793

...I had letters lately from Rome. I had given in mine an account of your settlement, & of the sweet odour of your example; and had taken the liberty to add, that, in order to render your usefulness still greater, I wished, that it were consistent with your constitution to employ yourselves in the education of young persons of your own sex. The Cardinal prefect of the Progapanda having laid my letter[3] before his Holiness, informs me, that it gave them incredible joy to find that you were come hither to diffuse the knowledge and practice of religious perfection, & adds, that, considering the great scarcity of labourers, & the defects of education in these States, you might sacrifice part of your institution to the promotion of a greater good; & I am directed to encourage you to undertake it; and now, in obedience to this direction, I recommend to your Revce & your holy community to take it into your consideration, & pray you all fervently to remember me in your supplications to the throne of grace, especially during this time. I am with the greatest esteem & respect, Hond. & Revd. Madam, Yr. Most obedt. Servt. in Christ. J. Bishop of Baltre [*JCP* 2:84–85].

c. To Charles Plowden, 1800

City of Washington Sept. 3rd 1800

...Those of the same [Carmelite] order from Hoogstraet[4] have multiplied themselves considerably, & give much edification by their retirement, & total seclusion from the world, and I doubt not of the efficacy of their prayers in drawing down blessings on us all: but their utility to the public goes no farther. They will not concern themselves in the business of female education, tho the late Pope, soon after their arrival, recommended it earnestly to them by a letter sent to me by Cardl. Antonelli, in consequence of the Popes own directions to him. As Mr. Charles Neale[5] governs that house with absolute sway, I suppose, that the opposition arose chiefly from him; tho' they have one Lady amongst

---

2. Bernadina is the first name spelling on the letter covering. A native of Maryland and sister of Ignatius Matthews [former Jesuit], she came to America in 1790. Mother Bernadina of St. Joseph was the name in religion for Ann Matthews.

3. See to Antonelli, Apr. 23, 1792.

4. Were at Port Tobacco, Md.

5. American-born Jesuit priest (1750–1823), who had accompanied the Carmelites from Hoogstraeten to Port Tobacco, Maryland, in 1790. He was twice superior of the Maryland Province (1808–12 and 1821–23). (Editor's note)

them, with superior talents for that employment; and she might form others [*JCP* 2:319].

> The John Carroll Papers, ed. Thomas O'Brien Hanley, S.J., 3 vols. (Notre Dame, Ind.: University of Notre Dame Press, 1976): 1:241–43; 2:32, 84–85, 319. Printed by permission.

## 21. Gabriel Richard's Petition to the Territorial Legislature of Michigan, 1808

*For more than thirty years Gabriel Richard (1767–1832) was the most promi-nent figure in the old Northwest. A French Sulpician missionary, pastor of the Church of St. Anne in Detroit, and U.S. congressman, Richard made numerous contributions to education, including his role with Rev. John Montieth in 1817 as cofounder of the future University of Michigan. In English still idiosyncratic, Richard petitioned the Michigan Legislature in 1808 for government aid to the numerous schools he was promoting in the Detroit area.*

to the Honourable Legislature of Michigan

Our neighbors on the British Side are now erecting a large stone building for an Academy. The undersigned being sensible that it would be shameful for the American Citizens of Detroit, if nothing should be done in their territory for a similar and so valuable Establishment, begs leave to call the attention of Legislature of Michigan to an object the most important to the welfare of the rising Generation — which cannot be but of little advantage, if it is not highly patronized by Government.

The Honourable Legislature partly knows what has been done by the Subscriber for the establishment of schools, and for the Encouragement of lit-terature, scientific knowledge and Useful Arts in this part of the Union. Besides tow [*sic*, throughout] English schools in town of Detroit there are four other Primary schools for boys and tow for young ladies, either in Town, or at Spring Hill, at Grand Marais even at River Hurons. Three of these schools are kept by three Natives of this Country who had received their first Education by the Rev. M[r]. J. Dilhet[1] and of whom tow under direction of the Subscriber have learnt the first Rudiments of English and Latin Languages, and some principles of algebra and Geometry so far as to the measurement of the figures engraved on the tomb of the immortal Archimedes. By necessity they have been forced to stop their studies and to become masters and teachers for others. at Spring Hill under the direction of Angélique Campeau and Elisabeth Lyons,[2] as early as the 9th of September last, the number of the scholars has been augmented by four young Indians headed by an old matron their grandmother of the Potowatamies tribe. Five or six more are expected to arrive at every moment.[3]

---

1. John Dilhet, a Sulpician, assistant to Richard at Ste. Anne parish. (Editor's note)
2. Campeau and Lyons were later associated with Richard in a failed attempt to establish a religious community of women. (Editor's note)
3. "This was the school at Springwells on the Matthew Ernest farm. ... It was in connection with this school that Father Richard wrote his well-known 'Outlines of a scheme of Education

In Detroit in the house lately the property of Captain Elliott, purchased by the Subscriber for the very purpose of establishing one Academy for young Ladies, under the direction of miss Elisabeth Williams there are better than thirty young Girls who are taught as at Spring Hill, reading, writing, arithmetic, knitting, sewing, spinning, &c. In these tow schools there are already nearly three dozen of spinning wheels, and one loom, on which four pieces of Linen or woolen cloth have been made this last spring or summer.

To encourage the young students by the allurement of pleasure and amusements, the undersigned had these three month past sent orders to New York for a spinning machine of about one hundred spindles, an air-Pump, an Electrical Apparatus &c. As they could not be found he is to receive these falls [*sic*] but an Electrical machine, a number of cards, and few colours for dying the stuff already made or to be made in his Academy.

It would be very necessary to have in Detroit a Public building for a similar Academy in which the high branches of Mathematics, most important languages, Geography, History, Natural and Moral Philosophy should be taught to young Gentlemen of our country, and in which should be kept the machines, the most necessary for the improvement of Useful Arts, for making the most necessary physical experiments and framing a Beginning of public Library.

In order to advance the foregoing Institution the undersigned, prays that the part of the old shipyard Laying between G. Meldrum, the River and the tow adjacent streets together with the buildings that are on it, may be appropriated to the use of the aforesaid Academies, that is to say, given for the aforesaid Academies, that is to say, given or exchanged for his donation Lot, for Mr. J[n]. Dilhet's donation lot or otherwise as it will appear more convenient to the Honourable Legislature.

The undersigned acting as Administrator for the said Academies further prays, that, for the Encouragement of Litterature and Useful Arts to be taught in the said Academies, one of the four Lotteries authorized by the Hon. Leg[re]. on 9th day of 7[ber], 1805, may be left to the management of the Subscriber as Administrator of the said Academies, on the conditions that may appear just and reasonable to the legislative Board. And to make a Trial the Subscriber is disposed to offer and from this moment he offers during this winter to make some lectures on such branches of mathematics or of Natural Philosophy that will be more agreeable to the wishes of a majority of those Gentlemen desirous to attend on every evening.

Detroit 8[ber] 18 A.D. 1808 Gabriel Richard

Gabriel Richard, Petition to the Territorial Legislature of Michigan, October 8, 1808, facsimile, Sister Mary Rosalita, I.H.M., Ph.D., *Education in Detroit Prior to 1850* (Lansing: Michigan Historical Commission, 1928), 79–81. [The original was apparently lost; only a photographic negative remains in the Burton Historical Collection, Detroit Public Library.]

for territory of Michigan which he addresses to President Jefferson and Congress.'" For a thorough study of this establishment see Sister Mary Rosalita, I.H.M., "The Spring Hill Indian School Correspondence," *Michigan History Magazine* 14 (Winter Number). (George Paré, *The Catholic Church in Detroit, 1701–1888* [Detroit: Gabriel Richard Press, 1951], 621, n. 17).

## 22. Black Catholics of Philadelphia Seek Education for Their Children, 1817

*St. Mary's in Philadelphia was one of the first parish schools in the country, begun in August 1782 by Robert Molyneux, S.J. Thirty-five years later, black Catholic parents called for the parish to give their children the same benefits "as you have... the poor of your own Colour."*

HOUSE OF THE CLERGY of St. Mary's Church Nov. 21ˢᵗ, 1817

At an adjourned meeting of the Trustees of St. Mary's Church.

Present     The Rev'ᵈ. L. De Barth    Denis McCready
                The Rev'ᵈ. T. McGirr      John Dempsey
                Hugh Christy            James Gartland
                John Doyle
                               ...

A Petition was also presented on behalf of the poor Catholics of Colour praying that the Board of Trustees would take the distressed State of their children into consideration which is as follows.

To the Revᵈ. Gentlemen and to the Laity who compose the Board of Trustees of St. Mary's Congregation

The Petition of the Catholic People of Colour residing in Philᵃ.

Humbly Sheweth

That your Petitioners are destitute of the means to give their Children a Catholic Education that the different Sectarians are seeking and encouraging us to send them that they may instruct them, but if we do they instruct them in their ways — That our Children are destitute of the means to acquire the Knowledge of our Religion & its duties whereby they might be able to repel the incessant attacks made on them by a set of beings who can quote the Scriptures with every phrase in order to seduce the ignorant — We tremble for the fate of our Children, some of whom have been already seduced from our Religion. Therefore we sincerely hope that your charitable Board will take them under your protecting Wing as you have taken the poor of your own Colour and to have ours also instructed in a common English Education and to appoint a teacher who will be careful above all things to cause them to know their catechism and how to say their morning & evening prayers and we and they shall ever Pray — Signed in behalf of ourselves and fellow Members — Joseph Burns, John Diamond, John Scott, Thomas Keen, Simon Hadock, John Carrell.

On motion it was resolved that a Committee be appointed to take the same into consideration & to report on the same.

Resolved that the Board of Trustees consisting of the Lay-Members be a committee for that purpose....

                                         Signed Jaˢ. Gartland, Secʸ

Adjourned at ½ past 10 OClock

Minutes of January 8, 1818

The Committee appointed to take into Consideration the Petition of the Catholic people of colour do also report.

That they most sincerely Consent that these poor People have not the means to give their Children a Catholic Education and that the Funds of the Corporation being at present so low in consequence of they [*sic*] owing a very large Sum on which they have to pay Interest until it is liquidated, the Board therefore cannot extend any relief from that Source that there are very heavy claims on the Congregation to support the St. Joseph's Society and the poor of the Congregation in the inclemency of the Winter by a public appeal to their Charity and that during that time trade & business are slack and unproductive hence your Committee are of the opinion they have it not in their power to set so necessary an institution on foot and they deem it prudent to wait until the approach of summer before they should make application to the charitable of the Congregation for aid by Subscription to establish so desirable an object as truly to instruct the Ignorant.

The same being read & considered it was on motion approved.

> Minute Book of the Trustees of St. Mary's Church, 1812–29, Philadelphia Archdiocesan Historical Research Center. Printed by Permission.

## 23. Pontifical Charter for St. Mary's Seminary, Baltimore, 1822

*French Sulpician emigrés headed by François Charles Nagot opened the first seminary in the United States at St. Mary's in Baltimore on October 3, 1791. The earliest of many contributions by the Society of St. Sulpice to the church in the United States, St. Mary's was chartered by the State of Maryland as a civil university January 19, 1805, and in 1822 it obtained the right to confer pontifical degrees.*

DECREE of the Sacred General Congregation of the
*Propaganda Fide* held on March 26, 1822.

If it is to be desired that inducements to and interest in virtue and knowledge be everywhere increased with the offering of honors and rewards, then nowhere do the practices of this kind seem more useful than in places where heresies are raging, in order that young men, instructed in all branches of study and especially in the sacred sciences and in sound doctrine, may lead others through right ways and promote the holy religion of Christ by removing errors. Since therefore there has been erected at Baltimore in Maryland, through the zeal of the archbishops and with the approbation of the civil authority, the illustrious College of St. Mary which is provided with excellent professors, with a library and with other conveniences, where young men are carefully instructed no less in piety than in the arts, and especially in the sacred sciences; and since the Most Reverend Lord, AMBROSE MARÉCHAL, the present Archbishop of Baltimore, has earnestly requested that, in order to incite more and more the students of this same college to learn the science of letters and particularly the sacred sciences, the power be granted by Apostolic Authority to him and to his successors of conferring the degree of Doctorate in Sacred Theology on those students of the aforesaid college who would be considered worthy of this very great honor, and that this same college be endowed with the privileges of other universities, a request of this kind has seemed just and highly conducive to an increase of holy Faith. Therefore our Most Holy Lord Pius VII, by Divine Providence Pope, at the request of the Sacred Congregation held in audience by R. P. D. Carolo Maria Pedicini, Secretary, on April 28 of the year 1822, kindly conceded and granted to the same college at Baltimore each and every privilege which other universities possess and enjoy; and to the present archbishop and to his successors *in perpetuum* the power of conferring the degree of Doctorate or the degree of Master in Sacred Theology, preserving the form of the Council of Vienne, and according to the custom of other universities, on those students who, in the same college, after completing the course of studies, have given proofs of their probity and learning, observing the following conditions, namely: I. that each one of the candidates have defended publicly and, in the judgment of the professors, rightly, questions proposed from the whole of philosophy; II. that he, as a Master of Arts, have taught in the same college the humanities for a year, and then the whole course of philosophy, in which, however, the archbishop, with just reasons concurring, may dispense; III. that he have studied Sacred Theology for four years, and canon law for a year; IV. that he have strenuously and cogently upheld on two successive days, for three hours each day public theses in all of theology, but especially in dogmatic and moral, and in canon law and Church history; V. finally, that he must, in the presence of the archbishop or another appointed by the same, undergo, in matters theological, a rigid examination, which is to be given by two Doctors in Sacred Theology. After each of the candidates, therefore, has undergone these tests and has been deemed worthy to be decorated with the degree, he will by Apostolic Authority be constituted and proclaimed by the archbishop, who will first have received in his hands the public profession of Faith according to the form handed down by Pope Pius IV of happy memory, as a *Licentiate emeritus*, and an outstanding Doctor and Master in Sacred Theology, with each and every indult, exemption, privilege, favor, preeminence, dignity and honor conferred on him which others thus promoted enjoy by law, or custom, or otherwise both in the city of Rome and in the universities of the whole world; with the faculty likewise given to the new Doctor of reading, teaching, glossing, interpreting, of ascending to the Magisterial Chair and of exercising publicly and privately all other magisterial acts. And in order that one who has gained a magisterial degree of this kind may likewise receive its ornaments, the accustomed insignia are to be conferred on him by the archbishop, the ring shall be placed on his ring-finger, and the birretum as a crown upon his head, the closed books shall be handed to him and opened in his hands, and finally he shall be placed in the Magisterial Chair, so that he may feel that he has been admitted and received among the Doctors of Theology, just as he ought to be admitted and received with a brotherly kiss by each teacher and Doctor there present, to the praise and glory of Almighty God and our Saviour Jesus Christ.

Granted freely without any recompense at all for whatever reason.

> Given at Rome in the hall of the Sacred Congregation of
> *Propaganda Fide* on the 1st day of May, 1822.

H. Card. Consalvi, Acting Prefect
Carlo Maria Pedicini, Sec'y

Decree of the General Sacred Congregation of the Propaganda Fide, March 26, 1822, trans. from the Latin, Sulpician Archives, Baltimore, Maryland. Printed by permission.

## 24. Sisters of the Visitation at Georgetown Petition Congress for Incorporation, 1828

*The Visitation Academy at Georgetown evolved from a small free school established adjacent to Georgetown College in 1799 by three Irish-born women known as the "Pious Ladies." Under the direction of Leonard Neale, S.J., they formed the nucleus of the future Visitation monastery. The nuns' request for legal incorporation in 1828 appended a detailed prospectus promoting a broadened scope of female education.*

### PETITION.

*To the Honorable the Senate and House of Representatives of the United States;*

The petition of the Sisters of the Visitation

RESPECTFULLY REPRESENTS:

That about twenty years ago their Institution was established in Georgetown, within the District of Columbia, and that they have, since that period, had the satisfaction of affording education to many young females, from different parts of the country. They have at present in their Academy, *fifty-three* boarders, and *forty-two* day scholars. They have also within their precincts a Benevolent School, attended annually by upwards of one hundred and fifty young females, who, for the sum of one dollar per quarter, receive a plain English education. For a description of the system and extent of the instruction afforded at their Seminary, they beg leave to refer your honorable body to the printed Prospectus accompanying this petition. To carry into effect the objects of their Association, it is necessary that they should possess both personal and real property, which, as a body, they cannot now do; and as individuals who compose their society, change by deaths and new admissions, they cannot hold property by any permanent tenure, which is sometimes the cause of difficulty and embarrassment, and might, by accident or neglect, produce serious consequences; nor can they protect themselves and the children placed under their charge from injury or assault, or from losses and injuries, which could alone be prevented or remedied by recurrence to law. The Sisters of the Visitation, therefore, pray your honorable body to pass an act of incorporation, granting them the privilege of holding property, and the power of suing and being sued; to have and use a common seal; with such other powers as may seem meet and just by your honorable body, to enable them to carry into effect the objects set forth in this petition; and, as in duty bound, they will ever acknowledge, with feelings of gratitude, the favor conferred.

    *Georgetown, D.C. April 7th,* 1828.

## PROSPECTUS

*Of the Ladies' Academy of the Visitation in Georgetown, D.C.*

    This Academy is located on the Heights of Georgetown, in the District of Columbia, contiguously to the eastern margin of the Potomac. It commands a view of the meanders of this magnificent river; and a distant perspective of Washington City. Notwithstanding the vicinity of so copious a stream, the salubrity of the air is uniform: no fevers, originating from the exhalations or miasmata, so prevalent in aqueous situations, having here exhibited their deleterious effects. The ladies, under whose superintendence and care the studies are conducted, are members of the religious order, founded in 1610, by St. Francis de Sales, and first governed by St. Jane Frances Fremiot de Chantal. Gentleness, benevolence, and temperate indulgence, swayed these venerated benefactors of society, in their guidance of youth. It is the study of their daughters to let these virtues appear conspicuous, in the discharge of the arduous duties imposed on them by the confidence of their friends.

    Of course, their religion is the religion of their holy founders; yet they have always enjoyed the patronage of their Protestant neighbors. To obviate acrimonious feeling, the rules of the Institution forbid all discussion on religious topics amongst the pupils, and no difference of doctrinal creeds, ever gives rise to ungenerous interference on the part of the ladies to whose care they are intrusted.

    Considering the rapid and unexampled progress of improvement, in the arts and sciences, during the last half century past, and the modification which has thence resulted in the forms of polite life, it would seem imperious on the guardians of youthful education, to widen the sphere of female tuition, and duly proportion it to the actual demands of society. This principle prompted the introduction of several new elements in the formation of the female mind, in various parts of Europe and America. To individuals who may have been tutored, in the age preceding this age of lights, the new branches ushered into the schools of young ladies, may seem fastidious innovation, or affectation of superior refinement. If trial be truth, as the vulgar adage would have it, the truth has glared in more than one popular city of our nation. Pursuing this noble scheme, for the improvement of an important half of the human family, the conductors of the Academy of the Visitation have in view to remove the land-marks yet further, and gradually to collect to one point, the newly introduced branches, seen disjunctively in various academies of Europe and of our own country.

Fenelon, in his invaluable treatise on female education, observes, that the conversation of a young lady should be ruled by present exigency — that an air of doubt and deference should accompany her utterence — that she should even be silent on the topics commonly beyond the sphere of her sex, although she number them among her own attainments. The taste of the age, however, has obtruded within the circles of polished life, branches of education, hitherto almost exclusively confined to Colleges or Universities. Such is the nature of the human character, that each individual of the circle wishes to give marks of information or intelligence on the subject in question, and none can be found insensible to the reproach of utter ignorance or mediocrity, where all would be equal. Hence, were the Archbishop of Cambray revived, and, with his intuitive view of the necessities of mankind, admitted to overhear the conversations of our brilliant saloons, would he not give latitude to his maxim, that the knowledge of ladies should be circumscribed within the pale of their functions, and that the character of their employment should induce the character of their studies. Moreover, as to the care of ladies is intrusted the guardianship of society in its earliest age, to them is frequently due the bias of the growing mind. It is often in their power to refine the taste, and to whet the appetite, for every virtuous and literary acquirement. The classic reader, continues Fenelon, well knows how Cornelia, the mother of the Gracchi, contributed by the elegance of her education, to adorn and inspirit the eloquence of her children, afterwards so illustrious at the rostrum.

The expansion of the youthful mind, in the more advanced stages of life, is generally the effect of impressions communicated to it, when first awakened to reason. It is then stamped for greatness, mediocrity, or paltriness. Its character remains, and acquires consistency. Its form is the form of the mould, and the man, seen in his important relations in society was the youth whose mind was quickened in its first operations by the mother. So the angle, in its more expanded dimensions, is still the angle at the vertex: obtuse or acute, at all its distances from the goal of increment, according to the impulse of the geometer's hand.

With the ancient Romans, the accomplished education of mothers was of special interest. To them, on the testimony of Quintilian, the fashion of the day allotted the task of superintending the language of their offspring, from their earliest lisp. That inappropriate terms, or a vicious form of expression, might not be interwoven in their habits, at the first development of their faculties, the gentle hand of the mother, smoothed and filed off the asperity of the first essays of infant enunciation. Thus were they prepared to lose no advantage that could be derived from future preceptors. In planning the education of the mother, if secondary were allowed to take the place of primary objects, the end would be frustrated, and the plan should be reprobated. But if the scheme be the dictate of society, as it now exists, such a scheme cannot fail of the patronage of the wise. From the centre, a ray is directed to each point of the circumference; and the female mind should be stored with the knowledge to fit her to inhabit the circle within which she is to move. In the choice of branches, should the Spartan principle guide our hand, the selection must be regulated by the refinement and civilization of the age with which we co-exist. It is not proposed to make orators of ladies, chemists, astronomers, or natural philosophers. Indeed, the limited period devoted to the literary improvement of females, would forbid the thought. Information, in these and other departments, will be diligently inculcated, with the help of individuals experienced in the education of youth.

The importance of taking the advantage of the years which a young lady spends with her preceptresses, is at once perceived, when it is considered, that on her return to the bosom of her family, she will never again have leisure or the inclination to apply to serious study. The season of busy communication has arrived. Many an avocation consumes her time, and improvement in the useful branches which she has once cultivated, not unfrequently retrogrades, rather than advances. The ladies of the Visitation, with proper counsel, have sent for *apparatus*,[1] by which they will be assisted in imparting an elementary insight, in at least fourteen branches of modern science. They have completed an edifice, named from an extension of the classic term ODEUM, adapted for its reception, and for the annual public Examination and Exhibition. Within its limits are also comprised an extensive hall for recreation, bath apartments, laboratory, and mantua-room.

On the annual recurrence of the examination and exhibition, the friends of the Institution will be admitted on presenting an authorized ticket.

The course of instruction, during the last term, embraced little more than the ordinary compass, commencing from the elements of a junior education, Orthography, Reading, Writing, Arithmetic, Grammar, English Composition, Geography, the use of Maps and Globes, Sacred History, Profane History, ancient and modern; Chronology, Mythology, and Rhetoric — French, Music on the Piano Forte and Harp; Dancing, Drawing, and Painting; Plain and Ornamental Needle-work in all its varieties; Tapestry, Lace-work, or Figuring on Bobbinet, and Bead-work, &c. To these will be gradually added, Algebra, Versification and Poetic Composition, Female Elocution, Popular Astronomy, with the assistance of the newly invented Geocyclic of Delamarche, Logic, Ethics, Metaphysics, Natural Philosophy in its various branches, Anthology, the Spanish, Italian and Latin Languages, if required; Vocal Music, the Guitar, and Painting on Velvet.

As parents have frequently expressed a wish that their daughters should be acquainted with mantua-work, to compose dress in its various forms, the knowledge and practice of this useful branch of female economy, will, if required, be taught by persons of experience.

Domestic Economy, comprising the various exercises in Pastry and the Culinary art, Laundry, Pantry, and Dairy inspection, &c: as conducted at the

---

1. "A common term to refer to materials used to demonstrate scientific and mathematical concepts and, in some cases, to allow female students to conduct scientific experiments" (information supplied by Thalia M. Mulvihill, author of "Community in Emma Willard's Educational Thought, 1787–1870," Ph.D. diss., Syracuse University, 1995). (Editor's note)

Academy of St. Denis Banlieue de Paris, will be an article which will occupy considerable attention in the enlarged system of education now laid before the public.

The ladies, charged with the duties of the Academy, will be vigilant in requiring an exact compliance with every rule of the Institution, and the forms of polite deportment.

At the exhibition, premiums will be awarded to the pupils, who shall have excelled in their respective classes. The young ladies are divided into two great circles, with respect to the exact observance of rules, polite deportment, and zeal for advancement. A crown will be allotted for the first in the *senior circle,* and another for the first in the *junior circle.* Both will inscribe their names in a book for special record.

During the hours which are not devoted to community-duties, the Sisters are seriously occupied in adding to their store of knowledge, and making every necessary research that may tend to accelerate the progress of their pupils.

The Protestant young ladies will attend at the church hours, and will be expected to observe the general regulations of exterior worship.

The *Academy doors* will be closed at half an hour after five in winter, and at half an hour after eight in summer.

The young ladies, when visited, will always be attended by a Sister.

The letters written or received by them will be examined by the General Directress of the Academy, previously to their delivery.

With the approbation of their parents or guardians, they may be allowed to visit once a month; they must, however, be returned before night, unless special permission, grounded on strong motives, be obtained.

Wednesday and Saturday evenings of each week, are allotted to recreation.

The Annual Recess, or Vacation, will commence on the last Thursday of July; the Examination will occupy the preceding Monday and Tuesday; and the Exhibition the afternoon of Wednesday.

The exercises will recommence on the second Monday in September.

### NOTICE TO PARENTS AND GUARDIANS.

No child will be received before the conclusion of her seventh year, unless strong reasons should be offered for her admittance at an earlier age. Young ladies above fifteen, must not expect to be received, if they be not recommended by a person who will be held responsible. Those who, during their course of tuition at this Academy, reach the ages above fifteen, are not subject to this regulation.

To be admitted into the *first class,* young ladies must have completed their studies in Grammar, Geography, and Arithmetic: must give satisfaction in Composition, and in their examination on Whelply's Compend of History, or other equivalent work.

The course of studies in that class, will be Select History and Chronology, Roman and Grecian Antiquities, Elements of Logic, Ethics, and Metaphysics,

Algebra, Rhetoric, Female Elocution, Poetry, Natural Philosophy, comprising Popular Astronomy, &c. &c. Chemistry, &c. &c. Domestic Economy.

### TERMS.

| | | | | | | |
|---|---|---|---|---|---|---|
| Entrance, | – | – | – | – | – | $5 00 |
| Board, tuition, &c. per annum, | | – | – | – | | 150 00 |
| Ink, quills and paper;   do. | | – | – | – | | 4 00 |

Books at the store prices.

Boarders in the 1st *class*, will pay an additional charge of ten dollars, for use of apparatus, &c.

| | | | | | |
|---|---|---|---|---|---|
| Day-scholars, per annum, pay | – | – | – | | 40 00 |

Those in the 1st *class* will pay the additional charge of boarders.

### EXTRA CHARGES.

| | | | | | |
|---|---|---|---|---|---|
| For each of the languages, except English, per annum, | | | | | $20 00 |
| Piano, per annum, | – | – | – | – | 48 00 |
| Drawing, Painting on Velvet, &c. | | – | – | – | 20 00 |

Harp, Guitar, and Vocal Music, at the Professor's charges.

Dancing, also, at the Master's charge.

Doctor's fees and medicines will entail no separate charge, except the case of protracted malady; then the Doctor's bill will be presented.

Boarders pay the current charges, semi-annually, in advance — Day-scholars quarterly.

As the recess forms a part of the exercises of the Academy, no deduction, on that consideration, will be made from the semi-annual account. Day-scholars are not subject to this regulation.

The winter-uniform of the young ladies, consists of a crimson bombazette dress and pelerine, with a black apron. Hitherto, they have been accustomed to dress in crimson crape on Sundays. It is wished that this practice should be continued.

In summer, on Sundays, the uniform is white, with a black silk apron; and on certain days, white, with a blue silk pelerine, and blue sash. The rule prescribes no particular dress for other days; blue gingham, however, is recommended.

Each boarder is required to bring with her the ordinary table furniture, consisting of knives, forks, silver spoons and silver tumbler, and be provided with bed and bedding, or pay $7 per annum, if furnished by the institution.

It is hoped that parents will conform to the established custom of placing all upon an equality, with respect to *pocket-money.*

The parents and guardians of the young ladies, who reside at a distance, are respectfully requested to designate some correspondent in the District, who will be charged to liquidate their bills when due.

It were much to be desired, that some merchant in town should be instructed to furnish the young ladies with apparel, or, if the office devolve on the Institution, that the requisite provision be made.

MICHAEL F. WHEELER,[2] M.A. *President,*
*Of St. Mary's College, Balt. And Director of the Convent and*
*Ladies' Academy of the Visit.*

*August* 14*th* 1827.

.*.* By this opportunity, it is notified, that the *Convent doors will, henceforward, remain closed on Sundays and festivals;* and, from the inconvenience resulting from the interruption of the duties of the community, that *no visit, at the parlors, will be prolonged beyond fifteen minutes, without special necessity.*

> Petition of the Sisters of the Visitation of Georgetown, D.C. Praying That an Act of Incorporation May Be Passed in Their Favor, April 8, 1828, 20th Congress, First Session [168] Washington: Printed by Duff Green. 1828.

## 25. Origins of St. Joseph Academy, Carondelet, Missouri, 1840

*Sisters of St. Joseph arrived in the diocese of St. Louis from Lyons, France, in 1836 and established communities in Cahokia, Illinois, and Carondelet, Missouri. At Carondelet the sisters taught village children and housed deaf-mutes and orphans in a small log cabin. With a brick building in progress, they took an initial class of seven boarders in 1840. The youngest, Eliza McKenney, later wrote memoirs that furnish an intimate glimpse of life at the primitive school.*

On the first Sunday in September in the year 1840, I entered St. Joseph's Institute although a child not yet nine years old....On arriving at St. Joseph's gate I saw sitting on the porch of the humble dwelling then called St. Joseph's, the future guides of my childhood and as they formed my character such I remained.

The revered form of our deeply revered and loved Mother Celestine occupied a central position: next to her, her "beloved disciple" Sister St. John and the other dear sisters whose names I give as memory best serves me. The saintly Felicité, the mild and gentle St. Protais who never reproved, but always found excuse for our failings: The sweet Philomene, humble, simple in her ways, who knew no will but ours, out of the sight of "notre mère," all hearts without guile. Then Sister Delphine our French teacher, Sister Mary Joseph our English teacher, and one more whose religious name I cannot remember but who was a Miss Valois of St. Louis as was also Sister Mary Joseph (Miss Dillon).[1]

When Mother Celestine received me from my mother's hands, she kissed me tenderly and said our "Bebé" [*sic*] and although in a few years pupils as young as I then was filled our home the name was never taken from me.

---

2. Baltimore-born Sulpician. (Editor's note)

---

1. The writer mentions six of the French pioneers from Lyons — Sisters Célestine Pommerel, St. Jean Fournier, Marguerite-Félicité Bouté, St. Protais Déboille, Philomène Vilaine, Delphine Fontbonne — and the first two Americans, Sisters Mary Joseph Dillon and Marie Josephine Valois. (Editor's note)

Our mother then called in the pupils to see me....All of these pupils with the exception of myself were young ladies all over seventeen years of age.

There were nine mutes all young with the exception of two of them....I could not recall the names of the younger ones as we seldom came in contact with them, they being Sister Philomene's help in the kitchen or as we called them her body guards.

The house we dwelt in was a poor one at its best: constructed of logs and weatherboarded over to screen us from the wintry blasts but it poorly fulfilled that duty.

It was a two story building with two rooms on the ground floor, the north room being mother's room and the south one being the refectory for both sisters and pupils. The second story which we entered from the outside only contained the pupil's dormitory and also one for the sisters and mutes. The rear of Mother's room and the refectory were two small rooms which were study and classrooms combined. The foundation for the first brick house on the north of the building we then occupied was being laid when I entered St. Joseph's and the following year we occupied it....

The winter was severe and our dear sisters were taxed to the utmost in order to make us comfortable; but always poverty was a great obstacle to their doing so. The house...offered a good target to the cold winds which had a high carnival in our dormitory, particularly during the snowstorms, and many a night did those dear self sacrificing pioneers spend their time in shaking the snow from our beds, regretting at the same time to be compelled to awaken us through their kind efforts in shielding us from the storm. There were porches above and below on the front of the old home, and the one upstairs facing the river was our lavatory. Seven tin basins, bright as silver were hung upon its walls and under them on the floor were some pails of water for our use....sometimes we would have to wait until we got downstairs to bathe our faces as the water in the pails would be one solid cake of ice....

The only discipline exercised over us was the one of love and we were obedient and docile pupils, and until Sister Mary Rose took charge of the pupils on Sr. Mary Joseph's death, discipline and punishment was unknown under St. Joseph's roof....

Sister Mary Rose (Miss Marstellar of Baltimore)...was a woman of marked ability and superior in education but constant ill health and bodily infirmities had soured a disposition that under other circumstances would have been that of a loving nature. But that same sternness and severity caused St. Joseph's to prosper as her ability became known both as a teacher and guide....Our mother [Sister Célestine] often told us that she herself was from the mountains of Savoy and her name was Marguerite Pomerel [sic]....

Being a privileged character and a spoiled child I often went to our mother's room unbidden, that I might feel her arms around me or her gentle hand under my chin and looking into my eyes with those soulful eyes of hers — would bend down and kiss me saying "What does Bebé want?" In many of these informal visits I found her in tears, and my little impulsive heart would melt into tears and I would ask her why she wept, and taking my pocket handkerchief from my pocket proceed to wipe away her tears, regardless of my own which were tracing their way down my face, in sympathy with her. Did we love her? Our love for her was our cult and what our mother said and did met with our own full approval....[U]ntil the next sett [*sic*] of sisters came to us...our recreations were spent with our sisters in our class rooms: but as our numbers increased—and that of the sisters also we were relegated to our study rooms and our sisters had a community room of their own very much to our disgust, as we were not pleased with any changes which interfered with our happiness and that happiness consisted in being with them at all hours....

There were two orphans besides the mutes as some of the last mentioned were orphans—but cannot recall names....

My mother's reasons for sending me from her when I was so young was that she was desirous of my acquiring a French education in all the purity of the language, which I certainly did, and I learned to speak it long before I could spell one word of the language as remember dear sister, none of the pioneers at that time could hardly make themselves understood in the English language. Sister Saint John spoke it better than any of them, and her grammar in that line was far from perfect, but in after years some of them did better and after I learned to speak French by routine, many a time was I interpreter for our mother when she met persons in a business way.

Sister Philomene was the sister we always loved to have with us at our evening recreations and we would assist her in washing dishes in order to have her sooner with us and many a night we retired to our beds shaking with fear from the horrid ghost and fairy tales with which she entertained us....When the north house was built the rear room on the ground floor became our refectory; and our sister's refectory became their private one, as previous to that we occupied the same refectory. Pupils, mutes and orphans at two tables our sisters at the third one....

The clock [in the new building] was hung on the wall near the staircase door where we ascended to our study room over the refectory and poor sister [Philomène] was kept in a frantic state of mind by our either retarding, advancing or entirely stopping the clock in its daily progress—giving us our dinner sometimes at eleven, and once at half past ten o'clock instead of twelve the regular time. Can you not see us dear sister playing these pranks and *still* our sisters enjoyed them....

Sister Felicité had charge of the dormitory and the sick besides her other manifold duties.

Sister had a serious and quiet disposition, and so much native dignity in her character. Her smile was contagious but I never knew her to laugh outright. An earnest and patient listener to us, and her replies given in the gentlest and sweetest of tones to which we replied in a like manner, as no one of our number was ever known to be guilty of a rudeness in the presence of that tall sweet sister.

How often, has she held me in her arms like a babe, in hours of sickness (as I was very small for my age) and with my head pillowed near her heart has she lulled me to sleep and forgetfulness of pain....

From the time I lost my mother, our mother [Sister Célestine] took her place, and when I was betrothed to the father of my children in 1853 I took him to see our mother for her consent to our marriage, spending the day with all my sisters. I was married May 12th 1853 and previous to taking this step I entered into retreat at St. Joseph at our mother's desire and occupied a bed in the same plaice I did whilst a pupil....

Our tuition for one year including board, washing, books, was the whole of eighty seven $87.00 dollars per year. We furnished our bed covers and sheets and paid physicians bills. Our beds were husk beds, *no more*, and it took an artist at the business to make that be level and presentable....

> Memoirs of Mrs. Eliza McKenney Brouillet (Series of letters to Mother Agatha Guthrie and Sister Monica Corrigan between February 23, 1890, and May 29, 1891), 912.2, Archives of Sisters of St. Joseph of Carondelet, St. Louis Province, Carondelet, Missouri. Printed with permission.

## 26. Archbishop Hughes versus the Public School Society, 1841

*John Hughes (1797–1864), coadjutor to the ailing Bishop John Dubois, used his noted oratorical skills and populist style at a large rally at Carroll Hall to mobilize New York Catholics behind a virtual third-party ticket in the election of 1841. The issue was education and freedom of religion. As an unforeseen result of Hughes's success, the religious aspect of education became increasingly restricted in public schools.*

### Great Meeting of the Friends of Freedom of Education in Carroll Hall, October 29th, 1841

A CROWDED and highly respectable meeting of citizens favorable to a just and equitable system of Common Schools in the city of New York, was held on the 29th of October at Carroll Hall, in this city, pursuant to public notice. ...Mr. O'Connor, one of the Secretaries, read the following requisition for the meeting from one of the public papers:

"SCHOOL QUESTION. — A general meeting of citizens favorable to such a system of Common Schools in the city of New York, as will extend the benefits of public education to the children of all denominations, without trenching on the religious rights of any, will be held at Carroll Hall, this evening, 29th inst., at half-past seven o'clock. By order of the Central Committee."

Bishop HUGHES then rose and said —

I am delighted, gentlemen, to find that the forlorn and neglected children of the city of New York have yet so many friends as I now see assembled around me. Amidst the passions and prejudices of public men, it is still consoling to observe that the rights of those children to the benefits of education are advocated by so many friends, and certainly if you were to abandon them in this emergency, their prospects for the future would be hopeless. When I speak of their forlorn condition with regard to education, I do not mean that there are not schools erected, but that those schools are conducted under such a system, and on such principles, as necessarily to prevent those children from attending them. The consequence has been as you know, that for sixteen years past, that portion of our citizens represented by this meeting have been obliged to provide separate schools, while they were taxed for the support of those from whose existence they derived no benefit.

Those facts determined the origin of this question. Some have supposed that the grievance had its origin only with the time when the agitation and explanation of it were publicly commenced; but let them look at your efforts for years past in providing education for your children, and ask themselves whether you would have gone to the second expenditure to provide a defective and inefficient education for your children if you could have permitted them to attend the schools already provided.

But first I must say a few words in explanation of my own position in this matter.

I was in Europe when the question was first brought before the public, and when I first heard of its agitation, I believed that we had but to make a full, fair and candid statement of our grievances to honorable men, in order to produce an acknowledgment of the injustice of employing the funds raised by taxing all for the benefit of a portion of Society, and to the exclusion of one entire class. [Cheers.] I have attended in this place and elsewhere, meeting after meeting, during which we have explained the grounds of our objection to the present system of education. We have uniformly avoided all questions of a political character, and I have more than once expressed publicly, as I do now, my determination to retire from such meetings the moment any political question was introduced. It is not my province to mingle in politics. The course which I have pursued hitherto in this regard I shall not abandon now, and I have therefore to request that you shall not look for forms here which may be usual in meetings of a political character, but to which I am a stranger, and which I do not desire to see introduced for the accomplishment of the object which we have in view.

The object of this meeting is, after all previous measures have been adopted, to see what means yet remain in your power for attaining the end for which you are contending....

In this as in all other undertakings, it is necessary that you proceed with firmness and perfect unanimity. Our adversaries accuse us of acting with interested motives in this matter. They say that we want a portion of the school fund for sectarian purposes to apply it to the support and advancement of our religion. This we deny now, as we have done heretofore.... There is no such thing as a predominant religion, and the small minority is entitled to the same protection as the greatest majority. No denomination whether numerous or not can impose its religious views on a minority at the common expense of that minority and itself. It was against that we contended. That was the principle from the unjust operation of which we desired to be released....

We do not ask for sectarian schools. We do not ask that any portion of the public money should be confided to us for purposes of education. We do not ask for the privilege of teaching our religion at the public expense — such a demand would be absurd and would richly merit the rebuke which it could not escape.

In the Public Schools, which were established according to the system now in force, our children had to study books which we could not approve. Religious exercises were used which we did not recognize, and our children were compelled to take part in them. Then we withdrew them from the schools and taught them with our own means. We do not want money from the school funds — all we desire is that it be administered in such a way as to promote the education of all. Now the Public School Society has introduced just so much of religious and sectarian teaching as it pleased them, in the plenitude of their irresponsible character, to import. They professed to exclude religion, and yet they introduced so much in quantity as they thought proper, and of such a quality as violated our religious rights. If our children cannot receive education without having their religious faith and feelings modeled by the Public School Society, then they cannot receive it under the auspices of that institution, and if for these reasons they cannot receive it from that institution, it is tyranny to tax them for its support. We do not ask the introduction of religious teaching in any public school, but we contend that if such religious influences be brought to bear on the business of education, it shall be, so far as our children are concerned, in accordance with the religious belief of their parents and families....

We first laid our case before the Common Council. They disposed of it in a manner with which you are familiar. We then applied to the Legislature. It is now in the order of things to be referred to yourselves. [Cheers.]... You are now to decide whether your children shall be educated as others shall prescribe — receive instruction from such books as are repugnant to your religious feelings, and whether you shall be constrained to give your voice in favor of those who would perpetuate such a state of things. And here see the effect of our admirable system of laws. We have it in our own power to remedy the evils of which we complain. It may truly be said to be a government of the people — based as it is on just and adequate representations, founded on a principle in which there is an implied contract, or what may be called an implied contract between the voter and the voted for. But in relation to the candidates who have been placed in nomination for your suffrage at the present time, mark the cunning of the gentlemen opposed to you. They have so managed it that those candidates, if elected, would go to the Legislature pledged to oppose your claim, so that when the representatives are assembled at Albany, it may be said that if you voted at all you voted in favor of that to which it has been said you were opposed — that you were satisfied with the schools of the Public School Society as they are, — that in your judgment those schools inculcate the proper amount of moral precept, and religion as we were once told in just the "legal quantity." [Cheering and laughter.] The time, then, has now arrived, when the fathers and the brothers and the uncles of the children who are excluded from those public schools should pass judgment on the evils of the present system....

But I call upon you to resist this Public School System, whether you are sustained by public men or not. You are called upon to join with your oppressors and they leave you no alternative in voting. It may appear uncommon — it may seem to be inconsistent with my character that I should thus take an interest in this matter; and I should not, were it not a subject of extraordinary import. But there has been an invasion of your religious rights, and, as the spiritual guardian of those now before me, I am bound to help their cause. If you are taxed, you must be protected. [Cheers.] Were the tax so imposed that each denomination might receive the benefits of its own quota, the case would be fair enough. We are willing to have any system that operates *equally;* but we will never submit to a direct violation of our rights, and an appropriation of the school fund in such a manner that we may not participate in its benefits....

I do not consider the question as it regards parties or men. I only speak for and advocate the *freedom of education* and the men who would stand up for it. I appear as the friend of him who would give justice to all classes. [Cheers.]

We have entirely kept out of sight all mere party distinctions, and have looked among public men for those who had just views of what we regard as our undeniable rights. We have now resolved to give our suffrage in favor of no man who is an enemy to us and the recognition of those rights, and to support every friend we can find among men of all political parties. [Great applause.]...

With political controversies and party questions I have nothing whatever to do. Such considerations enter not into anything with which I am concerned. But by my authority the only means left us to obtain justice have been sought, and this organization effected. The representatives of the neglected portion of the children in the various parts of the city have met, and have all united for the purpose of arranging a plan by which they may escape the miserable alternative of voting for their enemies, and they have prepared a ticket bearing on it the names of men who are all known as favourable to your cause. [Great cheering]...

It is impossible for me to say anything personally of those whose names have been recommended to be placed on the list of candidates, and I would not for one moment urge that they should be placed there, had I not been assured, on the most positive evidence and which I could not doubt, that they are friendly to an alteration in the present system of public education....

The Secretary then read the following list: — *Senators,* Thomas O'Connor, J. G. Gottsberger; *Assembly,* Tighe Davey, Daniel C. Pentz, George Weir, Paul Grout, Conrad Swackhammer, William B. MacLay, David R. F. Jones, Solomon Townsend, John L. O'Sullivan, Auguste Davizac, William McMurray, Michael Walsh, Timothy Daly....

You have now, gentlemen, heard the names of men who are willing to risk themselves in support of your cause.... You now, for the first time, find yourselves in the position to vote at least for yourselves. You have often voted for others, and they did not vote for you, but now you are determined to uphold with your own votes, your own rights. [Thunders of applause, which lasted several minutes.] Will you then stand by the rights of your offspring, who have for so long a period, and from generation to generation, suffered under the operation of this injurious system? [Renewed cheering.] Will you adhere to the nomination made? [Loud cries of "we will," "we will," and vociferous applause.] Will you be united? [Tremendous cheering — the whole immense assembly rising *en masse,* waving of hats, handkerchiefs, and every possible demonstration of applause.] Will you let all men see that you are worthy sons of the nation to which you belong? [Cries of "Never fear — we will!" "We will till death!" and terrific cheering.] Will you prove yourselves worthy of friends? [Tremendous cheering.] Will none of you flinch? [The scene that followed this emphatic query is indescribable, and exceeded all the enthusiastic, and almost frenzied displays of passionate feeling we have sometimes witnessed at Irish meetings. The cheering — the shouting — the stamping of feet — waving of hats and handkerchiefs, beggared all powers of description.] Very well, then, the tickets will be prepared and distributed amongst you, and on the day of election go like freemen, with dignity and calmness, entertaining due respect for your fellow-citizens and their opinions, and deposit your votes. And if you do not elect any of your friends, you will at least record your votes in favor of justice, and in favor of your principles, which must not — cannot be abandoned, and you will be guiltless of the sin and shame and degradation of electing men who are pledged to trample on you if they can!...I ask then, once for all — and with the answer let the meeting close — will this meeting pledge its honor, as the representative of that oppressed portion of our community, for whom I have so often pleaded, here as well as elsewhere — will it pledge its honor that it will stand by these candidates whose names have been read, and that no man composing this vast audience will ever vote for any one pledged to oppose our just claims and incontrovertible rights? [Terrific cheering and thunders of applause, which continued for several minutes, amid which Bishop Hughes resumed his seat.]

Silence having been at length restored, the ticket was adopted by acclamation, and the immense assemblage adjourned in the most peaceful and orderly manner.

> *Complete Works of the Most Rev. John Hughes, D.D., Archbishop of New York. Comprising his Sermons, Letters, Lectures, Speeches, etc.* Carefully Compiled and Edited from the Best Sources by Lawrence Kehoe, vol. 1, 2nd ed., revised and corrected (New York: For the Compiler, 1865), 275–84.

## 27. Orestes Brownson on Catholic Colleges, 1858

*Orestes A. Brownson (1803–76), a convert to Catholicism in midlife, had been a minister in the Universalist and Unitarian traditions and a founding member of the New England Transcendentalist Club. His religious and philosophical background provided a perspective quite different from that of the immigrant Catholic community in mid nineteenth-century America. From that viewpoint, he challenged the Catholic colleges of his day.*

Art. IV. — *Public Instruction, or Reflections on our own*
*Collegiate System as it actually exists.*

... We propose to offer some remarks on the present condition of this higher education among the Catholics of this country, for the purpose of unfolding our views as to the modifications most urgently required, and also as to the interest that should properly be manifested in the subject on the part of the community. The latter point seems to us of peculiar importance in order to place this species of education on a permanent foundation, to harmonize its equipment with the place which it holds in the economy of instruction, and to make it worthy of the prominent social position our Catholic community must necessarily occupy in the republic....

The arrangements for collegiate, or as we say, liberal education, are all embraced in a system complete and harmonious in all its parts. These arrangements comprise distinct kinds of official position, having diverse and well-defined duties....[A] college is a public institution of learning, favored by the law, with express functions in the economy of science, and possessing within itself all the powers requisite for discharging them....No system is so perfect as not to fall far short of the sanguine hopes of its framers, and none can be so unskillfully devised, or so defective in itself, that the self-sacrificing efforts of high-spirited men will not save it from entire failure. The question is not whether industry, ability, and experience can or cannot be ascribed to this individual or to that, but whether they are not all exerted in our present collegiate system under circumstances which hinder instead of favoring their proper success.

Our present collegiate system did not, at one bound, spring equipped into existence; nor was it, like the systems in operation around it, derived from the institutions of Great Britain, which, although withdrawn from Catholic control and direction, are even in our day administered, for the most part, in accordance with the statutes of their Catholic founders. So far, indeed, as a system of instruction, we are at a loss to ascribe to it any origin whatever....

Our present system, on its face, is ecclesiastical. It is appurtenant to various religious orders, or to the ecclesiastical polity of the Church at large. Adapted primarily to rudimentary instruction in the science of theology, and equipped in accordance with such a design, it was the offspring of necessities whose call was louder than could be that of collegiate education proper. In the absence, present and prospective, of the latter, the theological seminaries which from time to time arose to meet the wants of the former were obviously adapted to furnish instruction, to the general student, in Greek, Latin, and Geometry. To their directors the Catholic community of the day gladly committed the education of their children. Very soon, a flourishing condition led not a few of these institutions, although unendowed, to make successful application to various State Legislatures for the power of conferring degrees. Such action on the part of the executive officers may have been premature....The distinction implied by the new designation [of degree-granting college] is not practically important. The point to be considered is that there has been no adoption of the economy of collegiate education.

The principle of established classes and terms of admission, of regarding every pupil as a candidate for a degree, of uniform statutory regulations, of matriculation and of residence, does not enter into the system. Though empowered to confer degrees they are rarely conferred or applied for. The relations formed by students with the college are not essentially different from those between a well-grown child and the schoolmistress of a neighboring village. The institution continues to be an educational omnibus wherein the votaries of science enter unceremoniously, and continue up the ascent as far as suits either their curiosity or convenience, and no farther.

The designation has come to be applied, indifferently, to all institutions to which boys are sent from home to be educated, and every new institution prefaces its claims to the patronage of the community by the sounding title of COLLEGE. These institutions, so designated, are in fact only large boarding-schools, with the privilege, in some instances, of conferring the degree of Bachelor of Arts. This is done at the termination of the course of studies, which is divided into several classes, to the study of each of which an entire year is set apart. Pupils of all ages are received, and to each is furnished board, instruction, and a more or less assiduous care and supervision, inasmuch as the officers assume a responsibility for the moral conduct of the pupil....

If sufficient interest does not exist in the [Catholic] community to fully equip our present institutions of learning, or to establish institutions better suited to our wants, let the deficiency be ascribed to the proper source. Instead of pursuing the defects of the system through all its developments, and sympathizing with the sufferers from its vicious organization, let the community be aroused to a consciousness of the vital nature of their interest in the matter. All other difficulties will vanish as a mist, when the provision of means [for the erection and endowment of an institution of public instruction] is the only question to be presented for solution.

But if it be premature to demand what we have proposed, then the system should be changed. It should be adapted to the grade of attainment which is the community desire for their sons. The present system assumes that all who come up to college, come up for the purpose, except in case of impediment, of taking a degree at the end of the course. The number of students who actually demand the testimonial, as has been already stated, is comparatively insignificant. This artificial body, which we call a college, has then no appropriate functions to discharge, and it should be abolished....

> Orestes A. Brownson, "Public Instruction, or Reflections on Our Own Collegiate System as It Actually Exists," *Brownson's Quarterly Review* 15 (April 1858): 210–12, 229.

## 28. Petition to Leo XIII for a Polish Seminary in the United States, 1879

*Fr. Leopold Moczygemba, founder of the first Polish parish in the United States at Panna Maria, Texas, 1854, was president of the Polish Roman Catholic Union of America (PRCUA) from 1875 to 1878, when it resolved to establish a Polish national seminary in this country. During an extended stay in Rome, Moczygemba petitioned Leo XIII for permission to start the seminary and raise money to support it. Sts. Cyril and Methodius Seminary, founded in Detroit in 1885 by Fr. Jozef Dabrowski, is now located at Orchard Lake, Michigan.*

Most Holy Father:

Father Leopold Moczygemba, of the Order of Friars Minor Conventual, Apostolic Missionary in the United States of North America, and now for a short time Confessor in the English language at St. Peter's, prostrate to kiss your Holy foot, humbly makes known to Y[our]. H[oliness]. that, since there are more than two hundred thousand Poles in America scattered throughout different states and lacking sufficient Priests of the same nation for their spiritual needs, which are great, he proposes to establish a Seminary for young men of that nation who will dedicate themselves to the ecclesiastical life, and since he must begin with his own alms and trusts for the rest in the help of God and in the piety of the faithful, therefore begs Y[our]. H[oliness]. kindly to consent to grant him permission to devote to this purpose all the alms which he has presently and which he shall be able to obtain in the future.

That etc.

> To His Holiness
> Leo XIII
> happily reigning
>> From the Vatican Palace 14 Jan. 1879
>> We agree to everything
>> according to your request
>>> Leo P.P. XIII

Letter of Rev. Leopold Moczygemba to Leo XIII, The Central Archives of Polonia, Orchard Lake, Michigan. Trans. from Italian by Patricia Byrne. Printed with permission.

## 29. The Third Plenary Council of Baltimore on the Catholic Education of Youth, 1884

*The Third Plenary Council of Baltimore was the defining moment for the history of Catholic education in the United States. The assembled bishops issued binding decrees in regard to parish schools that recapitulated their developments in the first century of American Catholic education and established their direction for the next.*

Acts and Decrees of the Third Plenary Council of Baltimore, A.D. MDCCCLXXXIV

Title VI: On the Catholic Instruction of Youth
Chap. I: On Catholic Schools, Especially Parochial Schools
§1: On their absolute necessity

194. If ever in any age, then surely in this our age, the Church of God and the spirit of the world are in a certain wondrous and bitter conflict over the education of youth.... The Church, whose primary mission here on earth is to lead each man, reborn in the baptism of Christ, from the very first awakenings of reason to his supernatural end along the paths of truth and justice, cannot in any way allow Catholic parents whose right and natural and divine duty it is to look to the Christian education of their children, to obtain a merely secular education for them. Secular education cannot furnish the necessary means for the recognition and attainment of their final end.

195. Among those who strongly advocate this merely secular education are many who wish neither to bring any harm to religion nor to afford dangers to young people. From the very nature of the case, however, it follows that a merely secular education gradually breaks down so that it becomes irreligious and wicked, and especially dangerous to the faith and morals of the young....

196. And so we exhort Catholic parents not only because of our paternal love but we also admonish them with all the authority of which we are capable, to provide for that most beloved offspring given them by God, reborn to Christ in Baptism, and destined for heaven, a truly Christian and Catholic education, and to defend their children completely during the entire time of their infancy and childhood from the dangers of a purely secular education, and to place it in safe hands; Let them, therefore, send their children to parochial or other truly Catholic schools, unless perhaps the Ordinary, in a particular instance, judges that other arrangements can be tolerated.

197. That these are the schools in which at least very many if not all parents, using their own rights and following their duty, must seek and find a Christian education for their children was already decided by the Fathers of the 1st Plenary Council of Baltimore in clear fashion. In Decree 13 they say: "We exhort the Bishops, and in view of the very grave evils which usually result from the defective education of youth, we beseech them through the bowels of the mercy of God to see that schools are established in connection with the churches of their dioceses; and if it be necessary and circumstances permit, to provide from the revenues of the church to which the school is attached, for the support of competent teachers." In addition, the Fathers of the Second Plenary Council of Baltimore, no. 430, stated: "It seems that the best, or rather the only, remedy that remains by which these very serious and troublesome evils [that is, the deadly blight of indifferentism and the corruption of morals (no. 426) both of which are deeply deplored][1] can be met is that in every diocese, next to each and every church, schools be erected in which the Catholic youth may be imbued with literature and the fine arts as well as with religion and good morals."

The Sacred Congregation of the Propagation of the Faith, on the 24th of Nov., 1875, sent to our Bishops an instruction of the S. Cong. of the Holy Office[2] in which the Bishops are advised to protect the flock entrusted to them from a merely secular education with whatever power and effort they can. (They warned them) that "there is nothing according to common consent more necessary than that Catholics everywhere have their own schools, and that these be by no means inferior to the public schools. Therefore they must with all care look either to the establishment of Catholic schools where

---

1. Bracketed text appears, bracketed, in original Latin source. (Editor's note)
2. Latin text adds: "(Vide in *Appendice*, p. 279)." (Editor's note)

they are lacking, or to their enlargement and more perfect equipping and furnishing, so that they may be equal to the public schools in instruction and discipline."

Finally, it helps to bring to mind the Encyclical letter of Pope Leo XIII to the Bishops of France on the 8th of Feb. of this year, 1884, in which the necessity of Christian education in Catholic schools is taught by that highest authority....

198. Although from what has been said, the necessity and obligation of instructing Catholic youth in Catholic schools is clearer than light, it can sometimes happen — just as the instruction just praised intimated — "that Catholic parents can in conscience commit their children to public schools. They cannot do this, however, unless they have sufficient reason for so acting. Whether such a sufficient reason in any particular instance is present or not, will have to be left to the conscience and judgment of the Ordinary; this reason will generally be present when that which is at hand is ill-suited for properly or suitably instructing the youths in accord with their development. Before they can in conscience enter the public schools, fitting remedies and precautions must be taken to render remote the proximate danger of perversion which is more or less always connected with the very nature of such schools."

Since therefore for a sufficient reason, approved by the Bishop, parents may wish to send their children to public schools, provided that the immediate dangers are removed by the necessary precautions, we strictly enjoin that no one whether Bishop or priest, because the Pope through the Sacred Congregation clearly forbids it, dare keep from the Sacraments by rigorous threats or action parents of this kind as though unworthy. This is much more the case in regard to the children themselves. Wherefore, let pastors of souls be exceedingly cautious while they warn the faithful committed to their care of the dangers of these schools, lest, influenced by excessive zeal, they seem by words or deeds to violate the very wise counsels and commands of the Holy See.

199. Having carefully investigated all these matters, we decide and decree:

I. Near each church, where it does not exist, a parochial school is to be erected within two years from the promulgation of this Council, and is to be maintained *in perpetuum*, unless the Bishop, on account of grave difficulties, judges that a postponement may be allowed.

II. A priest who, by his grave negligence, prevents the erection of a school within this time, or its maintenance, or who, after repeated admonitions of the Bishop, does not attend to the matter, deserves removal from that church.

III. A mission or a parish which so neglects to assist a priest in erecting or maintaining a school, that by reason of this supine negligence the school is rendered impossible, should be reprehended by the Bishop and, by the most efficacious and prudent means possible, be induced to contribute the necessary support.

IV. All Catholic parents are bound to send their children to the parochial schools, unless either at home or in other Catholic schools they may be sufficiently and evidently certain of the Christian education of their children, or unless it be lawful to send them to other schools on account of a sufficient cause, approved by the Bishop, and with opportune cautions and remedies. As to what is a Catholic school, it is left to the judgment of the Ordinary to define.

§2. Concerning the ways and means of improving the Parochial Schools.

200. If on the one hand we, in the Lord, by the decrees given above place a very strict burden on the consciences of priests, faithful, and especially Catholic parents, on the other hand, we feel in our inmost hearts and profess with unmistakable words that this also is our duty, that in accord with our strength we see to it and effect that Catholic parents can find for their children not just any schools, but good and efficient ones by no means, as the Sacred Congregation warns, inferior to the public schools. And so we are pleased to propose and command some means by which the parochial schools can be raised to that level of usefulness and perfection which both the honor of the Church, and not only the eternal but also the temporal salvation of the children, and, finally, the wholehearted devotion of the parents in full accord with the law, demand and deserve. However these means seem to be principally those by which it is made possible that priests, laity and the teachers best understand and most faithfully fulfill their duties toward the schools.

First with regard to that which pertains to the priests, we have decided that already in the seminaries the candidates for Sacred Theology should be zealously taught that one of the principal duties of priests especially in these our times, is the Christian instruction of youth, and that this is not possible without schools whether parochial or other truly Catholic schools. And so in the studies of psychology, pedagogy and pastoral theology, special direction is to be given to the instruction of children. Likewise let the students learn the manner and method by which they can explain to the children clearly and solidly the catechism and sacred history.

Priests entrusted with the care of souls should rather frequently compare ideas concerning their very serious duty toward the schools in talks and meetings with their associates. Let them cherish their schools as the apple of their eyes, let them visit and look into them frequently, every part of them at least once a week; let them watch over the morals of the children, stir up their zeal with appropriate means. They themselves should teach catechism and sacred history, or certainly see to it that they are correctly taught by teachers who are members of a congregation; in addition, let them turn their attention to the other branches of knowledge; let them submit their schools to the attention of the faithful by public examinations once or even twice a year, and let them recommend these schools for approval. They are to do their utmost to see to it that only books prepared by Catholic writers are used in the schools. Inspired by holy motives, let them be solicitous for all these things; in addition, let them be aware that they will not be promoted to irremovable pastorates or other offices if they have neglected their duties toward the schools....

202. As to the laity, we exhort and command that they be so instructed by the Bishop and by the priests so that they regard the parish school as an essential part of the parish, without which the very existence of the parish in the future will be threatened. Let them, therefore, be taught clearly and convincingly that the school is by no means a work of supererogation, taken up as an outlet for the superabundant zeal of the priest, or as a pleasant and proper occupation, but that it is a burden and a duty laid upon the priest by the Church; a duty which is to be faithfully taken up by him and carried by him, but not without the aid of the laity. Let no less zeal and prudence be employed in rooting out the false idea that only those whose children attend the school have a stake in it; rather let the clergy show, as they easily can, that the benefits to faith and morals which result from the parish schools redound to the good of the whole community. After the church, let the faithful assign the place of honor to the school as a most powerful factor in the preservation of faith and morals, and as the nursery of youth, destined to prove later to us all a source of joy and consolation.

The laity are to give adequate and generous support to the schools. And so with united strength, they will be zealous in seeing to it that the parishes shall be equal to the costs and expenses of these schools. Let the faithful be reminded "whether through pastoral letters or sermons or private discussions, * * that they will seriously fail in their duty unless with all care they provide for the upkeep of Catholic schools. Those among the Catholics who surpass the others in wealth and influence have particularly to be reminded of this duty." (Instr. S.C.) Therefore in accordance with their means, parents are to pay promptly and freely that small monthly contribution which is customarily demanded for each child. However, the rest of the members of the parish are not to refuse to produce and increase the revenues of the Church insofar as is fitting and necessary for the support of the schools. Let everyone whether parents, or other heads of families, or the young who have their own source of income, be prepared to join some society especially recommended for each parish, particularly one already introduced and very richly blessed by the Holy Father himself, in which they might render help to the schools with modest but regular contributions and make these schools if not completely, at least partially, free schools. With the resources generously gathered by all for this very sacred purpose, this also will be effected, that the external glory of the schools and their internal luster will be enabled to grow, the number of teachers can be increased, the pupils can be divided into less crowded classes and the individual classes can be more suitably distinguished from one another and distributed according to grades; All this will be marvelously co-ordinated so that our schools may be promoted to a loftier degree of perfection.

Certain rights and privileges must be more accurately defined for the laity through the diocesan statutes, in as far as they are granted to the schools; safeguarding the rights of the Church, the rights and privileges of the schools must be defined insofar as the hiring and firing of teachers is concerned and the correctness of doctrine.

203. Since the status and growth of our schools depend especially on the fitness of the teachers, the greatest care must be exercised that none but good and competent teachers are set over them. And so we decree and command, that no one in the future will be admitted to the position of teaching in a parochial school unless he has by a previous examination proved himself suitable and competent.

Therefore the bishops, within a year of the promulgation of this Council, shall name one or more priests who are very well versed in matters pertaining to schools, to form a "Diocesan Commission of Examination." They shall be appointed until recalled, and those named shall solemnly promise the Bishop that they will perform their task according to the norms to be given them by the Bishop and to attain the end for which the examination is established in accord with their abilities. It will be the task of this commission to examine all the teachers, whether religious belonging to some diocesan congregation or secular, who desire in the future to teach in the parochial schools, and if they find them suitable to give them evidence of competency or a diploma, without which diploma no priest has the right to hire for his school any teacher (unless they have already taught before the deliberations of the Council). This diploma will be valid for five years and for all dioceses. When that time has elapsed, another and final examination will be required of the teachers. Moreover a diploma will by no means be given to those whom they do not find competent in one or the other examination, but they will relegate these persons to the following year's examination.

The examination will be set up once in a year; for members of a diocesan congregation, in houses and at times agreed upon by the examiners and the superiors; for seculars, at a time and place to be designated by the examiners. The materials and questions for the written examination will be prepared jointly by the commissioners, and on the day of the examination either by one of their own number or by another priest appointed by the president of the commission, they will be produced in a letter protected by the seal of the president, and opened in the presence of the ones to be examined; these latter shall write their solutions and answers under the surveillance of the commissioner or delegate. When the written part of the examination has been examined and reviewed by the examiners, an oral text will be conducted as soon as possible before the entire commission. Before they leave the place of the examination, the examiners shall prepare a summary in triplicate of those who have done satisfactorily in the examination. One of these lists they will give to the superior for a member of a diocesan congregation, or to the candidate himself if he is a secular; the second will be kept by the president of the commission; the third they will send to the chancery of the diocese.

When parochial schools have been assigned to regulars or congregations which have their own superiors or their own moderators general according to constitutions approved by the Holy See, the Bishop, should he from a visitation of the schools according to the approved constitution *Romanos Pontifices*, have knowledge that in some places there are teachers from those congregations who are unequal to the task and are appointed to teach, he shall warn the superior to rectify the situation within a reasonable time; if the superior neglects to do so, this neglect must be reported to the Sacred Congregation so that it may take appropriate action. If in assigning the parochial schools, definite agreements have either already been entered into by the Ordinaries or should be entered into in the future with the superiors of the congregations, regarding the appointment or removal of teachers or method of teaching the profane sciences, those agreements are to be kept in their entirety.

204. Besides this commission established to examine teachers for the whole diocese, the Bishops in proportion to the diversity of places and languages shall establish several "School Commissions" made up of one or more priests to examine the schools in the city and rural districts. Moreover it will be the duty of these commissions once, or even twice a year, to visit and examine each and every school in their district and to send an accurate report of the condition of the schools to the president of the diocesan commission for the information and action of the bishop.

205. In order that there may always be on hand a sufficient number of Catholic teachers, each one of them well prepared for the sacred and sublime duty of instructing the young, we warn the Bishops whose concern it is, either themselves, or if there is need, even calling upon the authority of the S. Congregation, to agree with the superiors of congregations dedicated to this task of teaching in those schools, to establish in their proper houses as soon as it can be done, normal schools where they do not yet exist and where their necessity is evident. In these schools for an extended period of time and with truly religious solicitude, the younger members shall be instructed by experienced and especially competent teachers in the different disciplines and sciences, in method, teaching skill and other matters relating to the beneficial guidance of the school.

206. If however, as has already in some places been done, priests whether secular or regular, should erect and properly conduct in our several provinces normal schools for training truly Catholic lay teachers, they are indeed performing a task worthy of every praise and assistance.

207. All these things should be considered with all appropriate reverence and observed with religious enthusiasm by those whose concern it is, especially by priests, lay men, teachers and Catholic parents, that our parochial schools may more and more grow both in number and excellence, and that they may daily become not only for the Church but also for the State a thing of respect, pride, hope and support.

Bernard Julius Meiring, *Educational Aspects of the Legislation of the Councils of Baltimore 1829–1884* (New York: Arno Press, 1978 [1963]), Appendix II, 293–312 (translation from *Acta et Decreta Concilii Plenarii Baltimorensis Tertii. A.D. MDCCCLXXXIV. Praeside Illmo. Ac Revmo. Jacobo Gibbons, Archiepiscopo Balt. Et Delegato Apostolico* [Baltimoreae: typis Joannis Murphy et Sociorum, 1894], 99–114).

## 30. Preserving Faith and Culture: A Polish Catholic Newspaper, 1891

*SS. Cyril and Methodius Seminary produced a Polish-language weekly, entitled Niedziela (Sunday). The issue pictured below is dated October 11, 1891.*

*Cover page of an early issue of* Niedziela (Sunday). *It synthesizes the Seminary's early educational mission under the patronage of "Mary—Queen of Poland": "Love God and Poland! Son, Love America Also! Mothers! Fathers! Speak to your Children in Polish!!!"*

Photo credit: Frank Renkiewicz, *For God, Country, and Polonia: One Hundred Years of the Orchard Lake Schools* (Orchard Lake, Mich.: Center for Polish Studies and Culture, Orchard Lake Schools, 1985), 53; original, Central Archives of Polonia, Orchard Lake, Michigan. Printed with permission.

## 31. Brothers of the Christian Schools: Teaching Latin in the United States, 1897

*St. John Baptist de La Salle founded the Brothers of the Christian Schools in France in 1680. In order to uphold both their commitment to poor scholars and the nonclerical nature of their institute, the Brothers did not as a rule teach Latin. The particular educational needs of boys in the United States, however, demanded they do so. By the end of the nineteenth century, in a climate suspicious of "Americanism," Brothers from the United States had difficulty in justifying this practice to the governing body of the congregation, located in Paris. The issue was not resolved until 1923, when Pius IX ordered the brothers to teach Latin.*

Copy of Memorial submitted to the Chapter of 1897, and read
in Public Assembly by Brother Justinus,[1] April 2, 1897.

I most respectfully beg your kind indulgence and patient hearing while I make known to you our position in relation to the Latin question in the United States.

In 1854 dear Brother Barbas began to teach Latin in our Academy of St. Louis, Mo., we have been informed with the permission of dear Brother Philippe, and continued to teach it until his death, three years ago, with the knowledge of all the Visitors and Assistants of America from that day to this.

The Second Plenary Council of Baltimore was held in 1867.[2] I was then Director of our Academy in that city. Archbishop Spalding, then Papal Legate to the U.S. and President of the Council, told me to call Brother Patrick to Baltimore as the Jesuits had made a protest against the Brothers teaching Latin. I accompanied dear Brother Patrick to Baltimore. The Archbishop asked him by what authority the Brothers were teaching Latin. Brother Patrick told him that he himself was the bearer of the letters from the Archbishops of the U.S. to the Chapter of 1854 in which the Bishops begged to have the Brothers teach the Latin. He said the permission was granted. The Archbishop replied that he would attend to the rest. The fourth day of the Council he sent for me and informed me that the Jesuits had withdrawn their complaint as they found that the Bishops were in favor of the Brothers teaching Latin.

In 1868 our Brothers were sent by our Holy Father Pope Pius IX to San Francisco to take charge of the Diocesan College. The undersigned (Brother Justian) was appointed Visitor and Director. The college was a Classical institution and our Brothers took up the course and have taught it ever since. In 1875 I asked the venerable Brother Irlide, after his election, if we would accept a High School in San Francisco under the Government in which the Classics were taught, and for which the Brothers would be obliged to undergo an examination. I proposed to put a note before the Chapter asking for the necessary faculties. The Très Honoré replied: "It is not necessary, whatever is not prohibited in the Bull of

---

1. Brother Justin (or Justian), an American. (Editor's note; information provided by Luke Salm, F.S.C.)
2. Actually 1866. (Editor's note)

Approbation, the Superior General has the right to grant, and if his Grace of San Francisco wishes you to accept the high School, I will give the necessary permission."

As most of you, venerable Brothers Capitulants, were at the Chapters of '82 and '84, I will not trespass on your time speaking of what occurred in them, nor will I go into many details about the introduction of Latin in our houses where it is now taught, as the history of one is the history of all. I now come to the Chapter of 1894. At the beginning of the Chapter I went to our late saintly and noble Superior, Brother Joseph, and begged of him to settle the Latin Question himself without submitting it to the Chapter. He declined. Before the last Session of the late Chapter, our dear Brother Exuperien, 1st Assistant, sent for me and requested me to ask my colleagues not to discuss the Latin Question when the report of the Committee would come before the Assembly as the Most Hon. Brother Superior was fatigued and could not bear such a discussion. Dear Bro. Justinus, Sec'y Gen'l, also requested me to say to the American Brothers not to discuss it. You, venerable Brothers Capitulants, will recollect that not a word was said when the Latin question came before the Chapter. Our lips were sealed through love and respect for our dear and beloved Superior. We were under the impression, however, that the Latin Question would remain as it was before the Chapter. After the Chapter, I called on the Très Honoré Superior and asked permission for two Brothers to study Latin for their Superior Diploma. He replied that in view of the action of the Chapter he felt he should not do it. "Then, Très Honoré, what shall we do about the contract signed by dear Brother Clementian, Assistant, in your name allowing Latin in Halifax?" "Tell the Archbishop that we cannot abide by the contract." Next day when we were taking leave of the Très Honoré, he asked us if we were pleased with the Chapter. Dear Brother Paulian said: "Yes, except the Latin." The Très Honoré replied: "Mes amis votre position n'est pas comprise ici."

The American deputies before leaving Paris discussed the sad situation created by the Latin Question and felt that an appeal to the Holy See would be made by the Archbishops through Mgr. Satolli,[3] and though the American Deputies were the cause of it, they did not figure in it. The decision was strongly and clearly unfavorable. Rome said we cannot grant the permission unless the Sup'r Gen'l of the Brothers asks it.

When Mgr. Satolli communicated the decision, I said "We have now exhausted all the means in our power and we must close our colleges." He said: "No; the case is grave, it is not closed; continue as you are for the present."

At this stage of the case our dear Brother Assistant Clementian called on Mgr. Satolli who proposed to him that as he was about to go to Rome, he would ask the Holy Father to call a certain number of Brothers to Rome to live in our house there and study Latin. When he made the same proposition to me I said that it could not be done: it would destroy us. He asked me what was to be done. I answered simply to have the permission for a certain number of Brothers to study Latin. He asked for the names and I gave them to him. At this

---

3. Francesco Satolli, apostolic delegate to the United States, 1893–96. (Editor's note)

time Archbishop Keane was Rector of the Catholic University, and he asked me to have our colleges affiliated to the University. I told him that it would be imprudent to do so as the Latin might be suppressed, and then we would be placed in a false position. He said: "When I go to Rome I will try to get the permission."

When Mgr. Satolli was recalled I saw Mgr. Martinelli and told him that we were tired of this affair and would have to close. He said: "No, I see by the correspondence in the office of the Delegation that the case is not closed. You can say to your superior that I am a friend of your Congregation and I would most respectfully suggest that it would be prudent in view of the great necessity that exists in this country to grant the permission to a certain number of Brothers under well-defined restrictions."

This, my very dear Brothers Capitulants is a plain statement of what we have done. Of course there are many details not mentioned.

Naturally you will ask, why did you go to Rome? Because we were requested not to appeal to the Chapter; our beloved Superior felt that he could not help us, and foreseeing, as we did, the great injury to our Institute, and the destruction of our principal houses — what else could we do but appeal to the Holy See to save us. But some may say to you that the Latin is not necessary. Do you not know us? Have we not always been loyal sons of the Blessed De La Salle? Do we not know our country and its wants better than strangers? But it is said we have abandoned the poor. We beg pardon. We have not abandoned the poor. We have about 1,000 boys studying Latin, yet this 1,000 gives us a standing we could not have without it; whereas we have over 3,600 orphans including 60 Negro children, while we have over 20,000 children in our parish schools. It is true we have not been able to observe the vow of gratuity as our Blessed Founder gave it to us, because the schools could not be supported without pay, and the great Brother Philippe obtained from the Holy See permission to take pay from the children.

Some reasons why Latin is necessary: —

I. In nearly all the Normal Schools of the United States the Latin is required for teachers in the primary schools.

II. Last year, as our dear Brother Assistant Clementian will tell you we had to close our house of Burlington because our income would not allow us to pay a professor of Latin.

III. In Dover, New Hampshire last year a commission was authorized by the State to visit our school to see if it was up to the standard of public education.

IV. Two years ago a bill was introduced into the Legislature of New York, requiring teachers in all Primary Schools to take Diplomas. Fortunately it was defeated. There is a bill now before the legislature of Missouri requiring the same thing. The dear Brother Visitor of Baltimore can show you a Report that the same is true in the State of Maryland.

V. The Catholics of New York are trying to have the Catholic Schools paid by the State. If this succeeds, some of our Brothers must have their Diplomas.

VI. Our dear Brother Quintinian, Visitor, made the visit to our house in Halifax on his way to this Chapter. His Grace, Archbishop O'Brien, said: "I am waiting for the decision of your Chapter on the Latin Question. If, unfavorable, I regret very much that you will have to withdraw from my Diocese." Dear Brother Malachy Edward, Aux. Visitor of Canada, will tell you that our Brothers must leave the District of Toronto on the same account, namely because they cannot study the Latin necessary for their certificates.

In 1867 the venerable Brother Philippe ordered several Brothers here in France to study the Latin, pass their examination and take their baccalaureate. I could mention some in the present Chapter but I have not the permission to do so.

The zealous Très Honoré, Brother Irlide, told me in 1875 that he would give the necessary permission for Latin if the Government required it. The ever-beloved Brother Joseph since the Chapter of 1894 gave dear Brother Anthony permission for several of his Brothers to study Latin.

Surely, venerable Brothers Capitulants, these great men had the spirit of our Blessed Founder and understood our mission. Yet, they granted permission taking into consideration "times and circumstances" as Benedict XIII says in the Bull of Approbation.

Is it possible, then that you our dear Brothers wish to destroy our young Districts? We beg of you not to mutilate them piece by piece; not to undo the beautiful work that has taken so much labor and so many sacrifices to build up.

But if you must strike your American Brothers, Strike! We are ready for the blow, and — notwithstanding our humiliation — you will find us at our post faithful to our duty and observing our Holy Rules.

But we are full of confidence that you will regard our position favorably and grant the petition.

Signed: –

|             |        | Brother Justian |   | Brother Paulian |
|-------------|--------|-----------------|---|-----------------|
| Attested: – |        | " Quintinian    | " | Felix John      |
| Brother Anthemian John | | " Bettelin | " | Christian of Mary |
| Brother Fabrician      | |            |   |                 |

Copy of Memorial submitted to the Chapter of 1897 and read in Public Assembly by Brother Justinus, April 2, 1897, New York District Archives of the De La Salle Christian Brothers, Manhattan College, New York. Printed with permission.

## Part 4

# CATHOLIC EDUCATION: TWENTIETH-CENTURY DEVELOPMENTS

## Introduction

The impulse toward Americanization dominated the development of Catholic education in the twentieth century. Originally a collection of isolated schools subject to individual pastors or religious superiors, Catholic education began to form a system at diocesan, then national levels in the years surrounding the turn of the century. The formation of the Catholic Educational Association (CEA) in 1904 meant inevitably an organization in which parts were regulated in their relationship to the whole. Outside forces — college entrance requirements, accrediting norms, and government standardization — tended to push Catholic education toward broad correspondence with its secular counterparts.

The Catholic University of America, established in 1889, was the first Catholic institution of higher learning in the United States founded on a university model. After 1900 other Catholic colleges began moving from the hybrid of seminary, secondary school, and college toward recognized university forms. By the 1930s Catholic universities started to revamp their graduate programs to meet criteria for accreditation.

Preserving the faith of Catholics from the dangers of secular education nevertheless remained a strong motive until mid-century. The scriptural and theological scholarship burgeoning at the turn of the century, epitomized in the *New York Review* published at the Dunwoodie Seminary between 1905 and 1908, was aborted in response to papal decrees against Modernism. In the United States as elsewhere, Catholic theology languished for decades. Catholic seminaries and colleges taught neo-Thomism as an antidote to modern philosophy. Educational policy strongly embraced the idea of a comprehensive Catholic culture as the alternative to modern decadence, heralded by the Catholic Revival of the interwar years. Voices that harbinged the future, however, were those of theologians and educators who risked thought in new directions.

The movement toward standardized education in the United States, accelerated after World War I, powerfully affected Catholic schools. After wavering between suspicion of state interference in education and the commitment to equality, the CEA (NCEA from 1927) opted for standardization through external agencies. The issue of accreditation prompted Mother Katharine Drexel to found Xavier College, New Orleans, in order to help African American Catholic students gain recognized degrees. Accreditation also meant degrees or certification for teachers, giving huge impetus to professional qualification, particularly among sisters. Catholic elementary and secondary schools retained the unmistakable marks of convent culture, but they, like the colleges, were on a path to educational parity with secular institutions. Catholic schools offered advanced mathematics, competed in science contests, and, by the 1950s, taught evolution.[1]

World War II was the unquestionable watershed for Catholic education in the twentieth century. With the GI Bill and baby boom, student populations mushroomed. Increased American affluence enabled parishes to build schools at record speed, mostly in the suburbs. This unprecedented growth caused a critical need for qualified teachers at all levels, and for increased finances in order to accommodate both students and standards. The Sister Formation Movement was initiated in 1954 to ensure the concurrent professional and religious preparation of young sister teachers. By the end of the 1950s conflicting forces strained the existing structures of Catholic education to their limits, a condition largely masked by the imperatives of relentless growth. In the early 1960s Catholic schools educated 14 percent of the elementary schoolchildren in the United States.[2] It was difficult to imagine their vulnerability in the avalanche to come.

The Second Vatican Council and the cultural revolutions of the 1960s precipitated drastic change in Catholic education. The council brought profound ecclesiological shifts, with immediate effect at the parish level. It turned the church firmly toward the world and prompted rethinking the meaning of "Catholic." A hemorrhage in membership among religious communities after 1967 added to a serious decline in Catholic elementary and secondary schools. Mary Perkins Ryan was not alone in raising questions about the disproportionate use of church resources for schools that served a minority of Catholic children. Relative neglect of other types of education, like the Confraternity of Christian Doctrine (CCD), rural vacation schools, or adult study groups seemed to highlight failures of the Catholic institutional model. College-level administrators, dependent on government support and facing the demands of academic freedom, worked out a redefinition of the Catholic university that was not so much a map for the future as recognition of what already had and would continue to evolve in higher education. Adaptation to American culture was

---

1. See Dale C. Braungart and Rita Buddeke, *The Study of Living Things* (Garden City, N.Y.: Doubleday, 1957), chap. 34, "Evolution of Man," 521–25.

2. McCluskey notes this meant "5.5 million pupils, in 10,633 Catholic elementary schools and 2,502 Catholic secondary schools, representing a $5 billion capital investment and an annual operating cost of $850 million" (Neil G. McCluskey, S.J., ed., *Catholic Education in America: A Documentary History* (New York: Teachers College, Columbia University, 1964), 1, citing unpublished statistics furnished by the Department of Education, National Catholic Welfare Conference, from a report of October 31, 1962).

no longer a question; it had become an acknowledged necessity and operative reality.

Over the past four decades Catholic education in the United States has had to reinvent itself — without the support of numerous religious personnel, and absent a defensive stance toward American culture. At the beginning of the twenty-first century, it faces dilemmas ironically new and old: a shortage of clergy and a large number of Catholics uneducated in their religion. Nearly two generations of Catholic youth have grown up with a religious education quite different from that of their elders. For many it has been erratic, or insecurely based on a jumble of new and old. Empty seminaries and novitiates offer little remedy, and the emergence of lay Catholics as primary religious educators has been slow, following two centuries of dependence on a specialized ecclesial workforce. Some parishes, however, have discovered education as ongoing communal conversion, notably through the new Rite of Christian Initiation of Adults. Cultural assimilation and decline of the institutional model have produced a new educational matrix from which new efforts have emerged, smaller in scale. Urban schools, though radically diminished in numbers, have produced creative programs for underprivileged, often non-Catholic, children, as in the Jesuit-inspired Nativity Network of schools, modeled on the Nativity Mission Center established in New York City in 1971. Catholic teachers, now overwhelmingly lay women and men, have sought to enliven old models and develop new ones. Elementary and secondary schools across the board are awake to the demands of social justice, including poverty and race.

The perennial question of adaptation and separatism resurfaced in the late 1980s when the Vatican questioned whether assimilation on the part of Catholic higher education had become loss of identity. The American Bishops' response in *Ex Corde Ecclesiae: The Application to the United States* (1999) affirms the academic autonomy of a college or university but also requires that Catholic professors of theological disciplines have a mandate from the bishop. On its side, the government has continued to engage the peculiarly American debate about church-state-school. Although the Supreme Court assured the right of American citizens to private education in 1922,[3] financial assistance to religious schools, with the exception of clearly extraneous benefits like busing, has repeatedly been ruled unconstitutional. In June 2002, however, the Supreme Court rendered a benchmark verdict, declaring the Ohio Pilot Project Scholarship Program not in conflict with the First Amendment, even though it allows parents in specific restricted circumstances to use state tuition vouchers in qualified public or private schools of their choice — including religiously affiliated schools. Writing the court's opinion, Justice Rehnquist explicitly stated it found the Ohio program "neutral in all respects toward religion."[4] The two recent statements by ecclesiastical and civil authority have proved highly controversial. Although too soon to infer their long-range effects, it is clear that from

---

3. *Pierce v. Society of Sisters.*
4. *Zelman, Superintendent of Public Instruction of Ohio et al. v. Simmons-Harris et al.,…* (June 27, 2002), *New York Times* [Online], available: http://laws.findlaw.com/us/000/00-1751.html [June 28, 2002].

different perspectives, each evokes enduring tensions about how the Catholic church and American society can relate to each other authentically over the central and permanent issue of education.

## 32. New Methods for Scripture Studies in Seminaries, 1900

*Francis E. Gigot (1859–1920) was perhaps the foremost Catholic biblical scholar of his day in the United States. French-born and a student of Alfred Loisy, Gigot served in various Sulpician seminaries in this country and authored significant texts on modern Scriptural scholarship. Although he left the Sulpicians at the time of the Modernist crisis, Gigot remained on the seminary faculty at Dunwoodie until his death. The following essay outlines a model for biblical studies in the Catholic seminary, incorporating methods of historical-critical interpretation then the subject of serious controversy.*

In the formation of a programme of studies taught in the seminary, there are few branches which present greater difficulty than the course in holy Scripture. The ground to be covered is so extensive, the important questions to be examined so numerous, the amount of time usually allotted for Biblical work so limited, and, more particularly, the present condition of Scriptural science so manifestly transitional, that it is impossible to do justice to the various topics connected with a complete course of sacred Scripture in our theological seminaries. The present paper will, therefore, offer only a few tentative remarks concerning the three following points: the scope of a course in sacred Scripture, study of the text, and higher criticism.

### Scope of Course in Sacred Scripture

...[T]he course of sacred Scripture in the seminary is recognized to be clearly distinct from a university course in the Scriptures, which presupposes the more elementary work of the seminary, and aims chiefly at training specialists; and it likewise differs from the teaching of sacred history in the Sunday-school or college class, which aims merely at giving a primary, and, at best, a disconnected knowledge of Scriptural topics.... The teacher in charge of an elementary [seminary] course must aim first of all at imparting a fair amount of knowledge concerning the questions which belong to general and special introduction, that is to say, such topics as are suggested by and gather around the text of the most important books of Holy Writ.... Furthermore, it behooves the teacher to make his students acquainted with the ever-increasing number of works bearing on Biblical subjects, and for this purpose he should be careful not only to mention but also to give judicious appreciation of such books or articles as he thinks may prove useful for present or future reference. Finally, a good teacher will not fail to initiate his pupils in strict scientific methods of study....

Such, in brief, seem to be the leading purposes of the professor who seeks to realize as far as he may the general scope of a seminary course of Scripture. In acting upon them he will not only impart the positive knowledge necessary to all, but he will at the same time introduce his students to the best available sources of information, while he fosters in them habits of personal scientific research.

Study of the Text

The ordinary course of Scripture in our seminaries comprises two series of regular classes: the one bearing directly on the text, the other on the questions pertaining to Biblical Introduction. The former is the much more important of the two; but I must confine myself to merely touching a few points regarding it.

The first consideration claiming our attention is that of the books to be selected for exegesis. As regards the New Testament, which naturally forms the subject-matter of textual study, there are the Gospels and the principal Epistles of St. Paul. Their contents will be all the more readily mastered by the student if he has already been made familiar with their historical aspect during one year of his philosophical course. For the Old Testament the problem is not so easily solved. It is much simplified, however, in those seminaries where during the second year of the philosophical course the historical books of the Old Testament are studied in connection with the history of the Jewish people, for in such a case a subsequent exegetical treatment of these books may be dispensed with. But even then there is still a serious difficulty of making a selection from the many remaining books. The Psalms, owing to their constant liturgical use, should certainly be taken up and studied with a certain fulness of detail. However desirable this might also be for the prophetical and sapiential books, lack of time makes it necessary to explain only a few of them, and these should be gone through in such manner as to illustrate the method of treatment for the others. One or another of the greater prophets, and such books as Proverbs, Wisdom and Ecclesiasticus naturally suggest themselves as the most available for this purpose.

Another topic which comes up for consideration regards the method the professor should follow in his treatment of the portions selected. Obviously all teachers cannot be expected to pursue the same method.... But, whatever be the method pursued, it should not fail to exhibit certain characteristics, the principal of which are the following: First, the treatment should be clear, concise, and generally within the reach of the average student. Secondly, proper deference should invariably be shown to legitimate authority, abiding by all the decisions of the Church and the unanimous consent of the Fathers in matters of faith and morals. Thirdly...the teacher should have constantly in view the various requirements, homiletic, controversial, doctrinal, etc., of a priest on the mission. Finally, the method should be scientific; none of the available data should be neglected; all the points, both of extrinsic and intrinsic evidence, should be judiciously estimated, and only such conclusions be admitted as are strictly warranted....

As a last suggestion a word may be said with reference to the general distribution of the subject-matter for textual study. It seems very desirable that students, in all stages of their scriptural work, be kept in direct contact with the sacred text. Obviously, no amount of information *about* the Bible can ever be so useful as a close and prolonged familiarity with the text itself, for the various purposes of the holy ministry. This end may be secured even from the beginning of the philosophical course by causing the young men to make a systematic study of both the Old and New Testament, simply from the standpoint of their historical contents. Such study will indeed appear almost necessary at this point to any one who bears in mind the regrettable fact that frequently the young aspirant enters the seminary without the necessary elementary knowledge of sacred history and geography. Moreover, the historical aspect of the inspired writings is the one most easily grasped, of greatest interest to the beginner, and one which, when conducted under the guidance of the professor and with the help of a concise text-book, will prove most useful in laying the indispensable foundation of all subsequent study of the text. Plainly, this method of initiating young men to the study of Holy Writ is preferable to that which launches them at the outset into the intricate, abstruse, and to them unintelligible questions of general introduction, which to our mind, can be studied profitably only when a real familiarity with the sacred text has been acquired.

In theology, the constant contact with the text here advocated may be secured by some such plan as the following: Taking for a basis of computation the ordinary three years' course with three classes a week, — one of these classes might be devoted throughout to questions of introduction, while the other two would be taken up with the work of exegesis. To cover the whole of the introductory ground, this weekly class might, during one year, deal with the topics of *General* Introduction and with *Special* Introduction during the other two years. As regards the exegetical work, it might be carried out by explaining the Gospels during one year, the Epistles during another, and the select passages or books of the Old Testament during the third, always at the rate of two classes a week. In this way the study of the text would never be interrupted, while that of Biblical Introduction would not only appear lighter, but also more complete, and, if we mistake not, better grasped and appreciated.

### The Higher Criticism

This brings us at once to the third part of the present paper. It has to deal with the Higher Criticism, which includes the most delicate topics connected with Biblical Introduction. To quote the words of Father Hogan: "There are extreme views on the subject. Some, struck by the evil following on the investigations of such questions, would have them almost entirely kept out of sight. Others, impressed by the fact that these are the live questions of the day, regarding which the priest is liable at any time to be interrogated, would have him give his chief care to them. The truth, as usual, lies in a middle course. It is inadmissible, on the one side, that the future defender of the true faith should be left in ignorance of the weak or threatened points of the position he holds. He cannot be expected to deal off-hand with difficulties he never heard of before; neither is it proper that his information on such subjects, even if he is compelled to discuss them, should be dependent on chance or on imperfect and, often, inaccurate information which he might derive from his intercourse with books picked up at random, or with men only a little less ignorant than himself. On the other hand, a special study of these more difficult problems, so much dwelt upon in our time, would be decidedly out of place. The beginner has neither the maturity of mind or the knowledge of facts which would enable him to form a personal judgment on the points at issue; he would soon lose his way amid the endless complexity of views and theories, and the final result would be a helpless confusion of thought, and it might be, the unsettling of his fundamental convictions."[1]

Several things of primary importance are implied in this judicious passage of the *Clerical Studies*. In the first place, the time is gone when the questions involved in the higher criticism might be simply identified with rationalistic attacks upon the revealed word. Again, one can no longer afford to be ignorant of the topics which, perhaps more than any others at present, engross the attention of the intellectual and religious world; which are continually discussed in books and periodicals, and in which so many lay people, Catholic as well as Protestant, take such a deep and ever-growing interest — whence follows the necessity for the future priest of being made acquainted with these subjects under the guidance of a prudent and competent professor, to whom he naturally looks for information on all such difficult matters. In fact, it is only thus that the acquisition of this very important knowledge can be surrounded by the proper safeguards.

The questions of date, composition, literary structure, and authorship, all of which belong to the domain of higher criticism, naturally present themselves for study in the special introduction to the various books. The higher critic deals with them chiefly from the standpoint of internal evidence, and no teacher can pretend to give a serious and adequate treatment of them without taking into account the many acquired results of modern critical research, or without giving due attention to the positions and arguments based upon intrinsic as well as extrinsic evidence. Nor in so doing can one be taxed with innovation; for in reality he is but following the best traditions of the past. Ecclesiastical writers, even as far back as St. Jerome, Origen, and Clement of Alexandria, worked on critical lines, and did not neglect to examine the literary style of the Epistles with a view to determine their authorship; and in our own century, as everyone knows, the same method of investigation has been carefully and successfully applied by such conservative scholars as Archbishop Smith, Lehir, Martin, Corluy, Hummelauer, Bacuez, and Vigoureux. Finally, it can hardly be denied that, besides its direct bearing on questions of introduction, higher criticism throws at times considerable light on the meaning of the sacred text itself by helping to place its various parts in their true historical setting. . . .

F. E. Gigot, S.S.

*St. Mary's Seminary, Baltimore, Md.*

Francis E. Gigot, "The Study of Sacred Scripture in Theological Seminaries," *American Ecclesiastical Review* 23 (September 1900): 227–35.

---

1. *Clerical Studies*, 441, sq. [*sic*].

## 33. Mother Katharine Drexel and Xavier University, 1924, 1930

*Xavier University of Louisiana is the only historically black Catholic college in the United States. Xavier now ranks first in the nation in the number of doctorates in pharmacy awarded to African Americans, and first in placing African American graduates in medical schools. Xavier evolved from a secondary school established in New Orleans in 1915 by the Sisters of the Blessed Sacrament. In 1924 Mother (now Saint) Katharine Drexel and her Council decided to introduce studies at the collegiate level.*

a. Annals of the Sisters of the Blessed Sacrament

[December] 1924.

Reverend Mother remained home about a week after the funeral and then departed to finish her visitation at New Orleans, taking with her as companion Sister Mary Frances.

Plans and specifications had been awarded for an extension to the Xavier Building. The extension was just as large as the old building. It contained Biology, Chemistry and Physics Laboratories, a Domestic Science Department and about twelve additional class or lecture rooms, also various offices. The contract was awarded to Ernest DuConge, the lowest bidder. The building cost, when completed, was about $70,000. The Mothers' Club furnished the three hundred new chairs for the auditorium and also blinds and curtains for the entire house.

One of the reasons for this extension was the contemplated College Work for Xavier. By its Charter, Xavier was authorized to confer degrees and the Colored People of this section were very desirous of having a Catholic College.

The matter was a cause for much discussion, first as to the upkeep of the College, second, the impossibility of having any Colored college, no matter how high its status or broadness of curricula, recognized by the Southern Association of Colleges. It was found that it could not be approved by the Middle West Association or by the East Atlanta Association because it was out of their zone.

After much discussion, however, it was decided to begin the College Work the next year as there was a great need of Catholic leaders among our Colored People and so few Catholic Colleges would admit them. The Councillors felt that where there was a need God would provide the means and that in some way or other recognition would be given....

> Annals of the Sisters of the Blessed Sacrament, Vol. 21, 153–54, Archives of the Sisters of the Blessed Sacrament, Bensalem, Pennsylvania. Printed by permission.

b. Appeal to the American Board of Catholic Missions, c. 1930

In discussing the missionary work of the Sisters of the Blessed Sacrament we confine ourselves to a single phase of their activity, one which, at this time presents the greatest difficulty, and in some respects the direst need in their missionary endeavor. This is the Higher Education of the Negro in a Catholic College.

No one can attempt to approach the study of this problem unless he is willing to face the issue with a viewpoint that is free from prejudice and misconception. Much has been said on the nature and feasibility of high education for this race; many there are insistent in the denial not only of its efficacy but even of its possibility. Actual contact with an intimate study of these questions will build proper concepts of their nature. After all, this is not a question to be studied from books but one to be gleaned from experience. If we want to know whether or not the Negro is capable of imbibing a complete college education, let us ask those who are actually engaged in giving it to him. They are quick to tell you that the Negro youth is fully capable of grasping, enjoying, and utilizing to the full, educational development of the highest order.

It is too late to argue the advisability or possibility of college education for the Negro. The Negro has settled the question himself. He is getting the education. In statistics recorded in "America" in the issue of January 4th, 1930, we learn that in 1924–1925 there were 4,825 Negro college students and that in 1928–1929 the registration jumped to 9,703. The question which the Catholics of America should raise is this: "Where is the Negro getting this education?" Listed in the 1929 report of the John F. Slater Fund are eighty-two denominational colleges exclusively for the Colored. We Catholics — we to whom the command of Christ: "Go ye forth and teach all nations" was directly given; we who hold, in the inspired words of our Holy Father in his recent encyclical on Christian Education, that "education consists essentially in preparing man for what he must be and what he must do here below, in order to attain the sublime end for which he was created," and that "there can be no ideally perfect education which is not Christian education"; we, over twenty millions of us in America, who believe all this — can boast of but one Catholic College for the education of Colored youth. That one Catholic College is Xavier College founded and conducted by the Sisters of the Blessed Sacrament in New Orleans, La.

With a Colored population of 112,752, the city of New Orleans has three exclusively Negro colleges — Xavier College, New Orleans University maintained by the Methodist Episcopals, and Straight College supported by the American Missionary Association. The situation facing the Catholic missioner in New Orleans is a perplexing one; the very atmosphere of the city breathes Catholicity. The staunch faith of the original French settlers has left an indelible mark on the lives of the New Orleanians. The colored population could not escape that influence. At heart, they are Catholic. Up until recent years, they have had to turn to sectarian institutions for higher education. Our non-Catholic brethren were quick to see the possibilities of this race, possibilities not only of elementary and high school education but of college development as well; they were quick to realize that they could guide the destinies of these people by the formation of educated leaders. Straight College was opened in 1869 and New Orleans University in 1873. Praise-worthy as were the first efforts of these two institutions to supply the needs of the Colored youth of New Orleans, they could not and have not given that religious formation so necessary for Catholic leadership to the many Catholic students trained within their walls.

Coming on the field at a late hour the Catholic missioner had strong competition facing him at the very beginning. He, too, realized the possibilities of this race, and, though late, made and is making strenuous efforts to preserve to them the rich inheritance of the Faith. Xavier High School was opened in 1915; in 1917 a Normal Department for the training of teachers was added; Xavier College evolved naturally from this Normal Department and opened its door in 1925. Since then the Teachers' College and the College of Liberal Arts have been functioning. In 1926 a two-year pre-medical course was added for those who wished to enter recognized medical schools. June, 1930, witnessed the conferring of the first degrees by the college of Pharmacy opened three years ago to supply the demand for registered pharmacists. Seven of these Pharmacy students took the State Board examinations and passed. During the scholastic year 1929–1930 ninety-eight students enrolled at Xavier and an additional forty teacher-students attended the evening extension courses. A summer School session conducted from June 13th to July 31st had an enrollment of over 100 students.

For the five years of its existence, Xavier College has been facing a gigantic task. It is true a splendid spirit of cooperation has been accorded by the Colored Students, their parents and friends working through the Alumni and the Parent-Teacher Association. But these people are not wealthy. In their appreciative gratitude, however, they have entered wholeheartedly into every movement for the extension and development of Xavier College. With that sense of confidence native to the Catholic heart, they have gladly brought their children to the Church and entrusted their education to its provident care. Xavier College has assumed the responsibility of their highest education. For five years she has borne this responsibility alone. Today she is in need of assistance.

Since their inception, the two sectarian colleges in New Orleans have been maintained by their respective Mission Boards. Recently, the Rockefeller General Education Board of New York and the Julius Rosenwald Fund of Chicago have offered these institutions $750,000 for a merger to take place in the near future. According to the terms of this agreement, the Board of Education of the Methodist Episcopal Church and the American Missionary Association will contribute conjointly $1,000,000. An additional $250,000 is to be raised by each of the two colleges. The grand total of $2,000,000 is to be expended in the erection of a Colored University to be known as the Dillard University. Seventeen trustees including prominent business men in New York, Chicago, and New Orleans will direct the operation of the new University in connection with which a School of Medicine and a Hospital will be built. Both Mission Boards have pledged $70,000 annually for the maintenance of the University which will begin to function in 1932.

How can Xavier hold its own or hope to compete with a university so heavily endowed and so splendidly equipped unless she keep pace with the progress? Official classification of colleges in the education world of the twentieth century rest not on faculty stamina or aspirations alone, but on grounds, equipment, facilities, etc., as well. Xavier College must plan for the future. Her present building is inadequate to meet the ever increasing student registration.

Already a site for a new college has been purchased, at a cost of $120,460.00. Of the $10,000 given to the Sisters of the Blessed Sacrament in February 1929, $2,115.00 was applied by them to the purchase of this site. But to what source can Xavier turn for the funds so necessary for the completion of her plans? Who will come to her aid and enable her to erect an institution that may worthily represent the zeal and faith of Catholic America?... Where can the young Negro receive the training in sound Catholic philosophy which will enable him to help bring his race into the true fold? Only a Catholic College holds the high ideal of training man to attain his destiny in the most perfect way, and for the Negro youth there is but one Catholic College which is devoted exclusively to his higher education.

The American Board of Catholic Missions will not be unmindful of this great and worthy cause.... May not the Sisters of the Blessed Sacrament add a fervent and specific request that in this hour of need, the Shepherd of souls, working through the aid of generous hearts in America, may bring the fruits of complete Christian education to the American Negro!

> Rev. Mother Catherine [*sic*] Drexel, "The Sisters of the Blessed Sacrament,"
> Report of Mother Katharine Drexel to the American Board of Catholic Missions.
> c. 1930, Archives of the Sisters of the Blessed Sacrament, Bensalem, Pennsylvania.
> Printed by Permission.

## 34. Religious Vacation Schools in the Diocese of Leavenworth, 1929

*Eulalia Erbacher, president of the Leavenworth Diocesan Council of Catholic Women, with her female collaborators, initiated a major project of the National Catholic Rural Life Conference in the diocese of Leavenworth by launching the Religious Instruction Vacation Schools during the summer of 1929. A few days after the first session began, Erbacher described the genesis of her enterprise to one of the Sisters of Charity of Leavenworth, the first religious community to teach in the summer schools. In 1938 Erbacher joined this community as Sister Mary John.*

St. Marys, Kansas
July 3, 1929

Dear Sister Mary Syra,[1]

At our Diocesan Convention [Leavenworth Diocesan Council of Catholic Women] here last fall, Miss Mary Burke, acting president of the Kansas City, Missouri, Council, selected as the subject of her address the religious Instruction Vacation School movement and its development in the Kansas City Diocese. The president, Miss Burke said, has been so intensely interested in this work that after the death of her husband she devoted her life and her fortune to the work.

---

1. Sister of Charity of Leavenworth (identification provided by Sister Leo Gonzaga, in the original transcription of Erbacher's letter).

Miss Burke's address was an inspiration to me, but it was during the National Convention of the Catholic Rural Life at Atchison some days later that I determined to do all in my power to establish several schools in our diocese. At Miss Lynch's kind invitation I served as chairman of the women's section at the Atchison meeting. My good fortune in being with Miss Lynch almost constantly during those three days afforded opportunities to learn more. Vacation schools too were discussed by many of the priests.

Close upon this convention came the national convention of the National Council of Catholic Women at Cleveland. The vacation school was one of the most important subjects discussed and it was truly inspiring to hear the wonderful reports of good accomplished through them in the various sections of the country. I made a special effort to attend every vacation-school session and roundtable discussion, and was thoroughly imbued with the idea of establishing several schools in our own diocese.

Our next quarterly meeting was in Topeka in January. There I presented my plans, but the Directors were far from responsive. Their chief argument against the plan seemed to be the question of securing teachers. I felt confident that we could secure teachers and even religious teachers and since our Right Reverend Spiritual Director, Monsignor Patrick McInerney, had expressed his approval of my plan I decided to go ahead. A few of us worked to produce a sentiment favorable to the schools before the April meeting of the directors in Kansas City. A great part of the business session of this meeting was devoted to the discussion of the schools. There was "a doubting Thomas" atmosphere but the directors who were themselves still unconverted were gracious enough to promise cooperation with my efforts if I secured teachers. Both Monsignor McInerney and Father Jacob Schmidt, (S.J.),[2] who were present spoke favorably of the schools and gave us some encouragement.

The day following our meeting in Kansas City I went to Leavenworth and requested Mother Mary Olive (then the Mother General of the Sisters of Charity of Leavenworth) to supply teachers. Mother was most generous in promising to give me all the teachers I needed within reason,... as the Sisters' contribution to the missionary labors in the Diocese of Leavenworth. The Little Flower in whose care I had placed the schools was doing her work beautifully and we were again encouraged.

After leaving St. Mary's Academy I visited Tonganoxie, Mount Olivet, Easton, and Kickapoo. Tonganoxie approved of the school but did not think it practical for that particular parish; the pastor at Easton was not home; Mount Olivet did not have a sufficient number of children in the parish to justify the services of two teachers, and the children there are beautifully cared for so that there is really no need for a school. Lansing accepted but found it necessary to write later that it would be impossible to have a school there.

Upon returning home I wrote to the other pastors who did not have parochial schools and with each letter I enclosed a copy of the special edition of

---

2. All material in parentheses and all ellipses apparently inserted by Sister Leo Gonzaga. (Editor's note)

*Rural Life* with Father O'Hara's article on Vacation Schools.... This is perhaps the most complete article I have read on the subject....

Waterville replied that there too the number of children would not justify the services of two teachers. The pastors at Kickapoo, Holton, Big Springs, Ottawa, Osage, St. Marys, Rossville, Belvue, and Perry replied and seemed eager to avail themselves of the opportunity to secure religious teachers for their children. My applications for teachers had to reach Mother Mary Olive by April 30. My letter to the pastor at Horanif was incorrectly addressed and was returned to me but as the time for submitting applications was up I did not remail the letter. That may have been one school lost.

Schools opened last Monday and I was happy to say that reports so far have far exceeded our expectations.

The Council aims to supply text-books for the teachers and for poor pupils. In a number of instances we are furnishing cars for daily transportation of teachers and pupils to and from school, and where we have affiliated societies we have asked them to take care of the living expenses of the Sisters so that the offerings made by parents may be sent to Leavenworth. I only hope that our plans will work out. I asked the pastor in every parish where we have no organization to arrange with the Altar Society to look after these details and I know of places where this is being nicely done. In other instances the Council (Leavenworth Diocesan) is paying bus fare or supplying cars to take the children to school. This is necessary especially [where] the father of the family is not a Catholic.

Several schools are preparing children for First Holy Communion; some for the reception of the sacrament of confirmation; all have organized choirs. The work is truly interesting and we are making every effort to have as many as possible of our women attend the classes occasionally to see what is being done. The Sisters are in love with the work. Those here at St. Marys [*sic*] are working overtime making posters, booklets etc. for use in the other schools too.[3]

The approbation of our Bishop was secured through our spiritual Director and Mother Mary Olive. At the diocesan priests' retreat at the college here the Bishop commended our Council for taking the initiative in the work, and after stating that there were eight parishes establishing schools he said, "I hope to see the establishment of at least 20 schools in this diocese next year."

Miss Lynch from Washington has written the Council and has also favored me with a personal letter of commendation for succeeding so far in this great work. Almost 400 children who would otherwise be deprived of religious instruction will through these schools be privileged to have it... and each day seems to bring more children.

> Letter of Eulalia Erbacher to Sister Mary Syra, excerpted and transcribed in typescript "History of the Religious Instruction Vacation Schools in the Diocese of Leavenworth," compiled by Sister Leo Gonzaga, 1945. Archives of the Sisters of Charity of Leavenworth, Vacation Schools — History. Printed with permission.

---

3. "Miss Erbacher does not mention that it was her home that was turned into a work shop and that she employed the whole family in getting this material together and sending it out to the other schools, but she did, as I was a witness to it. SLG" (inserted in transcription).

## 35. Teaching Theology in Catholic Colleges, 1939

*Before 1939 religion for lay students in Catholic colleges usually meant a course in apologetics. The introduction of theology as undergraduate subject matter inspired debate over whether it should be taught as scientia, in the Thomistic sense, or as a guide to the practice of religion. John Courtney Murray, professor of theology at the Jesuit seminary at Woodstock, supported teaching collegiate theology as a science but insisted on its relevance for laypeople. In his argument, Murray appealed to a renewed understanding of church, which, under the rubric of Catholic action, included profoundly communitarian and social dimensions.*

*The following excerpt is from Fr. Murray's response to a panel discussion on the topic of undergraduate theological education; it begins with his third point:*

...Thirdly, I think...there might be very genuine doubts in the minds of many—I know they exist in mine—as to just what this course in Catholic theology is going to be, and I believe it is about that point and that point alone that there could be any difference of opinion; and hence, I propose...that if you take Catholic theology as it is taught in our seminaries, and examine it, you cannot resist the impression (at least I cannot) that it does not adapt itself to becoming the basis of an effective program of Catholic action. There is my doubt.

Let me explain what I mean. By Catholic action I take it we do not mean any mere polemic against contemporary error. That is, it is true, a division of Catholic action. By Catholic action I think we agree in meaning, action that is co-extensive with the spirit of Christ in this world, action, therefore, that is wholly positive, that has as its supreme purpose *aedificatio Corporis Christi*, the building up of the Body of Christ; therefore in Catholic action that is what we are trying to inspire, vigorous social action, action that is characteristically social.

If you look now at scientific theology as it is taught in our seminaries, you cannot deny the fact — and I say this not on my own authority but on the authority of many other theologians who are teachers, professors of scientific theology — that Catholic theology in its contemporary form is shot through with a very individualistic current of thought. Catholic theology has not been able to resist the inroads of the great wave of individualism that poured into the world and has swept through it ever since the Renaissance. That is the first point. I could illustrate it. For instance, the Catholic theology of justification as is taught in the formal course of theology is a defense of the Catholic theology of justification against Martin Luther. Luther has said, "When my soul is justified, it merely means I have, myself, as an isolated individual, a consciousness that my personal sins have been remitted to me by a merciful God." Ah, no! says Catholic theology. Justification means that now there is a real relation between my individual soul and God; that God has put into my individual soul a theological reality which is the reality of grace; that is true, and it promotes the problem of justification on a purely individualistic basis and does not take account of what is the essential fact or theory of justification, or doctrine of justification — namely, that I am justified because I am inserted into the collective life of the Church, into the Body of Christ, in which the spirit of Christ dwells; in other words, I, as an individual, am justified because now a social life has become mine, the life that flows through all the members of the Body of Christ, who has given first of all to the Church, through the community, a collectivity, and through the community is given to the individual.

I could illustrate the same thing from the scientific theology of the sacraments as ordinarily taught in the seminaries, from the doctrine of the Church, the treatise on the Church but I will not delay you with that. I am merely leading to this conclusion, that if we are to introduce into our schools a course of theology worthy of the name, that will at the same time be the support and inspiration of a program of Catholic social action, it is imperative that we reform that course, that we do not simply take the course that is taught in the seminary, whose purpose is the formation, notice, of those who partake in the prophetic office of Christ, priests, and the equipment of them to defend the doctrine of the Church and explain it; but that we draw up a course that is specified, as we say, by its final object, its final cause.

We are not trying to do in our colleges and universities what we are trying to do in our seminaries. Perhaps I could put the thing this way: The formal object of theology as a science is the demonstrability of truth from the revealed Word of God, as kept and guarded by the Church. No theologian would quarrel with that as a fact, a formally accepted definition of a formal doctrine of theology by St. Thomas.

Is such a course of theology what we want in the colleges? I certainly do not think it is. I should say the formal object in colleges and universities is the livability of the Word of God as kept and given us by the Church; in other words, that our courses of theology must be wholly oriented towards life.

Theology deals with truth, it is true, but the truth that is an inspiration for the élan of the soul to God. That should be our purpose. I suggest the fact that the course must be reformed in some fashion, otherwise it will not be blended to the other courses in the colleges and universities.

Our courses in scientific theology as given in seminaries do not concern themselves directly — although I refuse to believe they should not concern themselves at least indirectly — with the religious value of the truth that they teach. When I address my class at Woodstock, I do not make it my primary object to energize their spiritual life. No, we discuss theology in a scientific, objective fashion, demonstrating the truth before us from the sources of revelation, Scripture, traditions, the Fathers, the Councils, the rest. On the contrary, these courses in scientific theology that we shall introduce, God willing, into our colleges and universities, must emphasize the value of the truth in life. That, I submit, must be their primary object. That is the finality that they have, and I would suggest the values of Catholic truth that they must emphasize, are these: that the Catholic religion is an objective thing, or rather, that the Catholic religion is essentially a theology; in other words it is a vision of God. It is not an instrument of humanitarianism; it is not even primarily an instrument for the constitution of a social order; it is first and foremost a vision of God, and a vision of God that comes to us in a very definite way, namely, through and in the concrete facts of a history; a history, namely, of a human life, the life of Christ; hence we have in basic Catholicism, two values: first, its objectivity; secondly, that it is historical; and of the ensemble of those two values a third, that Catholicism is essentially a social thing.

If we look up to God in the present order as He has been revealed to us by Christ, what is it that we see? A personal God? The philosopher sees that. When we look up to heaven as Catholics, what we see is a community. We see three persons, three distinct individuals, each of which preserves perfectly His own individuality, and yet whose life is One, and that is by definition, a community; and it is precisely from that vision of God as a community that there directly derives the essentially social character of Catholicism, because what God is determines His action in the world.

What is the purpose of God's action in the world? You tell me it is to save souls. That is and is not true, or rather, it is true but not complete. The purpose of God's action in the world is given to us by St John in the 12th Chapter, I believe, where he said that Christ died that He might gather into one the scattered children of God; God's action in the world, the reason why he sent His Son into the world to die, and why he sent His Spirit into the world to continue the work of His Son, is not merely the salvation of souls; it is the organization of society, the formation of a community which is the image upon earth of the divine community in heaven.

It is the insertion of the individual into the current of life that now is fully human, because that life is now divinized. That is the purpose of the action of God, and hence I say Catholicism is an essentially social thing.

Fourthly, the value I think should be brought out is this: that Catholic truth presents itself as a totality. I remember being very much impressed not long ago by reading a remark of Father Martindale, whose experience with converts has been very wide. He says that the ordinary cause that he has found for defections from the faith is this: that Catholics never grasped their faith as a whole; they grasped it as a more or less disconnected lot of things they had to believe, a disconnected lot of things they had to do, certain ceremonial practices that they had to frequent, the sacraments; but the notion that the object of their faith was a totality, an organized totality, had never dawned upon them; and hence, insistence upon the totality of Catholic truth and the totality of Catholic life, above all, its essential continuity (that is not a good word), the distinction between the divine and the human, and yet their unity — those are values that must be insisted upon.

Let me insist upon that, if we are to introduce courses in theology into the colleges and universities, I should say that the layman who is to have to submit to the course in theology, should be allowed to express very definitely what it is that he wants; and I say that for this reason, that if Catholic action means anything, it means that that which the Church emphasizes has changed; as the result of Protestant religious egalitarianism, it was necessary for the Church to insist upon the distinction between the hierarchy and the laity, between the Church teaching and the Church learning. The introduction of Catholic action as predominant in Catholic life today means simply this, does it not: that now

Catholic emphasis rests upon the unity of the Church teaching and the Church learning between the hierarchy and the laity?

*"Nos sumus Christi ecclesia,"* says the priest. You, we, you and I, are the Church of God, and it is right that those of us who teach should learn from those of you who learn from us.

> John Courtney Murray, S.J., "Necessary Adjustments to Overcome Practical Difficulties," in *Man and Modern Secularism: Essays on The Conflict of the Two Cultures* (New York: National Catholic Alumni Federation, 1940): 152–57.

## 36. Sister and at Least Forty-eight Pupils, 1948

Sister Ildephonsus Busse and Grade 1, Blessed Sacrament School, Wichita, Kansas, c. 1948.

> Photo credit: Archives of Sisters of St. Joseph, Wichita, Kansas. Printed with permission.

## 37. The Education of Sisters, 1949

*At the first regular meeting of the newly formed Section on Teacher Education of the NCEA, Sister Madeleva Wolff, C.S.C. (1887–1964) – president of Saint Mary's College at Notre Dame, a noted poet, essayist and lecturer – addressed an overflow crowd on a burning issue: the education of sister-teachers. Her talk sparked the beginnings of the Sister Formation movement.*

## THE EDUCATION OF OUR YOUNG RELIGIOUS TEACHERS

—

Sister M. Madeleva, C.S.C., St. Mary's College, Holy Cross, Ind.

—

This is an experience that many of us sisters have had more times than once. A mildly drunken man stops us on the street or in the railroad station. Magnanimously, he offers us some small change, saying: "I always help the sisters. They made me what I am." Usually we are glad to disclaim both the reward and the responsibility. Whatever this instance may lack in academic dignity and pertinence, it is not without its point.

A world genuinely sober in mind and fearfully sad can say to its teachers, "You helped to make me what I am." Everyone of us here can look back to our generation of teachers and realize how largely we are what they made us. Inevitably our students will have the same to say of us, for better or for worse. Knowing this we have every opportunity to make the report for better. That is the business of this present moment. We want to consider the education of our future religious teachers. We are intent upon posterity.

Those of my generation will recall how, when urged to think of posterity, and to try to improve the future of the race, Mr. Dooley used to protest, "What has posterity done for us?" The status quo, the condition in which we find ourselves at this moment, is the answer. We are the posterity to which he referred. We are makers of the present conditions.

Our opportunity to improve them is a responsibility and a duty. As teachers we can fulfill both by providing for the future better teachers than we are or than we had. We shall confine ourselves to the smallest and most select body of this professional group, the religious teacher. To simplify terminology and details of religious training we shall speak specifically of the teaching sister. Practically all of our recommendations can be adapted to the teaching priest and the teaching brother.

Let us consider a hypothetical high school graduate. Let us call her Lucy Young. She wants to be a teacher. To realize her desire on any level she knows that she will have to have a bachelor's degree and a teacher's license. She plans on all of this under whatever difficulties and demands of time and money. She expects to fulfill the minimum professional requirements for teaching. Any other procedure would be a sort of treason disqualifying her for the thing she wishes to be and to do. Before she begins her preparation she finds that she would rather be a teacher for God's sake than for two hundred dollars a month. She enters the novitiate of a religious community dedicated to education. She is simultaneously on two thresholds of one life. She is to be educated to be a teacher. She is to be formed to be a religious teacher. The two trainings are completely compatible, complementary, and can be perfectly synchronized.

For six months Lucy is a postulant and has no status save that of hope and anticipation in the community to which she has come. Her superiors, with wisdom and foresight, logically let her have her first semester of college preparation for teaching. Some superiors may give her the entire freshman year. At the end of her academic period she receives the holy habit of the community and begins her canonical year of preparation to be a religious teacher. No secular studies can intrude upon this important work. However, young Sister Lucy does study religion, Scripture, apologetics, dogma, Church history, perhaps.

At the end of her canonical year of formation she still has one year before her first vows and three additional years before her final profession. These are, I believe, the regular canonical periods and are fairly uniform in all our active orders. She still has three years and a little more of college preparation for her degree and her license. These are as important to her honest professional training as her canonical years are to her religious formation. We need not evade this by arguing the superiority of religious over secular subject. We do need to face the fact that the religious habit does not confer infused knowledge in any field nor justify the violation of the commonest requirements for teacher preparation. So let us give Sister Lucy these least qualifications.

In the second year of her religious life proper she should be allowed to take her regular sixteen hours of college work each semester. Good planning and budgeting of time can make this possible with an enrichment of rather than an intrusion upon her religious life. During summer session she can take an additional six hours. By the time that Sister Lucy makes her first vows she will or she can be a junior in college. Both her religious and her academic preparation are synchronously more than half completed. There still remain three years before her final profession. With less than two of these plus summer schools she will have finished her work for her bachelor's degree and will have over a year to go on mission as an unprofessed sister.

On the day of her final profession her religious superiors and her community can receive her as a sister completely prepared by her religious training, her vows, her academic education, to begin at once to carry on the work to which she is dedicated.

Perhaps all of this is high-handed, impossible, reckless planning. But we have been reckless to less worthy ends. Lucy and her companions are our most priceless and irreplaceable materials in the whole world of education. Let us treat them with much more than the care and caution bestowed on centers of atomic energy. Let us keep them out of the categories of our vacuum cleaners and our Bendix washers.

I need not tell you that Sister Lucy does not exist. But I know that we all should insist that she shall exist. We are here in part to bring her into existence. Sister Lucy is our 1949 model of the religious teacher of the future, her education and her training. She is the advanced payment of our debt to posterity.

After being utopian to this extreme of utter abandonment, let us pull ourselves back to the grim realities, things as they are. In the first place, Lucy's novitiate may not be at or near a college. This condition does not exist in many places and will have to be met by provisions too special to be detailed here. However, I know that any community operating a college will welcome Lucy and her sisters for any part of their college education that their superiors may desire.

Then there is the question of prudence. Should Lucy be educated before her community knows that she will persevere? Nothing can possibly do more to undermine her vocation than to send her out to try to teach without adequate, often without any preparation. Nothing can so disillusion her in her community as the dishonesty of assigning her to do in the name of holy obedience what professionally she is unqualified to do. Our secular accrediting agencies have been more than discreet and courteous in bearing with our practices in this matter. Our end does not justify our means.

Knowing that God is essential wisdom and infinite knowledge, that Christ is wisdom and knowledge incarnate, that Mary is the seat of wisdom, it is strange that we confide Lucy so much more confidently to premature teaching or laundry or floor waxing than to the study and the quest of wisdom for the development of her vocation. No group can deteriorate more quickly or more terribly than young girls of the type that enter our novitiates today without proper and adequate intellectual, cultural, and spiritual challenges. Nothing is more truly heavenly in human existence than the wonder of growth and expansion of these young people under the stimulus and inspiration of great teachers and great teachings. So let us educate Lucy in the name of the Holy Spirit. Her perseverance is in safer keeping than ours.

But this education is expensive. Can we afford it and how can we afford it? If we cannot afford to prepare our young sisters for the work of our communities, we should not accept them at all. We should direct them to communities that will prepare them. When Lucy comes to us, she gives up her own capacity to educate herself. In accepting her we deprive her of this capacity and these opportunities. Tacitly, we assume responsibility of providing both.

We need but consider for a moment that the material in our habits is some of the most expensive cloth made. We argue that it wears a long time. So does education. If we can afford to clothe Lucy's body, we can also afford to clothe her mind.

Community chapels are the object of our most generous contributions. Yet, nothing in the chapel, with the exception of the Blessed Sacrament, can so much honor God as the worship of our minds and wills. The unfolding beauty of Lucy's mind can mean much more to God than another statue or a new chapel carpet.

All of these difficulties communities will and can overcome. The chief and last, the difficulty before which they will all be helpless is that of pressure for more schools, more teachers. This pressure can come from our hierarchy, our clergy, our own ambitious selves. Never before have parishes been in a position to build schools before they could staff them. Naturally, there is a clamor for sisters to teach in them. Present schools have been enlarged with the inevitable demand for enlarged faculties. Mission fields have opened up small schools where three or four sisters can do apostolic work. Junior and senior colleges are being opened and expanded to meet the increasing educational demand. The story is too familiar to all of you to require elaboration. The point is that the need is going to continue for a long time. If all our religious communities begin this year to complete the education of our young sisters before sending them out to teach, practically all of the immediate generation will have their degrees and licenses in two or three years. After that, our teaching communities will have established this pattern of time and study training. They will have the same number of sisters to send out each year, with this incalculable difference, that they will all be adequately prepared. Summer schools thereafter can be devoted to graduate work, particularly in theology, and Sister Lucy will still be "young Sister Lucy" when her teacher training has been completed. She will have the vitality, the enthusiasm, the quick mind and generosity of youth to give to her best years of teaching. How shortsighted, how stupidly extravagant we have been in squandering these!

I ask every religious teacher present and over forty, what would you give to have had such a preparation? What will you give to procure it for our young religious? We can make them what we know they can and should be. We owe this to posterity.

Two years, three years is only a breath in the history of education, or even in the life of a generation. We can never spare them better than now. We would not be permitted to put a sister who is half prepared or unprepared on duty as a nurse. The care of minds is of much greater importance than the care of bodies. If we can take time to complete the professional training of our sister-nurses we can take time to complete the professional training of our sister-teachers.

The education of Sister Lucy and of every young sister is our great privilege, our great responsibility. Will we the superior generals, provincials, supervisors insist upon it? Will we college administrators and faculty provide for it? Will we pastors demand it? Will we bishops and archbishops, the great leaders and protectors of Catholic education, make the fulfillment of these conditions a requirement?

Let us remember that Lucy and her generation have been fed on the Blessed Sacrament all their lives. They have grown up on the doctrine of the Mystical Body of Christ. They are militant in Catholic action. They think and move with the instancies of aviation and television. They think in terms of super-atomic power. They are in spirit and in truth children of God. We must not frustrate the magnificence of their qualities by our lower-geared Victorian traditions and training.

God knows that we need ten thousand young Lucys in our novitiates this minute. When He sees that He can trust us with their education and their training, He will send them to us. Our teachers made us, in large part, what we are. We archbishops and bishops, we pastors and superiors, we school administrators and teachers can make Lucy in large part the kind of religious teacher that she should be. Will we?

Madeleva Wolff, C.S.C., "The Education of Our Young Religious Teachers," Report of the Proceedings and Addresses — Forty-sixth Annual Meeting, Philadelphia, Pennsylvania, April 19–22, 1949, *National Catholic Educational Association Bulletin* 46, no. 1 (1949): 253–56. Printed by permission of the National Catholic Educational Association.

## 38. Religious of the Sacred Heart at Stanford and Berkeley, 1954

*Although Religious of the Sacred Heart had studied at Stanford since 1924, American superiors had to defend it repeatedly to European Superiors General. In 1954 Rosalie Hill, R.S.C.J. (1878–1964), who governed an area including four Sacred Heart colleges,[1] explained to Very Rev. Mother de Lescure why the cloistered religious went there instead of to a Catholic university.*

Very Reverend Mother, I should like to say a few words to you about Stanford University, where, for twenty-five years, with your permission and before you with the permission of our venerated Mother Vicente and of Reverend Mother Perry, we have sent our religious to study for the degrees of M.A. and Ph.D. Among the Universities in the United States it has one of the highest scholastic reputations in the entire country. One of the reasons it suits us so well to send our religious there is that it divides the year into four parts, which allows our religious to do a whole quarter during the summer, while in the Universities which divide the year into semesters, the summer does not count for much. Each quarter is from 9 to 11 weeks with some weeks of vacation between each quarter. I cannot tell you the consideration shown us at this University, consideration we do not find elsewhere, even at the Catholic University of Washington. To give you only one example: for 18 years a large room has been reserved for the sole use of our religious in a part of the building where the library is located and where the public does not have access. In this room our religious can have their snack, read, study, [or] type, while others of our religious go to their classes, or between two class periods. The studies are very good at Stanford, Very Reverend Mother, but the professors show great thoughtfulness toward us, not requiring us to read books which would be objectionable to us, and not asking us to take more time than necessary in order to finish the work required for the degrees, which is not always true elsewhere. We always select the subjects that our religious should study and we never permit them to study philosophy in a university that is not Catholic. Before they go there we give them good courses in religion and philosophy...during the Juniorate.[2] For subjects like history or literature, we choose the courses given by Catholic professors or [those] who are favorable to the Church....

It is absolutely necessary for us, Very Reverend Mother, to have degrees for the Colleges and for the High Schools; even for the lower [that is, elementary] classes, the teacher must have a B.A. That is why with your permission, Very Reverend Mother, and before you with that of our venerated Mother Vicente, we have sent our religious to study at the University of California at Berkeley, where they were also considerate toward us. Several of ours have their degrees from this University, but we have not had anyone studying there for several years. Some have their degrees from the Catholic University at Washington, where two of ours are studying now with your permission. Two others are now

---

1. Barat College, Lake Forest, Illinois; Duchesne College, Omaha; San Francisco College for Women; and San Diego College for Women. (Editor's note)

2. The period before final profession, used by Religious of the Sacred Heart partly in preparation for teaching. (Editor's note)

studying at Saint Louis University. Besides St. Louis University, there are three other Jesuit Universities where ours have studied: Marquette University at Milwaukee, Loyola University at Chicago and Creighton University at Omaha. These Jesuit Universities only give the Ph.D. in a limited number of subjects, and therefore we cannot send those of ours there who must teach in other departments. Moreover, the "Accrediting Associations" do not give the same value to degrees from Marquette University, from Loyola or from Creighton, as to those of other Universities.

Although I understand your desire, Very Reverend Mother, that our religious receive their degrees from Manhattanville,[3] I believe I must tell you that, although the "Accrediting Associations" accept the B.A. and M.A. from Manhattanville, I really doubt that they would accept the Ph.D. from Manhattanville. Moreover, we cannot have a large number of degrees from Manhattanville, for the "Accrediting Associations" accuse a religious Order of "inbreeding" if that Order receives too many degrees from its own institutions. I submit all this very respectfully, Very Reverend Mother, but I truly do not believe that the Ph.D. from Kenwood[4] or Manhattanville would be accepted by the "Accrediting Associations," since even those of several Jesuit Universities are not accepted.

> Rosalie Hill, R.S.C.J., to R. M. de Lescure, San Diego, June 9, 1954, General Archives of the Society of the Sacred Heart, Rome, C-III 6b. Translated from the French by Patricia Byrne. Printed with permission.

## 39. Are Parochial Schools the Answer? 1964

*Before the end of Vatican II, when better than 12 percent of American schoolchildren were in Catholic schools, Mary Perkins Ryan (1915–) questioned the validity of that system. An author with publications in the area of liturgical renewal and Catholic life, Ryan based her critique on principles informing the Council: ecumenism, solidarity with humanity, and holiness in the world. Her book created a tempest, and the annual meeting of the NCEA in 1964 "focused on almost nothing else."[1]*

We may suppose, for the sake of argument, that the religious formation given in the Catholic school system of the future would be so reoriented as to further the aims of the renewal — and, as should be obvious from earlier chapters, this would indeed require a revolution. Religion class would no longer be just another subject, but something quite distinct from the regular school routine. Teachers of religion, all thoroughly trained in the spirit and methods of the new catechetics, would foster not only interest but a genuine spirit of inquiry. The school's prayer life would be patterned after that of the Church, integrated with

---

3. Manhattanville College of the Sacred Heart, Purchase, New York. (Editor's note)
4. Accredited normal school conducted by and for Religious of the Sacred Heart at their convent in Albany. (Editor's note)

---

1. Timothy Walch, *Parish School: American Catholic Parochial Education from Colonial Times to the Present* (New York: Crossroad, 1996), 177.

the Church's feasts and seasons, and steeped in Holy Scripture. School discipline would not bear on religious practice, school authority would not clothe itself in the authority of the Church, so that no child would be led to carry over resentment against school authority into resentment against the authority of the Church; his relation with Christ, his free commitment to Christ, would be fostered and not jeopardized. The school would, moreover, do everything possible to encourage friendliness and respect toward the public school and those who attend it.

But even if all this could be put into effect in the Catholic school system, it does not seem likely that an integrally Catholic education would result. It would be a case, rather, of new wine in old wine skins, for the old religious outlook harmonizes well enough with the present general ethos of public education; the new outlook would be at odds with it. An integrally Catholic education would be truly humanistic, in the sense that it would foster, above all, the development of each student's human powers and train him in the skills necessary for full human living; it would not mainly load him with facts and drill him in processes, as American education too generally does today. Such an education again would foster a sense of responsibility for self-development for the sake of serving one's fellow men, rather than, as at present, encouraging students to think of diplomas as magic passports to security and success. But until a revolution in the philosophy of public education itself has occurred in this country, it is hard to believe that the Catholic school system itself could be transformed along these lines and carry them even further so as to give a humanistic *Christian* formation. In the private Catholic school the possibility does exist. Bur for any large school system the pressures toward conformity are simply too great — the pressures exerted by standard, teacher-training agencies, texts, and the whole elaborate paraphernalia of present-day instruction. It is true that some hopeful trends are beginning to be discernible — for example, in the "new arithmetic," in various experiments with reading methods, and in allowing students to go ahead at their own pace. But it would seem as though Catholic educators and the Catholic public as a whole could work much more effectively to promote these tendencies from within the public school system than by trying to reform their own system separately. In the meantime, it would seem more fruitful to try to give Catholic young people, in the course of their outside-of-school formation, a truly humanistic and Christian motivation for pursuing their education than to try to do so within the framework of a Catholic education in which the greater part of the courses and teaching methods were differently oriented.

But this is not all. Even if it were possible to reform Catholic education completely, I am not convinced that attendance at a Catholic school would be the best way of preparing a young person for Catholic living in today's world. The atmosphere of a Catholic school is by nature a sheltered, even a hothouse one. True, outside of school the child or young person may have friends who are not Catholics. But most of his day is spent in Catholic surroundings; he does not become accustomed to the massive impact of the prevailingly secular atmosphere in which he will ordinarily be required to live his adult life. He is not prepared to stand up against the cold wind of indifference; he is more likely to be reacting against what seems like the over-religiousness of the Catholic school.

A Catholic education may perhaps fit a young person intellectually for some kind of dialogue with those of other faiths or of no faith at all. He may be taught the doctrines of the Catholic Church, and something about the doctrines that Protestant bodies hold in common with his own; he may learn to value the Judaic aspect of the Christian heritage. He may be equipped with reasonable bases for belief in God designed to meet the arguments of unbelievers. But except as his associations outside of school bring him into actual contact with different points of view, all this remains abstract. Learning his faith in school, learning general subjects in a Catholic atmosphere, he easily comes to feel either that religion is properly confined within the circle of one's co-religionists, or else that he knows all the answers — and neither of these attitudes is that of true dialogue.

It has already been remarked that by bringing about the association of Catholic parents with each other rather than with those of other faiths, by identifying their community interests with those of the parochial school, that school cannot help working against ecumenism in still another way.

It seems doubtful, consequently, whether the Catholic school system, however completely renewed, could compensate for the fact of being a system. What half a century ago still seemed to be its great advantages — getting the children together in a Catholic atmosphere and keeping them apart from non-Catholics — now appear to be serious disadvantages.

This is true whether we envisage our educational system as extending from the kindergarten through the Ph.D. or as being limited to some particular level. If a young person receives his whole education under Catholic auspices, he suffers the disadvantages of a hothouse atmosphere almost from the cradle to maturity. If we limit our efforts to maintaining our grade schools, as was mainly done in the past, we shall be training the children in this hothouse atmosphere and then leaving them, just at adolescence, to adjust to the atmosphere of a secular society as well as to their own new situation.

If we were, instead, to follow what has been the more recent trend and concentrate on high schools, we should be putting young persons into a segregated Catholic situation just when they need to begin to realize the impact of secularism and to learn how to resist it, just when they begin to become aware of other personalities and need to learn how to meet them in charity while differing from them on one or another conviction.

What if we were to drop the grade and high school systems entirely, and concentrate on colleges? Clearly, the result would be to cut young Catholics off from the intellectual currents of the general academic community just when they need to discover the relevance of Catholic truth to these currents and the reality of Catholic life in a secular world.

Neither, in the light of the renewal, does shared time seem to offer a truly satisfactory formation. Its effect on the students, as in our present school system, would be to make of religion simply another subject, taught in the same atmosphere and seemingly on the same level as history, literature, and the social sciences. It would also lend support to the notion that religion influences one's views of literature and the social sciences but not those concerning science or athletics, as well as to the assumption, already implicit in too much of today's student thinking, that what is taught in science classes is incontrovertibly true whereas what is taught in religion and the humanities is a matter of opinion.

Moreover, this plan would segregate Catholics, teachers and students alike, both from other believers and from nonbelievers in areas where the direct impact of other points of view is most crucial. Worse still, it would suggest that there must necessarily be a Catholic, a Protestant, and a Jewish version of each of the social sciences, instead of encouraging those of all faiths to work toward a truly ecumenical interchange. In spite of its apparent advantages, then, shared time may prove to be a kind of educational will-o'-the-wisp, with a tendency to distract concerned persons of all faiths from the basic problems of religious formation in our own day.

In the context of the new outlook, two major conclusions would seem to be inevitable: first, that a truly Catholic formation for all young people is a real possibility if we use all the resources at our disposal; and second, that a general education under Catholic auspices is no longer as necessary or even as desirable as in the past. As things are, the maintenance of our Catholic school system — not to speak of its extension — takes up a large part of our available human resources, resources now needed for urgent *religious* tasks. Even if some form of public aid were to relieve us of part of the financial burden, should we, then, plan for the continued maintenance of our Catholic school system in the future?

> Mary Perkins Ryan, *Are Parochial Schools the Answer? Catholic Education in the Light of the Council* (New York: Holt, Rinehart and Winston, 1964), 155–60. Printed with permission.

## 40. Defining the Contemporary Catholic University, 1967

*Two years after the Second Vatican Council, twenty-six representatives of nine Catholic universities, hosted by Theodore M. Hesburgh, C.S.C., met at Land O'Lakes, Wisconsin. In cooperation with the International Federation of Catholic Universities, they had come to prepare a statement about Catholic universities in accord with* The Church in the Modern World *(Gaudium et spes). The resulting "Land O'Lakes Statement" testified to the new situation of Catholic higher education in North America.*

### STATEMENT ON THE NATURE OF THE CONTEMPORARY CATHOLIC UNIVERSITY

*1. The Catholic University: A True University with Distinctive Characteristics.*

The Catholic university today must be a university in the full modern sense of the word, with a strong commitment to and concern for academic excellence. To perform its teaching and research functions effectively the Catholic university must have a true autonomy and academic freedom in the face of authority of whatever kind, lay or clerical, external to the academic community itself. To say this is simply to assert that institutional autonomy and academic freedom are essential conditions of life and growth and indeed of survival for Catholic universities as for all universities.

The Catholic university participates in the total university life of our time, has the same functions as all other true universities and, in general, offers the same services to society. The Catholic university adds to the basic idea of a modern university distinctive characteristics which round out and fulfill that idea. Distinctively, then, the Catholic university must be an institution, a community of learners or a community of scholars, in which Catholicism is perceptibly present and effectively operative.

## 2. The Theological Disciplines.

In the Catholic university this operative presence is effectively achieved first of all and distinctively by the presence of a group of scholars in all branches of theology. The disciplines represented by this theological group are recognized in the Catholic university, not only as legitimate intellectual disciplines, but as ones essential to the integrity of a university. Since the pursuit of the theological sciences is therefore a high priority for a Catholic university, academic excellence in these disciplines becomes a double obligation in a Catholic university.

## 3. The Primary Task of the Theological Faculty.

The theological faculty must engage directly in exploring the depths of Christian tradition and the total religious heritage of the world, in order to come to the best possible intellectual understanding of religion and revelation, of man in all his varied relationships to God. Particularly important today is the theological exploration of all human relations and the elaboration of a Christian anthropology. Furthermore, the theological investigation today must serve the ecumenical goals of collaboration and unity.

## 4. Interdisciplinary Dialogue in the Catholic University.

To carry out this primary task properly there must be a constant discussion within the university community in which theology confronts all the rest of modern culture and all the areas of intellectual study which it includes.

Theology needs this dialogue in order:

*a)* to enrich itself from the other disciplines;

*b)* to bring its own insights to bear upon the problems of modern culture;

*c)* to stimulate the internal development of the disciplines themselves.

In a Catholic university all recognized university areas of study are frankly and fully accepted and their internal autonomy affirmed and guaranteed. There must be no theological or philosophical imperialism; all scientific and disciplinary methods, and methodologies, must be given due honor and respect.

However, there will necessarily result from the interdisciplinary discussions an awareness that there is a philosophical and theological dimension to most intellectual subjects when they are pursued far enough. Hence in a Catholic university there will be a special interest in interdisciplinary problems and relationships.

This total dialogue can be eminently successful:

*a)* if the Catholic university has a broad range of basic university disciplines;

*b)* if the university has achieved considerable strength in these disciplines;

*c)* if there are present in many or most of the non-theological areas Christian scholars who are not only interested in and competent in their own fields, but also have a personal interest in the cross-disciplinary confrontation.

This creative dialogue will involve the entire university community, will inevitably influence and enliven classroom activities, and will be reflected in curriculum and academic programs.

### 5. The Catholic University as the Critical Reflective Intelligence of the Church.

Every university, Catholic or not, serves as the critical reflective intelligence of its society. In keeping with this general function, the Catholic university has the added obligation of performing this same service for the church. Hence, the university should carry on a continual examination of all aspects and all activities of the church and should objectively evaluate them. The church would thus have the benefit of continual counsel from Catholic universities. Catholic universities in the recent past have hardly played this role at all. It may well be one of the most important functions of the Catholic university of the future.

### 6. The Catholic University and Research.

The Catholic university will, of course, maintain and support broad programs of research. It will promote basic research in all university fields, but, in addition, it will be prepared to undertake by preference, though not exclusively, such research as will deal with problems of greater human urgency or of greater Christian concern.

### 7. The Catholic University and Public Service.

In common with other universities, and in accordance with given circumstances, the Catholic university is prepared to serve society and all its parts, e.g., the Federal Government, the inner city, et cetera. However, it will have an added special obligation to carry on similar activities, appropriate to a university, in order to serve the Church and its component parts.

### 8. Some Characteristics of Undergraduate Education.

The effective intellectual presence of the theological disciplines will affect the education and life of the students in ways distinctive of a Catholic university.

With regard to the undergraduate — the university should endeavor to present a collegiate education that is truly geared to modern society. The student must come to a basic understanding of the actual world in which he lives today. This means that the intellectual campus of a Catholic university has no boundaries and no barriers. It draws knowledge and understanding from all the traditions of mankind; it explores the insights and achievements of the great men of every age; it looks to the current frontiers of advancing knowledge and brings all the results to bear relevantly on man's life today. The whole world of knowledge and ideas must be open to the student; there must be no outlawed books or subjects. Thus the student will be able to develop his own capabilities and to fulfill himself by using the intellectual resources presented to him.

Along with this and integrated into it should be a competent presentation of relevant, living, Catholic thought.

This dual presentation is characterized by the following emphases:

*a)* a concern with ultimate questions; hence a concern with theological and philosophical questions;

*b)* a concern for the full human and spiritual development of the student; hence a humanistic and personalistic orientation with special emphasis on the interpersonal relationships within the community of learners;

*c)* a concern with the particularly pressing problems of our era, e.g., civil rights, international development and peace, poverty, et cetera.

*9. Some Special Social Characteristics of the Catholic Community of Learners.*

As a community of learners, the Catholic university has a social existence and an organizational form.

Within the university community the student should be able not simply to study theology and Christianity, but should find himself in a social situation in which he can express his Christianity in a variety of ways and live it experientially and experimentally. The students and faculty can explore together new forms of Christian living, of Christian witness, and of Christian service.

The students will be able to participate in and contribute to a variety of liturgical functions, at best, creatively contemporary and experimental. They will find the meaning of the sacraments for themselves by joining theoretical understanding to the lived experience of them. Thus the students will find and indeed create extraordinary opportunities for a full, meaningful liturgical and sacramental life.

The students will individually and in small groups carry on a warm personal dialogue with themselves and with faculty, both priests and laymen.

The students will experiment further in Christian service by undertaking activities embodying the Christian interest in all human problems — inner-city, social action, personal aid to the educationally disadvantaged, and so forth.

Thus will arise with the Catholic university a self-developing and self-deepening society of students and faculty in which the consequences of Christian truth are taken seriously in person-to-person relationships, where the importance of religious commitment is accepted and constantly witnessed to, and where the students can learn by personal experience to consecrate their talent and learning to worthy and social purposes.

All of this will display itself on the Catholic campus as a distinctive style of living, a perceptible quality in the university's life.

*10. Characteristics of Organization and Administration.*

The total organization should reflect this same Christian spirit. The social organization should be such as to emphasize the university's concern for persons as individuals and for appropriate participation by all members of the community of learners in university decisions. University decisions and administrative actions should be appropriately guided by Christian ideas and ideals and should eminently display the respect and concern for persons.

The evolving nature of the Catholic university will necessitate basic reorganizations of structure in order not only to achieve a greater internal cooperation and participation, but also to share the responsibility of direction more broadly and to enlist wider support. A great deal of study and experimentation will be necessary to carry out these changes, but changes of this kind are essential for the future of the Catholic university.

In fine, the Catholic university of the future will be a true modern university but specifically Catholic in profound and creative ways for the service of society and the people of God.

*Land O'Lakes, Wisconsin*
*July 23, 1967*

> "Statement on the Nature of the Contemporary Catholic University, Land O'Lakes, Wisconsin, July 23, 1967," in Neil McCluskey, S.J., *Catholic Education Faces Its Future* (New York: Doubleday, 1969 [1968]), 298–300. Printed with permission.

## 41. An Indian Sister Calls for Cultural Adaptation, 1972

*Following a century of mandatory assimilation as the norm for educating Native Americans through the Bureau of Indian Affairs, Congress passed the Indian Education Act in 1972. It implied more self-determination by providing financial assistance for education directly to the tribes. In the same year, Jeannette Kinlicheeny, principal of the school at Mission San Antonio de Pala, California, voiced the need for tribal teachers and ethnic cultural awareness in Catholic schools educating Native Americans.*

One aspect of education which is rarely included in the total concept of education in the United States today is Indian education. The education of the American Indian child is considered a problem of a different era and not a problem which is the main concern of many administrators and teachers covering a cross section of the Southwest and the Dakotas. Because of this, attention has been alerted to the educational problems of a minority within a minority.

There are now about 221,000 Indian students attending elementary and secondary schools operated by the Bureau of Indian Affairs (BIA). These students must board away from home because of the great distance from their hogan or village to the nearest public school. Over 10,000 Indian students attend American colleges and universities. Within recent years, the educational picture of the Indian has improved to such a degree that the small percentage of Indian dropouts has become a feather in our headband rather than a problem to be alarmed about in Indian country.

Within the Indian educational system there are only about 25 Catholic schools that are available to reservation Indians, and the total student enrollment at these schools numbers only 3,000. In the past century, these schools have made a barely perceivable surface impact on the education of Indians.

What accounts for the small percentage of Catholic schools on reservations? Lack of finances is one principal reason. Another is the lack of dedicated teachers truly interested in teaching Indian children. Early missionaries hoped that the Indian would receive the Christian faith in mission schools as well as an excellent education preparing him for life in a foreign society. From all appearances, this dream was realized to some extent, for the graduates of Catholic schools obtained employment with the BIA or with local reservation agencies. However, while living in a world of employment forms and weekly paydays, the Indian graduate clung quietly to his traditional way of life and Indian beliefs and longed for the weekends, when he could practice his religious beliefs. Moving within both cultures, the Indian had no thought for the preservation or the future growth of the mission school he had attended.

The history of Catholic education on the reservations embraces three generations of Indians. The alumni of these schools can be separated into three groups: 1) the students who have received an extraordinary gift of faith and who operate on an everyday level of belief in Christ without the security of their Indian practices (I say Indian practices and not Indian beliefs, for there is a difference.); 2) the majority of Indians who are sincere in their belief of the Catholic religion but who combine this belief with the Indian religious concepts of harmony with nature which are expressed in various Indian ceremonials; 3) an indifferent group of Indians who have lost all meaning in the truths of the Church and, sad to say, have lost all grasp of the total beauty of their Indian beliefs. This group is a new phenomenon not understood by either the missionaries or the traditional members of the tribes.

The existence and the preservation of Catholic schools depend upon the abilities and educational talents of the first group of Indians. Recognizing the importance of a Catholic education for their children, this group of adults willingly sacrifices the everyday luxuries of life. They want their children to have a solid foundation both in the Catholic religion and in the rudiments of basic subjects. This small force of conscientious parents is valiantly trying to keep the Catholic schools open on their reservations.

Within the existing 25 Catholic schools on the reservations, there is a unique spirit permeating each school. This spirit stems from the blending of the Indian culture with that of the Anglo world. An Indian adult who has received an excellent education, and whose reservation background has broadened it to wider horizons, is grateful for his Catholic education; but he is somewhat critical of the educational scene before him. The great unrest among the red, black, and brown powers and the questioning uncertainties of the Indian college graduates have alarmed the parents about the present administration of Catholic schools.

Many Indians are examining their schools' curriculum. Cultural awareness of traditional customs, the Indian language, and the inclusion of Indian board members in the governing of the schools are some of the topics now being deliberated by parents. As the parents become more secure in their role as average American citizens, they are assuming an attitude of equality and sometimes superiority in their judgment of current trends and practices relative to the total educational picture, especially in the area that they know best — Indian education.

As the Indian now comes into his own in the formal education of his child, he places himself in the shoes of the principal and the teachers in the administration of the school and the classroom. Parents are aware of the evident leadership of BIA schools. These schools have incorporated into their program Indian board members, Indian advisory boards, and Indian cultural programs. Comparisons of schools are being made, and, within inner family circles, parents are outlining programs they feel might advance their children to a higher level of learning.

It is time then that educational objectives be revised. An education-philosophy should be formulated recognizing and stressing Christian concepts but integrating these concepts within a framework of Indian thought. Branching out from this focal root, an Indian advisory board can aid the educational administration by its Indian thinking regarding finances, curricula, educational programs, and cultural awareness. Old and new members of the faculty should be subjected to an orientation program involving culture, Indian traditions, customs, and language. Formerly, teachers were unable to cope with the Indian student's mind because the child's heart radiated into the four Indian directions of nature, medicine man, family-clan relationship, and language. A child who may be indifferent to the newest teaching methods on the market may be reached by a person who understands his culture and background.

Every effort should be made to insure that teachers of Indian children have the same ethnic background as the child. Such leaders are better able to grasp the educational problems of the child and are more alert in zeroing in on the child's sensitive and silent pleas for help. Furthermore, a teacher of the same tribal background is able to act as an interpreter in the Indian language. Bilingual teachers are a great asset in the interpretation of the child's learning difficulties, and these teachers ease the communication between parents and teachers. If ethnic teachers are not available, volunteer Indian teacher-aides can be valuable in the effectiveness of the individualized programs.

The center of parish life is the school because it is there that all activities, social and financial, receive their stimuli. In recognition of this fact, innovative means should be forthcoming to motivate parents to become involved in their children's education. Ideas are not hard to find; a casual glance through *Navajo Times* may give administrators a few pointers. Once the parents become involved, a new spirit flows into the school, giving everyone an added interest and a personal feeling for the center of learning.

In looking back at what the Indian has done for Catholic education, we can see that Indian parents have given their own flesh and blood to the trust and guidance of Sisters, priests and lay teachers. The parents have gradually seen their own images transformed into adults who possess an ability to interweave their lives in the Indian and Anglo cultures. The parents are pleased with their children for they not only have the faith of the True God but have not lost the faith of the Indian mind, that of respect for the medicine man and his culture.

Many Indians with a college education are now returning to the reservation, and some of them are now finding teaching positions in the Catholic schools. Working as a silent force within the Catholic educational system, these teachers quietly guide their students to higher aspirations in the directions of professional employment, tribal government, and positions of leadership. We are pleased when we see our graduates become a success according to standards in the white man's world, but we are overjoyed when the students' success is surrounded by an aura of Indianness.

Jeannette Kinlicheeny, "Viewpoint: Indian," *Momentum* 3, no. 4 (December 1972): 44–46.

## 42. Catechesis and Renewal, 1977

*Five years after the promulgation of the Rite of Christian Initiation of Adults (1972), liturgist Aidan Kavanaugh used potential difficulties in its implementation to signal the revolutionary importance and extraordinary power of the restored rite as an instrument of renewal.*

### The *Ordo Initiationis Christianae Adultorum*

...among all the reformed initiatory rites — the *Ordo Baptismi Parvulorum* (1969), the *Ordo Confirmationis* (1971), the *Ordo Admissionis valide iam Baptizatorum, etc.* (1972), and the various permutations of these rites for pastoral reasons — it is clear that the rite of initiation of adults is the one that gives shape, articulation, and fundamental meaning to all the other rites which constitute the Roman initiatory economy. If this be true, then it represents a crucial restoration in the way Roman Catholics think about sacramental reality. Rather than regarding sacraments as separate entities, each containing its own exclusive meaning for theological exploitation, the *Ordo Initiationis Christianae Adultorum* [1972] presumes that all the initiatory rites form one closely articulated whole which, in turn, relates intimately with all the other non-initiatory sacraments and rites. Not only does this mean that infant baptism must be seen anew (perhaps as a legitimate abnormality out of which too much should not be made in theory and practice), but that confirmation as well must be revalued in a more rigorously baptismal context — the same context from which it gradually became separated in the West prior to the scholastic period....

Some Difficulties

I cannot emphasize too strongly my belief that in the restored Roman initiation polity lie the germs of a vastly revitalized sacramental theology and pastoral practice. At the same time I would be less than honest if I did not express my equally strong belief that the radical traditionalism of the documents is perhaps an Achilles' heel. By this I mean that, to have their salutary effects, the rites must be transferred from the printed texts into the lives of our churches. These churches, their clergy and people, are at present generally about as prepared to regard adult initiation as normative as they are ready for the Parousia. Nor are they prepared for the evangelical tasks that are necessary to produce, under God's grace, adult candidates for initiation. Even less do we possess the catechetical insights and structures necessary to form an adult catechumen's burgeoning personal faith adequately into that mature ecclesial faith the documents describe so splendidly as requisite for sacramental initiation. Religious educators in my country find it difficult to understand that catechesis is conversion therapy of a definite sacramental and ecclesial kind. What now dominates the field is much purely personal counselling on one hand and much formal religious education in school classrooms on the other. Neither of these is the catechesis of which I understand tradition or the Roman documents to speak.

To make a long matter short, the restored Roman initiation polity is, if truth be told, a major intimidation to many local churches because it is rightly perceived by those who study the documents to be explosive of the conventional patterns of church life. Most priests are horrified at the thought of dismissing catechumens from the Sunday eucharist, no matter how powerful a non-verbal catechesis this might be for the faithful on the grand dignity of their own baptism. Most bishops are quite incapable of viewing confirmation, along with ordinations and blessing chrism, as anything other than "their" sacrament. They perceive catechesis to be catechetics, and turn the matter over to their diocesan school board. And it has really never yet occurred, either to clergy or people in general, that a non-baptized catechumen of whatever age is not a pagan in some danger of hell should death transpire before the waters are poured. As long as this last assumption prevails, infant baptism will remain in place as our *de facto* initiatory norm, despite the affirmations of tradition and the recent Council that a catechumen is already in a degree of true communion with Christ in his Church.[1]

---

1. See, for example, the dogmatic constitution on the Church, *Lumen Gentium*, of the Second Vatican Council, para. 14; the decree on missions, *Ad Gentes*, para. 13–14. Also Hippolytus's *Apostolic Tradition* 19:2 (G. Dix, *The Apostolic Tradition*, London, 1968, 30), concerning the salvation of a catechumen who suffers death before baptism.

Because of these and other easily perceptible difficulties in the restored initiation polity, most clergy regard its implementation as problematic if not impossible. They are right. For what the Roman documents contain are not merely specific changes in liturgical rubrics, but a restored and unified vision of the Church. One might describe it as a concentric ecclesiology locked together by the sacramental discipline of faith shared on all levels, rather than as a pyramidal ecclesiology of juridical delegation of power that rests upon the base of a baptized proletariat.

Woven throughout the restored polity is a concept of "orthodoxy" as "right worship," a concept of the law of worship founding the law of faith (*lex orandi legem statuat credendi*), a concept of faith as a life lived in common under the law of the Gospel, a concept of the Church as a communion in faith as a commonwealth of discipline — a ministry of reconciliation. Scholars talk of these things as ideals: the Roman documents on initiation make them a norm that all must secure to some degree in practice.

Here is both the rub and the promise. One may turn an altar around and leave *reform* at that. But one cannot set an adult catechumenate in motion without becoming necessarily involved with *renewal* in the ways a local church lives its faith from top to bottom. For members of an adult catechumenate must be secured through evangelization; they must be formed to maturity in ecclesial faith through catechesis both prior to baptism and after it; and there must be something to initiate them into that will be correlative to the expectations built up in them throughout their whole initiatory process. This last means a community of lively faith in Jesus Christ dead, risen, and present actually among his People. In this area, when one change occurs, all changes. Few are able to bear the rub, but all desire the promise howsoever inchoately.

Aidan Kavanaugh, "Christian Initiation in Post-Conciliar Catholicism: A Brief Report," *Studia Liturgica* 12 (1977): 107–15. Printed by permission of Societas Liturgica.

## 43. A Catholic Senator on Government Funding for Private Schools, 1980

*Daniel Patrick Moynihan (1927–2003), senior U.S. senator from New York from 1977 to 2001 and a Catholic, brought extensive academic background to his long political career. Moynihan's contribution to a symposium sponsored by the Institute of Public Policy of the University of Notre Dame in 1980 critiqued the Supreme Court's interpretation of the Establishment Clause of the Constitution and reviewed his efforts in Congress to obtain government support for nonpublic education.*

I would like to make three simple points concerning various legislative proposals to fund aspects of nonpublic education. First, when taking up any subject for serious reflection, I have retained from my years in academe the practice of asking what the state of the subject is in the other industrial democracies, to what degree the subject is a generalized condition of this sort of social arrangement, and to what degree it is particular with us. To my knowledge, ours is the only industrial democracy in the world that does not routinely provide aid to nonpublic schools as part of its educational system. This is a problem unique to the United States. That fact alone says something, I think.

My second point is that the origin of this policy choice lies not in the intention of the framers of the First Amendment in the First Congress,...but in the Catholic-Protestant antagonisms of the 19th century. That is well known and amply documented, although it is surprising how much it has had to be rediscovered....

My third point is that when one reflects seriously on the quality of education provided in many of our urban centers, one is entitled to the judgment that the Supreme Court has been simply wrong in repeatedly telling state legislatures that they may not, consistently with the First and Fourteenth Amendments, provide a variety of forms of aid to elementary and secondary schools that are operated by a church or religious body. I offer just a former professor's judgment that the Supreme Court is simply wrong in this. This is not unprecedented....For example, the Court was plainly wrong in *Dred Scott*. The Court held in *Plessy* that separate but equal facilities were constitutional....

I would maintain that the Court has been egregiously wrong in much of the reasoning it has employed in defense of its decisions concerning public aid for nonpublic education. For example, the Court was reduced to saying in *Tilton* that a federal statue that provided aid to a Catholic college was constitutional, but that similarly direct subventions to a Catholic high school would be unconstitutional, because of a presumably well known difference in religious impressionability as between college freshmen and high school seniors. If you'll say that, you'll say anything. It was not an academically defensible statement....

Many other cases in this area are similarly embarrassing and confused. So poorly reasoned are the cases that one federal appellate judge, Joseph F. Weis, was led to ask recently in an opinion dealing with the New Jersey tuition tax deduction: "Where does this regime of judicial hostility to these schools arise from?" Acknowledging that the *Nyquist* decision bound the Court of Appeals, the judge nevertheless stated his opinion that the *Nyquist* decision was itself erroneous.

I have argued elsewhere the case that this judicial hostility to nonpublic schools does not derive from the Establishment Clause of the First Amendment, but from the Supreme Court's erroneous interpretation of that constitutional provision.[1] In that essay I likewise suggested that it was difficult to avoid the judgment that Justice Blackmun's dissent in the *Gannett* case was right and that the majority of the Court was wrong. Once such a judgment is posited, serious policy makers must face the question, "What do you do when the Supreme Court is wrong?" I think that the public response to *Gannett* provides us with an answer to this question. Heated debate began promptly. Some of the Justices, including the Chief Justice, got into the act of clarifying their

---

1. See Daniel Patrick Moynihan, *Counting Our Blessings: Reflections on the Future of America* (Boston: Atlantic-Little, Brown, 1980), 162–90 (all notes added by editor in original publication).

position and of half-apologizing for it in speeches off the bench. Legislation was contemplated. And litigation ensued. Even before remedial legislation was enacted, the Court had already begun the process of confirming its *Gannett* rule in Richmond newspapers.... [P]ublic policy makers who are clearly persuaded that the Court is wrong have a duty to engage in debate, to propose remedial legislation, and to correct an erroneous decision.

The debate should, in part, focus on the meaning of the Establishment Clause and the early history of state aid to church-related schools. I am persuaded that dispassionate scholars like Nathan Glazer, Mark DeWolfe Howe, Walter Berns and Michael Malbin have adequately demonstrated that the Courts' reading of that history is simply wrong. But I do not repeat their arguments here because I think that the public debate should likewise be focused on contemporary aspects of educational policy. Among those, racial justice in education remains a central issue. The alleged elitism of the private schools is a pseudo-issue. Access to public resources on an equitable basis is probably the principal issue.

The concern about racial justice in our educational policies is central because we cannot afford to compromise or delay the promise of quality education for all Americans held out in *Brown v. Board of Education.* But it would be wholly gratuitous to assert that nonpublic educators as a class are less concerned about racial integration in their schools than their counterparts in the public schools. Dr. James Coleman and Father Andrew Greeley have completed solid empirical studies that should lay to rest the silly contention that Catholic schools are elitist and racist in character. All too often, however, one hears the view that nonpublic schools are "bastions of white privilege and exclusivity." One doesn't have to be much of a political scientist to recognize that those words are politically loaded and are used to evoke certain symbols. I have been involved with the question of public support for nonpublic education for over two decades. When I came to Washington with President Kennedy, one of the principal arguments against providing aid to the parochial schools was that they were bad schools. Letting children remain in them, it was thought, would confine them to a life of educational disadvantage; the sooner they were closed down, the more access these children would have to equal education. In only two decades' time, these schools have turned from being inferior to being schools of such quality that opponents of aid for these schools now argue that if everybody had the slightest opportunity to enter them, there would be no public school system left.

This remarkable misuse of language has emerged in Congressional debates on two proposals that I have sponsored in recent years, the tuition tax credit proposal considered in the 95th Congress and the "baby BEOG" proposal considered in the 96th Congress. The people who have advocated this kind of financial support for nonpublic education were beaten badly in the 95th Congress, then very badly in the 96th. The tuition tax credit was defeated in 1978 in the Senate by a vote of 56 to 41. That was a large bill which would have cost about five billion dollars; it would have been a real transfer of money in education and in the society. In 1980, we proposed a much smaller program, to give elementary and secondary children from low-income families access to Basic

Educational Opportunity Grants. This would have cost about a hundred and twenty million dollars a year, which is not a large sum in terms of education appropriations. We lost 71 to 24.

We were beaten in no small part because of the implacable opposition of the Carter Administration, and much more importantly, that of all the major educational organizations of the country, most of which are involved in progressive political causes. . . .

It should be remembered that for six generations the Catholic schools have educated the children of the rural proletariat that landed in Manhattan. As Nathan Glazer and I tried to show in *Beyond the Melting Pot,* they were not thought to be "bastions of white privilege and exclusivity" until quite recently.[2]

Although Coleman and Greeley have shown that this characterization of parochial schools as racist and elitist is simply untrue, one has the impression that it has become fashionable to think that it is true. Perhaps this is because the people who most successfully control the media and who manage our symbols of progress have it all over the people who advocate proposals for broadening educational opportunity. Consider, for example, the view of the *Washington Post* and the *New York Times,* the two central organs of judgment in these matters. About tuition tax credits, the *Washington Post* said: "The bill threatens to do incalculable damage to the country's public schools." And the *Times* said: "The bill would encourage the dismantling of public education." These are very strong words and very threatening language. But no effective response was made by anyone who said, "You can't say that sort of thing without having me disagree with you." What is perhaps most regrettable about the editorial posture of the *Times* and the *Post* is that these influential shapers of public opinion have accepted the definition of this issue when public education is understandably anxious about its future. What previously was simply an adjunct school system has emerged as possibly an alternative school system, and that has roused deep anxieties and extraordinary fears.

Those anxieties and fears, I regret, now appear to be the basis for remarkable distortions of reality. For example, in the late 1960s, educational vouchers were generally regarded as a progressive proposal. All liberal faculty members would wish to be associated with it. Good foundations would support it. But with the space of a decade this proposal has somehow been transformed into a "bastion of white privilege and exclusivity."

Sometimes it takes a long time to overcome that kind of opposition in national politics. As a political scientist, I would not think that the Court would change its views on the Establishment Clause and church-related schools within this century. Although I am willing to be proved wrong on this one, I do not think that the prospect of change in this area is enhanced by the abandonment of pluralism and choice as liberal ideas and liberal values. It has, however, become increasingly clear that public funding of nonpublic schools will be advocated with vigor by persons on the political Right. As the issue becomes more

---

2. See Nathan Glazer and Daniel Patrick Moynihan, *Beyond the Melting Pot: The Negroes, Puerto Ricans, Jews, Italians and Irish of New York City,* 2nd ed. (Cambridge, Mass.: M.I.T. Press, 1970).

and more a conservative cause, it will, I suppose, become less and less a liberal one. If that happens, it will present immense problems for a person such as myself who was deeply involved in this issue long before it was either conservative or liberal. And if it prevails only as a conservative cause, it will have been a great failure of American liberalism not to have seen the essentially liberal nature of this pluralist proposition.

> Daniel Patrick Moynihan, "What the Congress Can Do When the Court Is Wrong," in *Private Schools and the Public Good: Policy Alternatives for the Eighties,* ed. Edward McGlynn Gaffney, Jr. (Notre Dame, Ind.: University of Notre Dame Press, 1981), 79–84.

## 44. The Catholic Identity of Colleges and Universities, 1999

*In November 1999, the National Conference of Catholic Bishops issued the Application of Ex Corde Ecclesiae for the United States, establishing norms for the implementation of the papal document issued in 1990 on the Catholic identity of colleges and universities. An earlier formulation of the same norms in 1996 had been rejected by Vatican officials, who required a more juridical form. The American bishops' final text provoked extensive controversy, particularly in regard to the relationship of passages concerning academic freedom and ecclesiastical control to Catholic higher education.*

Part Two: Particular Norms

The chief purpose of the following norms is to assist Catholic colleges and universities in their internal process of reviewing their Catholic identity and clarifying their essential mission and goals. They are intended to provide practical guidance to those committed to the enterprise of Catholic higher education as they seek to implement the theological and pastoral principles of *Ex corde Ecclesiae.* . . .

Art. 2. The Nature of a Catholic University

1. The purpose of a Catholic university is education and academic research proper to the disciplines of the university. Since it enjoys the institutional autonomy appropriate to an academic institution, its governance is and remains internal to the institution itself. This fundamental purpose and institutional autonomy must be respected and promoted by all, so that the university may effectively carry out its mission of freely searching for all truth.[1]

2. Academic freedom is an essential component of a Catholic university. The university should take steps to ensure that all professors are accorded "a lawful freedom of inquiry and of thought, and of freedom to express their minds humbly and courageously about those matters in which they enjoy competence."[2] In particular, "[t]hose who are engaged in the sacred disciplines enjoy

---

1. See above n. 15 [no referent in present excerpt].

2. Vatican Council II, Pastoral Constitution on the Church in the Modern World (*Gaudium et Spes*) 62. A university's commitment to Catholic ideals, principles and attitudes is not only consistent with academic freedom and the integrity of secular subjects, it requires "[f]reedom in research

a lawful freedom of inquiry and of prudently expressing their opinions on matters in which they have expertise, while observing the submission [*obsequio*] due to the magisterium of the Church."[3]

3. With due regard for the common good and the need to safeguard and promote the integrity and unity of the faith, the diocesan bishop has the duty to recognize and promote the rightful academic freedom of professors in Catholic universities in their search for truth.[4]

4. Recognizing the dignity of the human person, a Catholic university, in promoting its own Catholic identity and fostering Catholic teaching and discipline, must respect the religious liberty of every individual, a right with which each is endowed by nature.[5]

5. A responsibility of every Catholic university is to affirm its essential characteristics, in accord with the principles of *Ex corde Ecclesiae,* through public acknowledgment in its mission statement and/or its other official documentation of its canonical status[6] and its commitment to the practical implications of its Catholic identity, including but not limited to those specified in Part One, Section VII of this document.

6. The university (in particular, the trustees, administration, and faculty) should take practical steps to implement its mission statement in order to foster and strengthen its Catholic nature and character.[7] ...

### Art. 4. The University Community

*4. Faculty*

  a. In accordance with its procedures for the hiring and retention of professionally qualified faculty and relevant provisions of applicable federal and state law, regulations and procedures, the university should strive to recruit and appoint Catholics as professors so that, to the extent possible, those committed to the witness of the faith will constitute a majority of the faculty. All professors are expected to be aware of and committed to the Catholic mission and identity of their institutions.

  b. All professors are expected to exhibit not only academic competence and good character but also respect for Catholic doctrine.[8] When these

---

and teaching" and respect for "the principles and methods of each individual discipline." *ECE* [*Ex Corde Ecclesiae*], II, Art. 2, §5.

3. C[anon] 218.

4. See *ECE,* II, Art. 2, §5.

5. Though thoroughly imbued with Christian inspiration, the university's Catholic identity should in no way be construed as an excuse for religious indoctrination or proselytization. *See* Vatican Council II, Declaration on Religious Liberty (*Dignitatis humanae*), 2–4.

6. See footnote 31 for a listing of canonical categories [no referent in present excerpt].

7. In this regard, the university may wish to establish a "mission effectiveness committee" or some other appropriate structure to develop methods by which Catholics may promote the university's Catholic identity and those who are not Catholic may acknowledge and respect this identity.

8. The identity of a Catholic university is essentially linked to the quality of its professors and to respect for Catholic doctrine. The Church's expectation of "respect for Catholic doctrine" should not, however, be misconstrued to imply that a Catholic university's task is to indoctrinate or proselytize its students. Secular subjects are taught for their intrinsic value, and the teaching of secular

qualities are found to be lacking, the university statutes are to specify the competent authority and the process to be followed to remedy the situation.[9]

c. Catholic theology should be taught in every Catholic university, and, if possible, a department or chair of Catholic theology should be established. Academic events should be organized on a regular basis to address theological issues, especially those relative to the various disciplines taught in the university.[10]

d. Both the university and the bishops, aware of the contributions made by theologians to Church and academy, have a right to expect them to present authentic Catholic teaching. Catholic professors of the theological disciplines have a corresponding duty to be faithful to the Church's magisterium as the authoritative interpreter of Sacred Scripture and Sacred Tradition.

e. Catholics who teach the theological disciplines in a Catholic university are required to have a *mandatum* granted by competent ecclesiastical authority.[11]

1. The *mandatum* is fundamentally an acknowledgment by Church authority that a Catholic professor of a theological discipline is a teacher within the full communion of the Catholic Church.

2. The *mandatum* should not be construed as an appointment, authorization, delegation or approbation of one's teaching by Church authorities. Those who have received a *mandatum* teach in their own name in virtue of their baptism and their academic and professional competence, not in the name of the Bishop or of the Church's magisterium.[12]

3. The *mandatum* recognizes the professor's commitment and responsibility to teach authentic Catholic doctrine and to refrain from putting forth as Catholic teaching anything contrary to the Church's magisterium.

---

subjects is to be measured by the norms and professional standards applicable and appropriate to the individual disciplines. See *ECE*, II, Art. 4, §1 and above footnotes 24 and 27 [no referent in present excerpt].

9. C[anon] 810, §1.

10. *Gravissimum educationis* 10.

11. C[anon] 812 and *ECE*, II, Art. 4, §3.

12. *"Mandatum"* is a technical term referring to the juridical expression of the ecclesial relationship of communion that exists between the Church and the Catholic teacher of a theological discipline in the Catholic university. The prescription of canon 812 is grounded in the right and responsibility of bishops to safeguard the faithful teaching of Catholic doctrine to the people of God and to assure the authentic presentation of the Church's magisterium. Those with such a *mandatum* are not agents of the magisterium; they teach in their own name, not in the name of the bishop. Nonetheless, they are not separate from the Church's teaching mission. Responding to their baptismal call, their ecclesial task is to teach, write and research for the benefit of the Church and within its communion. The *mandatum* is essentially the recognition of an ecclesial relationship between the professor and the Church (*see* canon 229, §3).

Moreover, it is not the responsibility of a Catholic university to seek the *mandatum;* this is a personal obligation of each professor. If a particular professor lacks a *mandatum* and continues to teach a theological discipline, the university must determine what further action may be taken in accordance with its own mission and statutes (*see* canon 810, §1).

4. The following procedure is given to facilitate, as of the effective date of this Application, the process of requesting and granting the *mandatum*. Following the approval of the Application, a detailed procedure will be developed outlining the process of requesting and granting (or withdrawing) the mandatum.

a. The competent ecclesiastical authority to grant the *mandatum* is the bishop of the diocese in which the Catholic university is located; he may grant the mandatum personally or through a delegate.[13]

b. Without prejudice to the rights of the local bishop,[14] a *mandatum*, once granted, remains in effect wherever and as long as the professor teaches unless and until withdrawn by competent ecclesiastical authority.

c. The *mandatum* should be given in writing. The reasons for denying or removing a *mandatum* should also be in writing.[15]

---

13. The attestation or declaration of the professor that he or she will teach in communion with the Church can be expressed by the profession of faith and oath of fidelity or in any other reasonable manner acceptable to the one issuing the *mandatum.*

14. Although the general principle is that, once granted, there is no need for the *mandatum* to be granted again by another diocesan bishop, every diocesan bishop has the right to require otherwise in his own diocese.

15. Administrative acts in the external forum must be in writing (c. 37). The writing not only demonstrates the fulfillment of canon 812, but, in cases of denial or removal, it permits the person who considers his or her rights to have been injured to seek recourse. *See* canons 1732–1739.

*Part 5*

# CHURCH AND STATE

## Introduction

On the evening of September 12, 1960, presidential candidate Senator John F. Kennedy of Massachusetts stood before the Greater Houston Ministerial Association. It was a key moment in the 1960 presidential election. Kennedy had been invited to Houston to address what he termed the "so-called religious issue." He delivered a prepared statement and then responded to questions. With the last question of the evening, Robert McLaren of Westminster Presbyterian Church raised the issue of the Syllabus of Errors, a list of 80 statements condemned by Pope Pius IX in 1864. Sure to catch the attention of American readers was Proposition 55: The Church ought to be separated from the State, and the State from the Church.

Citing the authority of the *Catholic Encyclopedia* to show that the Syllabus was still binding on Catholics, McLaren noted "three very specific things which are denounced including the separation of state and church, the freedom of religion...and the freedom of conscience." He then asked Kennedy: "Do you still feel these being binding upon you...?" McLaren wanted to know if Kennedy held his oath of office above his "allegiance to the Pope on these issues." Kennedy cited a 1948 statement of the American bishops supporting separation of church and state. Surely they were not in error. Time was running out. He quickly affirmed his belief in freedom of religion and freedom of conscience and elided into his closing statement. This inconclusive confrontation between a Catholic senator and a Presbyterian minister gathered up nearly two centuries of controversy in which Catholics had to defend their full and conscientious commitment to "separation of church and state" and "religious liberty."[1]

In 1927 presidential candidate Governor Alfred E. Smith of New York defended himself in the pages of the *Atlantic Monthly* against allegations of divided loyalties arising from papal condemnations of separation of church and state. John A. Ryan came to Smith's defense with his own reading of the Syllabus of

---

1. For the texts of Kennedy's statement and the question-and-answer session, see the *New York Times,* September 13, 1960. The text of Kennedy's statement can also be found in *Public Voices: Catholics in the American Context,* ed. Steven M. Avella and Elizabeth McKeown (Maryknoll, N.Y.: Orbis Books, 1999), 361–64. See also propositions 15, 77, and 78 of the Syllabus of Errors on religious liberty and proposition 79 on freedom of conscience. The text of the Syllabus is available at newadvent.org.

Errors.[2] In his urbane postwar summary of the case against Catholic Americanism, Paul Blanshard reminded his fellow citizens that the Syllabus of Errors had branded religious freedom and separation of church and state as among "the principal errors of our time." He called Pius IX "one of the most reactionary men in all cultural history" and his Syllabus "probably the most famous document ever issued by a Pope."[3]

Despite Blanshard's claim about the notoriety of the Syllabus, probably neither Smith nor Kennedy were familiar with it prior to their presidential campaigns. But their theological advisors were. In 1927 Smith consulted Francis P. Duffy, former editor of the *New York Review* (1905–8) and a celebrated World War I chaplain. Kennedy consulted his campaign aide, John Cogley, a former *Commonweal* editor. John A. Ryan had described Chapter VII of John Henry Newman's *Letter to the Duke of Norfolk* as "undoubtedly the ablest, most comprehensive and the most convincing refutation of objections against the Syllabus on the score of civic loyalty that has ever been written."[4] In France Bishop Félix Dupanloup of Orléans wrote a pastoral letter on the Syllabus in which he distinguished between the "thesis," an ideal arrangement in which the Catholic Church would have the support of the state, and the "hypothesis," in which the Church bowed to circumstances and pursued a *modus vivendi* with particular governments. In this interpretation of the Syllabus, the American situation would always be a less-than-ideal example of Dupanloup's "hypothesis." Catholic thinkers in the United States tended to take a different approach to the Syllabus. When Duffy and Cogley were called upon to explain the Syllabus, they had at their disposal a long tradition of American Catholic interpretations of nineteenth-century Roman denunciations of liberalism.

At the time of the American Revolution, the papacy was foundering. Modern Catholic states had reduced the popes to near ceremonial stature. In 1773 Pope Clement XIV was forced to accede to Portuguese demands to suppress the Jesuits. Pope Pius VI, who had watched helplessly as the Revolution made havoc of French Catholicism, would die in exile in 1799 having literally been carried to France by the revolutionary army. It was not clear that he would have a successor. Pius VII did succeed him. But he too would be dragged off to France as Napoleon's prisoner. With his persecution of the popes, Napoleon had unwittingly set in motion a movement that, after the Congress of Vienna in 1815, would not only restore dignity to the papacy, but also "papalize" the face of Catholicism. This "exaltation of the papacy as the heart of Catholicism" was called "Ultramontanism."[5]

Though it had a theoretical basis in Count Joseph de Maistre's *Du Pape* (1819), this appeal "across the mountains" to the pope was primarily a counter-

2. "Catholic and Patriot: Governor Smith Replies," *Atlantic Monthly* 139 (May 1927): 721–28; John A. Ryan, *The Catholic Church and the Citizen* (New York: Macmillan, 1928), 32–39.

3. Paul Blanshard, *American Freedom and Catholic Power* (Boston: Beacon Press, 1949), 237, 22.

4. Ryan, *The Catholic Church and the Citizen*, 37.

5. Eamon Duffy, *Saints & Sinners: A History of the Popes* (New Haven, Conn.: Yale University Press, 1997), 216. The neologism "papalization" is from John W. O'Malley, S.J., "The Millennium and the Papalization of Catholicism," *America* 182 (April 8, 2000): 8–16.

revolutionary movement of popular religious devotion born out of European culture. It combined what Americans would call "politics" and "religion" in an inextricable mix. It had suited the Congress of Vienna to continue to recognize the pope as a "sovereign," the "temporal" ruler of the Papal States. In terms of "sovereignty," both Church and state in Europe made absolute claims. Nineteenth-century popes considered this "sovereignty" as essential to their struggle with modern states for what Americans would call "religious liberty" or "free exercise" for Catholics. Absolutist states did not consider themselves bound to grant such freedoms. Neither side had come to recognize them as "rights." This left the Church's freedom linked to the pope's sovereignty.

This is the context for understanding the terms *Church* and *State* as they were used by Pius IX in 1864 as Ultramontanist fervor moved toward its peak at the First Vatican Council in 1870. It is also the context in which Pastor McLaren could use the seemingly inappropriate term *allegiance* in his question to Senator Kennedy in 1960. With their own particular appeal to American exceptionalism, Catholics in the United States have generally insisted that "separation of church and state" does not mean the same thing in the United States as it did in the Europe of Pope Pius IX. But there remained the thorny issues of papal "sovereignty" and the persistent claim that in an ideal situation the Church should be supported by the state. This left American Catholic exceptionalism always vulnerable to the sorts of challenge brought by Paul Blanshard and Pastor McLaren. Herein lies the intellectual significance of John Courtney Murray.

In the years before the rise of Ultramontanism, both John Carroll and John England could matter of factly treat the pope's authority as "spiritual." When Carroll wrote to Plowden in 1784, Pope Pius VI had little inkling that the religious system of the United States "had undergone a revolution, if possible, more extraordinary, than our political one."[6] John England spoke before Congress during the largely ineffective papacy of Leo XII. But by 1864 the Ultramontane movement was in full swing. Kentucky-born and Roman-trained Martin J. Spalding was archbishop of Baltimore. On December 8, 1864, Pius IX issued the encyclical to which he attached the Syllabus of Errors. Immediately Spalding set to work on a pastoral letter. By February 20, 1865, it was printed. On that date he sent eight copies of it to his nephew, John Lancaster Spalding, then studying in Rome. The archbishop asked his nephew to deliver the copies of his pastoral letter to various people at Rome. He also asked him to see the papal secretary of state, Cardinal Giacomo Antonelli, and "ask explanations of the Nos. 55, 77, & 78 & 79 — which will be construed here as condemning our system of religious toleration so advantageous...to Religion." He feared that "these & some other propositions will furnish a pretext to the fanatics to persecute us...."[7]

---

6. Cited from the *The John Carroll Papers*, ed. Thomas O'Brien Hanley, 3 vols. (Notre Dame, Ind.: University of Notre Dame Press, 1976), 1:80–81, in James Hennesey, S.J., *American Catholics* (New York: Oxford University Press, 1981), 68.

7. Martin J. Spalding to John Lancaster Spalding, Baltimore, February 20, 1865, in John Tracy Ellis, "Some Student Letters of John Lancaster Spalding," *Catholic Historical Review* 29 (January 1944): 536. In a letter of January 5, 1865, to his uncle, the younger Spalding had already commented

Spalding's pastoral letter articulates what would become the standard Catholic reception of the Syllabus in the United States in terms of American exceptionalism. Spalding was delighted to see Bishop Dupanloup's pastoral letter and made reference to it in a supplement to the second edition of his own letter. But Dupanloup's distinction between the ideal or thesis and local accommodation or hypothesis was not Spalding's primary approach. Rather he distinguished between the unrestrained liberty advocated by "European Liberals" with their "anarchy and Jacobinism in politics" and liberty as understood in the United States. Central to American Catholic reception of the Syllabus would be the distinction between Europe and America, and the accompanying claim that, under the U.S. Constitution, the government is not indifferent to the moral law. "Is it not a sound canon of interpretation," Spalding asked, "to seek the meaning of a declaration, particularly if it be a solemn and official one, in the context and the circumstances which called it forth?"

> To stretch the words of the Pontiff, evidently intended for the stand-point of European radicals and infidels, so as to make them include the state of things as established in this country, by our noble Constitution, in regard to the liberty of conscience, of worship, and of the press, were manifestly unfair and unjust.[8]

In the same year as Spalding's pastoral letter, Orestes Brownson completed his major work, *The American Republic*. He too read the Syllabus in terms of the distinction between the Old World and the New. Brownson went so far as to claim that a real separation of church and state was "nowhere possible outside the United States" because "nowhere else is the state organized on catholic principles." To separate church and state as "external governing bodies" while "uniting them in the interior principles from which each derives its vitality and force" is the "religious mission of the United States."

This idea of a natural fit between American government and Catholic principles would be the hallmark of the Americanists of the 1890s. John Ireland called "America" "the providential nation." Both he and Isaac Hecker saw the relationship between church and state in the United States as a sign of the future for both church and world. Both were careful not to affirm separation of church and state as a universal theoretical ideal, but they promoted it as a providence for their time. By the 1920s, Michael Williams and John A. Ryan found themselves in a more defensive posture. Williams summed up the "real issue" of the Scopes trial in this question: "Are church and state to remain separate in the United States?" Separation of church and state would protect Catholics and others from laws that favored "what is called fundamentalist Protestantism." In entering the debate about Al Smith's candidacy in the 1928 election, Ryan could not avoid questions arising from Dupanloup's "thesis" position, or, what Ryan called the "Catholic doctrine on the union of Church and state." Ryan knew

---

on the Syllabus; see 532–33. Propositions 77, 78, and 79 dealt with religious liberty and freedom of conscience.

8. *Pastoral Letter of the Most Reverend Martin John Spalding, D.D.,* 2nd ed. (Baltimore: Kelly & Piet, 1865), 9–10.

that he could not deny the thesis. He could not affirm separation of church and state as an ideal but only the "existing separation of church and state." So he argued that the thesis or Catholic ideal applied only to Catholic states. It could never practically be realized in a nation such as the United States. With "But if it could...," always lingering over his arguments, this was an account of Catholic patriotism less robust than the Roaring Twenties might have required.

In the 1890s, Thomas Scott Preston, vicar general of the Archdiocese of New York, appealed against the Americanists to Proposition 55 of the Syllabus. Preston denied that "our republican form of government" is the best form of government. Rather he affirmed the thesis. The best form of government is "that where all believe in the true religion, or where the government supports the Church in the discharge of its high office, in leading men to their salvation." Denying one of the chief tenets of the Americanist position, Preston pointed to numerous examples where the state had failed to uphold the moral law. Joseph Clifford Fenton made similar arguments in the 1950s against John Courtney Murray. A Catholic "idea of a good civil society" had to include a "vigorous defence and support of the Church on the part of the government." Preston and Fenton considered history their strongest ally. Murray would try to steal it from them.

Murray's study of church and state in the 1940s and 1950s continued the familiar contrast between the American Revolution and the French Revolution. But Murray added a new twist. The distinction between church and state has its true origin in an older distinction in the European political tradition between the spiritual and temporal orders. The American Constitution embodies this pre-nineteenth-century distinction in a particularly fitting way. This was of "providential importance" for Catholics. "It serves sharply to set off our constitutional system from the system against which the Church waged its long-drawn-out fight in the nineteenth century, namely, Jacobinism...."

Murray had tried to restate the ideal in terms of an older distinction between the two realms. If he was correct, separation of church and state in the United States was not simply a privation of the ideal. In support of this historical retrieval, Murray had to explain religious freedom as a positive good. This would once and for all decouple religious freedom for Catholics in secular states from papal "sovereignty." Most importantly, Catholics could recognize freedom of religion and freedom of conscience as rights. No one could say that Catholics merely conceded these freedoms when they were not in the majority. Murray lived to see a major threat to the Americanist faith in the fit between America and Catholic principles and to the idea of a government that upholds the moral law. His image of the barbarian in a Brooks Brothers suit captures what Garry Wills calls, in this section's final selection, a "procedural" understanding of freedom.

## 45. John Carroll on the Pope as Spiritual Head of the Church, 1784

*Shortly after the American Revolution, the papal nuncio in Paris had contacted Benjamin Franklin to consult Congress for advice about the appropriate form of church government for the United States. It is the congressional reply to which Carroll refers here as testifying to Congress's lack of jurisdiction in spiritual matters.[1] In view of nineteenth-century developments, Carroll's understanding of the limitations of Pius VI's authority is noteworthy. In 1789 Carroll would be appointed the first American bishop.*

Dr. Franklin has sent in to Congress a copy of a note delivered him by the Nuncio at Paris, which I shall enclose in this. I did not see it before Congress had sent their instructions to their Minister in answer thereto; and the answer, I am well informed, is, that Congress have no answer to give, the matter proposed not being in their department, but resting with the different States. But this you may be assured of; that no authority derived from the Propaganda will ever be admitted here; that the Catholick Clergy & Laity here know that the only connexion they ought to have with Rome is to acknowledge the pope as the Spirl[*sic*] head of the Church; that no Congregations existing in his states shall be allowed to exercise any share of his Spirl authority here; that no Bishop Vicar Apostolical shall be admitted; and if we are to have a Bishop, he shall not be *in partibus* but an ordinary national Bishop, in whose appointment Rome shall have no share.

John Carroll to Charles Plowden, April 10, 1784, in *The John Carroll Papers, vol. 1 1755–1791*, ed. Thomas O'Brien Hanley, S.J. (Notre Dame, Ind.: University of Notre Dame Press, 1976), 146. Printed with permission.

## 46. John England Addresses Congress, 1826

*Six years after his arrival in the United States from Ireland, the first bishop of Charleston, South Carolina, and founder of the first Catholic newspaper in the United States was invited to address Congress. He affirms a distinction between civil authority and spiritual authority, established to testify to revelation.*

A political difficulty has been sometimes raised here. If this infallible tribunal [the pope], which you profess yourselves bound to obey, should command you overturn our government, and tell you that it is the will of God to have it new modelled, will you be bound to obey it? And how then can we consider those men to be good citizens, who profess to owe obedience to a foreign authority, — to an authority not recognised in our constitution, — to an authority which has excommunicated and deposed sovereigns, and which has absolved subjects and citizens from their bond of allegiance.

Our answer to this is extremely simple and very plain; it is, that we would not be bound to obey it, — that we recognise no such authority. I would not

1. On this episode, see James Hennesey, S.J., *American Catholics* (New York: Oxford University Press, 1981), 71.

allow to the Pope, or to any bishop of our church, outside this Union, the smallest interference with the humblest vote at our most insignificant balloting box. He has no right to such interference. You must, from the view which I have taken, see the plain distinction between spiritual authority and a right to interfere in the regulation of human government or civil concerns. You have in your constitution wisely kept them distinct and separate. It will be wisdom and prudence and safety to continue the separation. Your constitution says that Congress shall have no power to restrict the free exercise of religion. Suppose your dignified body to-morrow attempted to restrict me in the exercise of that right; though the law, as it would be called, should pass your two houses, and obtain the signature of the president, I would not obey it, because it would be no law, it would be an usurpation; for you cannot make a law in violation of your constitution — you have no power in such a case. So, if that tribunal which is established by the Creator to testify to me what he has revealed, and to make the necessary regulations of discipline for the government of the church, shall presume to go beyond that boundary which circumscribes its power, its acts are invalid; my rights are not to be destroyed by its usurpation; and there is no principle of my creed which prevents my suing my natural right of proper resistance to any tyrannical usurpation. You have no power to interfere with my religious rights; the tribunal of the church has no power to interfere with my civil rights. It is a duty which every good man ought to discharge for his own, and for the public benefit, to resist any encroachment upon either. We do not believe that God gave to the church any power to interfere with our civil rights, or our civil concerns. Christ our Lord refused to interfere in the division of the inheritance between two brothers, one of whom requested that interference. The civil tribunals of Judea were vested with sufficient authority for that purpose, and he did not transfer it to his Apostles. It must hence be apparent, that any idea of the Roman Catholics of these republics being in any way under the influence of any foreign ecclesiastical power, or indeed of any church authority in the exercise of their civil rights, is a serious mistake. There is no class of our fellow citizens more free to think and to act for themselves on the subject of our rights, than we are; and I believe there is not any portion of the American family more jealous of foreign influence, or more ready to resist it. We have brethren of our church in every part of the globe, under every form of government; this is a subject upon which each of us is free to act as he thinks proper. We know of no tribunal in our church which can interfere in our proceedings as citizens. Our ecclesiastical authority existed before our constitution, is not affected by it; there is not in the world a constitution which it does not precede, with which it could not coexist; it has seen nations perish, dynasties decay, empires prostrate; it has coexisted with all, it has survived them all, it is not dependent upon any one of them; they may still change and it will continue.

John England, "Address before Congress," January 8, 1826, in *The Works of the Right Reverend John England, First Bishop of Charleston,* ed. Sebastian G. Messmer (Cleveland: Arthur H. Clark Co., 1908), 7:32–33.

## 47. Orestes Brownson on the Political Destiny of the United States, 1865

*Philosopher, editor, and perhaps the most formidable intellect in the nineteenth-century U.S. church, Brownson is led by the Civil War to reflect on the nature of the American Republic. He articulates a providential understanding of its unique mission as a state truly organized on catholic or universal principles embodied in separation of church and state.*

The political destiny of the United States is to conform the state to the order of reality, or, so to speak, to the Divine Idea in creation. Their religious destiny is to render practicable and to realize the normal relations between church and state, religion and politics, as concreted in the life of the nation.

In politics, the United States are not realizing a political theory of any sort whatever. They, on the contrary, are successfully refuting all political theories, making away with them, and establishing the state — not on a theory, not on an artificial basis or a foundation laid by human reason or will, but on reality, the eternal and immutable principles in relation to which man is created. They are doing the same in regard to religious theories. Religion is not a theory, a subjective view, an opinion, but is, objectively, at once a principle, a law, and a fact, and, subjectively, it is, by the aid of God's grace, practical conformity to what is true and real. The United States, in fulfillment of their destiny, are making as sad havoc with religious theories as with political theories, and are pressing on with irresistible force to the real or the Divine order which is expressed in the Christian mysteries, which exists independent of man's understanding and will, and which man can neither make nor unmake....

But while the church, with her essential constitution, and her dogmas are founded in the Divine order, and are catholic and unalterable, the relations between civil and ecclesiastical authorities may be changed or modified by the changes of time and place. These relations have not always been the same, but have differed in different ages and centuries. During the first three centuries of our era the church had no legal *status,* and was either connived at or persecuted by the state. Under the Christian emperors she was recognized by the civil law; her prelates had exclusive jurisdiction in mixed civil and ecclesiastical questions, and were made, in some sense, civil magistrates, and paid as such by the empire. Under feudalism, the prelates received investiture as princes and barons, and formed alone, or in connection with the temporal lords, an estate in the kingdom. The Pope became a temporal prince and suzerain, at one time, of a large part of Europe, and exercised the arbitratorship in all grave questions between Christian sovereigns themselves, and between them and their subjects. Since the downfall of feudalism and the establishment of modern centralized monarchy, the church has been robbed of the greater part of her temporal possessions, and deprived, in most countries, of all civil functions, and treated by the state either as an enemy or as a slave.

In all sectarian and schismatic states of the Old World, the national church is held in strict subjection to the civil authority, as in Great Britain and Russia, and is the slave of the state; in the other states of Europe, as France, Austria,

Spain, and Italy, she is treated with distrust by the civil government, and allowed hardly a shadow of freedom and independence. In France, which has the proud title of eldest daughter of the church, Catholics, as such, are not freer than they are in Turkey. All religions are said to be free, and all are free, except the religion of the majority of Frenchmen. The emperor, because nominally a Catholic, takes it upon himself to concede the church just as much and just as little freedom in the empire as he judges expedient for his own secular interests. In Italy, Spain, Portugal, Mexico, and the Central and South American states, the policy of the civil authorities is the same, or worse. It may be safely asserted that, except in the United States, the church is either held by the civil power in subjection, or treated as an enemy. The relation is not that of union and harmony, but that of antagonism, to the grave detriment of both religion and civilization.

It is impossible, even if it were desirable, to restore the mixture of civil and ecclesiastical governments which obtained in the Middle Ages; and a total separation of church and state, even as corporations, would, in the present state of men's minds in Europe, be construed, if approved by the church, into a sanction by her of political atheism, or the right of the civil power to govern according to its own will and pleasure in utter disregard of the law of God, the moral order, or the immutable distinctions between right and wrong. It could only favor the absolutism of the state, and put the temporal in the place of the spiritual. Hence the Holy Father includes the proposition of the entire separation of church and state in the Syllabus of Errors condemned in his Encyclical, dated at Rome, December 8, 1864. Neither the state nor the people, elsewhere than in the United States, can understand practically such separation in any other sense than the complete emancipation of our entire secular life from the law of God, or the Divine order, which is the real order. It is not the union of church and state — that, the union, or identity rather, of religious and political principles — that is desirable to get rid of, but the disunion or antagonism of church and state. But this is nowhere possible out of the United States; for nowhere else is the state organized on catholic principles, or capable of acting, when acting from its own constitution, in harmony with a really catholic church, or the religious order really existing, in relation to which all things are created and governed. Nowhere else is it practicable, at present, to maintain between the two powers their normal relations.

But what is not practicable in the Old World is perfectly practicable in the New. The state here being organized in accordance with catholic principles, there can be no antagonism between it and the church. Though operating in different spheres, both are, in their respective spheres, developing and applying to practical life one and the same Divine Idea. The church can trust the state, and the state can trust the church. Both act from the same principle to one and the same end. Each by its own constitution co-operates with, aids, and completes the other. It is true the church is not formally established as the civil law of the land, nor is it necessary that she should be; because there is nothing in the state that conflicts with her freedom and independence, with her dogmas or with her irreformable canons. The need of establishing the church by law, and protecting her by legal pains and penalties, as is still done in most countries, can exist only in a barbarous or semi-barbarous state of society, where the state is not organized on catholic principles, or the civilization is based on false principles and its development tends not to the real or Divine order of things. When the state is constituted in harmony with that order, it is carried onward by the force of its own internal constitution in a catholic direction, and a church establishment, or what is called a state religion, would be an anomaly or a superfluity. The true religion is in the heart of the state, as its informing principle and real interior life. The external establishment, by legal enactment of the church, would afford her no additional protection, add nothing to her power and efficacy, and effect nothing for faith or piety — neither of which can be forced, because both must, from their nature, be free-will offerings to God....

The religious mission of the United States is not then to establish the church by external law, or to protect her by legal disabilities, pains, and penalties against the sects, however uncatholic they may be; but to maintain catholic freedom, neither absorbing the state in the church nor the church in the state, but leaving each to move freely, according to its own nature, in the sphere assigned to it in the eternal order of things. Their mission separates church and state as external governing bodies, but unites them in the interior principles from which each derives its vitality and force. Their union is in the intrinsic unity of principle, and in the fact that, though moving in different spheres, each obeys one and the same Divine law. With this the Catholic, who knows what Catholicity means, is of course satisfied, for it gives the church all the advantage over the sects of the real over the unreal; and with this the sects have no right to be dissatisfied, for it subjects them to no disadvantage not inherent in sectarianism itself in presence of Catholicity, and without any support from the civil authority.

Orestes A. Brownson, *The American Republic: Constitution, Tendencies, and Destiny* (New York: P. O'Shea, 1865), 411–18, 428.

## 48. Isaac Hecker on the Providential Relationship between Church and State in the United States, 1887

*A disciple of Brownson early in his life, Hecker shared Brownson's providential vision of America, especially with regard to separation of church and state. More hopeful than his mentor, Hecker insists that the U.S. government, while indifferent to ecclesiastical affairs, is not morally neutral. Rather it upholds the natural law and the gospel.*

No one can appreciate the depth of conviction and the strength of affection of Catholics for republican institutions unless he sees, as they do, the same order of truths which serve as the foundation of his religious belief underlying the free institutions of his country. The doctrines of the Catholic Church alone give to popular rights, and governments founded thereupon, an intellectual basis, and furnish their vital principle. What a Catholic believes as a member of the Catholic Church he believes as a citizen of the republic. His religion consecrates his political convictions, and this consecration imparts a two-fold strength to his patriotism.

What a Catholic believes as a citizen of the republic he believes as a member of the Catholic Church; and as the natural supports and strengthens the supernatural, this accounts for the universally acknowledged fact that no Catholics are more sincere in their religious belief, more loyal to the authority of the Church, more generous in her support, than the Catholic republican citizens of the United States. Catholicity in religion sanctions republicanism in politics, and republicanism in politics favors catholicity in religion....

He who does not see the hand of Divine Providence leading to the discovery of the western continent, and directing its settlement and subsequent events towards a more complete application to political society of the universal truths affirmed alike by human reason and Christianity, will fail to interpret rightly and adequately the history of the United States....

Here in America, when Church and state come together, the state says, I am not competent in ecclesiastical affairs; I leave religion its full liberty. That is what is meant here by separation of Church and state, and that is precisely what Europeans cannot or will not understand. They want to make out that the American state claims to be indifferent to religion. They accuse us of having a theory of government which ignores the moral precepts of the natural law and of the Gospel. Such is not the case, and never has been from the beginning. That is a false interpretation of the American state. By ecclesiastical affairs we mean that organic embodiment of Christianity which the Church is in her creeds, her hierarchy, and her polity. The American state says in reference to all this, I have no manner of right to meddle with you; I have no jurisdiction. By morals, on the other hand, we mean those influences of natural and revealed religion whose sway is general among the vast popular electorate of our country, uniform and definite enough to be a quickening influence upon our public life. To disregard this has ever been deemed a crime against good government among us, and punished accordingly....

If, as many think, democracy will soon assume control of public affairs in the old world, the question is, What kind of a democracy will it be; what influence will be powerful enough to guide it morally aright? No sectarian form of Christianity can be the guide of mighty human forces. So far as men are sectarians, so far do they deviate from the universal truth; and only the universal principles of reason and revelation grasped and wielded by such an organic world-power as the Catholic Church can guide aright the tumultuous masses of mankind when the transition from one phase of civilization to another has begun. The power that could tame the barbarian ancestors of the civilized world exhibits...a force competent to guide to its proper destiny the baptized democracy of our day.

Isaac Hecker, *The Church and the Age* (New York: H. J. Hewit, 1887), 86–87, 99, 113–14.

## 49. John Ireland on the Church as the Mother of Liberty and the United States as a Providential Nation, 1905

*Proclaiming a fit between Catholicism and the political institutions of the United States, the archbishop of St. Paul draws upon a counter-Enlightenment apologetic that presents the church as the civilizing agent of Europe. America's providential role is to continue the work of the church as mother of liberty.*

You ask: What is the attitude of the Catholic Church toward a republican form of government? The reply has substantially been given. The Church teaches that the choice of constitutions and of rulers lies with the people. Whether they shall have an empire, a monarchy, or a republic, it is their privilege to decide, according as their needs may suggest or their desires may lead. In this matter the Church is from her principles without a voice. This is the emphatic declaration of Pope Leo.[1]

It is for the people to speak; it is for the Church to consecrate and enforce their will. When, under due conditions, the people have constituted a government over themselves, whatever the form, in itself legitimate, this government may have, the Church commands obedience to it. It is, consequently, Catholic doctrine that in America loyalty to the Republic is a divine precept, and that resistance to law is a sin crying out to heaven for vengeance. To the Republic in America the Church accords the honor and respect due to the representative of divine authority in temporal matters, and her prayer for the Republic is that it may secure to the people what its professions permit them to expect — the largest possible share of civil liberty.

I lose patience when I hear prejudice still asserting that the Catholic Church is not the friend of free institutions. Could her teachings be more explicit? Has her history belied those teachings? The life, the soul of a republic is an intense love of civil liberty: has not the Church always labored to create and strengthen this love? Have not her efforts been always in the direction of personal dignity and of the rights of the individual? Was it not under her guidance that the Middle Ages gradually emerged from Roman despotism and barbarian feudalism into the possession of political liberty? Did she not, by abolishing slavery and serfdom, widen the ranks of freemen and citizens? Were not her bishops parties to all the charters of liberty wrenched from absolute monarchs? Were not parliaments and trial by jury the institutions of Catholic ages? Were not the fueros and communes of the Middle Ages the freest forms of municipal regimes? Are not the names of the Italian republics of Genoa, Pisa, Sienna, Florence, Venice, familiar to all students of history? Does not Switzerland, that classic land of mountain liberty, shoot into remote Catholic centuries the roots of her republican institutions? I may in all truth add that if the world is to-day capable of understanding and maintaining political liberty, it is due to the Church's long and painful elaboration of European civ-

---

1. Here Ireland cites Pope Leo XIII's encyclical *Diuturnum* (1881) and then a long passage from the same pope's letter to French Catholics (February 16, 1892) urging them to "rally" to the Third Republic.

ilization. Our radicals, I presume, wonder that the hordes led by Attila and Genseric were not at once educated by the Church into the intricacies of parliamentary debate and presidential campaigning. The action of the Church in the world is, as the action of God, strongest when mildest, sowing seeds in due season and awaiting due season to reap the harvest, educating nations as a parent educates the child. This much certainly is manifest from history, that the Church has encouraged the fullest development of personal freedom and personal rights, and that so far as political liberty is compatible with civil liberty, and avoids anarchy no less than despotism, she rejoices in its widest expansion.

I do not say that Catholics of all countries will profess, or that Catholics of all past ages would have professed, my own love and admiration for the republican form of government. The choice of governments the Church leaves to nations, and here, as in all questions open to free discussion, men differ. In other places Catholics see matters from local points of view; they judge from local experiences; they are influenced by the public opinion, or the prejudices, of their several countries. This much, however, I know, that if they prefer other forms, they are not compelled in their choice by Catholic principles or Catholic history. This much too, I know, that I do not transgress Catholic teaching when I speak forth my own judgment this evening, and salute the republic as the form of government which I most admire and love....

Let me state, as I conceive it, the work which, in God's providence, the Catholics of the United States are called to do within the coming century. It is twofold: To make America Catholic, and to solve for the Church universal the all-absorbing problems with which religion is confronted in the present age. Never, I believe, since the century the dawn of which was the glimmer from the Eastern Star, was there prepared for Catholics of any nation of earth a work so noble in its nature and so pregnant with consequences as that which it is our mission to accomplish. The work defines the measure of the responsibility.

The work is to make America Catholic. As we love America, as we love the Church, it suffices to mention the work, and our cry shall be, "God wills it," and our hearts shall leap towards it with Crusader enthusiasm. We know that the Church is the sole owner of the truths and graces of salvation. Would we not that she pour upon the souls of friends and fellow-citizens the gifts of the Incarnate God? The touch of her sacred hand will strengthen and sublimate the rich heritage of nature's virtues, which is the portion of America and America's children; it will add the deifying treasures of supernatural life. The Catholic Church will preserve as no human power, no human church can preserve, the liberties of the Republic. We know that by the command of the Master it is the bounden duty of the Church to teach all nations. To lose the apostolic spirit were, on her part, to give proof that she is unconscious of the truths which she owns and the commission under which she exists. The conversion of America should ever be present to the minds of Catholics in America as a supreme duty from which God will not hold them exempt. If we are loyal to duty, the record of our second century of Church history will tell of the wondrous spread of Christ's Church over the United States of America....

I have called America the providential nation. Even as I believe that God rules over men and nations, so do I believe that a divine mission has been assigned to the Republic of the United States. That mission is to prepare the world, by example and moral influence, for the universal reign of human liberty and human rights. America does live for herself alone; the destinies of humanity are in her keeping. No Monroe Doctrine confines her democracy within Atlantic and Pacific shores. American citizenship sustains the liberties of humanity. In Washington's day, the spirit of America, which the soldiers of Lafayette and Rochambeau had borne to their homes, hastened the French revolution. In Europe, however, Liberty was retarded in her progress by the wild excesses of her own champions; but, drawing courage and hope from America's democracy, she never ceased to struggle until Europe became, in fact, if not in name, free and democratic. To-day, France is a well established republic; Spain and Italy have reached the confines of republican regime; Germany elects her parliament, which a Hohenzollern emperor fears and obeys; in England suffrage is almost universal; in Belgium it is entirely so; in Russia the government must reckon with the masses of the population, and even in far-off Japan a representative parliament divides the supreme power with the occupant of the once deified throne of the Mikado; but towering amid them all, America rises before the whole world, in the power and majesty of personified democracy, the hope of liberty's friends, the despair of liberty's foes. O America, guard well thyself! For if thou fail, the hopes of humanity fail with thee.

> John Ireland, *The Church and Modern Society* (St. Paul: Pioneer Press, 1905), 1:60–63, 73–74, 192–93.

## 50. Thomas Scott Preston Invokes the Syllabus, 1891

*Having entered the Catholic Church in 1849 as part of the American Oxford movement, the vicar general of the Archdiocese of New York was vigorously Ultramontane in his theology. Dissenting in this text from Americanist faith in the moral character and providential role of U.S. political institutions, he affirms the ideal of a union between church and state in which the state supports the church.*

The doctrine that our republican form of government — good in itself, fitted to our state of society, and, in reality, having its source in the application of the principles of our religion — is the best form of government for all the nations of the earth, or the only form of government, cannot be held by any Catholics, whether they be Americans or of another nationality. We yield to no one in devotion to our own country; nevertheless, we cannot hold that the best form of government is that in which the Church is entirely separate from the State and the State from the Church. Such a proposition is condemned by the Holy See in the Syllabus of Pius IX. Proposition 55 declares:

"The Church should be separated from the State and the State from the Church."[1]

Undoubtedly, that form of government which does not interfere with the Church in any way is better than the form which persecutes the Church, which deprives it of its rightful liberty, which imprisons its priests and its ministers; but this does not make it the very best form of government. The governing authorities in any nation are as much bound to obey the Catholic religion as any individual. And nations, as such, are as much under the obedience of God as are individuals. The best form of government is that where all believe in the true religion, or where the government supports the Church in the discharge of its high office, in leading men to their salvation. This, although perhaps at the present time existing nowhere, is, nevertheless the best form, and although we do not ask a government like our own to interfere in any ecclesiastical matters — while on the contrary we deny its right to interfere in matters purely religious — nevertheless we cannot hold, as Catholics, that a Christian or a Catholic State should not work in harmony with the Church of God, to which are committed the highest interests of man. We cannot call our own form of government religious in any sense. There is a bare recognition of God and also an implicit recognition of many precepts of the natural law; still, we cannot call it a Christian government in the true sense of the word.

And it leads to a grave error to say that the State should always be separated from the Church and the Church from the State, as if they were different bodies, each one moving in its different sphere, and the spiritual having no authority, even indirectly, over the temporal.

The State has already, not only here but in the old world, interfered with the observance of the law of God, and has sanctioned that which, according to the divine law, is positively wrong. For example, the State has sanctioned divorce, thereby destroying the sacred character of Christian matrimony and allowing parties properly married to be separated, so as to annul the bond of matrimony....

Another most grave error which concerns the very foundation of Christianity is that which, unfortunately, is widespread, the error that religion and education can be separated without vital injury to the Commonwealth....

To a Catholic mind, to one who believes in Christianity, and to one who has studied at all the lessons of history, it is evident that education without religion is the source of infidelity, and therefore is destructive of human liberty, properly so-called. Catholics cannot approve of any system of education which is separated from religion or from the strict teaching of the principles of their faith. We are not by any means willing to hold that Americanism is infidelity, so therefore we do not understand why any of our fellow-citizens favor the separation entirely of religion from common education.

Thomas Scott Preston, "American Catholicity," *American Catholic Quarterly Review* 62 (April 1891): 401–2.

---

1. *"Ecclesia a statu, Statusque ab Ecclesia sejungendus est."*

## 51. Michael Williams on the Scopes Trial, 1925

*Commonweal had just begun publishing the previous November, when, in July
1925, founding editor Michael Williams traveled to Dayton, Tennessee, to cover
the Scopes Trial. Though he had little use for Clarence Darrow's public swipes
at biblical religion, and much sympathy for William Jennings Bryan's attempts to
defend revelation, Williams saw the key issue in the trial as separation of church
and state.*

The Scopes case was like a hall meant for a great debate on topics of the most
serious import: religion, science, human liberty, man's soul and God — a hall
in which clowns jostled the lecturers, and sometimes lectured themselves, while
so many gargoyles had been stuck on the walls and ceilings that the assembled
crowds could only stare, or guffaw, or shake their heads in bewilderment.

This journal stated before the trial began that the accompaniments of the
case, in the way of publicity stunts, circus features, and the preliminary bally-
hooing, were most likely to destroy whatever value it might otherwise possess
as an agency to turn men's minds to the serious consideration of the relation
between science and religion. The reality of what occurred at Dayton surpassed
anticipations. The above opinion still seems a valid one....

There remain still other observers of the case, however, who say that no matter what action is taken among the possible ones outlined above, the supreme
issue of the Dayton case had but barely been glimpsed during the somewhat far-
cical proceedings marking this fantastic trial. This issue they see as more vitally
important by far than the rather trite and factitious issues raised by Darrow, in
a somewhat mid-Victorian style about which clung the acrid dust of the justly
forgotten pages of Draper and White — the science vs. religion, and the conflict
between freedom of thought and dogmatism, out-moded now, but which was in
the air when both Mr. Bryan and Mr. Darrow were very young men.

The real issue was so simple that eleven words could express it — namely: Are
church and state to remain separate in the United States? Perhaps that was why
it was so seldom discussed by the prolix counsel representing the supposedly
embattled forces of freedom. Most of them required thousands of words with
which to say that two and two are four. They were orating about fundamentalism
and modernism, and about Galileo and Copernicus, or Darwin and monkeys,
when the great names that really mattered, and the fundamentalism that was
really concerned, were the names of the Fathers of the Constitution and their
fundamental principle that no religious body, whether a majority or a minority,
could or should write their religious tenets into the law of this republic.

There were a few newspapers that discussed this real issue, and at Dayton the
minds of those concerned in the trial were veering towards its full consideration before the trial blew up as if it were a giant motor truck thundering along
until all its tires burst with a "wow!" of hot air. Had the trial proceeded, however, this real issue would have received attention from both sides. The learned,
if somewhat tedious, professors of the 'isms and 'ologies would have had to
take a back seat. The summing-up speeches, in that case, would have been a real
summing-up of the real issue of the Scopes case.

Even so, the verdict, no matter what, would not have disposed of the matter. There will be other laws similar in essence to the Tennessee anti-evolution law, the intent of these laws being to give what is called fundamentalist Protestantism a favored and predominant position — protected, fostered, backed by the state. The verdict to be given as to whether the American people will, or will not, tolerate or permit this to come about, cannot be given for a long time yet. But that they will be asked — rather compelled by the pressure of events — to render such a verdict, can scarcely be doubted by any competent observer of the doings at Dayton. That this issue is supremely a political one is obvious.

There remains still another issue, which not only was not summed up at Dayton, but also could not be summed up by any judge, or any counsel, any more than it could be settled by the verdict of any jury. This is the issue which John Henry Newman had in mind, when in his Apologia he summed up the events and conclusions of his own religious struggle — the issue that comes when each man must face the ultimate realities of self and God.

Despite the crudities — many startling, some most deplorable, others socially dangerous — of the late Mr. Bryan and the fundamentalists, they have shouted, raucously it may be, yet in a way that compels attention, a question which each and every soul must face, as Newman faced it — even if not to the same answering act of faith.

The question is — "What think you of God?"

> Michael Williams, "Summing-Up at Dayton," *Commonweal* 2, no. 13 (August 5, 1925): 304–5.

## 52. John A. Ryan on Union of Church and State, 1928

*The 1928 presidential election placed the leading moral theologian at Catholic University and social action director for the National Catholic Welfare Conference in a difficult position. Even as he denies its practical possibility in the United States — or anywhere else that he can think of — Ryan affirms as Catholic doctrine a theoretical ideal of union between church and state.*

Within the last year, we in the United States have heard a great deal about the conflicts between civil and religious loyalty which are thought to arise out of the Catholic doctrine on the union of Church and state. Even if this doctrine were universally applicable, the resulting "conflicts" would not be nearly so serious as those persons have assumed who mistakenly think that it vitally affects American Catholics. In that hypothesis the Catholic citizen would be confronted by about the same difficulties and inconveniences that result from the discrepancies between the civil law and the canon law on the subject of marriage. The Church desires that marriage should be governed by certain regulations and endowed with certain qualities which the state does not accept. If the Church commanded a union of Church and state in our country, she would likewise be confronted by the refusal of the state to accept that arrangement. In this situation the Catholic citizen would not be forbidden by the state to do anything which the Church commanded; nor would he be required by the

Church to do anything which the state forbade. Even if the Church were to require her subjects to strive by constitutional means for the union of Church and state, compliance would not bring them into direct conflict with any organic or statute law of the land.

Of course, the Church is not going to do anything of the sort. The American Hierarchy is only well satisfied with the kind of separation which exists in this country but would oppose any suggestion of union between the two powers. No Pope has expressed the wish for a change in the present relation between Church and state in America, nor is any Pope likely to do so within any period of time that is of practical interest to this generation. The fundamental reason lies in the fact that a formal union is desirable and could be effective only in Catholic states. Only there does the Catholic doctrine of the union of Church and state find its specific application. What is a Catholic state? It is a political community that is either exclusively or almost exclusively made up of Catholics. A very high German authority, Father Pohle, declares that "there is good reason to doubt if there still exists a purely Catholic state in the world," and that the condemnation of Pope Pius IX of the public toleration of non-Catholic sects "does not now apply even to Spain or to South American republics, to say nothing of countries possessing a greatly mixed population." The following is his interpretation of the general rule, or general principle, on this subject: "When several religions have formally established themselves and taken root in the same territory, nothing else remains for the state than either to exercise tolerance toward them all, or, as conditions exist to-day, to make complete religious liberty for individuals and religious bodies a principle of government."[1]

Therefore, the Catholic citizen can conscientiously render full loyalty to the existing separation of Church and state, nor is he under any sort of obligation to strive for a union between them. Ignoring this decisive fact, more than one prominent person has within the last year adduced the general principle of union between Church and state as an evidence of conflict between the Catholic Church and the American State. The most conspicuous of these was Mr. Charles C. Marshall in his "Open Letter to the Honorable Alfred E. Smith."[2] His argument may be thus summarized: Pope Leo XIII declared it unlawful for the state "to hold in equal favor different kinds of religion," while the Constitution of the United States forbids Congress to make any "law respecting an establishment of religion or prohibiting the free exercise thereof"; the same Pope denied that it would be universally lawful or expedient for Church and state to be, as in America, dissevered and divorced, but this is precisely the arrangement which is provided for in our Constitution; the Church claims the right to draw the line which separates its jurisdiction from that of the state, while the Constitution asserts that right for the state; finally, the Catholic Church claims the right to fix the conditions for the validity of all marriages

---

1. *The Catholic Encyclopedia*, article, "Tolerance."

2. *The Atlantic Monthly*, April 1927. [For a selection from Smith's response to Marshall, see Steven M. Avella and Elizabeth McKeown, eds., *Public Voices: Catholics in the American Context* (Maryknoll, N.Y.: Orbis Books, 1999), 156–57. Eds.]

of baptized persons, but the various states of the American Union claim and exercise this function.

The first two of these statements imply that American Catholics are required to believe that a union between their Church and state should be maintained in America. As already noted, this is a false assumption. The other two describe in theory and in practice, respectively, the possibility of some kind of conflict between the Catholic Church and the American state. As pointed out above, however, a genuine conflict has rarely, if ever, occurred in their mutual relations; for the great majority of the differences between civil and canonical legislation on education and marriage do not exhibit contradictory commands. They consist in the fact that what the Church permits, the state invalidates, and what the Church invalidates or forbids, the state permits. The situations are extremely few in which the Church commands one thing and the state forbids that identical thing. Even in those very rare cases, Catholic citizens have been able so to conduct themselves, so to make concessions, that they have not placed themselves in a position of violating the civil laws, with regard to either education or marriage.

John A. Ryan, *The Catholic Church and the Citizen* (New York: Macmillan, 1928), 30–34.

## 53. Joseph Clifford Fenton Defends the "Thesis," 1950

*Arguing from the official liturgical ceremony for the benediction and coronation of kings, the editor of the* American Ecclesiastical Review *and Roman-trained Catholic University theologian defends as Catholic doctrine the ideal of a government that supports the church's mission.*

The essential point is, however, that under the circumstances to which the ceremony of the *Pontificale Romanum* looks, when the people and the rulers are members of the Catholic Church, the Church considers it the duty and the privilege of the government to act precisely as the government of a Catholic state, to protect and to foster the true faith, and to be of assistance in the work of the Church itself. The official prayer of the Church certainly gives no indication that a state composed of Catholics would be doing its duty merely in giving the Church the same liberties it would accord to some spurious religion.

Furthermore, we must realize that the *Pontificale Romanum*, in describing this sacramental, has in mind what authors dealing with the question of Church and state call the *thesis* rather than the *hypothesis*. This, in the absolute sense, is what a state should be with reference to the Church itself. Obviously the Church does not mean to imply that hereditary monarchy, or, for that matter, any other form of monarchy, is inseparable from the concept of a truly Catholic state. It does, however, imply that a vigorous defence and support of the Church on the part of the government (whatever form that government may take) is involved in the idea of a good civil society among Catholics.

Joseph Clifford Fenton, "The Relationship of the Christian State to the Catholic Church according to the *Pontificale Romanum*," *American Ecclesiastical Review* 123 (September 1950): 217.

## 54. John Courtney Murray on Religious Liberty and the Distinction between Church and State, 1960

*The editor of* Theological Studies *and professor of dogmatic theology at the Jesuits' Woodstock College was Msgr. Fenton's theological adversary during much of the 1940s and 1950s. Calling upon the unlikely pair of Roger Williams and Pope Pius XII, he affirms religious liberty as a good in itself and finds the source of the American distinction between church and state in pre-Enlightenment European political tradition.*

It remains only to insist that in regarding the religion clauses of the First Amendment as articles of peace and in placing the case for them on the primary grounds of their social necessity, one is not taking low ground. Such a case does not appeal to mean-spirited expediency nor does it imply a reluctant concession to *force majeure*. In the science of law and the art of jurisprudence the appeal to social peace is an appeal to a high moral value. Behind the will to social peace there stands a divine and Christian imperative. This is the classic and Christian tradition.

Roger Williams himself was a powerful spokesman of it. "Sweet peace" (the phrase he uses in *The Bloudy Tenent*) stands at the center of his doctrine; and he adds in the same context that "if it be possible, it is the express command of God that peace be kept." In a letter of 1671 to John Cotton the younger he recalls with satisfaction that his second great work, *The Bloudy Tenent Still More Bloudy,* was received in England "with applause and thanks" as "professing that of necessity, yea, of Christian equity, there could be no reconciliation, pacification, or living together but by permitting of dissenting consciences to live amongst them." There is also, along with others, the strong statement with which he concludes his pamphlet, *The Hireling Ministry None of Christ's.* As the sum of the matter he proclaims the duty of the civil state in the current conditions of religious division "to proclaim free and impartial liberty to all the people of the three nations to choose and maintain that worship and ministry their souls and consciences are persuaded of; which act, as it will prove an act of mercy and righteousness to the enslaved nations, so it is a binding force to engage the whole and every interest and conscience to preserve the common freedom and peace." This is the whereby "civil peace and the beauty of civility and humanity [may] be obtained among the chief opposers and dissenters."

Roger Williams was no partisan of the view that all religions ought to be equally free because, for all anybody knows, they may all be equally true or false. He reckons with truth and falsity in honest fashion. Yet even in the case of a "false religion (unto which the civil magistrate dare not adjoin)" he recommends as the first duty of the civil magistrate "permission (for approbation he owes not to what is evil) and this according to Matthew 13:30, for public peace and quiet's sake." The reference is to the parable of the tares.

It is interesting that this same parable is referred to by Pius XII in his discourse to a group of Italian jurists on December 6, 1953. This discourse is a strong affirmation of the primacy of the principle of peace (or "union" which is the Pope's synonymous word) when it comes to dealing with the "difficulties and tendencies" which arise out of mankind's multiple pluralisms and dissensions. The "fundamental theoretical principle," says the Pope (and one should underscore the word, "theoretical"; it is not a question of sheer pragmatism, much less of expediency in the low sense), is this: "within the limits of the possible and the lawful, to promote everything that facilitates union and makes it more effective; to remove everything that disturbs it; to tolerate at times that which it is impossible to correct but which on the other hand must not be permitted to make shipwreck of the community from which a higher good is looked for." This higher good, in the context of the whole discourse, is "the establishment of peace."

From this firm footing of traditional principle the Pope proceeds to reject the view that would "solve" the problem of religious pluralism on the ultimate basis of doctrinaire argument: Religious and moral error have no rights and therefore must always be repressed when repression of them is possible. In contradiction of this view the Pope says after quoting the parable of the tares: "The duty of repressing religious and moral error cannot therefore be an ultimate norm of action. It must be subordinated to higher and more general norms which in some circumstances permit, and even perhaps make it appear the better course of action, that error should not be impeded in order to promote the greater good." The Pope makes a clear distinction between the abstract order of ethics or theology, where it is a question of qualifying doctrines or practices as true or false, right or wrong, and the concrete order of jurisprudence, where it is a question of using or not using the coercive instrument of law in favor of the true and the good, against the false and the wrong. In this latter order the highest and most general norm is the public peace, the common good in its various aspects. This is altogether a moral norm.

Roger Williams had many a quarrel with the Roman papacy; in fact, he wanted it abolished utterly. It is therefore piquant in itself, and also a testimony to the strength of the hold that the central Christian tradition had upon him, to read this basic principle of Catholic teaching in the *Bloudy Tenent:* "It must be remembered that it is one thing to command, to conceal, to approve evil: and another thing to permit and suffer evil with protestation against it or dislike of it, at least without approbation of it. This sufferance or permission of evil is not for its own sake but for the sake of the good, which puts a respect of goodness upon such permission." The "good" here is the public peace. Williams concludes the passage thus: "And therefore, when it crosseth not an absolute rule to permit and tolerate (as in the case of the permission of the souls and consciences of all men of the world), it will not hinder our being holy as He is holy in all manner of conversation." In substance, Pius XII says the same thing, that it crosseth not an absolute rule to permit within the civil community, as he says, "the free exercise of a belief and of a religious and moral practice which possess validity" in the eyes of some of its members.

In fact, the Pope goes much further when he flatly states that "in certain circumstances God does not give men any mandate, does not impose any duty, and does not even communicate the right to impede or to repress what is erroneous and false." The First Amendment is simply the legal enunciation of this papal statement. It does not say that there is not distinction between true and false religion, good and bad morality. But it does say that in American circumstances the conscience of the community, aware of its moral obligations to the peace of the community, and speaking therefore as the voice of God, does not give government any mandate, does not impose upon it any duty, and does not even communicate to it the right to repress religious opinions or practices, even thought they are erroneous and false.

On these grounds it is easy to see why the Catholic conscience has always consented to the religion clauses of the Constitution. They conform to the highest criterion for all legal ruling in this delicate matter. The criterion is moral; therefore the law that meets it is good, because it is for the common good. Therefore the consent given to the law is given on grounds of moral principle. To speak of expediency here is altogether to misunderstand the moral nature of the community and its collective moral obligation toward its own common good. The origins of our fundamental law are in moral principle; the obligations it imposes are moral obligations, binding in conscience. One may not, without moral fault, act against these articles of peace....

As has been said, Roger Williams was not a Father of the Federal Constitution. He is adduced here only as a witness, in his own way, to the genuine Western tradition of politics. The point is that the distinction of church and state, one of the central assertions of this tradition, found its way into the Constitution. There it received a special embodiment, adapted to the peculiar genius of American government and to the concrete conditions of American society....

The area of state — that is, legal — concern was limited to the pursuit of certain enumerated secular purposes (to say that the purposes are secular is not to deny that many of them are also moral; so for instance the establishment of justice and peace, the promotion of the general welfare, etc.). Thus made autonomous in its own sphere, government was denied all competence in the field of religion. In this field freedom was to be the rule and method; government was powerless to legislate respecting an establishment of religion and likewise powerless to prohibit the free exercise of religion. Its single office was to take legal or judicial steps necessary on given occasions to make effective the general guarantee of freedom.

The concrete applications of this, in itself quite simple, solution have present great historical and legal difficulties.... In particular, we have not yet found an answer to the question whether government can make effective the primary intention of the First Amendment, the guarantee of the freedom of religion, simply by attempting to make more and more "impregnable" what is called in Roger Williams' fateful metaphor, the "wall of separation" between church and state. However, what concerns us here is the root of the matter, the fact that the American Constitution embodies in a special way the traditional principle of the distinction between church and state.

For Catholics this fact is of great and providential importance for one major reason. It serves sharply to set off our constitutional system from the system against which the Church waged its long-drawn-out fight in the nineteenth century, namely, Jacobinism, or (in Carlton Hayes's term) sectarian Liberalism, or (in the more definitive term used today) totalitarian democracy.

It is now coming to be recognized that the Church opposed the "separation of church and state" of the sectarian Liberals because in theory and in fact it did not mean separation at all but perhaps the most drastic unification of church and state which history had known. The Jacobin "free state" was as regalist as the *ancien régime,* and even more so. Writing as a historian, de Tocqueville long ago made this plain. And the detailed descriptions which Leo XIII, writing as a theologian and political moralist, gave of the Church's "enemy" make the fact even more plain. Within this "free state" the so-called "free church" was subject to a political control more complete than the Tudor or Stuart or Bourbon monarchies dreamed of. The evidence stretches all the way from the Civil Constitution of the Clergy in 1790 to the Law of Separation in 1905....

Moreover, this was done on principle — the principle of the primacy of the political, the principle of "everything within the state, nothing above the state." This was the cardinal thesis of sectarian Liberalism, whose full historical development is now being witnessed in the totalitarian "people's democracies" behind the Iron Curtain. As the Syllabus and its explicatory documents — as well as the multitudinous writings of Leo XIII — make entirely clear, it was this thesis of the juridical omnipotence and omnicompetence of the state which was the central object of the Church's condemnation of the Jacobin development. It was because freedom of religion and separation of church and state were predicated on this thesis that the Church refused to accept them as a thesis.

This thesis was utterly rejected by the founders of the American Republic. The rejection was as warranted as it was providential, because this thesis is not only theologically heterodox, as denying the reality of the Church; it is also politically revolutionary, as denying the substance of the liberal tradition. The American thesis is that government is not juridically omnipotent. Its powers are limited, and one of the principles of limitation is the distinction between state and church, in their purposes, method, and manner of organization. The Jacobin thesis was basically philosophical; it derived from a sectarian concept of the autonomy of reason. It was also theological, as implying a sectarian concept of religion and of the church. In contrast, the American thesis is simply political. It asserts the theory of a free people under a limited government, a theory that is recognizably part of the Christian political tradition, and altogether defensible in the manner of its realization under American circumstances.

John Courtney Murray, S.J., *We Hold These Truths* (New York: Sheed & Ward, 1960), 60–63, 66–69.

## 55. Garry Wills on Freedom, 1964

*Stimulated by a controversy over the* National Review's *less than enthusiastic reception of Pope John XXIII's encyclical* Mater et Magistra *in 1961, Wills wrote "the first complete book in English to deal with the problem of establishing norms for the interpretation of encyclicals in political discourse." Against a merely procedural approach to freedom, he argues that freedom is rule.*

There is not only freedom in the Church; the Church contributes to freedom in many directions. I shall not try to deal with the paradox of freedom — that service is rule — in its central mystery, in the love of God that is man's greatest liberation, but in one of its lesser manifestations, where it touches on politics: it is one of freedom's paradoxes that the Church's law, informing conscience, is a liberating thing in itself. Catholics not only love freedom, but love a *freeing* thing.

The riddle of liberty lies in the relation between achieved contacts with reality (offering alternatives for choice yet also creating ties), and spontaneous action along the gamut of these contacts. To define liberty in isolation from the *mind* that frees by *knowing*, by making the commitment involved in an apprehension of things as true or good, is to avoid difficulties only by settling for unlivable simplicities. Freedom, for instance, has been defined as "release from restraints." Release of *what* from restraints? Is a stone free if we remove it from the push and pull of surrounding objects? . . . Is frontal lobotomy the ultimate in liberation? If one says that freedom is the release of *man* from restraints, one comes closer to the problem; but then one must decide what *restrains* man and what *sustains* him. Do not free man of oxygen, or the company of his fellows, or the irritation of thinking. As Chesterton remarked, one can free a tiger of his bars; but if you try to free him of his stripes, you destroy him.

And so the merely *procedural* definition of freedom, the attempt to define by saying "do this" (remove restraints), fails in its secret aim — which was to avoid facing the complexity of the problem. This is the mental evasion that has become so common in our world of process and quantification: men say, let us have more of good, whatever good is; and, rather than define what good is, they opt for more of everything, hoping good will somehow get increased also. But it will not work. One must decide what is good if one wants to have more of it. In the same way, one must come to know the *quality* of human liberty before one can evaluate maxims on how to increase it *quantitatively* (e.g., the more restraints removed, the freer we are). Freedom is a word that demands completion — free of what, free for what? Freedom, for a man, is freedom to act as a man. And so one must face the whole problem of *what man is* if one hopes to discuss the freedom proper to him. One can free man of error, of responsibility, of danger, by brutalizing or imprisoning him. This action would fit the merely mechanical definition — restraints *are* removed — but it will not embody the complete concept of freedom.

Nor is it possible, at this point, to take the jump that tempts theocratic politicians — to say that freedom is the freedom *to do good.* Either this is tautology (*all* choices are made under the aspect of good, of something desired) or it is an evasion of the problem exactly parallel to the libertarian's procedure: if "freedom to do good" is taken in a procedural way — the more objectively good acts that, by any means, get done, the more freedom there is — then one is denying the *central* good at issue here, the structure of man's nature, which makes him *responsible* for his own actions, good or bad. The ruler who would prevent evil thoughts by censorship process meant to keep men children is trying to "free" the tiger of his stripes, to take away man's noblest (if most dangerous) gifts —

the judging intellect, the executing will. The theocrat tries to undo the creative work of that God in whose name he violates the human person. Man, to the extent that he is man, must become increasingly responsible for his own actions. All education, social pressure, and political restraint should work in this direction. The attempt to define freedom procedurally as freedom to do *what one ought* fails as drastically as the definition that says it is the freedom to do *anything.* The stone does what it ought. But if man is to follow his nature, he must exercise his ability to choose, to be responsible for his preferences, to have dominion over his acts.

And so we return to the fact that freedom is rule. It cannot be treated as mere lack. The irony of the "liberal" definition of freedom is that it tries to ennoble the individual by defining his most precious quality in a passive way — as the removal of restraints *from* him, the making of an environment permeable by him. Freedom is not a quantitative process, and certainly not the result of that process. It is the quality of a certain *act* with certain *objects;* it is a spontaneity toward alternatives. In the political order, the work of the state is to throw man back, as far as possible, on himself as the ruler of his inner forum. The free man, said St. Thomas, is the master of his own movements, *dominus actuum suorum.*[1] So anti-monarchical was "liberal" thought, so frightened of "rule" as a "necessary evil," that this essential aspect of freedom was blotted out in subsequent discussion of the problem. Tyrants are not bad because they *rule,* because power is bad or the state is bad. They are *usurpers,* who rule where another has right. They are kings who trespass against the monarchy that every man possesses over himself. Their sin is not in being kings, but in denying the fact that monarchy is a fellowship. The tyrant is a regicide; and the "regicides" who have overthrown kings were sometimes the truest defenders of monarchy.

If the discussion of freedom is to get back on the right track, then, we must stop discussing it as the lack of rule, and see the way in which it is dominion over the self, and the origin of all right rule in the state. The "laboratory" approach to freedom and order as opposites to be combined in palatable mixture is an outgrowth of nineteenth-century scientism at its worst. To start a more fruitful discussion of the matter, one must reflect on the ways in which freedom is an exercise of *rule.* "Freedom of conscience" must rest on the truth that, as Newman says, "Conscience is an authority."[2]

Garry Wills, *Politics and Catholic Freedom* (Chicago: Henry Regnery, 1964), 271–74.

---

1. *C[ontra]G[entiles]II, 47.3.*
2. Essay on Keble.

## Part 6

# MORAL THEOLOGY
# AND SOCIAL THOUGHT

## Introduction

Unknown to medieval theologians, the distinction between dogmatic and moral theology arose in the modern period. The phrase *moral theology* could refer in principle to any faith-inspired systematic reflection on Christian living. In fact, moral theology has been uniquely Catholic. The Christian practice that first generated the discourse of moral theology is sacramental confession. The reforms of the sixteenth-century Council of Trent called for auricular confession of sins by number and kind. Developments in confessional practice in response to those reforms have largely determined the shape of Catholic moral theology into the twentieth century.

The modern textbook or "manual" of moral theology came into existence in the institutional context of the seminary system set up by the Council of Trent as part of its effort to reform the clergy. Manuals were designed to prepare future priests to hear confessions. Seminarians learned a technical vocabulary they would eventually use to help penitents identify the sins of which they would accuse themselves in confession. Essential to this vocabulary was the distinction between mortal and venial sin and the conditions for each. Case-based moral reasoning or casuistry helped confessors learn to judge whether they could grant absolution in the unique cases they encountered in confession. An elaborate system of classification of sins and methods of determining their relative gravity helped confessors assign appropriate penances.

The project of modern moral theology has the feel of encyclopedic rationalism and *l'esprit géométrique*. But a wise confessor could use the mechanics of the manuals for the genuine care of souls. Sacramental confession played a central role in the parish missions and revivals of piety that punctuated the age of reason. This was the context for the work of St. Alphonsus Liguori (1696–1787), premier moral theologian of the eighteenth century whose three-volume *Theologia moralis* appeared in 1779. In lesser hands, manualist moral theology could trivialize moral life by encouraging lax consciences in their rationalizations and contributing to the agonies of the scrupulous or the self-righteousness of the puritanical.

It was in the form of the manual that Catholic moral theology came to the United States. The most formidable nineteenth-century representative of the manualist tradition in the United States was Francis P. Kenrick. Born in Ireland and trained in theology at Rome, he came to the United States in the 1820s as a one-man seminary faculty for the frontier diocese of Bardstown, Kentucky. From 1830 to 1850, Kenrick was bishop of Philadelphia. He established a seminary for his diocese and in the 1830s began work on the multivolume manuals of dogmatic and moral theology that would be published during the next decade for use in his seminary.

Kenrick wrote his manuals in Latin. His training initiated him into an international, Rome-oriented intellectual culture that was growing with Ultramontanism in the nineteenth century. In the years before Pope Leo XIII further standardized it with his encyclical *Aeterni Patris* and the Thomistic revival in 1879, Giovanni Perrone epitomized this eclectic modern Scholasticism. Kenrick relied heavily upon him. Kenrick's manuals were widely used in the nineteenth century. Theologians cited him as an authority during the debates on papal infallibility at the First Vatican Council.

Kenrick's manuals, his works of controversy, and his edition of the New Testament establish his credentials as a world-class scholar. But his treatment of slavery reveals a serious weakness in the manual tradition of moral theology. As a system of thought designed for individual confessional practice, modern moral theology is ill-equipped to recognize or deal with social evil or structural sin. Writing more than a century later, and using Catholic attitudes to slavery as one of his examples, sociologist Paul Hanly Furfey would ask "how Catholics can devote so much time and effort to the study of the moral sciences and yet fail to recognize obvious and large-scale affronts to everything that those sciences imply" (doc. 63).

Following Roman law, Kenrick treats slavery as a natural social institution that can be conducted either justly or unjustly. In order to avoid anachronism, it should be recalled that Kenrick was hardly in a position to take the lead in a national debate. During the riots of 1844, nativist mobs burned two Philadelphia Catholic churches and sent Kenrick temporarily scurrying from the city. His main concern in *De servitute* was whether Catholic slaveholders should accuse themselves of sin in confession and whether confessors should expect them to. But his classical presumption in favor of the past blinded him even to the obvious question that arose from his own system and might have sent him beyond it, namely, whether chattel slavery as practiced in the United States was ever or could ever be conducted justly. This question is present in the text but Kenrick does not emphasize it.

The classical treatment of slavery as an inherited institution that must be conducted justly corresponds closely with the classical treatment of warfare. A century after Kenrick, a leading manualist did ask the hard question about just conduct in the matter of warfare. Referring to the time of his own theological training and early teaching, Richard McCormick recalls John C. Ford and his coauthor Gerald Kelly as "the best American proponents of Catholic moral theology in this era."[1] Ford courageously published his analysis of the morality

---

1. Richard A. McCormick, S.J., *Corrective Vision: Explorations in Moral Theology* (Kansas City: Sheed & Ward, 1994), 42.

of obliteration bombing in 1944 at the height of American involvement in and support for World War II. He repeatedly reminded readers that his perspective was "that of one trying to solve the general moral problem, not of teaching confessors at what point they must draw the line and refuse absolution" (doc. 60). Ford worked within the just-war theory and pushed hard on the question about just conduct of the war. Where Kenrick had failed to get beyond the acts of an individual slaveholder, Ford was able, within his own system, to go beyond questions about the acts of an individual bombardier.

In 1966, in the aftermath of Vatican II, a seventy-year-old but still feisty Paul Hanly Furfey urged Catholic theologians to develop a moral theology that was more "actor-oriented" and less "act-oriented" (doc. 63). Still presuming sacramental confession as the practical context for moral theology, Furfey urged theologians to be clearer about Christian obligations in areas of social morality such as race and war. In his ongoing efforts to respond to Vatican II's call for renewal in moral theology, Germain Grisez has, without losing Furfey's concern for clarity about obligation, moved in the direction of a more "actor-oriented" approach by emphasizing the much neglected notion of personal vocation.

Vatican II had not been the only impetus for Furfey's call for a more "actor-oriented" and socially aware moral theology. During his long life, Furfey was deeply marked by two other currents in American Catholic thought. One was the Christian pacifism of the Catholic Worker as articulated by Dorothy Day's "On the Use of Force" in the face of widespread American Catholic support for Generalissimo Franco in the Spanish Civil War. The other was what has been referred to earlier as the "second Americanism."[2]

Dorothy Day brought something different to moral theology in the United States, an evangelical resolve that served as a constant prod to natural law stabilities and presumptions during the time of the Catholic Renaissance. Her principled commitments and long-term fidelity to them commanded the respect of Catholics such as Cardinal Francis Spellman of New York who would not otherwise have been inclined to listen to her. The generations of Catholic Workers, from James O'Gara and David Skillen and John Cogley to Michael Harrington and Daniel Berrigan and David O'Brien to Michael Baxter and William Cavanaugh, have had an influence on church and country far in excess of their numbers. Most important for moral theology, the practices of peace-making and corporal and spiritual works of mercy had generated different forms of moral discourse that came to lie down next to natural law, like the lamb and the lion but not always in the manner of the peaceable kingdom.

The second current that flowed into Furfey's proposal for an "actor-centered" moral theology was the long tradition of American Catholic social thought in which he stood. It is best represented by John A. Ryan, one of Furfey's teachers at Catholic University and author of the Bishops' Program of Social Reconstruction in 1919. Ryan is unquestionably the most important Catholic social thinker in the first half of the twentieth century. He is also a second-generation Americanist, a priest of the Archdiocese of St. Paul sent by John Ireland in 1898 to

---

2. See chap. 1, Introduction, n. 6.

study at Catholic University's recently founded School of the Social Sciences. Here Thomas Bouquillon and William Kerby introduced him to a form of social and economic thought that was as concerned about the poor as it was about science. After a stint at John Ireland's seminary, Ryan returned to Catholic University in 1915. He combined the neo-Scholasticism of the Catholic Renaissance with progressive social reform and the enduring Americanist spirit of positive engagement of the church with society and its needs.

For most of the twentieth century, Catholic moral theology would keep its connection to confessional practice and, to use Furfey's term, it would be thematically "act-oriented." During the 1950s and 1960s, one might have gotten the impression that the chief act with which moral theology was concerned was contraceptive intercourse among married couples. In 1951 Pius XII had given his blessing to "responsible parenthood" through periodic abstinence, popularly known as the "rhythm method." "Rhythm" was not to be undertaken casually but responsibly, and this might be a matter for discussion with a confessor. It was definitely not simply a choice. This already difficult and highly personal issue was immensely complicated in 1960 when the FDA approved the first oral contraceptive pill. A Catholic physician, Dr. John Rock, had pioneered research on the pill. Rock was an obstetrician-gynecologist and fertility researcher who taught at Harvard Medical School. He had initially used the pill in the treatment of infertility, hoping to "rest" the reproductive system and achieve a rebound effect.[3] Rock's 1963 book, *The Time Has Come,* posed this question: "If the specter of rape allows a woman to use the pills because by it [*sic*] she is relieved of the obligation to conceive, could a woman already relieved of the obligation by the 'serious reasons' of Pius XII [a woman who had made a conscientious decision to practice rhythm] also use them?" After five years of discussion and debate, Pope Paul VI, in his encyclical *Humanae Vitae,* issued in the summer of 1968, answered Rock's question in the negative. Moral theology would never be the same.[4]

In 1961 Pope John XXIII had written his first social encyclical, *Mater et Magistra.* The flap that surrounded its reception by the *National Review* and, especially by William F. Buckley's witticism (borrowed from Garry Wills) *Mater sí; Magistra no,* signaled the divisions between so-called liberals and conservatives that would intensify after 1968 over the legacy of Vatican II, and later over the pontificate of Pope John Paul II. Moral theology is now more of a mix than it was in the nineteenth century or in the first half of the twentieth. It is more like the discipline J. B. Hogan described in 1898. Some might say it is more vibrant. The final selections reflect continuing divisions in the Catholic community in the United States, but they also show Catholic thinkers

---

3. Loretta McLaughlin, *The Pill, John Rock, and the Church: The Biography of a Revolution* (Boston: Little Brown and Co., 1982), 115. See especially chaps. 7 and 8.

4. For a retrospective on the change, see McCormick, *Corrective Vision,* chap. 3. For an autobiographical statement by John Noonan on how he came to the perspective on doctrinal development from which his historical study of contraception was written, see John T. Noonan, *The Lustre of Our Country: The American Experience of Religious Freedom* (Berkeley: University of California Press, 1998), 25–31.

negotiating the tension between moral theology's "act-oriented" origins and its "actor-oriented" aspirations.

## 56. Francis Patrick Kenrick, "On Slavery," 1841

*The bishop of Philadelphia concludes that it is not unjust for slaveholders in the United States to keep their slaves in bondage.*

[Page 255][1] 35. Since all persons are equal by natural law, no one by nature is master of another. Nevertheless, by the law of nations,[2] human beings permit a person not only to be master *by jurisdiction,* but even *by right of possession.* The Old Law [Old Testament] confirmed this.[3] At one time those captured in war were quite often subjected to slavery when the victors "spared" the conquered. Those who inflict any other dreadful deed inflict on them the same penalty.[4] For such was the *patria potestas* that [a father] might sell his children to relieve his poverty, with the proviso that he might buy them back if a better day dawned.[5] Some people sold themselves [into slavery] in order to provide financial support for themselves. All of their children born of a slave mother, they considered slaves because, "Status at birth follows from the womb."[6] The Apostle [Paul] did not condemn the slavery flourishing among the various nations but he taught that they [slaves] had to be obedient: "Servants, be obedient to them that are your lords according to the flesh, with fear and trembling, in the simplicity of your heart, as to Christ."[7] He even recommended mildness and conformity to the owners: "And you, masters, do the same things to them, forbearing threatenings, knowing that the Lord both of them and you is in heaven; and there is no respect of persons with him."[8] The Church always keeps the apostolic writings before her eyes, and for that reason at the Council of Gangra[9] she anathematized those who under the pretext of religious obligation drove slaves away from their masters. Since [the Church] valued human liberty, it promoted the idea among masters that they should free their slaves. It would do this simply by exhortation until gradually slavery would be abolished by the force of public opinion. [p. 256] So in the year 1167 Alexander III

---

1. [The page numbers indicated in brackets are those of the original edition. That edition began the numbering of footnotes on each page. The words in brackets in the text and the notes are those of the translator.]

2. [The triple division of law into natural law (*jus naturae*), customary law (*jus consuetudinis*), and the law of nations (*ius gentium*), is found in Justinian's *Institutes* 1.1–2.]

3. Exodus 21 and Leviticus 25.

4. Cap. *Ita q[u]orundum, de Judaeis et Samaritanis* [concerning Jews and Samaritans].

5. 50.1 and 50.2ff. *De patribus qui filios suos distraxerunt* [concerning fathers who sell their children].

6. See the section of the Code [of Justinian] *de rei vindic.* [on legal claims].

7. Eph. VI.5. [This and all direct biblical quotations are from the Douay-Rheims translation. This version was translated directly from the Vulgate and was the English version of the Scriptures most widely distributed among United States Catholics in the nineteenth century.]

8. Ibid., 9.

9. [The Council of Gangra was a regional council which met in Pamphlagonia (modern Turkey) ca. 345. The records of this council were often copied with those of later ecumenical councils, thus giving them a broad impact. The Council condemned those who encouraged social upheaval, including a rejection of marriage and slavery (can. 3).]

forbade Christians to be held as slaves thereafter.[10] This most human ordinance was weakened over the following centuries as the abominable commercial trade was introduced.

36. More recently the humanitarianism of the Apostolic bishop Gregory XVI, who followed the example of his predecessor, made clear that Christian nations should be ashamed to be still practicing it, now that all vain and empty reasoning for continuing such an injustice had been exposed, and he condemned and prohibited it: "By [our] Apostolic Authority," says the Pontiff, "we admonish all believers of whatever status and we most strongly abjure them in the Lord, that in the future no one should dare to torment unjustly Indians, Negroes or any other kinds of persons or to rob them of their possessions or to subject them to slavery or to grant assistance or approval to any other persons performing those actions against them or to engage in this inhumane business in which Negroes, as if they were not human beings but simply and purely animals, were enslaved without any distinction, in opposition to their rights in justice and as human beings, are sold, bought, and are relegated meanwhile to the harshest and most oppressive labors, and, in anticipation of their imagined profit from trade with those who enslave the Negroes, they foment divisive and perpetual discord in whatever way they can. By our Apostolic Authority we condemn all the aforesaid actions as absolutely unworthy of the Christian name. By the same Authority we strictly prohibit and interdict any cleric or lay person from this particular commercial trade in Negroes and from presuming to preach or to teach in any way either publicly or privately that it would be licit anywhere by asserting either that they are only seeking to preserve the status quo or something else contrary to that which we warn with this Apostolic letter."[11]

37. Now how should we feel about domestic slavery which flourishes in many areas of the West and of the East? Should the descendants of those who had been abducted from Africa still be subject to this yoke? Certainly all who take pride in the fullness of liberty must grieve that from the beginnings of these undertakings they have been warned that laws have been promulgated which forbid them from being taught to read and which [p. 257] severely impede them from the exercise of religion wherever they are.[12] Finally, since these

---

10. See de Maistre, *Du Paple* [*Pape*] 1.iii. c.ii. [Joseph Marie de Maistre, *Du Pape* (Lyon: Paris, 1830). DeMaistre (1753–1821) was a French philosopher and supporter of papal supremacy.]

11. The Apostolic Letter begins: *In Supremo Apostolatus fastigio*, dated 3 December 1839. If the most learned theologian Carriere had seen this [letter], he would have changed his opinion concerning this commercial trade (in his work *De justitia et jure*, par. i, sect. i.c.iii.art.3, Paris, 1839) since he had great respect for the Apostolic See.

12. [In English:] "In Georgia, by an act, in 1829, no person is permitted to teach a slave, Negro, or free person of colour, to read or write. So, in Virginia, by statute, in 1830, meeting of free Negroes, to learn reading or writing, is unlawful, and subjects them to corporal punishment; and it is unlawful for white persons to assemble with free negroes or slaves, to teach them to read or write. The prohibitory act of the legislature of Alabama, passed in the session of 1831–2, relative to instruction to be given to the slave, or free coloured population, or exhortation, or preaching to them, or any mischievous influence attempted to be exerted over them, is sufficiently penal. Laws of similar import are presumed to exist in the other slave-holding states; but in Louisiana the law on this subject is armed with tenfold severity. It not only forbids any person teaching slaves to read or write, but it declares that any person using language, in any public discourse, from the bar, stage, or pulpit, or any other place, or in any private conversation, or making use of any signs or actions, having a

things are so, one should not attempt anything which contravenes the laws, nor should anything be done or said by which might promote emancipation or the bearing [of slavery] more lightly: but sacred ministers should exhibit prudence and charity on their behalf, so that slaves, formed in Christian habits, might distinguish themselves by their obedience to their masters, venerating the supreme God as Lord of all; and so that masters might distinguish themselves as just and kind, and might assuage the condition of their slaves by their generosity and their concern for their salvation. We have the apostles as authors who leave these testimonies to us. Those who neglect these, seeking to subvert all order in their desire for generosity, make the situation of their slaves much more difficult. In the previously praised Constitution the Pontiff does not neglect bringing this to the attention of all: "Inspired then by a divine Spirit, the Apostles taught these same servants to obey their earthly masters as they would Christ, and to do his will wholeheartedly. Similarly, they ordered masters to treat their servants well and to provide for them what is right and just and to forbear threatening them, knowing that the Lord in heaven is theirs [that of the slaves] and their own and there is not preferential treatment with him."[13]

38. Gerdil[14] rightly draws this to our attention: "We should not understand slavery as if one person could have the right to govern another person, which he owns like a beast. In the past those who refused to count slaves as persons were gravely mistaken on this issue,[15] [p. 258] and however maliciously and cruelly the master would hold his slave, nevertheless they believed that an injustice was done to the slave by the master. But slavery does not wipe out the equality of nature among human beings. In their view of slavery one person is conceived as the master of another such that the master holds a perpetual and total right to all the works of his servant. Even if it is right for one person to perform [labor] for another, by this particular law by which a master ought to take care of his servant, he must provide carefully to him all the obligations due to him by his nature, as we have stated elsewhere (*Specimen Element.* P. iii. §4.)[16] Slavery thus understood is not at odds with natural law in such a way that it might be considered a sin against natural law if a person holding slaves uses them moderately. Nevertheless, for the greatest good of the human race, slavery is endured

---

tendency to produce discontent among the free coloured population, or insubordination among the slaves, or who shall be knowingly instrumental in bringing into the state any paper, book, or pamphlet, having the like tendency, shall, on conviction, be punishable with imprisonment or death, at the discretion of the court." Kent's Comm. Vol.ii. p.iv. lec.xxxii. n. 253. (See James Kent [1763–1847], *Commentaries on American Law,* 4 vols. [New York: O. Halstead, 1826–1830].)

13. [Cf. Eph. 6.9.]

14. [Hyacinthe Sigismond Gerdil (1718–1802), a native of Savoy, now part of Italy, was a theologian, canon lawyer, provincial of the Barnabites and cardinal. His principal writings were against Locke and Rousseau.]

15. [Closer to home than any debate among European theologians was the controversy in the United States. The framers of the Constitution of the United States had debated whether or not slaves counted for census purposes. The "Three-fifths Compromise" (Article I, section 2) provided that a slave was to be counted as three-fifths of a person for purposes of apportioning members of the House of Representatives and for purposes of taxation. This was repealed by the Fourteenth Amendment, sec. 2, in 1868.]

16. [See Giacinto Sigismondo Gerdil, *Opere, edite e inedite* (Rome: V. Poggioli, 1806–21).]

with Christian kindness up to the present day among civilized nations."[17] "Why does a master injure his servant if he beats him cruelly, if he oppresses him with too much work, if he cheats him of the food and clothing he should have, if he bears his reputation? Rightly does Cicero say in *De officiis* I, chapter 13: so we must remember that justice must be served even for the lowliest. Therefore, those people who have the lowly situation and lot of the slaves at heart do not mistreat them when they order the slaves to be employed to accomplish a task as if they were hired servants to whom adequate provisions were rendered."[18]

39. We have to ask whether it is possible to keep those who had formerly been made slaves, since the majority of them were brought here from Africa by wrongful action. It seems that we must say yes, for the weakness of title after a long lapse of time must be considered healed, especially when the situation of the society as a whole would otherwise forever be in doubt, with the gravest danger to the masses. Those who took them away against their wills sin; but it does not seem that their posterity hold them in slavery unjustly. Specifically, they were born in that condition of which they cannot divest themselves. Finally, we must praise those who by their pursuit of humanity and religion give them freedom since there is an opportunity for them to settle the territory of Africa which is called Liberia. Religious help has been at their service as they have been making their plans and, with assistance from the Apostolic See, two priests from this diocese are now setting sail.

> Francis Patrick Kenrick, *De Servitute* ("On Slavery"), from *Theologia[e] Moralis*, vol. 1 (Philadelphia: Eugene Cummiskey, 1841), 255–58. Translated for this volume and annotated by Maureen Tilley. Translation printed with permission.

### 57. John B. Hogan Pleads for the Practical in Moral Theology, 1898

*With strong implied criticism of the approach represented by Kenrick, a long-time seminary professor and rector argues for a more "organic" approach with greater freedom and less reliance on the authority of the past in moral theology.*

Such, then, are the elements and methods of Moral Theology. Theories and principles, general rules, practical applications, constitute the whole science. The principles of themselves comprise all; yet to dwell exclusively in the region of principles would serve no practical purpose. Pure speculation and theory may suffice to make the moral philosopher, but not the moral theologian.

The principles of Moral Theology are almost exclusively rational; its rules, on the contrary, are gathered, as we have seen, from all manner of sources—the legislation of the Jews and the maxims of the Gospel, Roman law and canon law, councils and popes. But in their actual shape they are almost entirely due to the labor and thought of the schools through many ages. To the schools they owe in a great measure their precision and their authority. Yet, whatever their excellence may be in both respects, they still remain human, and consequently,

---

17. *Compendium institutionum civilium* L.I. p. 317. Vol. vii.
18. Gerdil, *De justitia et jure*, c. vi, prop. iii.

liable, more or less, to be reconsidered and recast. Even when they remain un-altered, they become fully available only through a knowledge of the principles from which they emanate; and without it they are often misleading. Casuistry, finally, is more accessible still and more helpful to the majority; but casuistry without the moral theories and rules from which it proceeds is little better than a child's form of knowledge.

In short, to the moral theologian the three classes of elements are almost equally necessary, and each one is the natural complement of the others. Prac-tice is as much a test of theory as theory is of practice. Many a principle seems unquestionable until an attempt is made to carry it out. But the practical im-possibility of applying it gives warning that it has to be dropped or modified. The happy working, on the contrary, of rule or principle is one of the surest signs of its correctness and truth.

The teacher of Moral Theology may take as his starting-point any one of the three spheres of the science. He may begin with the study of the theories or general principles, and from them come down to the rules and the practical applications; or, starting from the rules, he may proceed backward to the prin-ciples, and forward to the individual facts; or he can begin with what is nearest and most accessible, — specific cases, — and ascend gradually to what is more re-mote and more difficult. Each method has its peculiar advantages and attractions for a certain class of minds. Each has its special perils. Aristotle, in one of the opening chapters of his *Morals,* speaks of them as "reasoning from principles and reasoning to principles." He admits both, on condition that the starting-point shall be sufficiently known, and that it shall lead to a knowledge of the rest.

A better rule could not be laid down. No department of ethics is indepen-dent of the others — no single process sufficient to meet all its requirements. Moral Science is a structure, each portion of which borrows strength from the others, and helps to sustain them; an organism, every part and every function of which gives life to the whole.

John B. Hogan, S.S., *Clerical Studies* (Boston: Marlier & Company, 1898), 220–22.

## 58. John A. Ryan on Usury and Monopoly, 1919

*At the time he authored the Bishops' Program for Social Reconstruction, the NCWC's social action director cites* Rerum Novarum *to defend government intervention against monopoly.*

While Catholic teaching rejects the complete domination of industry by the state, as proposed in the socialist scheme, it is very far from advocating the opposite extreme of individualism and *laissez faire.*

Those who believe that the government should pursue an industrial pol-icy of non-intervention will find no comfort in the traditional attitude of the Church. And they will be grievously disappointed with the encyclical "On the Condition of Labor...."

The two supreme evils of our industrial system are the unreasonably small share of the national income obtained by the majority of wage-earners, and the unreasonably large share that goes to a small minority of capitalists. The remedies which Pope Leo offers for the former evil are, as we have just said, sufficient. The second evil he does not directly touch in the encyclical. His subject was the "Condition of Labor," not the wider topic of social reform, or social justice. Nevertheless, he makes two or three references to the evil of excessive gain that are not without significance when taken in connection with the traditional teaching of the Church.

He declares that the hard condition of the working classes "has been increased by rapacious usury, which, although more than once condemned by the Church, is nevertheless under a different guise but with the like injustice still practiced by covetous and grasping men." Again, he enjoins the rich to "refrain from cutting down the workmen's earnings, whether by force, fraud or by usurious dealing."

There can be little doubt that the new form of usury stigmatized in these sentences refers to the extortionate prices exacted from the working classes for the necessaries of life by the monopolists. A certain great meat packing industry last year obtained dividends of 35 per cent. During the same period this concern helped to promote an artificial shortage of hides, with the result that the price of shoes was kept at a much higher level than was required by the relation between supply and demand. Were Pope Leo alive, he would probably have little hesitation in classifying this coarse injustice as "usurious."

For centuries the Catholic teaching on monopoly has been that a combination which artificially raises the price of products above the market or competitive level is guilty of unjust dealing, and that such practices ought to be prevented by law. Taken in conjunction with the general principle of state intervention enunciated by Pope Leo, these doctrines constitute a sanction for the use of any legislative method that is necessary to meet the evil of monopoly.

Let us recall Pope Leo's general principle: "Whenever the general interest or any particular class suffers, or is threatened with mischief which can in no other way be met or prevented, the public authority must step in and deal with it." Therefore, if that "usurious dealing" which is practiced by monopolistic concerns for the sake of extortionate profits can "in no other way be met or prevented" than by the destruction of the monopoly, or by fixing maximum prices for its products, or by state ownership of the industry, in whole or in part, or by all these methods combined, the state will have not only the right but the duty to intervene in any or all of these ways.

Did space permit, it would be easy to show that all the other social questions, such for example as those of land tenure and taxation, and taxes on incomes and inheritances, can be adequately solved in conformity with the social and moral teaching of the Catholic Church. All the evils of our industrial system can be abolished by sane and progressive measures of social reform, against which the Church has not a hard word to say. There is no need to resort to socialism, even if that scheme would not leave the last state of society worse than the first.

John A. Ryan, *The Church and Socialism and Other Essays* (Washington, D.C.: University Press, 1919), 23–24, 33–34.

## 59. Dorothy Day on Nonviolence, 1936

*Widespread support among American Catholics for Franco's side in the Spanish Civil War drew from Day this reaffirmation of her commitment to gospel non-violence.*

Christ Our Lord came and took upon Himself our humanity. He became the Son of Man. He suffered hunger and thirst and hard toil and temptation. All power was His but he wished the free love and service of men. He did not force anyone to believe. St. Paul talks of the liberty of Christ. He did not coerce anyone. He emptied Himself and became a servant. He showed the way to true leadership by coming to minister, not to be ministered unto. He set the example and we are supposed to imitate Him. We are taught that His kingdom was not of this earth. He did not need pomp and circumstance to prove Himself the Son of God.

His were hard sayings, so that even His own followers did not know what He was saying, did not understand Him. It was not until after He died on the Cross, it was not until He had suffered utter defeat, it would seem, and they thought their cause was lost entirely; it was not until they had persevered and prayed with all the fervor and desperation of their poor loving hearts, that they were enlightened by the Holy Spirit, and knew the truth with a strength that enabled them to suffer defeat and martyrdom in their turn. They knew then that not by force of arms, by the bullet or the ballot would they conquer. They knew and were ready to suffer defeat — to show that great love which enabled them to lay down their lives for their friends.

And now the whole world is turning to "force" to conquer. Fascist and Communist alike believe that only by the shedding of blood can they achieve victory. Catholics, too, believe that suffering and the shedding of blood "must needs be," as Our Lord said to the disciples at Emmaus. But their teaching, their hard saying, is that they must be willing to shed every drop of their own blood, and not take the blood of their brothers. They are willing to die for their faith, believing that the blood of the martyrs is the seed of the Church.

Our Lord said, "Destroy this temple and in three days I will raise it up." And do not His words apply not only to Him as Head of His Church but to His members? How can the head be separated from the members? The Catholic Church cannot be destroyed in Spain or in Mexico. But we do not believe that force of arms can save it. We believe that if Our Lord were alive today he would say as He said to St. Peter, "Put up thy sword."

Christians, when they are seeking to defend their faith by arms, by force and violence, are like those who said to Our Lord, "Come down from the Cross. If you are the Son of God, save Yourself."

But Christ did not come down from the Cross. He drank to the last drop the agony of His suffering, and was not part of the agony, the hopelessness, the unbelief, of His own disciples.

Christ is being crucified today, every day. Shall we ask Him with the unbelieving world to come down from the Cross? Or shall we joyfully, as His brothers, "complete the sufferings of Christ"?

In their small way, the unarmed masses, those "little ones" of Christ, have known what it was to lay down their lives for principle, for their fellows. In the history of the world there have been untold numbers who have laid down their lives for Our Lord and His Brothers. And now the Communist is teaching that only by the use of force, only by killing our enemies, not by loving them and giving ourselves up to death, giving ourselves up to the Cross, will we conquer.

If 2,000 have suffered martyrdom in Spain, is that suffering atoned for by the death of the 90,000 in the Civil War? Would not those martyrs themselves have cried out against more shedding of blood?

Prince of Peace, Christ our King, Christ our Brother, Christ the Son of Man, have mercy on us and give us the courage to suffer. Help us to make ourselves "a spectacle to the world and to angels and to men." Help Your priests and people in Spain to share in Your suffering, and in seeming defeat, giving up their lives, without doubt there will be those like the centurion standing at the foot of the Cross who will say, "Indeed, these men are the sons of God."

Dorothy Day, *By Little and by Little* (New York: Alfred A. Knopf, 1983), 77–78. Printed with permission.

## 60. John C. Ford, S.J., on "Obliteration Bombing," 1944

*Working strictly within just-war principles, one of the preeminent moral theologians of his generation argues for the immorality of obliteration bombing.*

The present paper attempts to deal with the problem on a larger scale. The Popes have condemned as immoral some of the procedures of modern war, but they have abstained, as far as I know, from using terms which would put a clear, direct burden on the conscience of the individual subordinate in a new matter like the present one. Later on I shall attempt to show that obliteration bombing must be one of the procedures which Pius XII has condemned as immoral. But my viewpoint at present is that of one trying to solve the general moral problem, not of teaching confessors at what point they must draw the line and refuse absolution....

### The Contemporary Question of Fact

But it is obvious...that the conditions of modern war are changed, and that change makes it very difficult and sometimes impossible to draw accurately the line which separates combatants from innocent non-combatants according to natural law. Soldiers under arms are obviously combatants. It is not so clear what is to be said of civilian munitions workers, the members of various organized labor battalions not under arms, and so of others. Of these doubtful classes I do not intend to speak. In the end, only new international agreements will effectively and precisely protect the rights of these groups.

But it is not necessary to draw an accurate line in order to solve the problem of obliteration bombing. It is enough to show that there are large numbers of people even in the conditions of modern warfare who are clearly to be classed as innocent non-combatants, and then that, wherever the line is drawn, obliteration bombing goes beyond it and violates the rights of these people. It seems to me that an unnecessary attitude of defeat is betrayed by writers like Dr. McReavy, who seem to think that, because we do not know exactly where to draw the line, therefore we have to act as if there were no line at all between innocence and guilt (and hence find some other ground for protecting civilians from savagery). I think it is a fairly common fallacy in legal and moral argumentation to conclude that all is lost because there is a field of uncertainty to which our carefully formulated moral principles cannot be applied with precision.[1] It seems to me furthermore, that this mentality is encouraged if one is taking the view of a confessor who thinks in terms of absolution for the individual penitent, and who naturally does not want to deny it unless he is certain that he has to. Finally, in this present matter, I think this defeatist mentality is encouraged in moralists who, as it were, have been put on the defensive by public, "patriotic," and official opinion, and overwhelmed with talk of the radically changed conditions of modern war — as if everything were now changed, and all or almost all civilians now played a direct part in the war, and as if in the past, when the classical formulas were put together, the civilians who were declared untouchable in those formulas had little or nothing to do with the war effort of their countries. Is it not evident that the most radical and significant change of all in modern warfare is not the increased co-operation of civilians behind the lines with the armed forces, but the enormously increased power of the armed forces to reach behind the lines and attack civilians indiscriminately, whether they are thus co-operating or not?

And so the question arises, who has the burden of proof — the civilian behind the lines, who clings to his traditional immunity, or the military leader with new and highly destructive weapons in his hands, who claims that he can attack civilians because modern industrial and economic conditions have changed the nature of war radically and made them all aggressors. Do we start with the supposition that the whole population of the enemy is presumably guilty, and that anyone who wants to exempt a group from that condemnation is called upon to prove the innocence of the group? Or do we start with the view that only armed soldiers are guilty combatants and anyone who wants to increase the number of the guilty, and make unarmed civilians legitimate objects of violent repression, has the duty of proving his position? Is it not reasonable to put the burden of proof on those who are innovators? Do we not start from here: "Thou shalt not kill"? Seeing that the wartime rights of civilians to life and property are declared by centuries of tradition to be sacrosanct, what do we presume: a man's right to his life, even in war time, or my right to kill him? His right to his property, or my right to destroy it? Not merely the conscience of humanity, not merely international law, but the teaching of Catholic theologians for centuries, the voice of the Church speaking through her Councils and through her hierarchy and through the Supreme Pontiff down

---

1. We do not talk this way in the matter of the absolutely grave sum, even though it is impossible to draw the line with precision. Even in philosophy, when determining what is a miracle, we admit we do not know how far nature can go, but we are sure of some things that are beyond her powers.

to the present day, uniformly insist on the innocence and consequent immunity of civil populations. It is obviously the burden of those who think that distinction invalid (or, what comes to the same thing, completely impractical) to prove their contention. I can understand how a confessor, with thoughts of probabilism running through his head, would feel that when he refuses absolution he has the burden of showing he has a right to refuse it. But I cannot understand a moralist taking that point of view with regard to the rights of civilians. He has not the burden of proving these rights. On the contrary, those who want to increase the number of combatants, and include large numbers, even the "vast majority," of the civilian population amongst the guilty, must justify themselves.... The present demands of legislators, editors, and others for the indiscriminate bombing of *non-industrial* towns in Germany is a clear example of an inevitable tendency — once you get used to the idea of obliteration, and justify it.

This is another way of saying that the recognition of obliteration bombing will easily and quickly lead to the recognition of total war itself. Some may say, of course, that we recognize total war already and are waging it. But that would be a gross exaggeration. Dr. Guido Gonella tells us: "The totality of war is generally understood in a three-fold sense. It applies to the *persons* by whom and against whom warlike action is exercised, to the *means* which are employed in war, and to the *places* where warlike action takes place. (The term war-like action is taken in the broadest sense, including not only military action but also every form of manifestation of hostility, for example, by economic blockade, by the war of nerves etc....)" And again: "If total war is defended as a war which is fought without regard to any limitation affecting persons, or means of warfare, or places," then it must be condemned as immoral.[2] All Catholics, following the lead of the Pope, the hierarchy, and firmly established moral principles, condemn total war in this, its fullest sense. To say that war need to know no restraint in these matters is equivalent to asserting that men at war are no longer bound by the natural law at all. And so the elimination of total war was one of the main objectives of the Holy Father's Christmas message of 1941....

Now the air bombardment of civil centers is a symbol of total war in its worst sense. It is the first thing that comes to mind when the phrase "total war" is heard. The air bombardment of great centers of population lets down the bars, and opens up enormous categories of persons, hitherto immune, against whom warlike action can now be taken; it changes the scene of war-like activity from the battlefield to the city, and not only to the war factories but to the residential districts of the workers; and it uses explosives and incendiaries to a hitherto unheard of degree, leaving only one more step to the use of poison gas or bacteriological war. This means that obliteration bombing has taken us a long step in the direction of immoral total war. To justify it, will, I believe, make it exceedingly difficult to draw the line at further barbarities in practice. If the

---

2. Guido Gonella, *A World to Reconstruct: Pius XII on Peace and Reconstruction,* trans. T. Lincoln Bouscaren (Milwaukee: Bruce Publishing Co., 1944), chap. 12.

leaders of the world were well educated in moral matters and conscientious in the application of Christian moral principles to the waging of war, the danger might not be so real. But half of them are not Christian at all and worship material force as ultimate, while almost all of them are immersed in a completely secularized tradition. If *moralists* grant them the vast horrors of obliteration bombing, what will stop them from that point on? If one were merely applying the principle of the double effect to the act of an individual bombardier dropping a bomb, such considerations would not be very much to the point; but when the question is the whole strategy of obliteration, the larger considerations, the thought of future consequences for the whole civilized world, are the most important elements to be remembered in estimating proportionate cause. . . .

The conclusion of this paper can be stated briefly. Obliteration bombing, as defined, is an immoral attack on the rights of the innocent. It includes a direct intent to do them injury. Even if this were not true, it would still be immoral, because no proportionate cause could justify the evil done; and to make it legitimate would soon lead the world to the immoral barbarity of total war. The voice of the Pope and the fundamental laws of the charity of Christ confirm this condemnation.

*Theological Studies,* 5 (September 1944): 269, 280–82, 303–5, 308–9. Printed with permission.

## 61. William F. Buckley Jr. on *Mater et Magistra,* 1961

*Two weeks after this editorial comment on Pope John XXIII's first encyclical, NR included another comment in a group of items under the heading "For the Record": "Going the rounds in Catholic conservative circles: 'Mater, sí; Magistra, no.'" This commentary, which critics attributed to editor William F. Buckley, touched off a long-running controversy between liberal and conservative Catholics.*

The large sprawling document released by the Vatican last week on the seventieth anniversary of Leo XIII's famous encyclical *Rerum Novarum* will be studied and argued over for years to come. It may in the years to come be considered central to the social teachings of the Catholic Church, or, like Pius IX's *Syllabus of Errors,* it may become the source of embarrassed explanations. Whatever its final effect, it must strike many as a venture in triviality coming at this particular time in history. The most obtrusive social phenomena of the moment are surely the continuing and demonic successes of the Communists, of which there is scant mention; the extraordinary material well-being that such free economic systems as Japan's, West Germany's, and our own are generating, of which, it would seen insufficient notice is taken; and the dehumanization under technology-cum-statism, of the individual's role in life, to which there are allusions, but without the rhetorical emphasis given to other matters. There are, of course, eloquent passages stressing the spiritual side of man, as one would expect there should be. But it is not unlikely that, in the years ahead, *Mater et Magistra* will suffer from comparison with the American Catholic Bishops' hierarchy of emphases, in their notable annual message of November 1960.

*National Review* 9, no. 4 (July 29, 1961): 38. Printed with permission.

## 62. Dr. John Rock on "the Pill," 1963

*A Catholic obstetrician-gynecologist who played a key role in developing the birth control pill, poses the question of its morality. Widely translated, his book would stimulate the discussion of birth control in the 1960s.*

These statements [moral theologians on the question of intent], like many others, condemn the use of the "pill" for implementing the subjective intent to avoid conception, that sex may be used, perhaps only for love. Does such an attitude easily conform with the Church's justification of the rhythm method? The Papal documents sanctioning rhythm refer explicitly to the licitness of satisfying (by coitus) the secondary ends of marriage — sexual harmony and allaying of concupiscence — when procreation should be avoided for serious reasons: that is, when properly, there should be the subjective intent to avoid conception. Is this not a regard for sexual expression as a completely independent good, totally apart from procreation? Father Connery later in his article calls for the discovery of "some simple and reliable method of detecting and predicting ovulation" to make rhythm more reliable, a project which is theoretically, entirely possible. Is he not implying that when such means are found, their use will be intended to produce exactly "the same interference" as do the oral pills, separating sexual expression, as an independent good, from procreation?

I am persuaded that the Church has not concluded its examination of the morality of the progestational steroids when used for fertility control. The complex questions involved doubtlessly are still being studied and the results are not clearly predictable. Three eminent Vatican theologians, for example, have recently come to the conclusion that it is licit for at least some women in danger of rape to use the pills in order to prevent conception. Their findings, apparently occasioned by the rape of nuns in the Congo, were reported in the authoritative Vatican publication *Studi Cattolici*.[1] Monsignor Ferdinando Lambruschini, professor of moral theology at the Lateran University, pointed out that victims of rape do not have the alternative of abstention to which married couples can resort in order to avoid conception. Francis Hurt, a Jesuit professor at Gregorian University, noted that a farmer has the right to defend his property even with a machine gun and that human beings are justified, in certain circumstances, in suspending various bodily functions. Similarly, a woman threatened with rape would be justified in defending herself by suppressing ovulation. Monsignor Pietro Palazzini, the secretary of the Vatican's Conciliar Congregation, concurred in the Jesuit's views. Thus, it seems, willful suppression of ovulation is not in itself an evil deed.

---

1. New York *Herald Tribune* News Service, Dec. 19, 1961.

I do not know how broadly the Vatican theologians would construe this preventive use of the pills. Surely rape is not an uncommon threat in many countries. Among illiterate peoples, precariously living in poverty, women are in fairly continuous danger of sexual attack. (Doubtless some moralists would also tend to think that psychologically and physiologically, though perhaps not by secular or ecclesiastical law, a wife unwillingly subjected to brutal sexual attack by her drunken husband had indeed been "raped." St. Thomas' dictum, already quoted, that a man who uses his wife as a wanton sins against justice would seem to be relevant to such a circumstance. Could a wife who may justly avoid conception and knows the imminent danger of such a rapacious attack use the pill, by the same rule that applies to her maiden sister?)

Clearly the conclusions reached by the Vatican theologians have aroused great interest — and some concern — among American Catholics. Within ten days, the National Catholic Welfare Conference news service circulated a story quoting Francis J. Connell, C.Ss.R., former dean of the School of Sacred Theology at Catholic University, as declaring that this opinion "gives no leeway to the sin of contraception" for normal couples. However, he also declared that a woman who has been or very probably will be raped "has no obligation to undergo pregnancy, hence she may lawfully prevent it without being guilty of the sin of contraception."[2]

Father Connell in his formulation might seem to have legitimized the oral pills for millions of women who are not even potential victims of rape, for did not Pius XII make clear that serious medical, eugenic, economic, or social reasons may exempt couples from "the obligation" of pregnancy, "for a long time, and even for the whole duration of married life"?

If the specter of rape allows a woman to use the pills because by it she is relieved of the obligation to conceive, could a woman relieved of the obligation by the "serious reasons" of Pius XII also use them?

John Rock, *A Catholic Doctor's Proposals to End the Battle over Birth Control* (New York: Alfred A. Knopf, 1963), 175–78.

## 63. Paul Hanly Furfey on "Actor-Centered" Moral Theology, 1966

*The retiring chair of Catholic University's Sociology Department asks why Catholics failed to protest against slavery in the United States, Hitler's wars, and the bombing of noncombatants during the Second World War.*

Whatever may be said of the general spirit of the age, it is abundantly clear that at least Catholics profess to take ethics and moral theology seriously. In Catholic colleges ethics has a respected place and is quite usually a required course; in seminaries future priests take four years of moral theology; moreover, Catholic books and periodicals are constantly appearing with both popular and technical discussions of every conceivable moral question. Obviously, then, Catholics are very much in earnest about discussing morality. Yet Catholics did

---

2. *The Inland Register*, December 29, 1961.

not protest very vociferously or effectively against Negro slavery in America, against Hitler's wars in Germany, or against the bombing of noncombatants in the Second World War — to cite only those instances treated above. How Catholics can devote so much time and effort to the study of the moral sciences and yet fail to recognize obvious and large-scale affronts to everything that those sciences imply is a question that demands answering.

To understand the spirit of Catholic moral theology, one must grasp its relation to the sacrament of penance. Seminarians are taught morality so that later, as confessors, they can pass judgment on what penitents tell them. This usually means passing judgment on series of specific acts and omissions. This is the sort of thing that one is expected to mention in confession, as is evident from the standard forms for the examination of conscience available in prayer books and elsewhere. "Have I neglected my morning and night prayers?...Have I taken God's name in vain?...Have I taken pleasure in impure thoughts or desires?...Have I stolen?...Have I told lies?" Not surprisingly, this same preoccupation with the specific shows up in the technical literature. In recent issues of *The American Ecclesiastical Review* a distinguished moral theologian answered the following questions, among others. May an Episcopalian clergyman be called a "priest"? May Catholics patronize a drugstore in which contraceptives are sold? May a used car dealer repair a car so as to give the impression that it is in better condition than it actually is? If two good Catholics are eating in a restaurant on a day of abstinence and one inadvertently orders meat, must the other remind him of the day?

Moral theology is dominated by a concern with concrete instances. It would be fair to call it casuistical, were it not that this word has acquired a pejorative meaning which implies superficiality and sophistry. To avoid this unfair implication, it would be better to say that moral theology is *act-oriented*. In this it differs from ascetical theology, for example, which is less concerned with particular actions than with general personality trends, with habits and attitudes such as the spirit of prayer or detachment from worldly goods. It is concerned with the sort of person one is. It may therefore be called *actor-oriented.*...

Because moral theology is act-oriented, it emphasizes particularly those sins which are clear-cut offenses, sins such as stealing, lying, missing Mass on Sunday, and, above all, sexual sins. The latter are ideal material for the act-oriented approach because they are definite mental events or definite external acts which are so emotionally charged that they cannot be easily overlooked. The result is, as we know, that sexual sins receive an enormous emphasis in Catholic thought. In itself, of course, this may be all to the good. However, a preoccupation with this particular area can lead to an irrational prudery and it can also distract attention from important issues. The Catholic diocesan press has recently been carrying a great deal of detailed news about campaigns against pornography; but there has been little or no serious discussion about the morality of the war in Vietnam or about particular aspects of that war such as the alleged napalm bombing of inhabited villages.

The act-oriented approach is not very effective in defining the individual's duties in certain areas that are of grave importance socially. The sin of avarice offers a highly relevant example. Christ Himself made it clear that the rich find it very difficult to attain heaven; and St. Paul stated comprehensively, "The love of money is the root of all evils." It is clear that a preoccupation with material things, an excessive attachment to one's own possessions, coupled with a hard-hearted indifference to the poverty of others, is a contradiction of fundamental Christian ideals. But where, precisely, does one make the choice between God and mammon? What is the dividing line between a prudent concern for one's financial responsibilities and that gloating devotion to material things that distracts one from God and results in injury to one's neighbor? It is not enough to preach detachment as a counsel of perfection. It is a task of moral theology to identify sin. Society is to be reformed not merely by appealing to the generosity of the generous, but also by threats of punishment to wrongdoers. The reluctant Catholic must be told precisely what he *must* do if he is not to be corrupted by avarice.

Similarly, act-oriented theology is not very helpful in the complex field of race relations. One may take, for example, the case of a sincere Catholic who happens to be an influential citizen in a Mississippi town that is riddled with racial injustices. Negroes are paid on a wage scale of their own, much lower than the white scale. They do not receive equal justice in the courts. Their side of town has unpaved and poorly lighted streets, inadequate sewerage and water supply. And so on through the whole gamut of customary maltreatment. Under such circumstances there are many laudable things the Catholic might do: he might write letters to the local newspaper and to his representatives in the state legislature; he might contribute money to civil rights movements; he might use his personal influence with local officials; he might do these and much besides. However, the question now is: What *must* he do as a matter of strict obligation? What are his exact duties as a Catholic? Precisely how must he act to avoid mortal sin? If moral theology cannot answer these questions satisfactorily, a man is likely to conclude that, since he has no definable obligations, he has no obligations whatever. Undefined duties are not a sharp spur to conscience.

Recently, there has been a trend towards the development of a more actor-oriented moral theology, whose most prominent spokesman has been the distinguished Redemptorist, Father Bernard Häring, in whose view moral theology should be very much more than a catalogue of commands and prohibitions. This is a promising trend: however, to meet the need discussed here, the new moral theology will have to do more than describe the sort of person a Christian *should* be. It will have to describe what he *must* be.

Nevertheless, moral theology has sometimes been used very successfully in making the Christian social ideal more concrete. Father John LaFarge did much more than talk about interracial justice in general; he applied general principles to the concrete Negro-white situation in the United States. In the field of economics, Msgr. John A. Ryan was equally specific, and he greatly influenced contemporary thought on labor relations and in many other fields. It would be possible to name many others whose work made the Christian social ideal more concrete. Of course, the activities of all these men have simply been a

part of the modern Catholic social movement which is rooted in the great social encyclicals and has been expressed in many, many forms of social action in
various countries around the world.

To summarize the present discussion, it seems fair to state that Catholic
theology has been vastly more successful in defining the social ideal than in
defining sins against it. Devotion to the ideal has inspired very many lay people,
priests, and religious to make sacrifices in the service of their neighbors and in
the whole field of social action. Yet the definition of the individual's obligations
has been so imprecise that sincere Catholics could participate in Hitler's war
with untroubled consciences or could approve the slaughter of noncombatants
by the Allies. They could participate in the savage wrongs committed against
Negroes in the United States from the days of the Atlantic slave trade, through
the dreary history of slavery, down to the contemporary violation of justice in
segregation. Something is manifestly wrong.

> *The Respectable Murderers: Social Evil and Christian Conscience* (New York:
> Herder and Herder, 1966), 146–47, 148–51.

## 64. Richard McCormick, S.J., on the Preservation of Life, 1974

*Writing in the* Journal of the American Medical Association, *bioethicist Richard
McCormick (1922–2000) reflects on the distinction between ordinary and extraordinary means in the care and preserving of life. He relates extraordinary
means and questions about quality of life in cases of severely malformed infants.*

What has brought us to this position of awesome responsibility? Very simply, the sophistication of modern medicine. Contemporary resuscitation and
life-sustaining devices have brought a remarkable change in the state of the question. Our duties toward the care and preservation of life have been traditionally
stated in terms of the use of ordinary and extraordinary means. For the moment and for purposes of brevity, we may say that, morally speaking, ordinary
means are those whose use does not entail grave hardships to the patient. Those
that would involve such hardship are extraordinary. Granted the relativity of
these terms and the frequent difficulty of their application, still the distinction
has had an honored place in medical ethics and medical practice.... This distinction can take us just so far — and thus the change in the state of the question.
The contemporary problem is precisely that the question no longer concerns
only those for whom "biological death is imminent...." Many infants who
would have died a decade ago, whose "biological death was imminent," can be
saved today.... Contemporary medicine with its team approaches, staged surgical techniques, monitoring capabilities, ventilatory support systems and other
methods, can keep almost anyone alive. This has tended to shift the problem
from the means to reverse the dying process to the quality of life sustained and
preserved. The questions, "Is this means too hazardous or difficult to use?" and
"Does this measure only prolong the patient's dying?" while still useful and
valid, now often become, "Granted that we can save the life, what kind of life
are we saving?"...

If these reflections are valid, they point in the direction of a guideline that may help in decisions about sustaining the lives of grossly deformed and deprived infants. The guideline is the potential for human relationships associated with the infant's condition. If that potential is simply nonexistent or would be utterly submerged and undeveloped in the mere struggle to survive, that life has achieved its potential. There are those who will want to continue to say that some terribly deformed infants may be allowed to die *because* no extraordinary means need be used. Fair enough. But they should realize that the term "extraordinary" has been so relativized to the condition of the patient that it is this condition that is decisive. The means is extraordinary because the infant's condition is extraordinary. And if that is so, we must face this fact head-on — and discover the substantive standard that allows us to say this of some infants, but not of others.

Here several caveats are in order. First, this guideline is not a detailed rule that pre-empts decisions; for the relational capacity is not subject to mathematical analysis but to human judgment. However, it is the task of physicians to provide some more concrete categories or presumptive biological symptoms for this human judgment. For instance, nearly all would very likely agree that the anencephalic infant is without relational potential. On the other hand, the same cannot be said of the mongoloid infant. The task ahead is to attach relational potential to presumptive biological symptoms for the gray area between such extremes. In other words, individual decisions will remain the anguishing onuses of parents in consultation with physicians.

Second, because the guideline is precisely that, mistakes will be made. Some infants will be judged in all sincerity to be devoid of any meaningful relational potential when that is actually not quite the case. This risk of error should not lead to abandonment of decisions, for that is to walk away from the human scene. Risk of error means only that we must proceed with great humility, caution, and tentativeness. Concretely, it means that if err we must at times, it is better to err on the side of life — and therefore to tilt in that direction.

Third, it must be emphasized that allowing some infants to die does not imply that "some lives are valuable, others not" or that "there is such a thing as a life not worth living." Every human being, regardless of age or condition is of incalculable worth. The point is not, therefore, whether this or that individual has value. Of course he has, or rather *is* a value. The only point is whether this undoubted value has any potential at all, in continuing physical survival, for attaining a share, even if reduced, in the "higher more important good...." Is not the only alternative an attitude that supports mere physical life as long as possible with every means?

Fourth, this whole matter is further complicated by the fact that this decision is being made for someone else. Should not the decision on whether life is to be supported or not be left to the individual? Obviously, wherever possible. But there is nothing inherently objectionable in the fact that parents with physicians must make this decision at some point for infants. Parents must make many crucial decisions for children. The only concern is that the decision not be shaped out of the utilitarian perspectives so deeply sunk into the consciousness of the contemporary world. In a highly technological culture, an individual is always in danger of being valued for his function, what he can do, rather than for who he is.

It remains, then, only to emphasize that these decisions must be made in terms of the child's good, this alone. But that good, as fundamentally a relational good, has many dimensions. Pius XII, in speaking of the duty to preserve life, noted that this duty "derives from well-ordered charity, from submission to the Creator, from social justice, as well as from devotion toward his family."[1] All of these considerations pertain to that "higher, more important good." If that is the case with the duty to preserve life, then the decision not to preserve life must likewise take all of these into account in determining what is for the child's good.

Any discussion of this problem would be incomplete if it did not repeatedly stress that it is the pride of Judaeo-Christian tradition that the weak and defenseless, the powerless and unwanted, those whose grasp on the goods of life is most fragile — that is, those whose potential is real but reduced — are cherished and protected as our neighbor in greatest need. Any application of a general guideline that forgets this is but a racism of the adult world profoundly at odds with the gospel, and eventually corrosive of the humanity of those who ought to be caring and supporting as long as that care and support has human meaning. It has meaning as long as there is hope that the infant will, in relative comfort, be able to experience our caring and love, for when this happens, both we and the child are sharing in that "higher, more important good."

> "To Save or Let Die: The Dilemma of Modern Medicine," in *How Brave a New World: Dilemmas in Bioethics* (Washington, D.C.: Georgetown University Press, 1981), 344–45, 349–51.

## 65. Germain Grisez on Personal Vocation, 1983

*As part of a multivolume project for the renewal of moral theology after Vatican II, a contemporary moral theologian includes "personal vocation" in his treatment of Christian moral principles.*

Question E: Why does every Christian have a unique personal vocation?

1. Besides his basic commitment to do the Father's will — to reveal the Father and to respond as a man should to God's love — Jesus had a personal vocation (22-C). In this unique role he became the new Man, the saving Christ of humankind, the sacrificial Lamb who in his own blood reconciles all humankind to God and forms us into God's own human family.

2. Plainly, his personal vocation is not ours. Rather, each of us, in light of his or her personal gifts and unique situation, must make personal vocational commitments — a specific set of commitments made in the context of the basic commitment of faith. In other words, one's response to Jesus in faith must be a commitment to take up a personal cross, which takes a unique form. One's

---

1. Pope Pius XII, *Acta Apostolicae Sedis* 49 (1957), 1,031–32. The phrase "higher, more important good" also comes from this text, an allocution to physicians, November 24, 1957.

personal vocation must be executed in particular acts very different from those which made up the life Jesus yet very much influenced by him: We must try to do what he would if he were in our place.

3. "Vocation" has often been used to refer only to the special calling of some to the clerical or religious life. Vatican II sometimes speaks of "vocation" in this sense, but also takes note of marriage as a Christian vocation (see *G[audium et]S[pes]* 52). Even so, the concept of vocation is still that of a state of life rather than precisely that of a unique personal vocation. In even more general terms, the Council uses "vocation" to refer to the whole destiny which God has in mind for human beings in Jesus (see, e.g., *L[umen] G[entium]* 39, GS 11).

4. However, the Council also uses "vocation" to refer to the specific commitments, including any undertaken within one's state of life, which each and every Christian should make to shape his or her life into a responsible carrying-out of the basic commitment of faith (see *LG* 11, 46: *P[resbyterorum] O[rdinis]* 6; *GS* 31, 43, 75). So, for example, in a truly Christian home, "husband and wife find their proper vocation in being witnesses to one another and to their children of faith in Christ and love for him" (*LG* 35). Such specific witnessing within the context of one's state of life is a true Christian vocation and apostolate....

5. In his encyclical, *Redemptor hominis* [71], John Paul II refers to the teaching of St. Paul in emphasizing the principle of personal vocation:

> For the whole of the community of the People of God and for each member of it what is in question is not just a specific "social membership"; rather, for each and every one what is essential is a particular "vocation." Indeed, the Church as the People of God is also — according to the teaching of St. Paul mentioned above, of which Pius XII reminded us in wonderful terms — "Christ's Mystical Body." Membership in that body has for its source a particular call united with the saving action of grace. Therefore, if we wish to keep in mind the community of the People of God, which is so vast and so extremely differentiated, we must see first and foremost Christ saying in a way to each member of the community: "Follow Me."

6. One should not think of personal vocation solely in terms of large-scale commitments. The child who undertakes to become more like Jesus each day is making a commitment to implement faith; such a simple commitment is a basic one for personal vocation. It is later defined and articulated in a more sophisticated way, but it need never be replaced.

7. Similarly, a person who enters religion or marriage as a major vocational commitment must make various other commitments — for example, to justice in civil society, to groups of friends, and so on. And after taking one's religious or marital vows, one still has occasion to make additional commitments compatible with them. These need to be united to form a single, integrated identity. If they are, then the whole, complex self formed by commitments is determined by faith and is one's personal response to God's unique vocation.

8. God creates to manifest his infinite goodness. The multiplicity and diversity of created entities is important, for each embodies a facet of perfection absent in all the rest: God creates no mere duplicates (see *S.t.*, 1, q. 47, aa. 1–2; *S.c.g.*, 2, 39–45). Jesus' humanity is the most excellent of creatures, but it is very limited. As Jesus needs the Father and the Spirit to complete the uncreated part of the total fulfillment which centers in him, so he needs each of us, in all his or her uniqueness, to complete the created part of this total fulfillment. . . .

9. Jesus needs each of us and our unique gifts and opportunities to complete the universal work of redemption. It is through us that Jesus comes to the people of our time. It is through us that the human goods in our culture are to be gathered up and redeemed. Jesus' sacrifice, offered to the Father, is an unsurpassable gift, but without our self-gift, united with his, both the homage of creation to God and the gratitude of redeemed humankind to the Father are incomplete. Through Jesus we share divine life by his gift to us of his own Holy Spirit. The Spirit's work is to sanctify the whole of creation — utterly to renew the face of the earth. This work can only be completed by our acceptance and use of the Spirit's power to attain sanctity within our unique vocations (see *LG* 41).

Germain Grisez, *The Way of the Lord Jesus,* vol. 1: *Christian Moral Principles* (Chicago: Franciscan Herald Press, 1983), 559–62. Printed with permission.

## 66. Michael Novak on the Limits of Capitalism, 1993

*Published shortly after the fall of the Soviet Union in 1989, Pope John Paul II's 1991 encyclical* Centesimus Annus *has been hotly debated among American commentators. At issue is whether the encyclical is more an endorsement or a criticism of capitalism as it presently exists in the United States. A leading neoconservative offers his reading.*

Nevertheless, Pope John Paul II does not forget the cost of a new modern capitalism, based upon human creativity, whose other face is necessarily . . . "creative destruction." The Pope writes that "The constant transformation of the methods of production and consumption devalues certain acquired skills and professional expertise, and thus requires a continual effort of retraining and updating." (*CA,* #33) He particularly worries about the elderly, the young who cannot find jobs, and, "in general those who are weakest." He refers to the vulnerable in advanced societies as "the Fourth World." Meeting their needs is the unfinished work of *Rerum Novarum,* including "a sufficient wage for the support of the family, social insurance for old age and unemployment, and adequate protections for the conditions of unemployment." (#34) All such deficiencies of a market system need to be redressed with practical wisdom. In some cases government will have to take a leading role; in other cases various sectors of civil society. The Pope is no libertarian — but neither is he a statist. Christian ends leave a great deal of room within these boundaries for rival approaches to means, programs, policies. . . .

The Pope repeats three times that "It is unacceptable to say that the defeat of so-called 'real socialism' leaves capitalism as the only model of economic organization." (#35) But here as elsewhere his cure for unbridled capitalism is capitalism of a more balanced, well-ordered kind....In #42, after having introduced capitalism rightly understood, the Pope again attacks "a radical capitalistic ideology...." By "radical capitalistic ideology," the Pope seems to mean total reliance on market mechanisms and economic reasoning alone. In the United States, we usually call such a view "libertarianism"; it is the view of a small (but influential) minority. United States libertarians do not "refuse to consider" the poverty of multitudes; they offer their own sustained analyses and practical remedies, and with some success....

Ironically, nonetheless, the Pope prefers to call the capitalism of which he approves the "*business economy, market economy,* or simply *free economy.*" This is probably because of European emotional resistance to the word "capitalism." My own reasoning in preferring to speak of "democratic capitalism," rather than "the market economy," is to avoid sounding libertarian — that is, narrowly focused on the economic system alone. For in reality, in advanced societies the institutions of both the juridical order and the cultural order do impinge greatly on, modify, and "control" the economic system. Indeed, any religious leftist or traditionalist who still believes that the United States is an example of unrestrained capitalism has not inspected the whole thirty-foot-long shelf of volumes containing the Federal Register of legally binding commercial regulations. One might more plausibly argue that the economies of the capitalist nations today are too heavily regulated (and too unwisely) than too lightly.

In the real world of fact, the business economy is restrained by law, custom, moral codes, and public opinion, as anyone can see who counts the socially imposed costs they are obliged to meet — and the number of employees they must hire (lawyers, affirmative-action officers, public affairs officers, inspectors, community relations specialists, child-care custodians, etc.). The term "democratic capitalism" is an attempt to capture these political and cultural restraints upon any humane economic system. It is defined in a way broad enough to include political parties from the conservative to the social democratic, and systems as diverse as Sweden and the United States.

In a similar vein, the Pope notes three clear moral limits to the writ of the free market: (1) many human needs are not met by the market but lie beyond it; (2) some goods "cannot and must not be bought and sold"; and (3) whole groups of people are without the resources to enter the market and need nonmarket assistance. The market principle is a good one, but it is neither universal in its competence nor perfectly unconditional. It is not an idol.

In addition, the Pope thinks in terms of international solidarity. The whole world is his parish. The Pope's frequent travels by jet to the Third World are meant to dramatize the primary human (and Christian) responsibility to attend to the needs of the poor everywhere. Economic interdependence and the communications revolution have brought the Catholic people (and indeed all people) closer together than ever. This fact brings to his attention many moral and social imperatives surrounding and suffusing economic activities. For example, care must be taken not to injure the environment. (#37) States and societies need to establish a framework favorable to creativity, full employment, a decent family wage, and social insurance for various contingencies. (#34) The common good of all should be served, not violated by a few. Individuals should be treated as ends, not as means — and their dignity should be respected. (#34)

The tasks to be met by the good society are many. No system is as likely to achieve all these goods as is a market system, (#34) but in order to be counted as fully good, the market system must in fact achieve them. The Pope explicitly commends the successes registered in these respects by mixed economies after World War II. (#19) But he also stresses how much needs yet to be done. *Finding good systems is a step forward; but after that comes the hard part.*

On matters of population growth, the Pope's claim that human capital is the chief resource of nations may lead to a new approach to population control. Those who say dogmatically that a large population causes poverty have not thought carefully about highly successful societies of dense population such as Japan, Hong Kong, and the Netherlands.... The Pope's emphasis on the creative capacity of every human being offers one reason why densely populated countries can become wealthy. *The principle behind economic progress is the fact that most people can create more in one lifetime than they consume.* The cause of poverty is not "overpopulation." It is, on the contrary, a system of political economy that represses the economic creativity that God has endowed in every woman and man. Nations ought not to repress that creative capacity.

Michael Novak, *The Catholic Ethic and the Spirit of Capitalism* (New York: Free Press, 1993), 132–36. [Notes that do not refer to *Centesimus Annus* have been omitted. Ed.]

## 67. J. Bryan Hehir on the Thirtieth Anniversary of *Gaudium et Spes,* 1996

*A contemporary interpreter of Catholic social thought argues that* Gaudium et Spes *provides a new basis for Catholic social teaching in an anthropological rationale for the church's engagement with the world.*

While the council's statement lays stress on the continuity of human effort and divine intervention, the theology of *Gaudium et Spes* is not a unilateral affirmation that the kingdom of God is a human creature. The structure of the conciliar argument is anthropological in its foundation, eschatological in its culmination, ecclesiological in its focus and christological in its content.

[Yves] Congar's commentary on *Gaudium et Spes* argues that the shift in the church-world question manifested in the council is a move from a political-juridical conception of the church's role in the world to an anthropological perspective.[1] The person is the link between church and world; it is because of its ministry to the person that the church is engaged in enhancing the moral

---

1. Y. M.-J. Congar, "The Role of the Church in the Modern World" (Part I, Ch. 4), in H. Vorgrimler, ed., *Commentary on the Documents of Vatican II* (Freiburg: Herder, 1969), 208.

and material conditions of the world. Anthropology leads therefore to ecclesiology: the church's work in the world is at one level a response to the concrete needs of the person. Ecclesiology is tied to eschatology: the church responds to the needs of the person in the first instance because of the intrinsic moral value of meeting human needs, but the work of the church in the world has eternal meaning and value; it prepares for the kingdom. Finally a strong christological theme ties anthropology, ecclesiology, and eschatology together; each of the four chapters of Part I concludes with a christological summary.

The rich theological argument of *Gaudium et Spes* brings the earlier theological work of [Henri] de Lubac, Congar et al. to a new level of integration, and with new authority in the Catholic tradition. The principal achievement of the text was to provide a new basis for Catholic social teaching and social ministry. By rooting them in the service of the person and showing this ministry's relationship to the eschaton, Vatican II provided a rationale for the Church's engagement in the world which was previously lacking. A second value was the subordination of the classical church-state questions to the broader apostolic conception of the church as a servant in the world. The institutional questions of relationships with the state and other secular entities retain a crucial importance, but they are couched in a broader vision of ministry.

The consequences of *Gaudium et Spes* in the church are best evaluated at two levels in the life of post-conciliar Catholicism. First, the record of Catholic engagement with the world in defense of human dignity and in support of human rights, in public advocacy for peace and in support of social justice demands a systematic explanation. While this kind of secular engagement is hardly new with Vatican II, there has been a pattern of Catholic activism in diverse political and cultural settings which points toward a common source. The ecclesiological significance attributed to serving and shaping the world by *Gaudium et Spes* provides an authoritative impetus for such activity, giving it a substantive theological basis. This theological rationale, ecclesial and eschatological, has provided the basic motivation and even methods of ministry for the church in Latin America, the Philippines, Central Europe, South Africa, and the United States. A Catholic "activism" with solid theological credentials has been the signature of post-conciliar Catholicism.

Second, *Gaudium et Spes* has catalyzed distinctive theological movements since 1965. While both the Theology of Liberation and Political Theology move beyond the conciliar text, they reflect methodological and substantive themes found in it. In a more detailed treatment one could both find the lines of continuity from the council to post-conciliar theologies and specify the distinctive contributions which such theological reflection has added to the conciliar vision.

J. Bryan Hehir, "The Church in the World: Responding to the Call of the Council," in *Faith and the Intellectual Life,* ed. James L. Heft, S.M. (Notre Dame, Ind.: University of Notre Dame Press, 1996), 113–15. Printed with permission.

## Part 7

# SPIRITUALITY AND ART

## Introduction

The vast majority of Catholics living in the United States during the last quarter of the nineteenth century were European immigrants or children of immigrants. The process of their acceptance by, and assimilation into, American society was hindered by a frequently virulent nativism and anti-Catholicism, one expression of which was a claim that Catholics were "pagans" — that is, superstitious worshippers of "idols" (doc. 68).

U.S. Catholic religious culture was indeed characterized by the presence of both "low" and "high" art, from the statues of saints and the Virgin Mary adorning the humblest parish church, to the ornate stained-glass windows of the urban cathedrals designed in imitation of the magnificent Gothic churches of Europe. The charge of idolatry missed the mark, however. Catholics did not venerate icons, statues, crucifixes, or other material depictions of the sacred. But with the eyes of faith they did see, and encounter, the reality of God in and through the very things of creation.[1] This sacramental view of the world was typified in the way Catholics thought about and perceived the Catholic Church itself, namely, as a supernatural, divinely founded institution — a visible sign and source of invisible grace.

As Catholics succeeded in building their own religious subculture within the largely Protestant U.S. society, self-assertion and something approaching "Catholic smugness" replaced the old defensiveness. And, as the twentieth century dawned, Catholic love of beauty in nature and in art attained a certain respectability. "Tired with a surfeit of realism," as Katherine F. M. O'Shea put it, "a nauseated world is turning back to the uplifting idealism of Catholic art . . ." (doc. 68). The highly touted (if partly imagined) unity and coherence of Roman Catholic Christendom — especially during "the thirteenth, the greatest of centuries," as one American Catholic apologist entitled his book — was projected as the antidote to the fissiparous tendencies of modernity.

The neo-Thomist revival, representing a return to the theology and philosophy of St. Thomas Aquinas (see part 2), underscored the artistic and liturgical achievements of the High Middle Ages. One important vehicle of the revival of the ancient and medieval Catholic past was the Liturgical Movement the aim

---

1. Lawrence Cunningham, *The Catholic Heritage* (New York: Crossroad, 1983), 140.

of which, according to its U.S. promoters at St. John's Benedictine Abbey at Collegeville, Minnesota, was better to understand the "spiritual importance of the liturgy" and thus enhance the corporate life of the church. Emphasis on the spiritual dimensions of the liturgy led to a restoration of its literary, musical, artistic, and historical elements. For example, Gregorian chant — the plain chant of the Roman rite, named after Pope Gregory the Great (d. 604) — was the favored musical "art" of the Liturgical Movement (doc. 69).

Neo-Thomism also spawned a wide-ranging literary revival among American Catholics writing in a variety of genres, including spiritual autobiography (the Cistercian monk Thomas Merton's surprise bestseller, *The Seven Storey Mountain;* Catholic Worker founder Dorothy Day's memoir, *The Long Loneliness*) poetry (Merton; the celebrated converts Robert Lowell and Allen Tate); and novels and short stories (Katherine Anne Porter, Flannery O'Connor, J. F. Powers, among others). The most creative and talented of these authors drew on their Catholic identity as inspiration rather than as template. More often than not, they relied on irony, ambiguity, and paradox — literary devices that seemed a far cry, in effect, from Thomism's rational, precise, ordered, teleological worldview.

Some authors of this quality, such as F. Scott Fitzgerald, while retaining elements of a Catholic sensibility, had formally thrown off the church. But others, such as O'Connor and Powers, saw the destabilization of facile certitudes as part of their Christian vocation: the inversion of Catholic smugness in the face of a morally ambiguous world was, in itself, a moral act. Powers, for example, gently lampoons the self-congratulatory attitude of suburban, middle-class Catholics of the 1950s who felt they were "making it," finally, in America. Father Urban, the Midwest Catholic protagonist of Powers's first novel, *Morte D'Urban* (1962), notes with satisfaction that *Time* magazine has declared the Catholic Church a corporation whose efficiency rivals that of Standard Oil. As the literary critic Paul Giles comments, Urban "works to reincarnate the essence of spiritual truths amid the accidents of baseball and business life." The supreme irony of the Thomist revival, Powers seems to suggest, is that it did indeed prove to be a powerful force for the transformation of culture — that is, for the Americanization of Catholic culture or, as Giles puts it, for "the recasting of [the church's] otherworldly goals within the colloquial idiom of the American vernacular."[2]

More radical and profound in her reworking of the Thomist and Catholic paradigm is Flannery O'Connor (doc. 71). O'Connor's stories, on the one hand, are bluntly realistic, coldly rational and precise — terms also used to describe Thomist philosophy. On the other hand, she specializes in the unpredictable and irrational, the bizarre and the grotesque. In their "radical pruning of every romantic excess and in their aloof application of the letter of the Catholic law," Giles comments, O'Connor's texts are transparently Thomistic. Yet her "manipulation of the grotesque" renders impossible the "finality and

---

2. Paul Giles, *American Catholic Arts and Fictions: Culture, Ideology, Aesthetics* (Cambridge: Cambridge University Press, 1992), 429–30.

closure" characteristic of Thomistic theology. "The traditional function of the literary grotesque is to rip things open, to render moribund systems vulnerable to the very forces [the irrational, the ironic, the ambiguous] they are seeking to exclude." Giles concludes: "In O'Connor's case, this is, as she said, the advent of 'mystery' alongside 'manners,' the interruption of observable social reality by the latent force of divine truth."[3]

Not every Thomist appreciated the effort to translate Scholastic theology and philosophy into the more fluid and open-ended medium of modern fiction. The Jesuit critic Harold C. Gardiner (doc. 70) derided Fitzgerald for his post-Catholic "rootlessness" and found Powers to be an undiscerning and superficial observer of the U.S. Catholic priesthood.[4] Catholic novelists, in his conventional opinion, should stick to the straight and narrow task of embedding the lessons of "the One, True Faith" in the lives of the characters peopling their stories.

Gardiner's attitude was indeed typical of many culture critics of the Catholic generation that came of age before World War II. Nowhere was the didactic approach to literature and the arts more evident than in the reaction to the new visual art of American film. During the 1920s and 1930s, as the cinema came into its own as a premiere form of American popular entertainment, Martin Quigley, a devout Catholic and a newspaperman, built a publishing empire by covering Hollywood motion pictures in weeklies such as *The Motion Picture Herald*. Convinced that "indecent" movies were an affront not only to Catholic sensibilities but also to the movie industry's health, he induced Daniel Lord, a Jesuit priest, to compose a comprehensive movie Production Code that eventually came to govern the content of American films for a generation. In 1935, the National Catholic Welfare Conference formed the Legion of Decency, which began operating an official Catholic movie classification system. ("B" movies were morally objectionable in part for all viewers, for example, and "C" movies were condemned.) While the Code had its ups and downs, Hollywood did open its studio doors in the 1940s for a "golden age" of popular cinema celebrating U.S. Catholicism in such priest-lionizing films as "Going My Way" and "The Bells of St. Mary's," both starring the charismatic American movie icon, Bing Crosby.[5] Yet the didactic approach in literature yielded to a sentimental approach in film, and Catholicism, as well as the nation, lost a truly golden opportunity to present a compelling portrayal of the church's complex and multidimensional contributions to building the moral fabric of U.S. society (doc. 72).

The most enduring legacy, then, rested with the self-consciously Catholic artists whose faith — and doubt — subtly yet vividly shaped their depiction of the world. Author Paul Elie has argued that a shared sense of spiritual pilgrimage set O'Connor, Merton, Day, and the novelist Walker Percy apart from their

---

3. Ibid., 361.
4. Stanley Poss, "J. F. Powers: The Gin of Irony," *Twentieth Century Literature* 14 (1968): 67.
5. Charles Morris, *American Catholic: How the Saints and Sinners of American's Most Powerful Church Built an Empire* (New York: Times Books, 1997).

more secure, less alienated predecessors in American Catholic literature.[6] Existential angst filtered through Catholic hope produced in the work of these writers gripping and odd yet recognizable evocations of a world wounded by sin and inhumanity but simultaneously awash in grace. In realistic and often bleak works like *Final Payments* (1978), one of the inheritors of that complex legacy, the contemporary novelist and short fiction writer Mary Gordon (doc. 73), has effectively explored the indelible wounds as well as the hard-won personal victories associated with coming of age in a post-Thomist, postenchanted Catholic world.

## 68. On the Mission and Influence of Christian Art, 1900

*The following excerpt is taken from a defense of the Catholic sacramental imagination, and its expression in great works of Catholic art, against the charge of "idolatry" and "paganism." Like other apologetic works, Katherine F. M. O'Shea's essay combines a spirited explanation of controversial Catholic practices with a celebration of the church's decisive contributions to Western culture and civilization.*

*Written at the dawn of the twentieth century, O'Shea's apologia strikes a note of vindication. The emergence in 1833 of the Oxford movement from within the Church of England signaled the gradual return of the English-speaking world to "Catholic ideals and methods of teaching" through immersion in the arts. The Catholic World, a Paulist journal dedicated to the evangelization of the United States through conversion of the educated and elite classes to a Catholic Christian sensibility, was the natural home for such an essay.*

The return to Catholic ideals and methods of teaching, in the adoption of music and of beautiful and uplifting pictures as great moral influences in the education of the young, is one of the most striking fulfilments of the poet's prophecy that many cycles of years have given us.

For nearly four centuries the Catholic Church has been called "idolatrous" just because of her appreciation of and devotion to Art, but now a blinded world is beginning to acknowledge that it was blind by adopting the very "idols" it so long abhorred. Aye! and is falling before them with a sentiment more nearly akin to idolatry than aught else, for the present trend of popular appreciation is to apotheosize the artist and his skill. Catholics venerate primarily the ideals represented.

Well, it is not the first time in this variable world's history that persecutors have become advocates, and that anathematizing Balaams have been forced to bless. " 'Tis but the law of the pendulum over again!"

What the church sought was not merely to please the eye and train the aesthetic faculties, by the representations of beautiful forms and faces, in the most harmonious colors and groupings conceivable. Her prime motive was to elevate the weak and earth-bound soul of man to the contemplation of things divine, to enter his heart through his sense of the beautiful, and thus conquer for the

---

6. Paul Elie, *The Life You Save May Be Your Own* (New York: Farrar, Straus and Giroux, 2003).

Lord this secret empire of the soul, over which he so longs to reign. Here, then, is the *raison d'être* of Christian Art!

All psychologists now understand what the church has always understood — that beautiful pictures, as well as beautiful music, have wondrous power over the souls of men; and thus it is that Catholic art, after an eclipse of centuries, is shining forth from the darkness of prejudice with a radiance more glorious than ever; for the "rejected stone" has once again "become the head of the corner" in the great work of education.

It is a curious and interesting study to remark the wonderful reaction in favor of Catholic ideals and teaching which the present century discloses. It began in the Oxford movement, in which mighty intellectual forces shook the foundation of Protestantism, as Samson the temple of the Philistines, until it is falling in shattered ruins everywhere about us.

That great movement was like to the explorations of buried cities, whence discovery brings to light treasures hidden for ages beneath the hardened lava tide of volcanic eruptions. It resurrected ancient doctrines and re-wrote religious history, setting in motion the reactionary forces of man's thought that have brought tens of thousands back to the church of their fathers, and restored Christian Art to her rightful place in the minds of men as one of the most beneficent gifts which the Spirit of God has scattered upon the face of the earth, or that his church has ever employed in its great apostolate.

Wonderful, indeed, is the change in our Protestant brethren's ideas, when pictures of the Blessed Virgin and of saints are hung upon the walls of public schools, and are found even in Protestant churches!

If such things happened a quarter of a century ago, nothing short of a public revolt would have resulted. Let us, indeed, be grateful that better knowledge prevails, and that broader culture is dispelling for ever, we hope, the narrow-mindedness and blind fanaticism that, for so many centuries, have made abhorrent all things Catholic.

The church knew from the first that the enervated and susceptible human soul needs many aids to lift it heavenward; therefore, those beautiful twin arts, painting and music, were cultivated to highest perfection for the service of the Lord in the conversion of the human race. Christian Art is but the hand-maiden of Religion; a teacher and preacher of Christian truths. Her eloquence touches every heart, her expression reaches all intelligences....

Never has the art of printing so well taught the truths of the Bible as those glowing picture stories of mediæval days! And what has not Catholic art done for the Book of Books itself? It treasured its sacred pages as jewels beyond price. It wrote the Scriptures on rarest vellums, in letters of gold, and bound them in precious metals adorned with gems! No mother ever guarded the precious heirlooms entrusted to her for her children as the Catholic Church cherished and defended and safeguarded that precious heritage of truth.

The Scriptures were her joy and her glory — the sole proofs of her claims; the foundation stones of her every doctrine. The church building, its forms and divisions, were all biblical. It was the Ark, or Ship of Christ, sailing over the stormy billows of the world. It was built in the form of a cross. The vestibule was the outer court; the nave, aisles, and transepts formed the holy place; the sanctuary and altar, the "holy of holies"; and so on, throughout the entire structure, form the cross-crowned pinnacles of steeple and towers to the huge foundation stones; from the foliated, many-hued windows of the chancel to magnificently sculptured doors of bronze, the Scriptures were taught in the unsurpassed eloquence of art; and thus found echo in the big, ungoverned but nobly disposed hearts of the Northmen, whom beauty could teach and music could tame.

With the revival of learning in the twelfth century was laid the foundation of that "new birth" of art which took place in the thirteenth, and grew to its zenith in the genius of Michael Angelo and Raphael, in the sixteenth century.

During the reign of the popes was the Golden Age of Art, for they have ever been the most ardent and liberal promoters. But for them and their devotion to its cause, not one of the art treasures of the world to-day would be in existence.

Not only did they promote the highest ideals of Christian art, and encourage and stimulate it to still greater perfection, but they gathered the remains of ancient art from desolate ruins and devastated cities, even digging down into the earth, where the accumulations of ages had buried them, for the beautiful remains of pagan sculpture. These they restored, as best they might, that the exquisite productions of those old Greek masters might teach the new world of artists, thirteen hundred years after them, the lost arts of expression and proportion. Under the kingdom of the Papacy art, science, and letters flourished with a degree of brilliancy never excelled.

During the days of Michael Angelo Buonarotti and Raphael da Urbino art attained its highest degree of excellence, and its greatest power of expression, because they were the living results of an æsthetic culture and an intellectual development unknown since the days of ancient Greece, and brought into the world again by that "revival of learning" begun in the twelfth century by the popes and fathers of the Catholic Church.

The monks were the most learned of men in the world; and, next to the popes, the most ardent promoters and lovers of art....

How many know that Roger Bacon was a Franciscan, and Albertus Magnus, Fra Angelico, and Fra Bartolommeo were Dominicans?

Art was the expression of man's delight or wondering comprehension of God's work. Its aim was to teach men that they are not beasts; involving, necessarily, spiritual or religious information about themselves.

Pagan art was sensual — of the body; Christian art was spiritual — of the soul; teaching lessons of immortality.

The idolatry of the human, as in Greek art, was but the apotheosis of self; expressing the idea of God in human beauty, drawing down the Infinite to the finite — lowering the Creator to the place of a creature.

The mission and aim of Christian art was to lift man's thoughts to God and place restraints upon sensualism and selfishness, by the preaching of higher ideals in the sublime eloquence of holy pictures.

Before the invention of printing every Benedictine abbey had its library and its scriptorium, where silent monks were employed from day to day and month to month in making transcripts of valuable works, especially the Scriptures. In those days a copy of the Bible was worth a king's ransom. To these monks the world owes the multiplication and diffusion of copies of the Bible, as well as the preservation of the greater part of the works of Pliny, Sallust, and Cicero. They were the fathers of Gothic architecture; they were the earliest illumina-tors and limners, and the first inventors of the gamut, and first to institute a school of music, in the person of the Benedictine Guido d'Arezzo. They were the first agriculturists who brought intellectual resources, calculation, and sci-ence to bear upon the cultivation of the soil. Of them it can be truly said: "They made the desert to bloom and the wilderness to blossom as a rose."

The sublime conceptions of Michael Angelo, the exquisite idealism of Raph-ael, and the tender holiness of Fra Angelico's spirituality are but the exponents of a culture more noble, more perfect, more complete in its intellectuality, its refinement, its all-embracing "progressiveness," than any culture the world can boast of before or since.

That was the Golden Age of Art, when color and form and expression, united in a perfect whole, blossomed forth upon the world in ideal beauty. Then it was that Angelo's sublime conceptions awed and charmed a world, while Raphael's heavenly ideals lifted men's thoughts to the skies. Then it was that Christ and his Mother were the undying inspirations of artists' souls — the sweet and gracious sovereigns of their hearts. That was the time when, as in days of patriarch and prophet, men delighted in bringing every best and perfect gift as "first-fruits" to the service of the Lord, in the adornment of his temples. "The Last Judgment" made men "think in their hearts" of the reward of sin; and the Madonna di San Sisto shamed them into sorrow with its mysterious pathos! The church, ever alert to the wants of the times, preached repentance and salva-tion in every marvellous picture of that time, when Art was the hand-maiden of the Lord, and her glory was supreme.

At that time Catholicity had contributed everything which civilization could boast. Slavery had been abolished, woman elevated, gentleness of manners im-planted by chivalry. In the moral world Christian charity ruled; in the æsthetic, architecture, music, and art. Universities were established in all nations, those of Oxford, Cambridge, Louvain, Prague, Bohemia, Vienna, Basle, Salamanca, Leipsic, Alcala, Paris, Bologna, and Ferrara being the most renowned.

In the scientific world and the world of letters the greatest savants were all children of the church; whilst in the world of eloquence, if we may so call it, the oratory of the Christian priesthood outshone the glories of Demosthenes and Cicero....

"The surest sign of the decadence of art, or of anything," says an eminent critic, "is when it falls into sensualism, for realism is the lowest idea of it; on the contrary, idealism is the highest, for it bases itself on universal truth." Tired with a surfeit of realism, a nauseated world is turning back to the uplifting idealism of Catholic art, with sick souls longing for the "good things" of the Father's table. "Broken cisterns" cannot long assuage the thirst of the human soul!

Katherine F. M. O'Shea, "Christian Art: Its Mission and Influence," *Catholic World* 71, no. 46 (September 1900): 815–26.

## 69. Gregorian Chant as Art: Translating the Liturgy into Music, 1908

*The author of the following passage, Justine B. Ward, was an associate of Virgil Michel, the founder of the U.S. branch of the Liturgical Movement of the twentieth century. Ward served for a time as a contributing editor of Orate Fratres, the journal of the movement, which first appeared in 1926 (and was renamed Worship in 1948).*

*The fervor of the reformers is reflected in Ward's presentation of Gregorian chant as the ideal melding of form and idea, for the purpose of "translating the liturgy into music."*

*Diffused throughout the Frankish Empire as part of the romanizing policy of the imperial court, Gregorian chant eventually supplanted most other forms of local or regional plain chant. Gregorian chant is monodic, i.e., one vocal part or melodic line predominates. It needs no instrumental accompaniment, and its scales or modes run from D, E, F, and G, rather than from C or A, as in modern music. With the rise of polyphony (music with two or more independent melodic parts sounded together) and measured music (music using metric units between two bars on the staff), the Gregorian chant tradition entered upon a serious decline compounded, after the Council of Trent (1545–63), by the publication of the Medicean edition of the Mass and Divine Office chants (1614 and 1615).*

*In the nineteenth century, however, the French Abbey of Solesmes led the effort to recover the original tradition. Ward wrote the following words at a time when Gregorian chant was enjoying a revival in the United States and Europe.*

One can trace a certain definite sequence in the development of every art. First we have the idea which strives to express itself in form. This form, at first crude, gradually perfects itself, until the point arrives when idea and form become synonymous. Then we have the classical period. Any further development of form is at the expense of the idea; it is the beginning of decadence, the lowest ebb of which is reached when art has descended to pure matter without idea. When form has thus submerged the idea, the painter uses color for color's sake, the musician revels in mere sound, in "tone color," the orator in "fine words," sonorous phrases, tickling sound, dazzling color, *vox et praeterea nihil*, — and art lies dead. Perfection of form is good art, display of form is decadence; and so the psychological moment when idea and form coincide must remain the classical period for all time, the highest expression of that particular idea. A true development in art can only be brought about by the entrance of a new idea. Thus after the vocal idea comes the instrumental; after the melodic idea, the contrapuntal. One succeeds the other, but one does not improve upon the other. Gregorian Chant represents the culmination of the melodic idea, the highest conceivable development of unisonous music, and further development had to take the form of polyphony.

The important question, then, is not whether we ought to go back to antiquity, but whether, by so going, we shall or shall not find the classical period in the art of musical prayer: the moment when the idea — prayer — and the form — music — became identical.

Let us briefly examine the characteristics of liturgical prayer; for Chant, as an art, stands or falls on the basis of its adaptability to this purpose. If it can be proved that the Gregorian form, and that form only, succeeds in translating the liturgy into music, in fitting that particular idea with form, then its value as an art is proved.

The liturgy of the Catholic Church serves a twofold purpose: to pray and to teach. The latter, her teaching function, is defeated by the use of any but unisonous music, because polyphony makes the words, in a greater or less degree, incomprehensible. In Chant the words are not repeated, twisted, turned upside down, inside out, and hind part before; they are uttered slowly, distinctly, pensively, each syllable lingered over as though with tenderness. It is a "musing," a quiet spiritual breathing. We can hear the Word of God and absorb it. Thus the teaching function of the Church demands the use of Chant.

Her prayer function demands it no less. Structurally, her prayers were conceived in a spirit of Chant and not of music, their very length precluding a more elaborate setting. A single illustration will suffice: during Holy Week the history of the Passion is read in all Catholic churches as the gospel of the day, while the congregation stands. Bach has given the Passion a musical setting, — one of the greatest of all pieces of devotional music. Yet it has one fatal objection: its performance takes no less than five hours, — a somewhat severe test upon the bodily strength of the congregation. Thus the musical structure of the period prevented even the great Bach from clothing his great idea with a suitable form. Chant merely enunciates the words, music embroiders on them; one is the principle of concentration, the other that of diffusion. Chant is, therefore, the only form in which the whole liturgy can be sung at all.

So much for the merely structural demands of the liturgy. Its æsthetic demands are no less clear.

Liturgical prayer is not the expression of individual reaching up to God, as in private devotion; it is the Church praying as a Church, officially, as a corporate whole. Her prayer has a fixed form, the outgrowth of the spiritual evolution of the Church, a survival of the fittest in the realm of religion. This prayer has, first of all, dignity: it is addressed to Almighty God. For this reason our modern rhythm, the outgrowth of the dance movement, is out of place, the form being too trivial to express the idea. I am speaking on purely artistic grounds. Again, prayer must have spontaneity; any insincerity kills prayer as prayer. For, as we have seen, a form attracting attention to itself detracts from the idea, and the idea in this case is God. Thus a prayer in rhyme would so obtrude its form as materially to detract from the idea. In precisely like manner is a prayer in music inferior to a prayer in Chant. Music, with its fixed measure, its regular strong and weak beats, is a formal garden, cut and trimmed into conventional avenues, adorned with hothouse plants. Chant is nature, the beauty of the fields and the forests. The formal garden has indeed its own place, its proper function; but prayer trimmed into a formal garden is an anomaly. The spirit bloweth where it listeth. Music moves with the regular rhythm of poetry; Chant with the free rhythm of prose, the cadence of a fine oratorical period. Chant has feet but no measure, and these feet succeed each other naturally, not artificially, so that there is no conflicting form to obstruct Chant in its effort to take the identical shape of the words and phrases of the prayers.

Modern music has two scales, or *Modes*. Chant has eight. It is evident that eight modes give a greater variety of expression than two, — an advantage for which even our modern indiscriminate use of the chromatic does not fully compensate. A mode is a manner. As in speech the speaker's manner shades the meaning of his words, sometimes even alters it, so in music the mode, or manner, determines the character of the composition. The meaning of a triad, for instance, depends entirely upon whether its manner be major or minor: lower the third, and its manner is sad; raise the third, and its manner is gay. Our present musical system is limited, then, to two manners, the major and the minor; and so Chant has the advantage of greater scope and variety. But more than this: the character of these two modern scales compels us to choose between a gayety almost frivolous on the one hand, and, on the other, a sorrow savoring of despair; neither of which emotions has any place in the Christian soul at prayer. The eight modes of the ancients, on the contrary, were devised to meet the requirements of prayer in an age when art was exclusively the servant of religion. They enabled the composer of the period to seize the subtle prayer-spirit, that elusive characteristic of Christianity, the rainbow tints of *joy in suffering.* Chant is joyful, but with the joy of the Cross, as distinguished from the joy of the revel. Chant is fervent, but with the passion of asceticism, as distinguished from the passion of the world. Prayer-sorrow is never despair, nor is prayer-joy ever frivolous. Chant is the artistic embodiment of this spirit; the minor idea and the major idea are so interwoven, their relation is so intimate, that to disentangle them is impossible. We are never left in sorrow, yet our joy is never without a cloud. Even in those bursts of ecstatic joy of the Easter Alleluias lurks the memory that we are still a part of earth, still in the valley of tears. Light and shadow play tantalizingly in and out, like the sun shining through a forest; glimpses of heaven caught through rifts in the clouds of the world.

We do not find in the ancient modes the same violent contrasts of mood as in the modern. They combine a solemnity, a grandeur, with the most tender and fervent devotion. Their minor tendency gives not so much the impression of sadness as of great solemnity and awe; their major tendency, not so much the impression of merriment as of a tender and ardent devotion. Thus we have the combination that makes true prayer: reverence and love, — the prayer that, like David's, rises as incense before the altar....

If the Christian ideal in its fullness produced the truly Christian art-form, may it not be possible, by an inverse process, to enter into the ideal by means of the art; by studying the effect to arrive at a better understanding of the cause? Familiarity with this classic prayer-music must reveal something of the prayer ideals which gave it birth, and thus bring about a new era of faith. Does art seem an insignificant approach to such a renaissance of spirituality? Not necessarily, for the language of art is, in a sense, universal, in so far as it touches the subconscious personality, and creates a receptive mood. Art cannot do the work, but it can at least pave the way. Piety is not, it is true, a mere matter of the emotions, but real piety, which lies in the intellect and the will, can often be approached and set in motion by means of the emotions; a permanent result be achieved through a transitory cause. The emotions are simply a motive power, but not on that account to be despised. They are to piety what appetite is to physical life: not the food, but the impetus to take food. They are a means to an end. But it is the food itself, and not merely the appetite, which supports life; the appetite simply makes easy and natural what might otherwise be difficult. To stimulate appetite is not, in itself, unsanitary, nor is to stimulate the emotions necessarily unspiritual. But as the emotions are prone to run away with us along false paths, we strive to stimulate them as much as possible along the lines of true piety, that we may absorb food and not poison. That is the theory of ascetic art as a whole, the test of whose value lies simply in the quality of its stimulus.

One more aspect of this movement, which must not be forgotten, is its democratic character. For the carrying-out of the full ideal demands the coöperation of the entire people, who will no longer assist at, but take part in, the liturgy. This may not be accomplished in a day, but the Church works for the future, and already she is sowing the seeds. The little Catholic school child is learning to pray, not only in words but also in song; not only in the Church's language, Latin, but in her musical language, Chant; and when these children grow up, our choirs will be the whole Catholic world. While the variable and the more elaborate parts of the liturgy will demand the great genius, the great artist, the simpler parts will be taken up spontaneously by the entire congregation; producing the superb contrast of, on the one hand, the perfection of art, and on the other, the majesty of numbers. This is, indeed, nothing new: it is thus that the liturgy is intended to be rendered; it is thus that it has been rendered in the past, and is still rendered in a few centres of Catholic life. It is simply a return to the true ideal, a "renewing of all things in Christ," a revitalizing, through art, of the spirit of Catholic democracy and universality.

Justine Bayard Ward, *The Reform in Church Music* (Philadelphia: American Ecclesiastical Review, 1908), 9–14, 22–24.

## 70. Literature as a Moral Activity, 1953

*Harold C. Gardiner, S.J., the author of* Norms for the Novel, *from which the following passages are excerpted, was the literary editor for* America, *the Jesuit weekly review. Adhering to what he understood to be the fundamental principles of Thomism, Gardiner adopted a strictly didactic approach to literature. In 1951, for example, Gardiner had offered "a Christian appraisal" of the American novel during the first half of the twentieth century. Novels were judged according to their fidelity to an orthodox Christian worldview, and novelists ranked according to their "realization of man as fundamentally a religious being." He made clear his disdain for Protestant authors such as Edith Wharton, "who lacked a sense of heaven and glory," and Sinclair Lewis, who, Gardiner claimed, rendered "Creation a fairy story, the Incarnation an impossibility and*

*the redemption a joke."[1] The following passage is taken from a chapter entitled
"Literature as a Moral Activity."*

This Aristotelian concept is still, in the main, the concept that dominates
Catholic writing and ought to dominate Catholic criticism and reading. The
fact that it *is* held, though perhaps implicitly and unconsciously, is revealed by
a sort of congenital uneasiness among Catholic readers over the photographic
and reportorial type of writing that bulked so large in the American fiction of
the 'twenties and 'thirties and which still crops up today. The Catholic who
has read books like Steinbeck's *The Wayward Bus* (1947) or Jones' *From Here
to Eternity,* though he is in all honesty impelled to admit that the slices of life
have been caught vividly and can be verified in actual experience all around
him, still feels a vague suspicion that this kind of book somehow *cannot* really
be called literature. What this reader is unconsciously saying to himself is that
these books have fallen short of the Aristotelian concept of what art is and
ought to be.

Such books have photographed a montage of contemporary life; their click-
ing of the shutter has often been marvelously timely and vivid. But they have
merely caught men acting as they do and not rather as they "ought." In these
books and others like them there is no clear perception of ultimate ends and
purposes. A frozen moment of social or marital life, let us say, is caught in
the story, but the problems and acts of *this* particular social group receive no
illumination from any clear vision of the goals and purposes of social life in
itself; *this* particular marriage is not illuminated by any light flowing from a
clear realization of the intrinsic ends and purposes of the very institution of
marriage.

This is why, in Aristotle's concept, art is essentially, if indirectly, a moral
activity — the individual act captured in the creative activity always implies a
relationship toward ends and purposes. Such a relationship is a moral fact and
the portrayal of such a relationship is a moral activity. It is in this sense that
art is always, at least implicitly, didactic, for if "man learns first by imitation,"
says Aristotle, and if it is "natural for all to delight in works of imitation," it
is further true that "to be learning something is the greatest of pleasures not
only for the philosophers but also for the rest of mankind, however small their
capacity for it; the reason for the delight in seeing the picture is that one is at the
same time learning." Think back, here, if I may suggest it, to the earlier remarks
on the *rational* pleasure which is literature's first purpose.

Perhaps an illustration may be taken from portraiture. It will be admitted,
I suppose, that photography is not, strictly speaking, an art. It must be admitted if you are an Aristotelian. For the photograph, catching the subject in the
split second of the shutter's release, immobilizes the human features, just, and
only, as they instantaneously are. The portrait painter, on the other hand, working over days and weeks, will complete a human face which at no time during
the sittings looked exactly and completely as it does in the finished product. It

---

1. Harold C. Gardiner, S.J., "A Christian Appraisal: The Point of It," in Harold C. Gardiner,
S.J., ed., *Fifty Years of the American Novel: A Christian Appraisal* (New York: Gordian, 1951), 1, 4.

will, however, and marvelously enough, by having caught the varying shades of mood, temperament and personality that played over the features during the sittings, be a truer picture because of its composite growth. The painter will have reproduced the human face as it "ought" to be to reflect this particular personality; the photographer will have merely caught the human countenance as it actually was merely at a particular point of time.

This moral approach to the function of art is admittedly a narrow gate and a strait [*sic*] path. If interpreted in a doctrinaire and apologetic way it leads directly to preachment through art. This was all too evident some two decades ago in the Marxist line that was to be clearly traced in some fairly mature fiction. Such an approach may lead to Catholic preachment as well, if one forgets that the morality — the "oughtness" — of the Aristotelian concept is an inherent relationship of the reality with the ideal and not an overt elaboration of the ideal superimposed upon the reality....

This basically Aristotelian concept is still operative, and it is by no means confined to Catholic novelists and critics. It is the leaven working away in almost any literature which is not purely naturalistic.

It is lamentable, therefore, to find viewers of the current literary scene announcing so flatly that the literary tradition of the Western world is cold and stiff in a morgue. A Proust, a Joyce, if you like, or a Sinclair Lewis or a James Jones, may be uttering the "dying gasps of European culture," but I cannot see that a Greene or a Waugh or a Bernanos are. The society these Catholic writers are portraying may indeed be "decadent" (as reviewers are so fond of saying without telling us what they mean), but the cardinal point is that the authors' approach to that society, their proposing to that society of the fundamental purposes and ideals of life, are *not* decadent. In other words, to go back to the ideals of Aristotle, such authors show us their sophisticated, unpleasant, weary and blasé gallery of characters as indeed they are, but against an unmistakable background of implications of what they "ought" to be. There are no such "oughts" in Farrell, Lewis, Jones and the like.

Not all critics, indeed, fail to realize that this great Western literary tradition, being as it is but part of the *philosophia perennis,* is a still-enduring thing. R. Ellis Roberts, for example, in reviewing Cyril Connolly's *The Condemned Playground* (*Saturday Review of Literature,* July 13, 1946) and remarking that Connolly must be presumed to know Eliot, Mauriac, Dubos, Bernanos, Baring, Belloc and many others writing in the Christian tradition, goes on to say: "Yet [Connolly] makes no effort in writing of the past or of the present, estimate the part played by Christianity and the Catholic revival. Here he remains, indeed, an insular Victorian." This lack of sympathy, Mr. Roberts continues, is all the more odd since Connolly "sees so clearly the vice in modern art...it is the exaltation of self-expression over communication... nothing can effectively deal with 'elephantiasis of the ego'" save religion, which means that "purely humanist and psychological values must be superseded by spiritual and mystical values."

This, then, is the common critical approach — common to the literary traditions of historical Christendom, and common across the international boundaries of today, wherever worthy Catholic craftsmen are working. A voice identical in two-fold wise speaks through all real Catholic literature. It is identical in its statement of theological and philosophical principles. It is no less identical in its reiteration of literary and critical principles....

The charge most likely to be raised in a discussion of literature from Aristotle's viewpoint of its morality is the charge that literature is *ipso facto* being burdened with an undue concern with religion or being viewed from a specifically ecclesiastical point of view....Actually this whole discussion has nothing to do with any ecclesiastical viewpoint. It is not an *ex cathedra* definition of what Rome thinks about modern literature. Our discussion is simply a mulling over of what a great thinker once thought, a great thinker whose thought has been incorporated into the thinking of the whole civilized Western world. It is, as a matter of fact, only since the rise of the modern ultra-realistic school of fiction that the thought has been seriously challenged in its application to literature.

> Harold C. Gardiner, S.J., *Norms for the Novel* (New York: America Press, 1953), 120–23, 125–28.

## 71. Flannery O'Connor on the Prophetic Vision of the Fiction Writer, 1969

*In the following passage, Flannery O' Connor (1925–64), the Catholic novelist of the Deep South, articulates a view of Catholic literature which stands at some distance from the simple didacticism of Harold Gardiner. O'Connor's short stories, although engaged directly with Catholic theology, explore the incongruity between the Catholic faith and a secularized modern world; the lack of a cultural context in the Bible Belt South for conveying the complex Catholic view of the relationship between fallen human nature and grace lends irony and, at times, the quality of the macabre to her fiction.*

*The surface appearances of the world, O'Connor's art suggests, hide a deeper significance that is rooted in the paradoxical but redemptive event of Christ's death on the Cross. To portray the subtle presence of grace amid human sinfulness, O'Connor created vivid, often bizarre characters and placed them in surreal situations. "Distortion," she writes elsewhere in the work from which the following passage is taken, "in this case is an instrument; exaggeration has a purpose, and the whole structure of the novel or story has been made what it is because of belief. This is not the kind of distortion that destroys; it is the kind that reveals, or should reveal."*

I have found that people outside the Church like to suppose that the Church acts as a restraint on the creativity of the Catholic writer and that she keeps him from reaching his full development. These people point to the fact that there are not many Catholic artists and writers, at least in this country, and that those who do achieve anything in a creative way are usually converts. This is a criticism that we can't shy away from. I feel that it is a valid criticism of the way Catholicism is often applied by our Catholic educational system, or from the pulpit, or ignorantly practiced by ourselves; but that it is, of course, no valid criticism of the religion itself.

There is no reason why fixed dogma should fix anything that the writer sees in the world. On the contrary, dogma is an instrument for penetrating reality. Christian dogma is about the only thing left in the world that surely guards and respects mystery. The fiction writer is an observer, first, last, and always, but he cannot be an adequate observer unless he is free from uncertainty about what he sees. Those who have no absolute values cannot let the relative remain merely relative; they are always raising it to the level of the absolute. The Catholic fiction writer is entirely free to observe. He feels no call to take on the duties of God or to create a new universe. He feels perfectly free to look at the one we already have and to show exactly what he sees. He feels no need to apologize for the ways of God to man or to avoid looking at the ways of man to God. For him, to "tidy up reality" is certainly to succumb to the sin of pride. Open and free observation is founded on our ultimate faith that the universe is meaningful, as the Church teaches.

And when we look at the serious fiction written by Catholics in these times, we do find a striking preoccupation with what is seedy and evil and violent. The pious argument against such novels goes something like this: if you believe in the Redemption, your ultimate vision is one of hope, so in what you see you must be true to this ultimate vision; you must pass over the evil you see and look for the good because the good is there; the good is the ultimate reality.

The beginning of an answer to this is that though the good is the ultimate reality, the ultimate reality has been weakened in human beings as a result of the Fall, and it is this weakened life that we see. And it is wrong, moreover, to assume that the writer chooses what he will see and what he will not. What one sees is given by circumstances and by the nature of one's particular kind of perception.

The fiction writer should be characterized by his kind of vision. His kind of vision is prophetic vision. Prophecy, which is dependent on the imaginative and not the moral faculty, need not be a matter of predicting the future. The prophet is a realist of distances, and it is this kind of realism that goes into great novels. It is the realism which does not hesitate to distort appearances in order to show a hidden truth.

For the Catholic novelist, the prophetic vision is not simply a matter of his personal imaginative gift; it is also a matter of the Church's gift, which, unlike his own, is safeguarded and deals with greater matters. It is one of the functions of the Church to transmit the prophetic vision that is good for all time, and when the novelist has this as a part of his own vision, he has a powerful extension of sight.

It is, unfortunately, a means of extension which we constantly abuse by thinking that we can close our own eyes and that the eyes of the Church will do the seeing. They will not. We forget that what is to us an extension of sight is to the rest of the world a peculiar and arrogant blindness, and that no one today is prepared to recognize the truth of what we show unless our purely individual vision is in full operation. When the Catholic novelist closes his own eyes and tries to see with the eyes of the Church, the result is another addition to that large body of pious trash for which we have so long been famous.

It would be foolish to say there is no conflict between these two sets of eyes. There is a conflict, and it is a conflict which we escape at our peril, one which cannot be settled beforehand by theory or fiat or faith. We think that faith entitles us to avoid it, when in fact, faith prompts us to begin it, and to continue it until, like Jacob, we are marked.

For some Catholic writers the combat will seem to be with their own eyes, and for others it will seem to be with the eyes of the Church. The writer may feel that in order to use his own eyes freely, he must disconnect them from the eyes of the Church and see as nearly as possible in the fashion of a camera. Unfortunately, to try to disconnect faith from vision is to do violence to the whole personality, and the whole personality participates in the act of writing. The tensions of being a Catholic novelist are probably never balanced for the writer until the Church becomes so much a part of his personality that he can forget about her — in the same sense that when he writes, he forgets about himself.

This is the condition we aim for, but one which is seldom achieved in this life, particularly by the novelists. The Lord doesn't speak to the novelist as he did to his servant, Moses, mouth to mouth. He speaks to him as he did to those two complainers, Aaron and Aaron's sister, Mary: through dreams and visions, in fits and starts, and by all the lesser and limited ways of the imagination.

I would like to think that in the future there will be Catholic writers who will be able to use these two sets of eyes with consummate skill and daring; but I wouldn't be so reckless as to predict it. It takes readers as well as writers to make literature. One of the most disheartening circumstances that the Catholic novelist has to contend with is that he has no large audience he can count on to understand his work. The general intelligent reader today is not a believer. He likes to read novels about priests and nuns because these persons are a curiosity to him, but he does not really understand the character motivated by faith. The Catholic reader, on the other hand, is so busy looking for something that fits his needs, and shows him in the best possible light, that he will find suspect anything that doesn't serve such purposes.

Flannery O'Connor, *Mystery and Manners: Occasional Prose* (New York: Farrar, Straus and Giroux, 1969), 177–82.

## 72. The Impact of the Legion of Decency on American Film, 1951

*In the following passage the film critic Walter Kerr, in an essay that was later anthologized by* Commonweal, *the lay Catholic foundation and magazine, looked back on fifteen years of the code and lamented what he saw as the devastating effect of censorship on the creativity and quality of American cinema. In 1953, two years after Kerr's essay was first published, Otto Preminger's* The Moon Is Blue *became the first movie successfully to defy the code office.*

Bad taste is not one of the seven deadly sins, and nobody is going to hell for having preferred "Quo Vadis" over "God Needs Men." But neither is there any wisdom in elevating bad taste to the level of a virtue, or in confusing it with virtue itself. And it does seem to me that American Catholic criticism of the popular arts — especially the sort of criticism that is generally meted out to the motion picture — is rapidly driving itself into just such an unattractive, and philosophically untenable corner.

However inadvertently, and with whatever genuine concern for the moral health of its membership, the Church in this country has permitted itself to become identified with the well-meaning second-rate. In effect, it has seemed to say: "I don't care what the quality of the art work is, so long as its content is innocuous, or perhaps favorably disposed in our direction."

In the most publicized Catholic "art" award of 1952, the Christophers selected "Quo Vadis." This essay in calculated vulgarity represented, we were told, "creative work of enduring significance." It was "outstanding," not merely because it threw a certain number of Christians to a certain number of lions, but because it lived up to the highest esthetic "standards." The truth, of course, slips out; in presenting the award, Father Keller immediately launched into praise of the film for showing "how a handful of human beings, fired with the love and truth of Christ, were able to overcome the might of Pagan Rome." The esthetic norm is clearly the proselytizing content, if, with a little effort of the imagination, "Quo Vadis" could be considered as really having proselytizing content.

But this avowal — that Christians ought to like "Quo Vadis" because "Quo Vadis" likes Christians — was not a frank one. There was the additional insistence that the film's special pleading, its fairly dim and remote hoeing of the Catholic row, be equated with artistic merit. Because Saint Peter had been given a certain amount of footage in the production, this form of logic demands that therefore the movie in question be praised for its craftsmanship.

The intention is virtuous; the execution must therefore not be called into question, must indeed be lauded as supremely desirable. The makers of motion pictures were explicitly urged to go on in the same vein, with the assurance that they would thereby arrive at unparalleled esthetic glories. The *Christopher News Notes* announced that "outstanding personalities in the entertainment and literary fields...predict that if similar Christopher Awards are made for the next three or four years, they may do more to stimulate high quality work in these spheres of influence than any other single factor."

The sort of judgment which at best reveals an alarming innocence of the very texture of art, and which at worst smacks suspiciously of cant, has pretty much become rule-of-thumb for the American Catholic moviegoer. A film featuring a saint is a film of majestic technical excellence. A film showing a nun driving a jeep is a superbly made comedy. A film embracing a jolly priest, a self-sacrificing Catholic mother, and an anti-Communist message must be defended in the diocesan press from those irresponsible esthetes and conspiratorial leftists — and even worse, those maverick Catholics — who have had the meanness and the malice to question it.

When there is no recent film of obviously Catholic sympathies — no priest in the pulpit, no nun in the backfield, no early-Christian Deborah Kerr in the jaws of a Technicolor lion — the next-best bet, in the current practice of Catholic criticism, is to play it safe. An earlier Christopher Award — I am not really out after the Christophers; they got out there by themselves — went to "The Father of the Bride." Now "The Father of the Bride" was a pleasant little film, certainly a harmless little film. That it represented the peak of creative achievement, of imaginative artistry, in its given year is, however, fairly doubtful. (If one wanted to be parochially picky about it, one might even raise some doubt about its suitability for an explicitly Catholic award; if the film reflected any social concept at all, it reflected precisely that slick, sentimental, materialistic concept of the two-child, two-car family against which pulpit orators have so long and richly fulminated.) But it was a film that was kind to babies, kind to parents, generally optimistic about the domestic scene. It was therefore qualified for praise on the highest level of esthetic achievement. The identification of good will with good work is commonplace in the Catholic press. Unfortunately, the sort of art which Catholics are urged to admire is commonplace, too — and the power which Catholic spokesmen have come to wield over the motion picture even more commonplace than it need have been.

The penalties of this inverted esthetic — the notion that what is pure is also necessarily perfect — have thus been double. Catholic taste in motion pictures has been frozen at the "unobjectionable," or purity-with-popcorn level, a level that if pursued down the ages would have called into question nearly every literary or dramatic masterpiece ever produced. (We need not think of such rowdy samples as "Volpone" or "Tartuffe," a "Phèdre" or a "Hamlet" will do.) And the American film has, through the rigid circumscriptions of the production code and the terrors of an unfavorable Legion of Decency rating, been dissuaded from attempting anything complex enough in the way of human behavior to serve as the basis for a new masterpiece.

The first of these penalties — the petrifaction of taste — cannot seem of much moment to men whose urgent concern is the saving of souls. Yet it has far more serious consequences than many an honest moralist realizes: it discredits the entire Catholic intellectual tradition. The man who had been to see "Quo Vadis" might reach certain conclusions: that the "Catholic" concept of art is a decidedly primitive one; that it probably rests on similarly primitive philosophical principles; that the Church, when its true colors are showing, is essentially antipathetic to the creative spirit, essentially in league with the vulgar.

The fact that each of these assumptions is thoroughly false, and would seem strange indeed to an Augustine, an Aquinas, or a Newman, is nothing for which the contemporary observer can be held responsible; the impression is thrust upon him, paraded before him, drummed in his ears by the most vocal Catholic spokesmen in the field.

And this conviction that bad taste among Catholics is due to an ineradicable defect deep down in the Catholic philosophical minds leads to new damage: it tends to shut off Catholic intellectual influence altogether. We hear a great deal about the "influence" Catholicism has had on the American Screen. We forget that this influence has been wholly of one kind: the influence of the pressure group. The Legion of Decency is an economic weapon; the production code was written under the standing fear of boycott. Neither represents an intellectual victory in the sense that an esthetic principle has been stated with such clarity and force as to bring about free assent. The only persuasiveness we have been able to whip up is the persuasiveness of the dollar.

The barbed-wire barriers of the production code may be up; but the lines of communication are down. The theatergoer, the critic, or the creative artist who stands outside the Church looking in, sees only a forbidding tangle of precaution and proscription, over which hovers a halo of bad taste. He does not notice much lively discussion of esthetic value; indeed, he will quickly discover that "esthetic" is a bad word in vast areas of the Catholic press. He does not notice much effort to liberalize parochial taste; indeed, he will quickly find most such effort labeled "art for art's sakeism." He will nowhere run across any frank recognition of home truths—such as that a work of art may be perfectly clean and perfectly terrible. That he should feel vaguely uncomfortable in this environment is understandable. That he should reject it is perhaps inevitable. That he should feel, in rejecting it, that he is thereby rejecting the whole body of Catholic thought on the arts, the central content of Catholic philosophy itself, is tragic. Yet by stubbornly praising what is safely banal, by strenuously encouraging a low level of taste, we are fostering such an impression.

Our fear that any recognition of the claims of the "esthetic" may undermine the Catholic accomplishment to date, our reluctance to encourage any study of the nature of art as art, our insistence that the Catholic contribution stop dead at the cautionary level, have also brought about the second penalty mentioned above: the discouragement of the creative filmmaker pursuing the ultimate possibilities of his craft.

Walter Kerr, "Movies," in *Catholicism in America: A Series of Articles from "The Commonweal"* (New York: Harcourt, 1954), 209–14.

## 73. A Celebrated Novelist Examines the Catholic Roots of Her Craft, 1988

*To non-Catholic Americans in the first half of the twentieth century, the Catholic Mass was an arcane world unto itself: bread and wine miraculously transformed into body and blood by a priest intoning ancient Latin prayers; women called "nuns" shrouded in forbidding black gowns known as "habits"; the splash of holy water, the echo of bells, the aroma of incense. In this passage, the novelist Mary Gordon, author of* Final Payments *and other works of fiction that betray a profound Catholic sensibility, reflects on the ways in which the memory, ritual, and symbols of her Catholic childhood shaped her perceptions and imagination.*

To begin speaking about the words "spiritual quests" in relation to myself fills me simultaneously with amusement and alarm. Amusement because the words "spiritual" and "quest" conjure up the imagery of the knight consecrate, Galahad after the Holy Grail, dying picturesquely at the very moment he fulfills his goal. I can't see myself in the part. And alarm because the very word "spiritual" suggests to me the twin dangers of the religious life: dualism and abstraction.

Abstractionism I define as the error that results from refusing to admit that one has a body and is an inhabitant of the physical world. Dualism, its first cousin, admits that there is a physical world but calls it evil and commands that it be shunned. I'd venture to say that these two what I call "sins" — dualism and abstraction — are the cause of at least as much human misery as pride, covetousness, lust, envy, hatred, gluttony and sloth. Those names come very easily to my mind — names learned in childhood, memorized in childhood. They're one of those lists, those catalogues, that made the blood race with the build-up. So many catalogues there were in the church I grew up in, so many lists: seven capital sins, three theological virtues and four moral ones, seven sacraments, seven gifts of the Holy Ghost. A kind of poetry of accumulation, gaining power like an avalanche from its own momentum — perhaps a small influence, but in my prose an important one that I grew up hearing every day of my life, for my childhood days were shaped and marked by the religious devotions of my parents, by the rhythmic, repetitive cadences of formal prayer. It bred in me a love for strongly rhythmic prose.

I can never talk about the spiritual or the religious life without talking about early memory, which is anything but disembodied. Whatever religious instincts I have bring their messages to me through the sense — the images of my religious life, its sounds, its odors, the kind of kinesthetic sense I have of prayerfulness. These are much more real to me than anything that takes place in the life of the mind. I want to say that I've never been drawn to systematic theology except as a kind of curiosity, though as soon as I say this I want to qualify it, because what makes me even more nervous than the word "spiritual" are the words "evangelical," or "charismatic." The religious impulse mediated by reason terrifies me, and it seems to me that we are always having to mediate between the emotions, the body, the reason. So even though I can't be moved forward in any way by systematic theology, I like it to be there, in the same way that I like modern architecture to be there, even though I don't want to live in it.

And the body must be not left out. I was born into a church shaped and ruled by celibate males who had a history of hatred and fear of the body, which they lived out in their lives and in the rituals they invented. They excluded women from the center of their official and their personal lives. When I tried to think of any rituals that acknowledged the body, except for rituals involving death and in a very oblique way birth, the only one I could think of was what used to be called "the churching of women," which is a blessing for the mother, a kind of purification after the mess of birth. It's a remembrance of the purification of the Virgin Mary; she would have been actually submerged in water, not merely symbolically cleansed, for the reentry into the legitimate world where body life could once again be hidden.

I keep having to backtrack; every time I say something I instantly think that I haven't quite told the truth, because I have to confess and acknowledge my own dualism. Much of what is beautiful to me in my religious experience is its bodylessness. I remember the early morning Masses of my childhood. In my memory the atmosphere is always gray, a kind of false dawn, air without heat or light. I'm walking with one of my parents, never both, because these memories are the *tête à têtes* of the anointed "only child," the child of parents who preferred her to each other. The women in my memories are wearing coats of muted colors, kerchiefs, round-toed nunlike shoes. The nuns themselves are disappearing in their habits, faceless. They are only forms. The church is coldish. It is silent. In the sacristy you can hear the mysterious, inexplicable, untraceable noises of the priest and the altar boy — the cruet's tinkle, the vestments' rustle. There are whispered words.

And then there is the Mass. In preparing this talk, it occurred to me for the first time what an excellent training ground the regular attendance at Mass was for an aspiring novelist. First, there's the form of the Mass itself, which popularly has been compared to drama, but the likenesses with the novel are also not at all unapt. The central event of the Mass occurs — interestingly for the novelist, I think — way past its middle. It's the consecration, the turning of bread and wine into the body and blood of Christ. I have to say a word about this, because for orthodox Catholics this is an actual transformation of substance. (The doctrine is called transubstantiation.) That is to say, for an orthodox Catholic the bread and wine is no longer believed to be bread and wine; it has changed in its essence, in what the scholastic philosophers called its substance, so that it is no longer bread and wine but has been actually transformed into the body and blood of Christ. Somewhere there's a conversation I like between Mary McCarthy and Flannery O'Connor in which Mary McCarthy tries to get Flannery O'Connor to admit that she really believes that transubstantiation is only a symbolic act. And Flannery O'Connor is reported to have said, "If I thought it were just a symbol, I'd say the hell with it."

For the novelist, then, there is a central dramatic event. But, interestingly, there is also a regular alternation of levels of language and types of literature within the Mass itself. There's scriptural invocation, reflective prayer, the poetry of the Psalms, the Old Testament and Gospel narratives and the repetitions: the Sanctus, the Agnus Dei, the *Domini non sum dignus,* repeated three times, the first and last time to the accompaniment of bells. Different types of Masses offer to the sensitive ear examples of different kinds of formality and embellishment, from the simple daily Low Mass to the more formal Sunday Low Mass to the High Mass, complete with choirs, chants and all the liturgical stops pulled out.

I'm not saying that as a child I consciously understood this. Obviously I didn't. As a matter of fact, I don't think I thought of it at all until I was preparing this talk. But I absorbed it unconsciously, this elaborate and varied and supple use of language. From a very early age it wove itself into my bones. Once again, Flannery O'Connor says that the writer learns everything important to him or her before the age of six. So every day, for however often I was taken to daily Mass, I was learning lessons in rhetoric.

And I was learning a lot of other things. If we accept the truism that all writers are voyeurs, then we can say that an hour a day in a confined space like a church, where one has the leisure or the boredom to observe others of one's kind when they imagine themselves to be in private communion with their deepest souls, is as useful for a prospective novelist as a wiretap. Daily Mass was the home ground of the marginal, the underemployed; you always wondered why they weren't at work or getting ready for work. A child at daily Mass got to observe at close range the habits of old women, of housewives at eight-thirty already tired out for the day, men down on their luck praying for a reversal of their bad fortunes.

You also got wonderful lessons in structure. The structure of the Mass, like that of the parish, composed itself around the figure of the priest, the center of all our earthly attentions, the center of parish life, at an observable distance on the altar for an hour of our time. The erotically charged yet unreachable figure of the priest! And around him, theoretically invisible, and yet of course the pulse of parish life, the women: jockeying, serving (except on the altar, where they were forbidden to be), dreaming, losing and gaining lives against the backdrop of history. And the single figure of the priest, who could contain in himself the whole world. The priest was theoretically available to all, and yet available to no one, just as the Church was in theory open to all and in theory welcoming of all, but in fact operated on principles of initiation and exclusion. For all that, it has always contained a membership that includes representatives from all of Europe and all the places where the Europeans set down their iron-shod feet.

So to be a Catholic, or even to have been one, is to feel a certain access to a world wider than the vision allowed by the lens of one's own birth. You grew up believing that the parish is the world, and that anyone in the world could be a member of the parish. But of course the parish was a fiercely limited terrain: the perfect size and conformation for the study of the future novelist. Anachronistically limited, its hierarchies clear, its loyalties assumed and stated and then in practice always undermined, it has at its center issues of money. You learned from the parish how the watermarks of class and privilege work. You could see how the impressive personality, the personality of the clergy, can change life.

A novelist builds a fence enclosing a certain area of the world and then calls it his or her subject. To be a Catholic, particularly in Protestant America, made one an expert at building the limiting, excluding fence. Inside the paddock there were shared assumptions about everything from the appropriate postures for kneeling to the nature of human consciousness. But there was always a right way and a wrong way, and you always knew which was which.

One could be, at least in the time when I was growing up, a Catholic in New York and deal only in the most superficial of ways with anyone non-Catholic. Until I went to college I had no genuine contact with anyone who wasn't Catholic. The tailor and the man who ran the candy store were Jews, and the women who worked in the public library were Protestants, but you only allowed them the pleasantries. Real life, the friendships, the feuds, the passions of proximate existence, took place in the sectarian compound, a compound, like any other, with its secrets — a secret language, secret customs, rites, which I now understand must have been very menacing at worst or at the best puzzling to the outside world.

But we never knew that, because we never understood that the rest of the world was looking. We weren't interested in the rest of the world. If some of us did assume that the rest of the world was looking, our response was to be all the more zealous in keeping the secrets secret. One of the greatest treasures a novelist can have is a secret world which he or she can open up to his or her reader. When I turned from poetry to fiction in my mid-twenties, I had a natural subject — the secrets of the Catholic world. And since the door had not been very widely opened before I got there, I was a natural. I think that accounts to a great extent for the popularity of *Final Payments.*

Mary Gordon, "Getting Here from There: A Writer's Reflections on a Religious Past," in *Spiritual Quests: The Art and Craft of Religious Writing,* ed. William Zinsser (Boston: Houghton Mifflin, 1988), 27–35.

## Part 8

# THEOLOGY AND SCIENCE

## Introduction

The debate over evolution stood at the center of the Catholic encounter with modern science. "Evolution" — a broad and seminal concept that took several related forms from the 1870s through the end of the twentieth century — emerged in scientific and popular lexicon when the nineteenth-century European biologists Jean Baptiste Lamarck and Charles Darwin attempted to account for the origin, development, and proliferation of animal species. Darwin's milestone, *On the Origin of Species by Means of Natural Selection* (1859), argued (against Lamarck) for the priority of the environment over the inheritance of acquired characteristics in determining which species would survive. In *The Descent of Man* (1871) Darwin scandalized much of the Christian world by applying the theory of evolution to the human race.

Catholics, like Protestants, were forced to confront this apparent challenge to the biblical accounts of creation and the doctrines of providence and the immortality of the soul. But Catholics found a way to accommodate the emerging general theory of evolution while condemning certain specific versions thereof. In 1931, after the Darwinian revolution had finally gained widespread acceptance in the scientific community, the *Catholic Encyclopaedic Dictionary* defined "evolutionism" as "the theory of the transformation of species only." Absolute evolutionism, the author continued:

> . . . is not justified by physical science which has established without doubt the stability of species, without ever discovering veritable specific transformations; moreover, it is condemned by metaphysics which refuses to admit that effects can be more perfect than their efficient causes; and "extreme" evolution denies the special act of creation of life, attributing the whole process to a natural development from inorganic matter. The doctrine of the natural development of all the species of the animal and vegetable world from a few primitive types created by God is *moderate* evolution. Catholics are free to believe in moderate evolution, excluding the evolution of man. Animals, as distinguished from man, are devoid of reason. Hence the animal soul, i.e., the principle which gives an animal life, is essentially material. Hence, man's soul, though depending on

material things for its activities, being essentially spiritual, the evolution of man *as a whole* from the lower animal is impossible.[1]

This tortured appraisal of evolution reflected six decades of conflict within the church.[2] In the United States the Roman Catholic response to Darwinism and evolution (two different things) reflected developments in American Catholicism and in the theory of organic evolution itself. From roughly 1870 to 1910, at the same time as two camps formed within the American Catholic community, Darwinism generated a lively and intense debate. The progressive camp, including dozens of priests and perhaps a dozen bishops sometimes described as "Americanists," attempted to blend religious faith and a scientifically informed worldview. Cardinal James Gibbons, archbishop of Baltimore, along with Archbishop John Ireland of St. Paul, Bishop John J. Keane of the Catholic University of America, and John Lancaster Spalding, bishop of Peoria, endorsed the research of Father John Zahm, a Holy Cross priest-scientist at the University of Notre Dame, who was interested in reconciling Catholic doctrine and evolution (doc. 74). The conservative camp, made up of the majority of Catholic prelates (led by Archbishop Michael A. Corrigan of New York) and priests, feared that the faith would not survive a direct encounter with liberalism, Protestantism, scientific materialism, and other perceived ideological threats to supernatural religion. They saw Zahm's attempts at reconciliation with the modern science of evolution as foolhardy and dangerous.

The two camps vied for the attention and loyalty of a growing Catholic middle class which was beginning to send its children to colleges and universities in significant numbers at the turn of the twentieth century. The progressives were dedicated not only to scientific investigation, but also to educational and economic adaptation to American institutions. While they won some important battles, the progressives, or "Americanists," experienced several setbacks in their efforts to adapt Catholic thought to modernity, including the silencing of Zahm in 1897 by the Vatican. (The Holy Office ordered Father Zahm to withdraw his book, *Evolution and Dogma*, from publication.) Some European and American Catholic priests, however, continued to maintain that theistic evolution did not fall under the 1907 ban on "Modernism" and that a modified form of Darwinism was therefore acceptable.

The Zahm affair had larger ramifications. The encounter with Darwinism and neo-Darwinism prompted Catholics to hone the distinction between the empirically tested and universally accepted findings of science, on the one hand, and the new evolutionist philosophies inspired by those findings, on the other. The distinction proved decisive for American Catholic attitudes toward

---

1. Donald Attwater, ed., *The Catholic Encyclopaedic Dictionary* (New York: Macmillan, 1931), 187.

2. The discussion of the Zahm affair and the turn-of-the-century Catholic debate over evolution is adapted from R. Scott Appleby, "Exposing Darwin's 'Hidden Agenda': Roman Catholic Responses to Evolution, 1875–1925," in Ronald L. Numbers and John Stenhouse, eds., *Disseminating Darwinism: The Role of Place, Race, Religion and Gender* (Cambridge: Cambridge University Press, 1999), 173–207; and R. Scott Appleby, *Church and Age Unite! The Modernist Impulse in American Catholicism* (Notre Dame, Ind.: University of Notre Dame Press, 1992), chap. 2.

science throughout most of the twentieth century: Catholic theologians, bishops, and popes tended to approve the science, while roundly condemning the philosophy.

According to this view, the real enemy was not science, per se, but the emerging materialist worldview of secular modernity, with its disastrous social and religious implications. Darwinism as a scientific theory was not entirely innocent, of course; it reflected the epistemological assumptions of the secular worldview and advanced it in the realm of science. But Darwinism as a philosophy, that is, as "a more general and universal theory which is applied to the physical world, to the realm of ethics, to man and to society," as the 1931 dictionary article put it, loomed as a powerful verification of materialism. The reference was to "social Darwinism," the application of Darwinism to the social conditions of the industrial age. As developed and popularized by the British philosopher Herbert Spencer in the late nineteenth century, social Darwinism viewed social and economic classes as falling along an evolutionary continuum, with the poor and illiterate classes doomed to their fate because nature had not endowed them with the intelligence and other survival skills necessary to compete with the "fittest."[3]

For U.S. Catholics, then, "modern thought" evoked the specters of materialism, atheism, and naturalism (i.e., a desupernaturalized world). The resulting society was seen as "irreligious" or, only slightly less catastrophic, as "Protestant." And Darwinism, in all its forms, was a product of modern thought, the culmination of its irreligious tendencies. Hence, scientific theory was suspect in large part because it was transmuted so rapidly into cultural material.

The debate over evolution, it must be remembered, occurred in the context of turn-of-the-century nativism (the social movement which sought to protect Anglo-Saxon privilege in the United States) and the twentieth-century rise of social engineering. Most American Catholics found both movements morally questionable, offensive, and potentially threatening. Eventually, these Catholic concerns transcended the progressive-conservative divide, and the priests who helped to shape popular Catholic opinion on evolution came to see a dangerous connection between Darwinism and the darker implications of eugenics (doc. 75).

In order to appreciate the specific nature of the threat to Catholicism, one must consider the social profile of the Roman Catholic Church in the latter half of the nineteenth century. American Catholicism was primarily a lower working-class phenomenon, a religion of un-Americanized immigrants.[4] Cities

---

3. For a mid-twentieth-century appraisal of Herbert Spencer, see Richard Hofstadter, *Social Darwinism in American Thought* (Boston: Beacon Press, 1955 [1944]), 31–50.

4. From 1820 to 1920, the United States attracted 33.6 million immigrants. See Philip Taylor, *The Distant Magnet: European Emigration to the U.S.A.* (New York: Harper & Row, 1971). Between 1851 and 1920, 3.3 million Irish immigrants, the vast majority of them Roman Catholic, settled in the United States, bringing the total Irish migration to the United States during the century of immigration, 1820–1920, to 4.3 million people. See Patrick J. Blessing, "Irish," in *Harvard Encyclopedia of American Ethnic Groups*, ed. Stephen Thernstrom (Cambridge, Mass.: Harvard University Press, 1980), 524–45. Jay P. Dolan notes that the typical Irish immigrant was young, unmarried, and poor.

were clogged with Irish, German, Polish, and Italian immigrants willing to take low-paying jobs and to crowd into urban tenements. With the influx of so many uneducated, "unwashed" foreigners, nativism took a distinct anti-Catholic turn with the Know-Nothing movement immediately prior to the Civil War. In the 1880s anti-Catholicism was on the rise again, in the form of the American Protective Association (A.P.A.), at just about the time that Catholic priests and lay leaders were pondering the social and cultural implications of a scientific theory that held that humans had evolved from lower forms of life and that only the fittest deserved to survive. They found terrifying the notion that the social and economic class hierarchy in industrial society, with rich, middle-class, and working poor vying for resources, reflected and was rooted in immutable genetic and biological differences.

Cultural and political implications of Darwinism were also being drawn by conservative social Darwinists and progressive social scientists, neither of whom looked with favor on the "character" of the immigrant Catholic. Conservatives used social Darwinism to defend the social and economic hierarchy; liberal reformers and social scientists embraced the Darwinian notion of progress to legitimate a program of eugenics and social engineering. To them, social progress consisted, in part, of "the rearing of the greatest number of individuals in full vigor and health, with all their faculties perfect under the conditions to which they are subjected." In 1891 the naturalist Joseph LeConte, a Protestant exponent of theistic evolution, could have been speaking for Roman Catholics when he worried that "if selection of the fittest is the only method available, if we are to have race improvement at all, *the dreadful law of the destruction of the weak and helpless* must, with Spartan firmness, be carried out voluntarily and deliberately." Against such a course, LeConte stated, "all that is best in us revolts."[5] Darwin, in short, left an opening for racist conclusions and policies to be drawn from his work.[6]

Indeed, in the early twentieth century social scientists who embraced eugenics proposed public policies (or supported others' proposals) to prevent the reproduction of mentally defective, feeble-minded, or criminally inclined people. The most common method resorted to was sterilization. Bills authorizing the sterilization of the so-called unfit came before the Michigan legislature in 1897 and Pennsylvania assembly in 1905; the first bill signed and written into law was enacted in Indiana in 1907.

In this trend the battle lines were joined for an early-twentieth-century version of culture wars. "That the socially conservative Roman Catholic Church invariably opposed all sterilization laws wherever they might be proffered," historian Carl Degler notes, "further convinced reform-minded or

See Dolan, *The American Catholic Experience: A History from Colonial Times to the Present* (Notre Dame, Ind.: University of Notre Dame Press, 1992), 129.

5. Joseph LeConte, "The Factors of Evolution," *The Monist* 1 (1890–91): 334.

6. Charles Darwin, *The Descent of Man*, is quoted to this effect in Carl N. Degler, *In Search of Human Nature: The Decline and Revival of Darwinism in American Social Thought* (New York: Oxford University Press, 1991), 15.

Progressive Americans that permanently preventing the unfit from procreating was forward-looking as well as socially necessary."[7]

During the 1920s the use of I.Q. tests spread beyond the identification of the mentally deficient; increasingly they were drawn upon to compare the intelligence of the various ethnic and racial groups in the United States, a practice "sparked by the enormous influx of immigrants into the United States during the previous fifteen years" and defended by nativists like Madison Grant, author of *The Passing of the Great Race* (1916). This wealthy New York socialist and amateur zoologist contended that southern and eastern European immigrants — particularly Polish and Italian Catholics and Russian Jews — were decidedly inferior mentally, morally, and physically to the Irish, English, Germans, and Scandinavians who had entered the country in earlier years. The movement to limit immigration culminated in the Immigrant Act of 1924.[8]

With this social and cultural battle in the foreground, in the early twentieth century Catholic anti-evolutionism took the form of warnings, like the one presented by the editors of the conservative *Ecclesiastical Review*, about "the constant diminution of the birth rate over almost the entire civilized world, [which] is one of the most appalling signs of degeneration in our time, and a subject for the most earnest consideration on the part of our pastoral clergy, since our own country is fast taking a conspicuous part in this triumph of the modern paganism." The culprit was "materialistic education and the overwhelming deluge of Socialistic literature" celebrating "the rapidly decreasing birth rate and the no less rapidly ascending proportion of divorces." In the socialist-materialist scheme of things, "continence, when demanded by the Church, is spoken of as immoral because opposed to nature; the laws of civilized nations in matters of sex are proclaimed as unjust because hindering the free development of normal instincts; the bounds set to the full satisfaction of sexual inclinations are stigmatized as degrading because destructive to character and detrimental to the harmonious expansion of the human faculties." Socialism, the editors continued, "is popularizing among the masses the teachings it has gathered from Darwin...and Spencer," among others. Socialist doctrine, which should be made "the center of attack on the part of the clergy from pulpit and platform as well as in our schools of ethics," is quite specific in its prescriptions:

Woman, in the first place, is to be made economically independent of man.... Every additional child born into the midst of the great class struggle and not demanded by economic necessity, we are told, is only a burden and an encumbrance to render the winning of a strike less possible, to swell the ranks of competition in the search for employment, and to delay by so many hours, days or weeks the coming victory of an inevitably conquering Socialism.[9]

---

7. Degler, *In Search of Human Nature*, 48.
8. Ibid., 53.
9. "Editorial," *The Ecclesiastical Review* 15 (September 1911): 276–79.

Thomas Dwight, the lay Catholic anatomist at Harvard Medical School, added his voice to the debate at this point. Having earlier seen "no contradiction between evolution on the one hand and design and teleology on the other,"[10] Dwight noted in 1911 that "Catholics have [accepted evolution] upon the understanding that the question is an open one" and that "God breathed into it the breath of life of an immortal soul." He also voiced sympathy for the opposition of conservative Catholic clergy to the social and philosophical applications of Darwinism, in light of "the misuse of Darwin and modern science."[11]

Catholics fought vehemently against birth control and associated its advocacy with a growing acceptance of evolutionism and materialist philosophy. In the second and third decades of the twentieth century, when birth-control activists such as Margaret Sanger came to prominence, American Catholics warned that a host of errors would follow from the American embrace of this scientific-*cum*-materialist trend.

Throughout this long saga the progressive members of the Catholic clergy attempted to balance what they perceived to be the needs of the immigrant community — specifically, the need to gain access to the mainstream institutions of American society — with theological orthodoxy as defined by the Vatican. This balancing act produced an inconsistent, tentative, and sometimes confused response to evolution. On the one hand, the progressives sought to demonstrate that Roman Catholics would take a back seat to no one when it came to scientific research and freedom of inquiry. On the other hand, these same men were clergy of a church that perceived a pervasive threat to religious belief in most of the modes of modern scientific thought. When American Catholics welcomed Darwinism in its modified form, cited Protestant and secular authorities on the question, and began to develop their own theological accommodations to it, their opponents within the church raised charges of Americanism and Modernism. By the 1920s the response to evolutionary theory had become a litmus test for orthodoxy, a marker of allegiances in the contest for influence over Catholic education.[12]

In sum, the American Catholic response to the Darwinian revolution revealed as much about the mindset and internal struggles of the polyglot, urbanizing, immigrant Catholic community as it did about the scientific theory. Darwinism was engaged critically by only a few Catholic elites, while most Catholic commentators and publicists quickly framed it within ongoing intraecclesial controversies. The debate over Darwinism itself, for all its virulence, was actually an occasion for American Catholics to work out a number of identity-defining issues facing the immigrant community. Perhaps for this reason the debate did not leave a strong anti-evolutionist legacy to future Catholic educators, in quite the way Protestant fundamentalism did. The advent of

---

10. Thomas Dwight, "Description of the Human Spines Showing Numerical Variation in the Warren Museum of the Harvard Medical School," *Memoirs of the Boston Society of Natural History* V (January 1901): 242–43.

11. Thomas Dwight, *Thoughts of a Catholic Anatomist* (New York: Longmans, Green, 1911), 12.

12. See Appleby, "Exposing Darwin's 'Hidden Agenda,'" 198–200.

evolutionary theory, in other words, served as a catalyst for the resolution of internal Catholic issues rather than as a sustained evaluation of Darwinism and evolutionary theory in itself. Despite the seeming victory of the conservatives, moreover, the scientific theory of evolution was never formally condemned, and Roman Catholicism modified its general anti-evolutionist stance several times in the twentieth century, a process that culminated in the conditional approval of the theory by Pope Pius XII in 1950.[13]

In the same encyclical, *Humani Generis,* however, the pope made it quite clear that modern science must be incorporated within the framework of Thomism, lest so-called scientific evidence be marshalled in support of agnostic, atheistic, and materialist philosophies (see doc. 76). It was not clear to all Catholic scientists or theologians, however, that the thought of Thomas Aquinas was up to the task of absorbing the complexities of modern science.

The cultural acceptance of modern science grew steadily in the United States during the course of the twentieth century. One manifestation of this growing acceptance was the challenging or displacement of religious categories and "explanations" by secular, scientific ones. Nowhere was this more apparent than in the young field of psychology. Psychology (Greek, "study of the soul") was a branch of philosophy until the late nineteenth century, when the experimental laboratories of Europe established it as a science of behavior with objective methods of measurement. As a result of Sigmund Freud's pioneering research and theorizing, psychoanalysis emerged as a form of clinical psychology that placed great emphasis on unconscious or "subconscious" motivations that relegated the rational choices of the mind to a secondary role in explaining human behavior. Psychoanalysis became a force in American clinical training shortly before World War II due to the forced migration of many Jewish psychoanalysts from Europe. By 1942, despite the misgivings of many religious leaders, the United States had become the center of psychoanalysis.[14]

Following a pattern similar to the American Catholic response to evolutionary biology, a few intrepid Catholic priests practiced the new science and attempted to demonstrate that it could be reconciled with Catholic doctrines and values. Among the most significant of these Catholic psychologists were Edward Pace, a priest who helped to establish the American Psychological Association in 1892 and taught a range of courses in psychology for forty-four years at Catholic University of America; and psychiatrist Thomas Verner Moore, a Paulist priest who later left the Paulists and joined the monastic Order of St. Benedict (Benedictines). Moore served for twenty-five years as the chair of Catholic University's department of psychology and psychiatry. Departments

---

13. Pope Pius XII, "The Encyclical Letter *Humani Generis,*" in *The Teaching of the Catholic Church,* ed. Joseph Neuner and Heinrich Roos (New York: Alba, 1978). This papal teaching "settled the matter" of evolution by claiming that it is acceptable within the framework of Christian doctrine as long as Catholics confess the individual creation of each human soul, the authority of revelation in speaking to us of the source of our being, and the unity of the human race.

14. C. Kevin Gillespie, S.J., *Psychology and American Catholicism: From Confession to Therapy* (New York: Crossroad, 2001), 1, 14–15.

of psychology were also established at St. Louis University (1926), Loyola University of Chicago (1934), and Fordham University (1934).[15]

The Sisters of St. Joseph, a religious order of women, produced a remarkable pioneer in the field of psychology and behaviorism — Sr. Annette Walters, C.S.J., whose fascination with and expertise in experimental psychology grew over the course of nearly half a century, from the early 1930s to her death in 1978. Walters's tenure as executive secretary of the Sisters Formation Conference came during the crucial years of 1960 through 1964, when the Second Vatican Council was in session and a new Catholic openness to the modern sciences, including psychology, reached unprecedented heights. She took good advantage of the post, from which she effectively conveyed the benefits of psychological insights for spiritual growth and the religious life.[16]

The Catholic acceptance of psychology was sporadic and halting, however, before Vatican II. To some Catholics, the advent of modern psychology was a threat to traditional beliefs and practices: the "soul," they feared, would be displaced by the "psyche," sin by mental illness, the sacrament of confession by psychoanalysis. In the final analysis, these critics charged, the uncritical proponents of psychology ran the same risk as the uncritical proponents of evolution — namely, the error of infusing scientific method with materialist philosophies. Only Thomism could safeguard against the reduction of the human being to the sum of subconscious processes — or, so argued the great popularizer of the thought of St. Thomas, Monsignor Fulton Sheen (doc. 77).

The Roman Catholic encounter with evolution was by no means unprofitable for the church. It produced, among other results, the extraordinary, innovative theology of Pierre Teilhard de Chardin (1881–1955), a French Jesuit and a distinguished geologist and paleontologist. (He worked on the team that discovered Peking Man — Sinanthropos — in China.) From an evolutionary perspective Teilhard reconceptualized all of life and its relationship to the gospel. Through a process he called "complexification," molecules had evolved into life, whose habitat Teilhard called the "Biosphere." From life came the human mind, the highest level of complexity, whose layer of existence he called "Noosphere." Evolution, for Teilhard, is an ongoing process on both levels; eventually, the human consciousness will evolve into a new consciousness which Teilhard calls the "Christosphere," leading humankind to the Omega Point — that is, to union with God.[17]

Teilhard's thought, banned by the church prior to the Second Vatican Council, was extremely influential among a generation of American priests who came of age in the 1960s and 1970s (doc. 78). His emphasis on the beauty and inherent goodness of nature helped transform concern for the environment into a deeply held ethical and religious commitment among some Catholics. Teilhard's theology of "the cosmic Christ," the One who brings all things to completion in Himself, drawn from the Gospel of John and from St. Paul's

---

15. Ibid., 32–45.
16. Ibid., 69–81.
17. Lawrence S. Cunningham, *The Catholic Heritage* (New York: Crossroad, 1983), 102.

descriptions of Christ as the originator and end of all creation, inspired hope in the inevitability of progress toward a rising religious consciousness. Priests took special pride in Teilhard's analogy of the consecration of the Eucharist to Christ's sanctification of the world.

Catholic thinkers who examined the relationship between theology and science in the postconciliar period (1965–2000) took a cue from Teilhard by re-conceptualizing premodern doctrines and theological understandings in light of the findings of modern science. The most creative of these thinkers, in ex-ploring the implications of science for Catholic self-understanding, used these insights to support their retrieval of previously overlooked or underdeveloped dimensions of the gospel message. Elizabeth Johnson's illumination of feminist themes through reflection on ecology and the Christian call to stewardship of the earth (doc. 79) is a case in point.

## 74. A Notre Dame Priest Explores the Possibility of "Theistic Evolution," 1896

*Born in Ohio in 1851 to immigrant parents, John Augustine Zahm entered the seminary at the University of Notre Dame at the age of fifteen. Gifted with a natural aptitude for science, he rose rapidly in the ranks of the Congregation of Holy Cross, and by the age of twenty-three was a professor of chemistry and physics, codirector of the science department, director of the library, curator of the museum, and a member of the board of trustees of the fledgling university. From 1875 to 1883 Zahm concentrated on building the science department at Notre Dame into a first-rate facility; Catholics lagged far behind American Prot-estants in experimental capabilities. In 1883 he entered the public controversy over evolution.*

*Initially, Zahm attacked* The Descent of Man *and Darwinism in general as an insubstantial and unprovable hypothesis. Like other Catholic priests and ed-ucated laymen, he was most disturbed by "those agnostics, materialists, and atheists" who transformed a "shaky" scientific theory into a "full-blown" philo-sophical system. Zahm asserted the priority of dogma over the claims of science, for "no liberalism in matters of doctrine can be tolerated.... What the Church teaches must be accepted as divine truth."[1] Yet one must distinguish between official teaching of the magisterium and the private opinions of theologians and commentators. The "official church" had never and would never define the exact age of the world or of the human species, for such matters "have nothing to do" with faith and morals. Similarly, the church permitted an understanding of biblical inspiration that allowed for errors on the part of the authors in mat-ters of history, biology, geology, and other scientific disciplines. (Zahm made this assertion in 1886; twenty-one years later, in 1907, the Pontifical Biblical Commission ruled otherwise.)*

*Zahm rejected Darwinism, as he understood it, as based on a number of highly questionable assumptions: the spontaneous generation of life from inor-ganic matter, against which stood "conclusive scientific evidence"; the "nebular hypothesis" that the earth and all heavenly bodies were originally in a state of*

---

1. John Augustine Zahm, "The Catholic Church and Modern Science: A Lecture" (Notre Dame, Ind.: Ave Maria, 1886), 6–7.

*incandescent vapor* — "mere speculation"; and the "unprovable" notion that one species evolved from another by a process of transmutation. On the other hand, Zahm argued that, should evidence in favor of Darwin's general theory be established, Catholics could accept a form of divinely guided, or theistic, evolution. The Catholic definition of creation could be broadened to include derivative creation "when God, after having created matter directly, gives it the power of evolving under certain conditions all the various forms it may subsequently assume." Neither church teaching nor Scripture stood in the way of this understanding of creation; in fact, "according to the words of Genesis, God did not create animals and plants in the primary sense of the word, but caused them to be produced from preexisting material." The evolutionist simply maintained that "God did potentially, what the ordinary Scripture interpreter believes he did by a distinct, immediate exercise of infinite power."[2]

The passage below is taken from Zahm's most controversial work, Evolution and Dogma, which appeared in February 1896. Here Zahm described this general theory of evolution as shared by Darwin and Lamarck alike as "ennobling" and "uplifting." Older views regarding creation, he contended, must be materially modified to harmonize with modern science: "Between the two theories, that of creation and that of Evolution, the lines are drawn tautly, and one or the other theory must be accepted.... No compromise, no via media, is possible. We must needs be either creationists or evolutionists. We cannot be both."[3] For Zahm, evolution was a question "of natural science, not of metaphysics, and hence one of evidence which is more or less tangible." In delineating the reasons for "the almost universal acceptance of the theory by contemporary scientists," Zahm followed a procedure he believed to be at the heart of Catholic wisdom: seek truth wherever it may be found, separate it from error, and reconcile it with other truths. In evaluating the thought of the leading naturalists of the modern era, he found "elements of truth" in Darwin, Lamarck, Mivart, and others.

Neither "a Darwinist nor a Huxleyist," he was equally comfortable quoting the creationist Louis Agassiz against certain implications of natural selection and Darwin against the theory of abiogenesis held by the creationists. His one allegiance was to the general theory of evolution which, he was convinced, eventually would absorb and incorporate salient aspects of each modification of merit. Zahm predicted the development of a "true, comprehensive, irrefragable" theory demonstrating the "ordained becoming of new species by the operation of secondary causes." This ideal theory would admit "of a preconceived progress 'towards a foreseen goal' and disclose the unmistakable evidence and the certain impress of a Divine Intelligence and purpose." Zahm hastened to add that "the lack of this perfected theory, however, does not imply that we have not already an adequate basis for a rational assent to the theory of Organic Evolution.... Whatever, then, may be said of Lamarckism, Darwinism, and other theories of Evolution, the fact of Evolution, as the evidence now stands, is scarcely any longer a matter for controversy."[4]

Evolution and Dogma attracted international attention. It was translated into Italian (1896), French (1897), and Spanish (1904) and was promoted with an

---

2. Ibid., 44.
3. Ibid., 75.
4. Ibid., 200–201.

advertising campaign by publisher D. H. McBride that played up the controversial aspects of the book. It is not surprising, therefore, that Evolution and
Dogma incited the antagonisms of curial officials whose worldview it seemed
to subvert.

## Faith Has Nothing to Apprehend from Evolution

Suppose, then, that a demonstrative proof of the theory of Evolution should
eventually be given, a proof such as would satisfy the most exacting and the
most skeptical, it is evident, from what has already been stated, that Catholic Dogma would remain absolutely intact and unchanged. Individual theorists
would be obliged to accommodate their views to the facts of nature, but the doctrines of the Church would not be affected in the slightest. The hypothesis of
St. Augustine and St. Thomas Aquinas would then become a thesis, and all reasonable and consistent men would yield ready, unconditional and unequivocal
assent.

And suppose, further, that in the course of time science shall demonstrate —
a most highly improbable event — the animal origin of man as to his body.
There need, even then, be no anxiety so far as the truths of faith are concerned.
Proving that the body of the common ancestor of humanity is descended from
some higher form of ape, or from some extinct anthropopithecus, would not
necessarily contravene either the declarations of Genesis, or the principles regarding derivative creation which found acceptance with the greatest of the
Church's Fathers and Doctors.

Mr. Gladstone, in the work just quoted from, expresses the same idea with
characteristic force and lucidity. "If," he says, "while Genesis asserts a separate creation of man, science should eventually prove that man sprang, by a
countless multitude of indefinitely small variations, from a lower, and even
from the lowest ancestry, the statement of the great chapter would still remain
undisturbed. For every one of those variations, however minute, is absolutely
separate, in the points wherein it varies, from what followed and also from what
preceded it; is in fact and in effect a distinct or separate creation. And the fact
that the variation is so small that, taken singly, our use may not be to reckon it,
is nothing whatever to the purpose. For it is the finiteness of our faculties which
shuts us off by a barrier downward, beyond a certain limit, from the small, as
it shuts us off by a barrier upward from the great; whereas for Him whose faculties are infinite, the small and the great are, like the light and the darkness,
'both alike,' and if man came up by innumerable stages from a low origin to the
image of God, it is God only who can say, as He has said in other cases, which
of those stages may be worthy to be noted with the distinctive name of creation, and at what point of the ascent man could first be justly said to exhibit
the image of God."

But the derivation of man from the ape, we are told, degrades man. Not at all.
It would be truer to say that such derivation ennobles the ape. Sentiment aside,
it is quite unimportant to the Christian "whether he is to trace back his pedigree
directly or indirectly to the dust." St. Francis of Assisi, as we learn from his life,

"called the birds his brothers." Whether he was correct, either theologically or zoölogically, he was plainly free from that fear of being mistaken for an ape which haunts so many in these modern times. Perfectly sure that he, himself, was a spiritual being, he thought it at least possible that birds might be spiritual beings, likewise incarnate like himself in mortal flesh; and saw no degradation to the dignity of human nature in claiming kindred lovingly with creatures so beautiful, so wonderful, who, as he fancied, "praised God in the forest, even as angels did in heaven."

## Misapprehensions Regarding Evolution

Many, it may here be observed, look on the theory of Evolution with suspicion, because they fail to understand its true significance. They seem to think that it is an attempt to account for the origin of things when, in reality, it deals only with their historical development. It deals not with creation, with the origin of things, but with the *modus creandi,* or, rather, with the *modus formandi,* after the universe was called into existence by Divine Omnipotence. Evolution, then, postulates creation as an intellectual necessity, for if there had not been a creation there would have been nothing to evolve, and Evolution would, therefore, have been an impossibility.

And for the same reason, Evolution postulates and must postulate, a Creator, the sovereign Lord of all things, the Cause of causes, the *terminus a quo* as well as the *terminus ad quem* of all that exists or can exist. But Evolution postulates still more. In order that Evolution might be at all possible it was necessary that there should have been not only an antecedent creation *ex nihilo,* but also that there should have been an antecedent involution, or a creation *in potentia.* To suppose that simple brute matter could, by its own motion or by any power inherent in matter as such, have been the sole efficient cause of the Evolution of organic from inorganic matter, of the higher from the lower forms of life, of the rational from the irrational creature, is to suppose that a thing can give what it does not possess, that the greater is contained in the less, the superior in the inferior, the whole in a part.

No mere mechanical theory, therefore, however ingenious, is competent to explain the simplest fact of development. Not only is such a theory unable to account for the origin of a speck of protoplasm, or the germination of a seed, but it is equally incompetent to assign a reason for the formation of the smallest crystal or the simplest chemical compound. Hence, to be philosophically valid, Evolution must postulate a Creator not only for the material which is evolved, but it must also postulate a Creator, *Causa causarum,* for the power or agency which makes any development possible. God, then, not only created matter in the beginning, but He gave it the power of evolving into all forms it has since assumed or ever shall assume.

But that is not all. In order to have an intelligible theory of Evolution, a theory that can meet the exacting demands of a sound philosophy as well as of a true theology, still another postulate is necessary. We must hold not only that there was an actual creation of matter in the beginning, that there was a potential creation which rendered matter capable of Evolution, in accordance with the laws impressed by God on matter, but we must also believe that creative action and influence still persist, that they always have persisted from the dawn of creation, that they, and they alone, have been efficient in all the countless stages of evolutionary progress from atoms to monads, from monads to man.

This ever-present action of the Deity, this immanence of His in the work of His hands, this continuing in existence and developing of the creatures He has made, is what St. Thomas calls the "Divine administration," and what is ordinarily known as Providence. It connotes the active and constant coöperation of the Creator with the creature, and implies that if the multitudinous forms of terrestrial life have been evolved from the potentiality of matter, they have been so evolved because matter was in the first instance proximately disposed for Evolution by God Himself, and has ever remained so disposed. To say that God created the universe in the beginning, and that He gave matter the power of developing into all the myriad forms it subsequently exhibited, but that after doing this He had no further care for what He had brought into existence, would be equivalent to indorsing the Deism of Hume, or to affirming the old pagan notion according to which God, after creating the world, withdrew from it and left it to itself.

Well, then, can we say of Evolution what Dr. Martineau says of science, that it "discloses the method of the world, not its cause; religion, its cause and not its method." Evolution is the grand and stately march of creative energy, the sublime manifestation of what Claude Bernard calls "the first, creative, legislative and directing Cause." In it we have constantly before our eyes the daily miracles, *quotidiana Dei miracula* of which St. Augustine speaks, and through it we are vouchsafed a glimpse, as it were, of the operation of Providence in the government of the world.

Evolution, therefore, is neither a "philosophy of mud," nor "a gospel of dirt," as it has been denominated. So far, indeed, is this from being the case that, when properly understood, it is found to be a strong and useful ally of Catholic Dogma. For if Evolution be true, the existence of God and an original creation follow as necessary inferences. . . .

As to man, Evolution, far from depriving him of his high estate, confirms him in it, and that, too, by the strongest and noblest of titles. It recognizes that although descended from humble lineage, he is "the beauty of the world, and the paragon of animals;" that although from dust — tracing his lineage back to its first beginnings — he is of the "quintessence of dust." It teaches, and in the most eloquent language, that he is the highest term of a long and majestic development, and replaces him "in his old position of headship in the universe, even as in the days of Dante and Aquinas."

John Zahm, C.S.C., *Evolution and Dogma* (New York: Arno Press, 1896 [1978]), 428–35.

## 75. The Struggle against Eugenics in the Early Twentieth Century, 1926

*From the 1880s through the 1920s Roman Catholics in the United States ob-
served with growing trepidation the apparent social consequences of Darwinian
evolution, including the advocacy of sterilization of the "feebleminded," a notion supported by the anti-Catholic American Protective Association, and the
move by some Protestant groups to administer intelligence tests to Eastern European immigrants to demonstrate their "inferiority."[1] In 1886 the New York
Evening Telegram printed a caricature of an Irish servant girl "with the mouth of
a baboon and horns upon her."[2] Meanwhile, diatribes against the high birth rate
of the (inferior) immigrant population began to appear, and the public campaign to restrict population growth, though not restricted to nativists, found
some measure of legitimation in the Darwinian argument that morality itself
had evolved over time along with other human traits; it was time once again,
the birth-control advocates argued, for humanity to move to a higher plane of
moral existence.*

*Such arguments obviously troubled and offended many Christians and Jews,
against whom the xenophobic diatribes were also aimed. Catholics in particular fought vehemently against birth control and associated its advocacy with
a growing acceptance of evolutionism and materialist philosophy. In the second and third decades of the twentieth century, when birth-control activists
such as Margaret Sanger came to prominence, American Catholics warned that
a host of errors would follow from the American embrace of this scientific-cum-
materialist trend. The* Catholic Encyclopaedic Dictionary *defined "eugenics" as
"the science which aims at improving the well-being of the race by studying the
factors which affect bodily and mental health, with a view to the encouragement of the beneficial and the elimination of the harmful. Statistics are adduced
to show that the chief obstacle is the marriage of the unfit, leading to an increase of hereditable evils, such as insanity, addiction to drink, consumption,
venereal disease. The Church has nothing but praise for the aim of eugenics and
has no objection to the positive methods proposed as a remedy of the evil,
e.g., granting diplomas to the fit, endowing them to encourage the rearing of
a large family, providing healthy homes, educating public opinion; but she cannot approve of the negative methods suggested by some eugenists, viz., 'birth
control' or the compulsory sterilization of degenerates....When eugenists go
astray, it is because they forget or deny that spiritual well-being is of far greater
importance than material, and that even a tainted existence is better than no
existence at all."[3]*

*In the following passage, an American Catholic commentator laments and
ridicules the tendency of the proponents of eugenics to equate human worth
with material and social prosperity.*

---

1. Degler, *In Search of Human Nature*, 25–40. For a popular and influential presentation of the
mentality behind these social policies, see the writings of A.P.A. activist Madison Grant, *The Passing
of the Great Race* (New York: Scribner, 1916).

2. *New York Evening Telegram*, December 10, 1886; reported also in the *Catholic News*, December 15, 1886.

3. Attwater, ed., *The Catholic Encyclopedic Dictionary*, 190.

Just to what degree is worldly failure to be considered a crime? Once the question could not have been asked. Crime was supposed to have a black core, theologically known as sin, and sin was generally believed to imply an imperfection in one's relation with God. Now it seems to mean a misunderstanding with one's banker or an inability to get into "Who's Who." A new criterion is being applied, and in a way which will probably cause profound astonishment to those good people who depend upon the daily newspapers for their news and quickly forget the great bulk of that — often with considerable advantage to their minds.

The science of human betterment began with an excellent purpose, but it made the mistake of not taking the trouble to find out clearly whither it was bound. You may know exactly what you mean when you say "better," but your neighbor will not know unless he knows what you consider good, and why. The science in question, however, having elected to call itself Eugenics, felt ready to set sail. The port in view was not in view, exactly, but, they said, must be somewhere below the horizon. Besides, the object of any science is to reach the truth, and the way to reach it is to watch and see what comes — all of which was precisely like starting on an ocean voyage without chart or rudder.

Now one of the strangest things in nature is the path taken by a rudderless vessel, perhaps because, strictly speaking, a rudderless ship is outside of nature. It is a delusion. There is a helm and a guiding hand, visible or not, to the wildest barque that ever turned blindly before stupid winds. Yet, to the merely human eye, the course of the Flying Dutchman is unpredictable, and unbelievable are the harbors of which it comes in sight.

Not for long did Eugenics remain without giving some further sign of *its* destination. Crime and insanity are hereditary, it announced, and it would abolish them. Asked for a definition of crime and insanity, and for a description of the method with which it proposed to cope with heredity, it mildly suggested that marriages should be controlled, while crime and insanity — everybody knew what they were.

I remember a correspondence I had a few years ago with a well-known writer on the subject, in which I pressed him to be more specific. And I finally succeeded in getting a declaration from him to the effect that the essence of crime was non-conformity. He had hit the nail squarely on the head. That is the essence of crime exactly, non-obedience to some law. But what law? Here my correspondent showed that he was entirely at sea. He could refer to nothing but the statute law momentarily in effect in the place where crime was committed.

The rudderless predicament of a science was never more clearly demonstrated. For surely a willingness to conform to any and every statute which a human legislature anywhere might see fit to pass, would be a curious test of human virtue. And as to insanity, he was willing to leave that to the doctors, even after I reminded him that Prof. Lombroso, just then quite prominent, was a doctor, and had pronounced insanity as practically synonymous with genius. I knew better than to remind him that some of the saints had been pronounced insane — by doctors. It would have pleased him too well.

The other eugenic pronouncement, that marriages should be controlled, failed, when stated that way, to arouse much attention from anybody — for one reason because marriages have always been controlled to a certain extent, the very institution implying control of some sort. Even the Church has done its eugenic bit by seeking to control marriage, and if a man be free anywhere to marry his grandmother it is not in a Catholic country.

But this vagueness has at last disappeared. A port, however unlooked for, looms into view, and we know not where we are going for we have almost arrived. Prof. Lewis M. Terman has written what critics term "a monumental book," entitled "Genetic Studies of Genius," recently published by Stanford University. It forms the basis of a series of articles by Mr. Albert Edward Wiggam, now running in the *World's Work*, where the curious reader may find not only Prof. Terman's data but a number of arguments and conclusions of Mr. Wiggam's own.

Unfitness, we now learn (and I mean it literally) is indeed to be measured by inability to get into "Who's Who" and similar volumes, and the war against unfitness has not only declared itself to be (again literally) a war to the knife, but is already sanctioned by law and practice in no less than twenty-three states of the Union.

I confess that I was astounded to discover, only the other day and from the chance reading of an essay by J. B. Eggen (an opponent of the eugenic philosophy and a contributor to *Current History* for September), that 6,244 citizens of the United States have, without public clamor, been legally pronounced unfit to leave their impress upon future generations, and rendered incapable of disobeying the judicial ukase by surgical interference. California claims 4,636 of these cases (in at least one of which the sentence was for "drunkenness").

But it remained for Prof. Terman, and more especially for his exponent, Mr. Wiggam, clearly to indicate the far voyage upon which it is proposed to take the race. Crime and insanity were but island stops on the way. The grand harbor is the elimination of everybody who is not considered a credit to society, merit and demerit marks to be awarded by the dominant element of the society in question. In the United States as at present constituted that could only mean the Puritanic, Protestant, moralistic, dry and pietistic Nordic.

Prof. Terman confines himself chiefly to collecting material and giving a new trend to the inquiry. It is Mr. Wiggam who suggests what action should be taken. Yet Mr. Wiggam is a soft-spoken gentleman with a voice like anything but a pirate's, and he beguiles us at the beginning — shanghais us, so to speak — with an interesting discussion of the old legend regarding the poor country boy and his supposed chance of becoming distinguished. It is not much of a chance, a formidable array of statistics is brought out to prove. The advantage all lies with city children. Three per cent of the people (those belonging to the professional classes) have in America produced nearly one-half of our artists. Likewise, one-third of the population (described as being above early struggles) have been responsible for three-fourths of America's writers.

To quote directly from Prof. Terman himself, "Superior intelligence is approximately five times as common among children of superior social status as among children of inferior social status." Gone is the chimera, the self-made man, and our foolish belief in the presidential possibilities of rail-splitting and selling newspapers.

To clinch the matter and give it a thoroughly international character, Dr. Cyril Burke, the English psychologist, devised a problem which he put before various classes of school children. Slum children required an average of 123 seconds to arrive at a solution, while merchants' children took but 91, and "the children of professors and bishops" (doubtless Anglican bishops) 74 seconds. Nor do I wish to conceal the fact, vouched for in one of Mr. Wiggam's articles, that "in the general run of people there is one eminent man out of every four thousand," while "among the sons of English judges there is one eminent man out of every eight."

It would be interesting if we could pause here to criticize the method. All of the "famous" biologists and psychologists and sociologists upon whose findings these arguments are based, took their successful men either from "Who's Who," some dictionary or biography, or measured it frankly in dollars and cents, and it might be suggested that not all desirable human traits are those which lead to wealth or conspicuous position. Attention might also be called to one strange omission. No *Lives of the Saints* are consulted to show the effect of poverty and self-denial upon the growth of holiness. The nearest approach to it is Prof. Terman's statement that nearly all gifted children come from good homes.

But Mr. Wiggam hurries on and we must hurry with him, for more horrendous matters are in store. Readers of Genesis have long been familiar with the fact that every living creature bringeth forth after its kind, and I call attention to this comforting corroboration merely because another school of psychologists flatly denies it, holding that what we call heredity is merely environment of a very early variety. Incidentally, they carefully limit themselves to the mind, all but the toughest of them, not yet being quite ready to explain the difference between a Negro and a Chinaman in purely educational terms.

Mr. Wiggam even goes so far in the direction of Genesis as to quote with approval from Adams Wood's "The Diminishing Influence of Environment," wherein it is held that as we come up in the scale from the amoeba there is an increasing ability of the individual to mould circumstances to suit himself. Good old amoeba! He always gives me the feeling, when I meet with him in an argument, that the digging down for the foundation has been thoroughly done. And he is always with us these days — unlike the poor, who, under eugenic treatment, seem about to disappear....

But if the poor are to be eliminated, why not the recalcitrant? Why not those, who, in the old phrase of Grover Cleveland, show "offensive partisanship" — for some cause not approved of by the ruling party? Granted the principle, why should Protestants tolerate Catholics, or Baptists Presbyterians, or Old-school Baptists New-school Baptists? Why, even, should Prof. Terman and Mr. Wiggam tolerate Mr. Eggen? Or, for that matter, Prof. Terman Mr. Wiggam himself? If we are to have uniformity of this sort, let us have it. Let there be a driving from life's stage, and — well we know who it is who is usually called upon to take the hindmost.

Harvey Wickham, "Straining the Quality of Mercy," *America* 36, no. 8 (December 4, 1926): 180–82.

## 76. The Proper Relationship between Theology and Science, 1950

*In 1950 Pope Pius XII issued the encyclical* Humani Generis *("Of the Human Race"), which warned against certain aspects of "the new theology" emanating from Europe, primarily from France. Certain (unnamed) theologians writing on nature and grace, original sin, ecumenism, and liturgical renewal had embraced schools of modern philosophy and science such as existentialism, evolutionism, and historicism. In so doing, these Catholic philosophers and theologians had failed to avoid some of the errors of these schools of thought, the pope charged. Pope Pius restated the church's commitment to Thomism as the true Christian philosophy, and he asserted that when a pope carefully pronounces on a controverted theological subject, it "can no longer be regarded as a matter of free debate among theologians."*

*The encyclical cast a chill in Catholic intellectual circles, where the new theology was widely touted as a path to the renewal of the church. Indeed, many of the ideas of the French and other Continental theologians were refined and incorporated into the theology informing the documents of the Second Vatican Council (1962–65), which passed over Pius's attempt to enhance papal authority in silence.*

*The following passages are taken from an extensive commentary on* Humani Generis *written by Cyril Vollert, a Jesuit priest teaching at St. Mary's College, Maryland. Note how, within a generally receptive treatment of the encyclical, Father Vollert underscores the distinction between the accepted conclusions of science (e.g., "evolution in the narrower sense"), which the church does not condemn, and the partly erroneous philosophies constructed around them. Note also the description of theologians as "scientists" in their own right, a claim that theologians themselves came to reject.*

Since the encyclical *Humani Generis* treats of "some false opinions which threaten to undermine the foundations of Catholic doctrine," its exceptional gravity is apparent at first glance....

To root out doctrinal weeds that have grown up rankly during the past hundred years, the Church has repeatedly issued official pronouncements. Action was taken against Guenther, Hermes, Froschammer, Rosmini, the Rationalists, the Liberalists, and the Modernists. The basis of most such aberrations was the desire to accommodate the teaching of Christ to the state of science and philosophy as it ran its course from generation to generation. Sincere Catholics have always welcomed papal directives with joy, for they know that the light which enlightens every man is found in the Church....

The science that seeks intelligence of the faith is theology. The principles of this science are truths revealed by God. Therefore the Church, to which these principles have been committed, has charge over the whole science that derives from them; and theologians receive the principles of their science from the Church that is living today.

In its effort to understand divine revelation, theology employs all the resources of reason and seeks to gather information from any science that holds forth some promise of contributing to clarification. The theologian taps all channels of knowledge for facts and data that may aid toward a comprehension of his own science. Every advance in civilization and learning can be the occasion of a more explicit formulation of dogma or of progress in theological elaboration....

Of all the problems that plague the Catholic mind today, perhaps the most pressing is that of the relations between evolution and transcendence. No phase of thought is more characteristic of the modern mentality than the idea of evolution. With regard to evolution in the narrower sense, the evolution of living species, a paleontologist or a biologist who is not an evolutionist would indeed be hard to find. But the evolution of species is only one aspect of the question. The significant trait of modern thought is the hypothesis, if not conviction, of universal evolution. And if everything in the universe evolves, there is no changeless truth; no values are stable, nothing is permanent.

The problem cannot be shrugged off; it has to be faced. How, in an intellectual atmosphere of universal evolutionism, can we safeguard transcendental truth? Evolution has captured the very vocabulary of the natural sciences, and from there has seeped into the common outlook. The theologian likewise is induced to consider the possibility of its consonance with Christian faith.

In some respects this question is more vexatious than that problem St. Thomas had to solve; for the discoveries of modern science reach farther than the rediscovery in the Middle Ages of the works of an ancient philosopher. As in those days, theologians divide into three camps. A few refuse to pay any attention to evolution. Others founder on the rocks of relativism and suffer shipwreck in their faith. A third class tries to emulate the attitude St. Thomas took when one day Aristotle rose up and stared him in the eye.

To our grief, no St. Thomas has been born in our century. But colleges of Catholic scientists and groups of Catholic philosophers and theologians have bent their energies to the solution of this many-angles puzzle, with the aim of demonstrating permanence in the midst of evolution and of showing that evolution demands the transcendent God. Thanks to their labors biological evolution, which had been mechanistic and materialistic, has become finalist and, no less than the view of the separate creation of distinct species, has been shown to require God at its beginning and throughout its course. On the other hand, the evolutionary hypothesis has released a number of theological difficulties that have by no means found a convincing solution.

Modern evolutionary theories, though mainly the product of paleontology, also stem from a philosophy of history; widely remote at their origin, the two sources have mingled their waters. Some Catholic philosophers have set themselves the arduous task of comprehending Hegelianism from within, proposing to enrich Catholic thought with any truth it might contain. Others have made similar forays into dialectic materialism, pragmatism, and existentialism, on the theory that they might be able to express dogma and theology in new categories if they could but correct such philosophies and purge them of error, somewhat as Aquinas had done with Aristotelianism. It is now clear that the explorations have ended in failure; the modern philosophies are incompatible with dogma, not in rectifiable details or tendencies, but in their basic principles....

Theology has to be keenly alive to all modern discoveries and currents of thought. But involvement in new movements and facts uncovers a danger as well as a benefit. The benefit is a deeper and enriched knowledge of a traditional doctrine; and that is a precious acquisition. The danger is a premature attempt to assimilate an insufficiently criticized opinion that may turn out to be theologically indigestible. A diseased relativism may be the unsuspected result. The desire to present dogma in forms acceptable to modern philosophies, so different from one another and so divergent from Scholastic teaching, may issue in the view that none of them is wholly true; and if all of them are only approximations, they can be interchanged and some notions can be replaced by others that may be opposed at points yet are roughly equivalent. In this way Catholic doctrine is made available to various cultures in terms of their own cherished ideas. Dogma may come to find expression in notions that are relative; misgivings are quieted by the comforting assurance that such notions reflect rays of revealed light that in the last analysis is too radiant for human eyes. In the case of scientific discoveries the danger may be a superficial and ephemeral concordism. An instance that now appears faintly ridiculous is afforded by the innumerable attempts made during the last century to match the six days of creation with the successive geological ages variously reconstructed by naturalists....

Ill-advised excursions of this sort remind the theologian that he must always check his proposals with tradition, the common teaching of his brother theologians, and especially with the mind of the official magisterium. For theology is an instrument in the hand of the Church and is employed by the Church to guard intact, to transmit, and to develop the wealth of the deposit of faith. In the researches he institutes at his own risk the theologian is exposed to error. That is why Christ appointed a living magisterium, to preserve us from doctrinal peril.

Yet to perform its task theology requires liberty. Unlike the official teaching authority, which has the function of preservation and continuity and is charged with the office of transmitting to each generation the revealed truth received at the beginning, theology has the function of exploitation and progress, of research and discovery....

Theologians are not mere recorders of received doctrines. They are not clerks busy filing side by side the opinions of various schools. They are scholars, with courage to reflect for themselves. They are experts well acquainted with the work of their predecessors and with theories current among their contemporaries. Like all scientists, they desire to contribute researches of their own leading to a fuller clarification of their specialty. And, like all scientists, they may make mistakes. The possibility of error grows with the distance from revealed data their quest of truth takes them....

The Church does not wish to halt or suppress any creative movement that has been inaugurated. Theological research may go on and must go on; it is needed for the effective presentation, to the men of our day, of revealed truth that is ever fresh and vital. But the teaching authority must insist that all such currents remain within the right channel, because it has to safeguard fidelity to the deposit of revelation.

The encyclical confers an incalculable benefit on Catholic theology and life. In the first place, it points a sure finger at the goal toward which some contemporary movements were tending and which they would risk reaching if they were not checked and redirected. That is a valuable service benefiting theologians as well as the faithful....

The Catholic theologian will have no difficulty in following the directives of this encyclical. He can confidently carry on his researches and he can still pursue his apostolic ambition to make the changeless profundities of Catholic truth intelligible to the minds of our time. But in his freedom of investigation and boldness of speculation he must keep his ears open to the voice of the Church. The personal ideas of the Catholic theologian are not indispensable to the life of the Church; and when not guaranteed by the directions of the magisterium, his teachings remain merely human opinions. Without ecclesiastical approval of his labors, the theologian cannot hope to influence Catholic life....

As a public function, the work of theology is a work of the Church. The Church has been commissioned to teach. And because it has to teach, it has to know the explanations given of its teaching and oversee the science wrought from that teaching. Otherwise such teaching would not be basically its own. That is why the Church guides theologians, as it does in *Humani Generis;* the sacred truth to which theologians devote their lives is the Church's own truth.

> Cyril Vollert, S.J.: "*Humani Generis* and the Limits of Theology," *Theological Studies* 12, no. 1 (March 1951): 3, 5, 6, 8–14, 20–23.

## 77. Monsignor Fulton Sheen on the Problem with Modern Psychology and Psychoanalysis, 1949

*The most visible U.S. Catholic prelate of the day, Monsignor Fulton J. Sheen, a professor of apologetics at Catholic University of America for twenty-five years, dedicated his considerable rhetorical skills and philosophical training to opposing the secularist trends reshaping American society, not least of which was what he called, in a sermon delivered in 1947 from the pulpit of St. Patrick's Cathedral in New York City, "a particular type of psychoanalysis called Freudianism which is based on four assumptions, materialism, hedonism, infantilism and eroticism."[1]*

*In the following excerpt from his 1949 book,* Peace of Soul, *Sheen offers a searing critique of psychoanalysis, the chief error of which is its encroachment upon the realm of spiritual counseling and confession, which is the arena of the church.*

A few decades ago, nobody believed in the confession of sins except the Church. Today everyone believes in confession, with this difference: some believe in confessing their own sins; others believe in confessing other people's sins. The popularity of psychoanalysis has nearly convinced everyone of the necessity of

---

1. Quoted in C. Kevin Gillespie, S.J., *Psychology and American Catholicism: From Confession to Therapy* (New York: Crossroad, 2001), 16.

some kind of confession for peace of mind. This is another instance of how the world, which threw Christian truths into the wastebasket in the nineteenth century, is pulling them out in isolated, secularized form in the twentieth century, meanwhile deluding itself into believing that it has made a great discovery. The world found it could not get along without some release for its inner unhappiness. Once it had rejected confession and denied both God and guilt, it had to find a substitute.

Our particular concern here, as usual, *is not with either psychiatry or the psychoanalytic method, both of which are valid in their spheres.* We limit the discussion solely to that single psychoanalytic group who assert these things: Man is an animal; there is no personal responsibility and therefore no guilt; the psychoanalytic method is a substitute for confession.

To begin positively: The Sacrament of Penance, or Confession, was instituted by Our Divine Lord, and it satisfies the deepest aspirations of the human soul. Experience reveals these three aspirations: When a man does wrong, he wants to avow it. Because he knows it to be wrong, he will not tell it to anyone who happens by, but only to some representative of the moral order, for what he seeks is pardon. And, to get back on the right track, man wants some ideal higher than himself or even his fellow man, some unfailing absolute standard, with a spokesman willing to help him to that ideal....

It is on this point of avowal that there appears the first difference between psychoanalysis and confession. Psychoanalysis is an avowal of attitudes of mind in unconsciousness; confession is an avowal of guilt in conscience. Psychoanalysis is the probing of mind by mind; confession is the communion of conscience and God. The revealing of mental attitudes asks nothing of our pride and never craves pardon: as a matter of fact, one can be proud of an unhealthy state of mind. Some men delight in boasting of their atheism, their agnosticism, their perversities, but no conscience ever boasted of its guilt. Even in isolation, the sinner is ashamed.

If the moral order is denied, the avowal becomes only the acknowledgment of a mistake or a misfortune, not the acknowledgment of sin. Guilt is moral, not physiological or animal; therefore it cannot be known objectively and scientifically, any more than a poem can be known by a study of its meter alone. As against the escapism of some analysis which makes the self blameless, confession to a priest assumes that the ego can be at fault, that the seething lava of unrest below the surface is due to the repression of a *willful* disorder, and that only by acknowledging it as one's own can one be restored to a fellowship with self, with nature, with fellow man, and with God. It takes no courage to admit that one is guiltless, but it takes a heroism of which few are capable to take the burden of one's guilt to Calvary and to say to the Christ on the Cross, "That Crown of Thorns my pride placed there; those nails were driven by the hammer of my avarice; the scourges that fell on Thy flesh were swung by my lusts and my cupidities." Guilt is guilt only when it is subjectively felt as one's own. If a man does not know within himself that he is harsh or spiteful or proud, he does not know himself. The Agony in the Garden was the supreme subjective knowledge of the world's guilt, for there it was Our Lord permitted

Himself to feel the guilt due to the sins of man; and the Agony resulted in the Bloody Sweat.

A further difference is this: No person likes to have his mind excavated according to a fantastic, unscientific theory that sex must be at the bottom of all his problems. This was one of the most general complaints of soldiers during World War II against mental examinations; some Army doctors assumed that continence was abnormality. Even in the occasional case where sexual conflicts are really to blame, no one is made better by having someone else tell him how queer he is or how rotten he is. Everyone wants to do his own telling, for he knows he can be made better only by avowing the guilt himself. "Let me tell it" expresses a primary right of the human heart. The individual alone has the right to repudiate a part of himself as the condition of betterment. He resents probing and analysis by alien minds. He wants to swing open the portals of his own conscience; he wants no one breaking them down from the outside. The very uniqueness of personality gives him the right to state his own case in his own words. No soul likes to be studied like a bug. No trial is complete unless the defendant has a chance to take the witness stand to testify in his own case. The worst in the self, through self-avowal, ministers to one's betterment and peace. But each person wants to be his own witness for the prosecution — to conduct his case against himself, not that he may be condemned, but that he may not....

The modern world is full of mentally normal but harassed people who seek peace wherever they have heard that it is offered — even from men who have been trained to deal with the insane. But they are sane enough. For them, the world needs a revival of the Rights of Sanctuary: during the ages of Faith, a fugitive from justice was considered immune from prosecution by civil law if he succeeded in grabbing the big iron ring which was attached to the front door of a church. By this token, he threw himself upon the mercies of church laws. Such sure and solitary harbor is needed today for the poor souls who long to pour out their guilt for the sake of pardon and reparation and peace. And the Church does have such a haven in the confessional box, where the Divine Mercy Our Lord extended through His human nature to a penitent thief, Magdalene, and the woman taken in sin is made available to our equally broken hearts. It is not easy to go into that box, but it is a wonderful feeling to come out!

More than any form of psychoanalysis, the world needs psychosynthesis; some psychiatrists have recognized this — Jung, in his idea of "rebirth," and some followers of Freud, who have called their theory "active psychoanalysis." For human beings need to be put together more than they need to be taken apart. Sin divides us against ourselves; absolution restores our unity. Most people today have a load on their minds because they have a load on their consciences; the Divine Psychologist knew how miserable we should be if we could not unload that burden. Hospitals are built because men have sick bodies, and the Church builds confessional boxes because they also have sick souls. Regular confession prevents our sins, our worries, our fears, our anxieties from seeping into the unconscious and degenerating into melancholy, psychoses, and neuroses. The boil is lanced before the pus can spread into unconsciousness. The

Divine Master knew what is in man; so He instituted this Sacrament, not for His needs, but for ours. It was His way of giving man a happy heart. The left side of the physical heart and the right side of the heart have no direct communication with each other; they are joined through the medium of the blood circulating through the body. Our hearts become happy, too, by communicating with Christ's Mystical Body and His Blood. We are not made worse by admitting the need for absolution. We are not made worse even by admitting we are all brokenhearted; for unless our hearts were broken, how else could God get in?

Fulton J. Sheen: "Psychoanalysis and Confession," *Peace of Soul* (Garden City, N.Y.: Garden City Books, 1949), 124–25, 127–29, 145–46.

## 78. Pierre Teilhard de Chardin, S.J.: Reconceptualizing Creation, Cosmology, and Christology through the Lens of Evolution, 1964

*In the following passage, Christopher F. Mooney, an American Jesuit priest, celebrates Teilhard's accomplishment in establishing the connection between "Christianity and the Outcome of Evolution" (the title of the second chapter of Mooney's 1964 book,* Teilhard de Chardin and the Mystery of Christ, *from which this excerpt is taken).*

In 1936 Teilhard de Chardin summarized in the short space of a few paragraphs the broad lines of his whole life's work. The passage deserves to be quoted in its entirety, since it is perhaps the clearest statement of the triple direction taken by his thought in its search for unity in the Christian life.

If we want to reach the modern religious current at its deepest level and change its course, three steps seem to me to be necessary, each linked to the other.

*a* A first step would consist in developing (along the lines of the 'perennial philosophy': primacy of being, act and potency) a correct physics and metaphysics of evolution. I am convinced that an honest interpretation of the recent achievements of scientific thought justifiably leads not to a materialistic but to a spiritualistic interpretation of evolution: — the world we know is not developing by chance, but is structurally controlled by a personal Centre of universal convergence.

*b* The second step concerns dogmatic theology and would consist in articulating a Christology which would be in keeping with the dimensions of the universe as we know them today. This would mean a recognition that, along with those strictly human and divine attributes chiefly considered by theologians up to now, Christ possesses, by virtue of the mechanism of the Incarnation, attributes which are universal and cosmic, and it is these which constitute him that personal Centre hypothetically invoked by the physics and metaphysics of evolution. Such a perspective is in striking harmony with the most fundamental texts of St. John and St. Paul, and with the theology of the Greek Fathers.

*c* A third step concerns the spiritual life and would consist in developing an evangelism of human conquest. This third step follows automatically from the second, since it is indeed impossible for Christians to have a clearer vision of Christ as the summit of the world's evolution without at the same time appreciating more deeply the supernatural value of human effort carried out *in Christo Jesu*. The universal Christ enables us to understand that the most direct way to heaven is not to let go of earth as quickly as possible, as could sometimes appear, but to bring this earth to fulfilment, since we see it now as a much vaster thing, more unfinished than we ever suspected. In this way fundamental Christian attitudes would thrive and move ahead forcefully, without in the least deviating from their traditional course....

Teilhard de Chardin's ultimate purpose in developing the "hyperphysics" of evolution we have just summarized was in no sense exclusively scientific. He was a man who, as we have already noted, experienced a very acute sense of anxiety before the mystery and apparent futility of human life. Up to his very last year he was acutely aware of the world's power to discourage and oppress, and it is this awareness which to a large extent conditioned his own personal search for unity between God and the world. Hence the frequent references to modern anxiety in *The Phenomenon of Man,* for Teilhard was convinced that his own experience was typical of twentieth century man. "In all my work I am conscious of being merely a sounding-board, amplifying what people around me are thinking."

In addition to this sense of anxiety there was his almost mystic attraction for some absolute, present as we have seen from his earliest childhood, and this made it imperative that the evolutionary pattern to which he had committed himself as a scientist, should also be related intrinsically to some absolute. On the strict level of the physical sciences this was obviously impossible, since by its very nature evolution is relative. This explains Teilhard's constant preoccupation with the future, the end of the process, the terminus where all the radii converge at the Omega Point. Here it was possible for him to locate an absolute for cosmogenesis which, though itself outside the process, would provide that assurance of ultimate success which alone was capable, in his mind, of assuaging the anxiety and fear of modern man. Consequently he continues his analysis of evolution into convictions "strictly undemonstrable to science,...faith in progress,...faith in unity,...faith in a centre of personality exerting an infallible attraction." Again, what we shall attempt here is the barest summary. The following text will serve as our point of departure and also help avoid any misconception about what he is going to do:

On the strictly psychological plane...I mean by 'faith' any adherence of our intelligence to a general view of the universe.... The essential note of the psychological act of faith is, in my opinion, to see as possible and to accept as more probable a conclusion which, because it envelopes so much in space and time, goes far beyond all its analytical premises. *To believe is to achieve an intellectual synthesis.*

Teilhard begins his "act of faith" with two factors, two phenomena, which have profoundly changed the whole character of noogenesis. The first is modern man's sudden awareness of what is taking place in him and by means of him. This awareness of evolution is indeed the specific effect of the process peculiar to our present age. *The Phenomenon of Man* links the whole psychology of modern disquiet with the confrontation of space-time. "What has made us in four or five generations so different from our forebears (in spite of all that may be said), so ambitious too, and so worried, is not merely that we have discovered and mastered other forms of nature. In the final analysis it is, if I am not mistaken, that we have become conscious of the movement which is carrying us along, and have thereby realized the formidable problems set us by this reflective exercise of human effort.... What makes and classifies modern man... is having become capable of seeing in terms not of space and time alone, but also of duration,... and above all of having become incapable of seeing anything otherwise — anything — not even himself... — the definitive access of consciousness to a scale of new dimensions." The result is the "malady of space-time," the feeling of both anxiety and futility, the sense of being crushed by the enormities of the cosmos.

Far more decisive, however, is the second factor, that of human freedom. For it is not only *in* man that the movement of evolution is now carried on, but *by* man. It is man who invents and discovers and who has, by taking into his own hands the direction of the world, gradually replaced nature in the progress of life. Through man evolution has not only become conscious of itself but free to dispose of itself, — it can give itself or refuse itself. Upon man therefore falls the awful responsibility for his future on earth. In the great game being played "we are the players as well as being the cards and the stakes. Nothing can go on if we leave the table. Neither can any power force us to remain. Is the game worth the candle, or are we simply its dupes? The question has hardly been formulated as yet in man's heart, accustomed for hundreds of centuries to toe the line; it is a question, however, whose mere murmur, already audible, infallibly predicts future rumblings. The last century witnessed the first systematic strikes in industry; the next will surely not pass without the threat of strikes in the noosphere.... If progress is a myth, that is to say, if faced with the work involved we can say 'What's the good of it all?' [then] the whole of evolution will come to a halt — *because we are evolution.*"

Teilhard's first assurance to modern man is to point to the pattern he has uncovered through his generalized physics of evolution. Time and space are terrifying only if they are thought to be motionless and blind; they immediately become humanized as soon as a definite movement appears which gives them a physiognomy and shows them to be part of a developing whole. "What matters the giddy plurality of the stars and their fantastic spread, if that immensity (symmetrical with the infinitesimal) has no other function but to equilibrate the intermediary layer where, and where only in the medium range of size, life can build itself up chemically? What matters the millions of years and milliards of beings that have gone before, if those countless drops form a current which carries us along?" In Teilhard's mind we are not simply face to face with "change" in the world but with "genesis," which is something quite different. It should be noted that the French word *genèse* is much wider in meaning and more common in usage than the English "genesis." It applies to any form of production involving successive stages oriented towards some goal. The law of complexity-consciousness is thus an assurance that there has been "genesis," that the universe has been pursuing an aim, that a single pattern has thus been running through the whole and that this pattern has been oriented towards man. Man is the key to the whole biological process, since it was through him and him alone that evolution crossed the threshold of reflection into the mysterious realm of the person.

But Teilhard sees clearly that what the present generation needs most is assurance not about the past but about the future of evolution. The universe has always been in motion and at this moment continues to be in motion. But will it be in motion tomorrow?...

Such a guarantee must be given in the context of human freedom; it cannot come from an order imposed by coercion or sustained by fear. In Teilhard's mind this is precisely the reason for the world's present discouragement with the whole human aspiration towards unity. Up to now every gigantic effort to reduce the multitude of mankind to some order seems to have ended by stifling the human person. Communism, nazism, fascism have produced the most ghastly fetters; men hoped for brotherhood and found only ant hills.... Yet what men forget is that, monstrous though it is, modern totalitarianism is really a distortion of something magnificent, and thus quite near the truth. When an energy runs amok, the engineer, far from questioning the power itself, simply works out his calculations afresh to see how it can better be brought under control. And in our modern world what has gone wrong is that we have neglected those forces of freedom which emerge from the depths of the human person and therefore constitute a unitive force which is interior, a force based not upon coercion or fear but upon love....

But how then are we to explain the appearance all around us of growing repulsion and hatred? If such a strong potency is really besieging us from within and urging us to unite, what prevents it from passing into act? One thing only: "that we should overcome the 'anti-personalist' complex which paralyzes us, and make up our minds to accept the possibility, indeed the reality, of some source of love and object of love at the summit of the world above our heads. So long as it absorbs or appears to absorb the person, the collectivity kills the love that is trying to come to birth." Unless the modern impetus towards union is leading us towards "Someone," it must certainly end up by plunging us back into matter. In order to turn this failure that threatens us into success, what we must do is to recognize "not only some vague future existence, but also, as I must now stress, the radiation *as a present reality* of that mysterious Centre of our centres I have called Omega."

Christopher F. Mooney, S.J., *Teilhard de Chardin and the Mystery of Christ* (New York: Harper and Row, 1964), 34–35, 48–53.

## 79. "An Ecological Ethic Grounded in Truth": Feminism, Environmentalism, and Women's Spirituality, 1993

*Two important Catholic intellectual currents of the postconciliar era — women's spirituality informed by feminism, and environmental ethics — converged in the writing of leading American Catholic theologians such as Elizabeth A. Johnson, C.S.J., a professor of theology at Fordham University and the author of the influential book,* She Who Is: The Mystery of God in Feminist Theological Discourse *(1992). The following passage is excerpted from the 1993 Madeleva Lecture in Spirituality, delivered by Professor Johnson. In the chapter entitled "A Taproot of the Crisis: The Two-Tiered Universe," Johnson decries the "hierarchical dualism" which, she argues, has provided justification for the exploitation of both women and the Earth by patriarchal societies, including the institutional church. Writing with a keen awareness of the ecological crisis that threatens the earth (and with Teilhard de Chardin in mind), Johnson critiques the dualist pattern of thought and action — which separates humanity from nature, man from woman, and God from the Earth — from the vantage of a Teilhardian worldview more directly informed by modern biology and evolutionary thought. The "law of complexity-consciousness," she writes, leads us to recognize that the "human spirit is rightly interpreted* within *rather than* over against *human kinship with nature."*

I am persuaded of the truth of ecofeminism's insight that analysis of the ecological crisis does not get to the heart of the matter until it sees the connection between exploitation of the earth and the sexist definition and treatment of women. As a theologian I am further convinced that the distortion found in those two instances also influences the Christian experience and doctrine of the mystery of God. This, I suggest, is the genius of women's spirituality in our day, informed by feminist analysis: that it sees the deficient pattern as a whole rather than in bits and pieces. Having faced something of the devastating result, let us cut to a major taproot of the crisis, namely, the dominant form of western rationality called hierarchical dualism.

This is a pattern of thought and action that (1) divides reality into two separate and opposing spheres, and (2) assigns a higher value to one of them. In terms of the three basic relations that shape an ecological ethic, this results in a view in which humanity is detached from and more important than nature; man is separate from and more valuable than woman; God is disconnected from the world, utterly and simply transcendent over it, as well as more significant than it. Hierarchical dualism delivers a two-tiered vision of reality that privileges the elite half of a pair and subordinates the other, which is thought to have little or no intrinsic value of its own but exists only to be of use to the higher....

Women, Earth, and Spirit

Hierarchical dualism also shapes the classical Christian doctrine of God, who is depicted as the epitome of the masculine half of the dualistic equation. The all holy Other is uncontaminated by matter, utterly transcendent over the world and unaffected by it. The way in which patriarchal authority commands the obedience of women and other creatures on earth serves as a prime analogy for God's relation to the world. Absolutely omnipotent, "He," for such a concept is always designated by the grammatically masculine, is the victorious sovereign whose will is law and whom all are meant to serve. Even when this monarchical model graces the Supreme Being with a benevolent attitude, "He" is still intrinsically remote, ruling the universe while not affected by it in any significant way....

The logic of hierarchical dualism sheds light on why this is the case. Valuing spirit over body and transcendence over immanence, it concentrates on the one high God who creates by "His" word to the neglect of the indwelling, sustaining presence of God within the fragility of matter and historical process. When this pattern of thought turns to Trinitarian theology it keeps the focus on the relation of Father and Son, one generating and the other being generated, finding it difficult even to know what proper name to give the Spirit. Dualism has trouble with threes.

But it is not only the framework on which the doctrine of God is built that excludes the Spirit. In a subtle way this mindset connects the Spirit with the female side of the dualistic equation, with women's reality and functions, which it disvalues. The Spirit brings forth and nurtures life, keeps all things connected, and constantly renews what the ravages of time and sin break down. This is surely analogous to traditional "women's work" which goes on continuously in home and society, bringing forth life, holding all things together, cleaning what has been messed up, while unnoticed and unremunerated. Neglect of the Spirit has a symbolic affinity with the marginalization of women and is an inevitable outcome of a sexist, dualistic lens on reality, which also, let us remember, disvalues nature.

The extent of what is lost to the richness of faith can be glimpsed when we realize that what is being neglected is nothing less than the mystery of God's personal engagement with the world in its history of love and disaster; nothing less than God's empowering presence active within the cosmos from the beginning, throughout history and to the end, calling forth life and freedom. Forgetting the Spirit is not ignoring a faceless, shadowy, third hypostasis but the mystery of God vivifying the world, closer to us than we are to ourselves, drawing near and passing by in liberating compassion.

Three basic relationships: human beings with nature, among themselves, and with God. In each instance the major classical pattern of relationship is shaped by hierarchical dualism, that is, modeled on the dominance of ruling male elites and the subjugation of what is identified as female, cosmic, or foreign, an underclass with only instrumental value. As the ecological crisis makes crystal clear, the polarization of each pair's terms is nothing short of disastrous in its interconnected effects. Our eyes have been blinded to the sacredness of the earth, which is linked to the exclusion of women from the sphere of the sacred, which is tied to focus on a monarchical, patriarchal idea of God and a consequent forgetting of the Creator Spirit, the Lifegiver who is intimately related to the earth.

In the quest for an ecological ethic grounded in religious truth, these three relationships need to be rethought together. But we must be wary of roads that lead to dead-ends. I think it is a strategic mistake to retain the dualistic way of thinking and hope to make an advance simply by assigning greater value to the repressed "feminine" side of the polarity. This is to keep women, earth, and Spirit in their pre-assigned box, which is a cramped, subordinate place. Even if what has previously been disparaged is now highly appreciated, this strategy does not allow for the fullest flourishing of what is confined to one pole by pre-assigned definition. In truth, women are not any closer to nature than men are; this is a cultural construct. In truth, women are every bit as rational as men, every bit as courageous, every bit as capable of initiative. At the same time, precisely because women have been so identified with nature, our voices at this moment in time can speak out for the value of despised matter, bodies, and nature even as we assert that women's rational and spiritual capacities are equal to those of men. What we search for is a way to undercut the dualism and to construct a new, wholistic design for all of reality built on appreciation of difference in a genuine community. We seek a unifying vision that does not stratify what is distinct into superior-inferior layers but reconciles them in relationships of mutuality. Let us then listen to women's wisdom, discern our kinship with the earth, and remember the Spirit, as vital steps toward an ecological ethic and spirituality....

## Kinship

The human race along with all living creatures is physically made of the dust of the earth which is the fallout of stardust. But, one might argue, what about intelligence and freedom which so distinguish the human species? Does this not break the kinship that humanity shares with the rest of creation? Not at all. Human consciousness is in continuity with the energy of matter stretching back through galactic ages to the Big Bang, being a special, intense form of this energy. The law of complexity-consciousness reveals that ever more intricate physical combinations, as can be traced in the evolution of the brain, yield ever more powerful forms of spirit. Matter, alive with energy, evolves to spirit. While distinctive, human intelligence and creativity rise out of the very nature of the universe, which is itself intelligent and creative. In other words, human spirit is the cosmos come to consciousness. Teilhard de Chardin broached this point years ago as he wrote, "The human person is the sum total of fifteen billion years of unbroken evolution now thinking about itself...."

This makes us distinct but not separate, a unique strand in the cosmos, yet still a strand *of* the cosmos. Consciousness is the flowering through us of deeply cosmic energies. Thus human spirit is rightly interpreted *within* rather than *over against* human kinship with nature.

Since nature is a dynamic web of interconnected processes of which we are one part, it becomes clear that each species that has evolved has an intrinsic value of its own, apart from immediate human use. The kinship paradigm appreciates this even as it knows our own human difference. For it arises from an experience of communion which at its deepest level is religious. From a religious perspective, all diverse strands in the web of life are expressions of the creative power of the cosmos which is ultimately empowered by the Creator Spirit. The enormous diversity of species itself points to the inexhaustible richness of the Creator, whose imaginative goodness these species represent.... Realizing this, the religious kinship attitude cherishes and seeks intelligently to preserve biodiversity, for when a species goes extinct we have lost a manifestation of the goodness of God.

To sum up: appreciating the deep patterns of affiliation in the cosmos, the kinship model knows that we are all connected. For all our distinctiveness, human beings are modes of being of the universe. Woven into our lives is the very fire from the stars and the genes from the sea creatures, and everyone, utterly everyone, is kin in the radiant tapestry of being. This relationship is not external or extrinsic to who we are, but wells up as the defining truth from our deepest being.

Elizabeth A. Johnson, *Women, Earth, and Creator Spirit* (New York: Paulist Press, 1993), 10–11, 17–22, 37–39.

## Part 9

# THE PATH TO VATICAN II

## Introduction

"Tridentine Catholicism" — the practices, institutions, movements, and theology fostered by the Council of Trent (1545–63) — prevailed within the Roman Catholic Church for four hundred years. By the second decade of the twentieth century, however, a revival of the teachings of St. Thomas Aquinas, endorsed by Pope Leo XIII in 1879, was stimulating Catholic intellectual life and spiritual renewal in Europe and the United States. Thomism, or neo-Thomism, as the revival was called, proved to be an important path from Tridentine Catholicism to a new, modern form of Catholicism endorsed in broad outline by a very different ecumenical council, Vatican II.

The dominant theory of the church during the nineteenth century, inherited from the Council of Trent and reinforced by the First Vatican Council (1869–70), emphasized the bishops' subordination to the pope, the laity's subordination to the clergy, and non-Catholics' spiritual inferiority to Catholics. This model endured well into the twentieth century; indeed, the Thomist revival was initially intended to shore up "traditional" ecclesiology in the face of modern trends that threatened to undermine it. Thomism's doctrine of revealed truths essential to salvation and entrusted to the church (and, specifically, to the magisterium) provided the theological foundation for this top-heavy form of institutional Catholicism. In addition Thomism, which adduced a universal moral law that is embedded in nature and accessible to rightly ordered reason, was presented as a beacon of hope for Christian societies whose faith in humanity and God was shaken by the brutality of the world wars.

This one-two punch made Thomism the perfect antidote to "Modernism." The original Modernists, a small network of European Catholics with a few supporters and admirers in the United States, had undertaken the critical study of the Bible; the historical study of the development of Christian doctrines, practices, and institutions, and the comparative study of religions. Before the so-called Modernists gained much momentum or achieved maturity as a company of thinkers, Pope Pius X condemned the "movement," in 1907, and instituted an anti-Modernist oath required of all priests thereafter. The Modernists' fundamental error, according to their detractors in the curia, was their departure from the neo-Scholastic or neo-Thomist paradigm for theology and philosophy.[1]

---

1. R. Scott Appleby, *Church and Age, Unite! The Modernist Impulse in American Catholicism* (Notre Dame, Ind.: University of Notre Dame Press, 1992), 236.

The Catholics who feared a conspiracy of Modernists arising within the church worried that modern man was veering away from the supernatural reality pointed to and embodied by the church. In the Tridentine mass, by contrast, the anti-Modernists believed, the proper respect for the radical otherness of the divine was preserved. The priest at the altar, his back to the congregation, ritually reenacted the sacrifice of Christ at Calvary. Representing the bishop and sharing in his sacerdotal power, the priest properly stood apart from the faithful. By virtue of ordination, his soul had received a special mark or character. When speaking about "the church," in fact, the laity referred primarily to those men, from the lowliest parish curate to the pope, who had been set apart in this way for apostolic life. The sacraments, especially the Eucharist, were sacred mysteries, solemn moments when, at the behest of the church, the divine penetrated and transformed the mundane. The sacred, in short, was understood to be utterly transcendent — remote from ordinary experience and inaccessible apart from the mediation of the church.

The Modernists' doctrine of "vital immanence," or the indwelling of the Holy Spirit in the soul of each baptized Christian, was therefore anathema to the neo-Scholastic theologians of the period, the most prominent of which were Jesuits. They advanced a theory of divine revelation and biblical inspiration called "extrinsicism." It held that revelation is completely extrinsic to, or independent of, subjective human needs or horizons of understanding.[2] Society, increasingly rudderless and vulnerable to the reckless autonomy of the secular individual, needed the church, more than ever, to preserve the right relationship between God and humanity. The church did so, not least by safeguarding the "deposit of faith" — the revealed teachings of Jesus Christ and his apostles.

For fulfilling this divine mandate, a robust institution was indispensable. Like the modern state, Catholicism grew more centralized and bureaucratic during the course of the nineteenth and twentieth centuries. The papacy consolidated its power over the college of bishops. The Roman rite of the Mass, celebrated in Latin, the "universal" language of the church, fostered a fundamental unity, even as missionary orders carried the gospel to diverse cultures. Vatican-approved manuals of moral theology standardized the sacramental practice of confession and penance. The clergy and religious orders cultivated the virtue of obedience among their ranks and in the laity.

In the political order, the church aligned itself with or against nation-states, depending on the concessions or privileges it won from the latter. The concordat the church signed with Germany, for example, was apparently one factor that Pope Pius XII (d. 1958) took into consideration when he failed to speak out frequently and unambiguously against Adolf Hitler and the atrocities being committed by Nazi Germany against Jews and other minorities.

With this background in place, one can better appreciate the fact that reformers within the church, in the early decades of the twentieth century, were planting the seeds of reform that would spring forth dramatically in the Second

---

2. Gabriel Daly, *Transcendence and Immanence: A Study in Catholic Modernism and Integralism* (Oxford: Clarendon Press, 1980), 175–76.

Vatican Council. Neo-Thomism, although rooted in the medieval past and often used by some proponents of the twentieth-century revival to resist the incursions of modernity, provided subtle encouragement for this work of "updating." The modern Thomists took history seriously. They studied the thought of Aquinas in its original context, which had been obscured to some extent by his eighteenth- and nineteenth-century neo-Scholastic interpreters. Significantly for the nascent reform process, the very practice of retrieving historical models for theology led some Thomists, or scholars writing under the canopy of Thomism, to probe other Christian historical periods, most significantly the apostolic era. These would-be reformers included German and American Benedictine monks who were engaged in the study of Catholic liturgical traditions.

Lay Catholics as well as priests contributed to the revival. Professors at Catholic universities (Fordham, Notre Dame, St. Louis University, and Catholic University of America, in particular) founded scholarly societies and professional journals to explore the relevance of natural law philosophy and "Christian Aristotelianism" to the major moral and cultural questions of the day. Even radical Catholicism, given striking expression in the Catholic Worker movement founded by Dorothy Day and Peter Maurin, took Thomism as its philosophical starting point. The 1920s and 1930s were the heyday of the revival in the United States.[3]

Eventually, however, Thomism itself split into rival schools, in response to theological ferment taking place in Catholic Europe. One such school, known as the "transcendental Thomists," advocated a shift to a neo-apostolic paradigm for Catholic self-understanding.[4] The influential Jesuit theologian Karl Rahner argued, for example, that the church in the modern world, a world that was increasingly "post-Christian" and neo-pagan in orientation, had more in common with the early church (situated, as it was, within the pagan world of ancient Rome) than with medieval Christendom. The church of the first three Christian centuries thus became a source of guidance for the liturgical, catechetical, and ethical reformers of the mid-twentieth century.

The popes, ironically, were inadvertent agents of the diffusion of Thomistic thought, in that they contributed to the opening up of Catholic modes of inquiry. Two papal encyclicals, both issued in 1943, were particularly influential; themes from both were later incorporated into the documents of Vatican II. Thirty-six years after the condemnation of Modernism, Pope Pius XII issued *Divino Afflante Spiritu*, a forward-looking document that gave conditional approval to the use of historical-critical methods in the study of the Bible. Neither the cautious tone of the papal approval, nor the great import of it, were lost on

---

3. Philip Gleason, *Contending with Modernity: Catholic Higher Education in the Twentieth Century* (New York: Oxford University Press, 1995), 146–63.

4. On the fragmentation of Thomism after the world wars, see Benedict M. Ashley, O.P., "The Loss of Theological Unity: Pluralism, Thomism and Catholic Morality," in *Being Right: Conservative Catholics in America*, ed. Mary Jo Weaver and R. Scott Appleby (Bloomington: Indiana University Press, 1995), 63–87.

the editors of the *Catholic Biblical Quarterly*, a journal established at the Catholic University of America in Washington, D.C., four years earlier to promote the scholarly study of the Bible (see doc. 80).[5]

In the encyclical *Mystici Corporis*, Pius XII defined the church as the Mystical Body of Christ, an image taken from the New Testament (Romans 12 and 1 Corinthians 12). Although *Mystici Corporis* employed juridical and hierarchical language to describe the relationship between the head of the body and its members, the pope also emphasized the interior reality of grace and the role of the Holy Spirit as the soul of the Mystical Body. By providing a model of the church to complement the previously exclusive focus on the papacy and the hierarchy, the encyclical underscored the spiritual and supernatural dimensions of the church. In addition to developing spiritual rather than institutional criteria for participation in the true church of Christ, the Mystical Body model, with its biblical basis, was far more congenial to Protestant and Orthodox Christians, with whom Catholics would enter into sustained ecumenical dialogue following Vatican II.[6]

Papal approval of studying the Bible in its cultural and historical contexts and turning to the Bible for models of the church was welcomed by the proponents of the so-called "new theology." The term refers to the writings of, among others, the French Dominicans Marie-Dominique Chenu and Yves Congar, and the Jesuits Henri de Lubac and Jean Daniélou. From the 1930s onwards, these European thinkers salvaged what was crucial in Modernism and went on to revolutionize Catholic theology. Arguing that the transcendent word of God is always expressed in historically contingent, imperfect, incomplete — and therefore revisable — forms, Chenu pioneered the incorporation of the historical-critical method into theology. Congar's theological reflections on the laity were both forward-looking and enormously influential in the preparation of the documents of Vatican II, especially *Lumen Gentium*'s chapter on the laity. Daniélou, a critic of Scholastic theology, urged the integration of insights from modern science and philosophy into Catholic thought. He called for a renewal of biblical theology through a return to the sources — the scriptures themselves, the fathers of the early church, and the ancient liturgy. In the return to patristic thought, he wrote, Catholics will recover "categories which are those of contemporary thought but which Scholastic theology had lost."[7] De Lubac challenged the Scholastic notion of a "double finality" for human beings — the state of nature and the elevated state of supernature — as alien to patristic theology. Faith, he contended, is born of one "graced nature" and is rooted in the heart, not the intellect.[8]

---

5. Ibid., 303.

6. "Mystici Corporis," in Richard P. McBrien, gen. ed., *The HarperCollins Encyclopedia of Catholicism* (New York: HarperCollins, 1995), 900; Avery Dulles, S.J., *Models of the Church* (New York: Image/Doubleday, 1987 [1974]), 58.

7. Jean Daniélou, quoted in Paul Lakeland, *The Liberation of the Laity: In Search of an Accountable Church* (New York: Continuum, 2002), 36.

8. Lakeland, *The Liberation of the Laity*, 40.

These European Catholic intellectuals, taken together, offered a radically new approach to theology, one that departed in certain fundamental respects from the neo-Scholastic model that had upheld Tridentine Catholicism in the nineteenth century. Daniélou, for example, chided Scholastic theology for ignoring the pressing questions of historicity and subjectivity that informed modern philosophies such as existentialism and Marxism. "Locating reality in essences rather than in subjects," he wrote, "[Scholastic theology] ignores the human world, the concrete universes that transcend all essences and are distinguished only by existence...."[9]

Neo-Thomism, as we have seen, was a broad canopy. In the United States, as in Rome, it was often the lens through which champions of the Tridentine model read new developments in Catholic theology. Document 83 provides an example of the conservative function of Thomism. Taken from an article in *The Thomist,* a quarterly journal of philosophy and theology founded in 1938 and based at the Dominican House of Studies in Washington, D.C., the excerpt takes aim at the "new theology" for being insufficiently Thomistic in orientation. In so doing, the author anticipates concerns that were shortly to be voiced by Pope Pius XII in his 1950 encyclical *Humani Generis.*

Neo-Thomism also provided the putative framework within which vitriolic debates unfolded in the United States on the proper relationship between church and state, on the desirability of religious freedom, and on cooperation with Protestants. Taking the progressive, change-oriented side of these debates were the American Jesuit John Courtney Murray and his colleagues such as Gustave Weigel, S.J. The most prominent and persistent of Murray's opponents were two priests at Catholic University of America, Joseph Clifford Fenton and Francis J. Connell, who edited and published numerous articles and essays in the *American Ecclesiastical Review.*

Fenton and Connell were not only theologians, but also pastors who sought to preserve and bolster the social, cultic, and ideological barriers that protected the integrity of the Catholic Church as a distinct subculture within American society. They were ardent Thomists, and equally ardent skeptics regarding theological innovation. In the 1930s, for example, when many American Catholic intellectuals publicized their expectation that Thomism would serve as an integrating force in an apparently philosophically exhausted Western culture, Fenton expressed his doubt that Aquinas might "ever become 'the fashion.'" Fortunately, he observed, Thomistic philosophy "has not, and could not be made to have, the Sunday Supplement flavor requisite for that position." There is hardly room for Thomas "in the gatherings of the sophisticates," for he is "a little too mature for that sort of thing.... He would hardly have cared for the exclusive atmosphere of a 'social set.'"[10]

---

9. Jean Daniélou, quoted in ibid., 37.
10. Joseph Clifford Fenton, "Popular Thomism," *Commonweal* 24 (1936): 554–55. On the confidence of the Thomist revival between the wars, see William A. Halsey, *The Survival of American Innocence: Catholicism in an Era of Disillusionment, 1920–1940* (Notre Dame, Ind.: University of Notre Dame Press, 1980).

Fenton's opposition to religious liberty (doc. 81) was based in part on his evaluation of the relatively undiscriminating religious environment created in the Unites States as a consequence of the nation's experience in the travails of the twentieth century, leading up to and including the Second World War. The worldwide turmoil of the 1930s — the Depression, the collapse of democracy and the rise of totalitarianism in Europe, the war in Spain, and other catastrophes — had alarmed Catholic intellectuals such as de Lubac, Jacques Maritain, and Murray (who was studying in Europe at the time). The outbreak of World War II confirmed their generalized sense of crisis in the social order.[11]

Murray responded by calling for interreligious cooperation, but Fenton and Connell were unwilling to accept the risk, for they perceived a rising tide of Catholic indifferentism that threatened the very core of distinctive Roman Catholic identity in the United States.[12] Fenton and Connell addressed this problem of indifferentism — the idea that religious differences are of little or no importance — by addressing what they saw as common errors in most American Catholics' understanding of religious liberty and church-state separation. In 1941 Connell, lamenting the fact that "in present-day America the frequent intermingling of Catholics with non-Catholics is inevitable," wondered whether some Catholics, "in their laudable efforts to be broadminded and charitable toward the members of non-Catholic religious bodies, are not becoming unduly tolerant toward their doctrines. Is not the pendulum swinging from bigotry to indifferentism?"[13] The wartime mobilization of millions of Americans hailing from diverse religious backgrounds had strengthened the attitude of indifferentism, Connell worried, and he excoriated "the governmental attitude so consistently practiced in all matters pertaining to religion, that all forms of religious belief are equally good...."[14]

In their subsequent attacks on Murray's positions on these matters, Fenton and Connell posed a distinction between freedom and license. Patriotic but misguided Americans often confused the two: the ability to choose from a variety of options regardless of their source or orientation, they contended, is the essence of license. Genuine freedom, by contrast, is the natural and God-given freedom to embrace the one true religion. The minimal obligation of the state is to place no obstacle in the path of the person pursuing this inherent human

---

11. See R. Scott Appleby and John Haas, "The Last Supernaturalists: Fenton, Connell, and the Threat of Catholic Indifferentism," *U.S. Catholic Historian* 13 (Winter 1995): 23–48.

12. Despite differing occasionally in particular judgments and in temperament, Fenton and Connell formed a team; that each checked and corrected the other's work before it was published no doubt added to the impression of unanimity between them on the central issues they addressed. In 1958, Fenton expressed gratitude to "the Very Reverend Dr. Francis J. Connell, C.Ss.R., for these last fourteen years my brilliant and faithful associate in the work of *The American Ecclesiastical Review*. He has been kind enough to read and to correct the manuscript of this book with the same charitable care he has given to the reading and correction of all I have written for publication since our association began." The quote is taken from the introduction to Monsignor Joseph Clifford Fenton, *The Catholic Church and Salvation* (Westminster, Md.: Newman Press, 1958), xi.

13. Francis J. Connell, C.Ss.R., "Catholics and 'Interfaith' Groups," *American Ecclesiastical Review* 105 (November 1941): 340–41.

14. Francis J. Connell, "Pope Leo XIII's Message to America," *American Ecclesiastical Review* 109 (October 1943): 254.

right and obligation. "One who sincerely believes himself bound to practice some form of non-Catholic religion is in conscience obliged to do so," Connell admitted, "but this subjective obligation, based on an erroneous conscience, does not give him a genuine right. A real right is something objective, based on truth." Accordingly, he concluded, "a Catholic may not defend freedom of religious worship to the extent of denying that a Catholic government has the right, absolutely speaking, to restrict the activities of non-Catholic denominations, in order to protect the Catholic citizens from spiritual harm." A Catholic "may indeed uphold the feasibility of complete freedom of religious worship *as far as the United States is concerned*. For, all things considered, the most practical policy for our land is equality for all denominations."[15]

In 1944, a year after Connell's article appeared, Fenton picked up the theme and posed the question that would preoccupy him off and on for the rest of his life: how might American Catholics affirm the doctrine *extra Ecclesiam nulla salus* while also upholding the constitutional definition and actual practice of religious liberty in the United States? (See doc. 81.)

For his part, Murray responded with arguments drawn from history and, more importantly, from an awareness that the church was itself subject to history. The question facing U.S. Catholics in the age of Nazi and communist totalitarianism, he argued, is whether "the religion of the state" — in this case, the separation of church and state enshrined in the U.S. Constitution — is an appropriate historical expression, correct for its day and age, of the "freedom of the Church." Answering in the affirmative, Murray took into account the concrete historical, psychological, and spiritual conditions of the mid-twentieth century. These include not only "the dechristianisation of society" and the rise of totalitarianism that threatens to crush the individual subject, but also the fact that "the significance of human personality [is] more acute and profound than the nineteenth century knew." Here Murray specifies what is new in the understanding of the person, namely: "the rights of conscience," "a concept of a living personal faith as the goal of the apostolate (the nominal Catholic is something of a social menace)," and "a more exact appreciation, and likewise distrust, of the methods of constraint and coercion, in the light of fuller experience of their sociological and psychological effects" (doc. 82). Father Murray's analysis of this question would eventually win the day at Vatican II.

Murray's positive approach to budding ecumenism was also vindicated by history. Gustave Weigel, S.J., Murray's friend and colleague, devoted much of his career to the thorny question of "cooperation with non-Catholics." During World War II both Catholics and Protestants seized upon the rise of Nazism and the dramatic collapse of France before the German onslaught as illustrations of the moral and military decrepitude of an increasingly secular West. Protestants urged the citizenry to strengthen the republic by a return to religion. The personal liberties and democratic polities of the West, they argued, had been derived from a biblical anthropology that nurtured respect for the inalienable dignity of the human person. The war had demonstrated the need

---

15. Ibid., 255–56.

for a bolstering of the spiritual and moral foundations of democracy. Catholic apologists, meanwhile, had been using socialism and communism as examples of human autonomy gone awry since the nineteenth century, and it was not difficult to incorporate Nazism into the litany of ills with which to flay liberalism. Fenton momentarily grabbed this opportunity, arguing that the perennial philosophy is the "great weapon of civilization" for it provides "the fundamentals upon which an enduring civilization can be based."[16]

In wartime relief efforts and pastoral work no less than in sociocultural criticism, the menacing power of a revitalized paganism required a coordinated Christian response. Intercreedal collaboration during the war led to a makeshift ecumenism, the justifications for which were left to theologians of the several cooperating Christian denominations. The exigencies of this international crisis raised a "strictly theological issue" for Catholics, which Murray posed as follows: "Can Catholics and non-Catholics form a unity by the fact of co-operation without thereby compromising the Catholic Unity of the Church?"[17]

Weigel's general answer to this question, which he elaborated in the fifties and early sixties, was "yes," but his affirmation took the form of a nuanced and sometimes ambiguous discussion rather than a straightforward endorsement of inter-Christian unity (docs. 87a and 87b).

Liturgical reform also assumed a distinctively American cast in the postwar years leading up to the council. The most important leader of the movement in the United States was Virgil Michel, a Benedictine monk of St. John's Abbey in Collegeville, Minnesota. In everything he did as a liturgist, from founding the journal *Orate Fratres* (later *Worship*) and The Liturgical Press to preaching and teaching constantly across the United States until his death in 1938, Michel emphasized the organic connection between the Catholic Mass and the Christian commitment to social justice. By incorporating worshippers into the Body of Christ, the celebration of the Eucharist forged a community of compassionate sufferers who were called to participate with the living Christ in service to humanity.[18]

In Europe as in the United States, the Liturgical Movement gained momentum after the world wars. In 1947, it received a considerable boost from the pope. Four years after *Mystici Corporis* and *Divino Afflante Spiritu* opened up the areas of ecclesiology and biblical studies, respectively, Pope Pius XII issued a third major encyclical promoting reform in Catholic self-understanding. *Mediator Dei* laid the groundwork for the eventual renewal of Catholic worship; the papal letter was received in most quarters as an official (if cautious) endorsement of the Liturgical Movement.[19]

---

16. Joseph C. Fenton, "The Perils of Consistency," *Commonweal* 21 (1935): 733–34.

17. John Courtney Murray, S.J., "Intercreedal Co-Operation: Its Theory and Its Organization," *Theological Studies* 4 (1943): 257.

18. For a succinct summary of Michel's career, see Patrick Carey, "Virgil Michel," in Carey, *The Roman Catholics* (Westport, Conn.: Greenwood, 1993), 281–82.

19. *"Mediator Dei,"* in McBrien, gen. ed., *The HarperCollins Encylopedia of Catholicism*, 847–48.

In the wake of *Mediator Dei*, proposed reforms in the liturgy were subjected to unprecedented scrutiny. American followers of Michel were challenged to justify their linking of Catholic worship to Catholic social justice. Conservative critics charged the reformers with reducing the sacred, ineffable mysteries of the Catholic Mass to slogans in support of a typically American, Protestant, pragmatist version of the gospel, which confused redemption from eternal damnation with improvement in social conditions. The reformers responded vigorously to these charges. "The beauty of the liturgy and its sacred order must be a thorn in my side," wrote the reformer H. A. Reinhold, "if at the same time the socio-economic order of my country is a mockery of the Gospel and if Christ's friends, the poor, are ignored while the well-washed, well-dressed, well-housed and respected are given practical preference as the 'good' Catholics" (doc. 84).

The transformation of the "socio-economic order," in turn, was seen as the work of the laity. As in other areas of reform that paved the way to the council, however, the hierarchy and the clergy provided impetus at crucial moments. Lay initiative was not a new idea when Pope Pius XI promoted "Catholic Action" in the 1920s and 1930s, but the concept and practice flourished thereafter; indeed, the derivative nature of the laity's mission was signaled in the pope's definition of Catholic Action as "the participation of the laity in the apostolate of the hierarchy."

In the United States, however, Catholic Action took a distinctive shape that included greater levels of lay autonomy. As in Europe, priests were nonetheless its initial founders. During his studies in Louvain, Belgium, Father Donald Kanaly of Oklahoma met Joseph Cardijn, a priest who had developed the "inquiry method" of Catholic Action. This "observe, judge, act" method called for lay Catholics to observe and discuss their work environments, judge the situation in light of the gospel, and act to transform the situation. Kanaly popularized this method in the United States, and influential labor priests such as Raymond A. McGowan, who organized workers in defense of their rights, embraced Catholic Action. From the 1920s through the 1940s a host of movements flourished in this vein, including the Young Christian Students, the Young Christian Workers, the Catholic Worker, and the Christian Family Movement.[20]

Though each reform movement had its own leaders and internal dynamics, the various streams of reform were inherently interrelated. The Liturgical Movement, the historical and cultural approach to the Bible, the developments in church-state theory, the ecclesiology embodied in the theology of the Mystical Body, Catholic Action — all followed a certain logic flowing from a new/old image of the church as a light to the world, the salt of the earth. Monsignor Fulton Sheen, an advocate of Thomism who became a popular Catholic radio and television personality, explained to his vast audiences that "Catholic Action has

---

20. Jay P. Dolan, *The American Catholic Experience: A History from Colonial Times to the Present* (Notre Dame, Ind.: University of Notre Dame Press, 1992 [1985]), 415.

its foundation, its deepest reason, in the brotherly communion of the Mystical Body."[21]

The underlying unity of the reform impulses was on display in the American Catholic campaign against racism, initially pioneered by John LaFarge, S.J. (doc. 85). A native of Newport, Rhode Island, LaFarge entered the Jesuit seminary in Innsbruck, Austria, in 1900. There he came into contact with Catholic social teaching, especially the ideas expressed in Pope Leo XII's social encyclical *Rerum Novarum* (1891). His subsequent pastoral work among African American Catholics in Maryland inspired the young priest to work for racial justice, and he became affiliated with an organization known as the Federated Colored Catholics. By the end of the 1920s LaFarge and a fellow Jesuit, William Markoe, had engineered a major shift in the organization's direction. "Instead of a race-conscious push for equality," writes historian John McGreevy, "Markoe and LaFarge came to favor an interracial doctrine that eliminated racial categories."[22] LaFarge clearly understood the connection between the notion of the Church as a mystical communion united in the Eucharist, and the imperative to build a socioeconomic order untainted by discrimination and injustice. Thus, in his words, "the practical remedy of the [African American's] condition, [is] found in the religious and social program of the Church, embodied in Catholic Action."[23] Using his position as the editor of the Jesuit magazine *America*, LaFarge founded the first Catholic Interracial Council in 1934; the interracial movement, which launched a generation of progressive Catholic initiatives in opposition to racism, was yet another American Catholic reform movement based on the model of Catholic Action.

The American Catholic preparation for Vatican II, then, was not insignificant. But the Americans made strides by adapting to the U.S. context a series of ideas and lessons learned from Catholic social teaching, from the popes, and from great European reformers such as Congar, Rahner, de Lubac, Chenu, and others. Not least, American Catholics learned to think historically, and to apply the hard-won historical consciousness to their own self-understanding as Catholics. As the brilliant American Jesuit scholar Walter Ong explained, thinking historically and innovatively about a past they had seen as "static" was a considerable challenge for American Catholics (doc. 86).

## 80. The Founding of the *Catholic Biblical Quarterly,* 1939

*The renewal of Catholic theology in the twentieth century was linked inextricably to the "updating" of scholarly understanding of the Bible through the use of historical, literary-critical, and archaeological investigations. In the United States the first stirrings of a new energy in Catholic scriptural studies was evident in October 1936, when fifty scholars of the Bible established the Catholic Biblical Association (CBA). Several of the founders had come together earlier*

---

21. Monsignor Fulton J. Sheen, quoted in John T. McGreevy, *Parish Boundaries: The Catholic Encounter with Race in the Urban North* (Chicago: University of Chicago Press, 1996), 44.

22. Ibid., 45, 47.

23. John LaFarge, S.J., quoted in ibid., 45.

*that year, at the invitation of Bishop Edwin V. O'Hara, to plan a revision of
the Challoner-Rheims New Testament. (The revised version appeared in 1941
as the Confraternity of Christian Doctrine [CCD] New Testament.) In 1939 the
officers of the CBA founded the* Catholic Biblical Quarterly *for the purpose of
promoting scholarly exchange and dialogue among biblical scholars and for "the
personal edification of priests." Their efforts to incorporate new methods and
approaches were given a critical boost in 1943, with the promulgation of Pope
Pius XII's encyclical,* Divino Afflante Spiritu, *which encouraged the prudent
application of historical-critical methods in the study of the Bible.*

*In the following passage, the president of the CBA, William Newton, reflects
on the purposes of the association in light of Pope Pius XI's warning against
complacency in biblical studies and the pontiff's exhortation that "in the matter
of criticism alone — not the study of one translation... but indeed the criticism
of the Sacred Text — of the divine word it must be said nil actum, since, in truth,
there remains so much to be done" (Pius XI, quoted in* Osservatore Romano,
*May 21, 1938). Newton's address, excerpted below, was published in the first
issue of the* Catholic Biblical Quarterly, *apparently as a statement of purpose
for the journal.*

There pervails [*sic*], as we know, a lamentable and growing disregard of the Bible
in our generation. Were this found only in the people, we might be inclined to
look for excuse to the disturbed conditions of the times. But when we discover
it embodied in a statement of doctrine emanating from what is usually a conservative religious body we are inclined to look upon it as a portent. In reference
to the inspiration of the Scriptures this statement proclaims that "The tradition
of the inerrancy of the Bible commonly held in the Church until the beginning
of the nineteenth century... cannot be maintained in the light of the knowledge now at our disposal." As long as this conviction remains we may expect
but an increase of that indifference which voids the influence once enjoyed by
the Word of God.

Nor are we much consoled when examining into the acceptance and use of
the Scriptures by our own people; for we must allow that there too, unfortunately, there has been induced a comparable neglect of the Bible, particularly as
a book of private devotion. This is not the place to search out the causes for this
situation, but we should not close our eyes to the fact, nor be indifferent to its
effects. In this connection we think at once of the continued effort of the Fathers, of the concern of Leo XIII, and of the ardent blessing of Benedict XV, all
aiming at the spread of devotion towards the Word of God. When daily reading
of the Scriptures is the ideal, we can understand how far we have fallen beneath
it in modern practise [*sic*].

This general condition is closely related to another which comes within our
acquaintance, and which is the cause of no little concern. I refer to the disposition towards destructive criticism so manifest in a great deal of the scholarly
activity outside the Church. How much this has to do with the increasing dis-
respect for the Bible may be a question. But it can be taken for certain that if
this type of criticism is accepted for real scientific study there is small hope for
an improved attitude towards the Bible. Too often the confidence that was once

shown the divine Author is now turned towards the scholar who dresses error in a cloak of erudition. We all deplore this especially since there is no reason to doubt the good intentions of many a scholar who has fallen into this type of criticism, and since there is so much room for admiration of their diligent enterprise and exceptional attainments. Such a state of affairs only makes more emphatic the degree of our own inactivity.

With these reasons for energetic effort before us, we are obliged to say "nil actum." We should be able to appreciate that the words of Pius XI contain for our Association a call to undertake anew the task always sponsored by the Church, the office of protector of the divine Scriptures. The more clearly we can vision the field in which our labours lie, the more keenly will we regret our past inactivity and the more firmly resolve upon a ready response to this summons....

One danger of complacency in regard to the Sacred Scriptures has always been clear to Catholic scholars: that since the Church has declared the Vulgate an authentic text nothing remains for us to do. The sense of the decree of Trent, the story of St. Jerome, the history of the Vulgate — all have protected us against this danger....

Since Trent, however, and particularly within recent generations, much has been done towards the recovery of the Scriptures in their original languages. It is expressly to this work of criticism that the Pope is calling attention, and it may be no less against complacency in this regard that he is warning us. The very progress that has been made here justifies the warning. The majority of those intimate with the Scriptures in their original languages will admit at once that the Masoretic Text and the critical editions of the New Testament bring us close to the original autograph, much closer than any other text. Some will go farther, so far as to fall into the illusion that we have the autograph itself. There existed just this misapprehension at the close of the 16th century, as we know from the preface to the first edition of the Rheims New Testament. The error had to be fought by those who first undertook to give us our critical editions of the New Testament. It would now be sad indeed were we to fall into the same snare of thinking that, since "something of value has been done," we have nothing more to do. And here the Holy Father reminds us, *Nil actum si quid agendum.*

It would be wrong to conclude that the Holy Father is in any sense condemning what has been done, or that he is diverting our attention from the Sacred Text as it stands today in its original dress. His intention is rather in the opposite direction: he is pointing out to Catholic scholars the duty incumbent upon them of entering into this basic phase of biblical study. This is something more than an academic enterprise. Its subject is the original message which God has deigned to send the human race. As scholars and lovers of truth it is our duty to seek out this message and to represent as the original form of the message only that which we can establish was really part of it....

If we should require any further motivation for entering earnestly into the labours that are ahead of us, it might be found in the practical good we can do. Few if any sciences are purely theoretical; even the most abstract have brought culture and benefit to mankind. If this may be verified at all, it will be found true of the biblical sciences. At least from our point of view, taking our direction from the call of the Church, biblical studies tend always to make the divine message more certain, more understood by our generation, more effective....

What we have in the way of opportunity for practical work requires no detailing at present. The general objective is patent, and that is the main thing. We must restore confidence in the Word of God, we must make available a text that will be within the capacity of the people, we must produce aids for the better understanding of that text, we must do all in our power to enable the divine message to reach those for whom it was destined. If we had nothing further to consider, here is a great and worthy occupation.

William L. Newton, "Nil Actum Si Quid Agendum," *Catholic Biblical Quarterly* 1, no. 1 (1939): 10–13, 13–14.

## 81. Joseph C. Fenton on Defining "Religious Freedom," 1944

*The meaning of religious liberty, both in Catholic thought and as enshrined in the religion clauses of the First Amendment of the U.S. Constitution, was a matter of serious internal controversy in the Catholic Church in the two decades prior to the Second Vatican Council. One of the staunchest American advocates of the official Roman Catholic position on the question was Rev. Joseph Clifford Fenton (1906–1969). Ordained in 1930, Fenton began his teaching career in 1934, arrived at the Catholic University of America in 1938, and became editor of the* American Ecclesiastical Review *in 1944, serving in that capacity until he suffered a heart attack in 1963. He published 189 articles in the AER alone. In the excerpt below, he refers to his colleague, Francis Jeremiah Connell (1888–1967), a Redemptorist priest ordained in 1913, who taught theology for twenty-five years before moving to Catholic University in 1940, where he authored more than six hundred pieces in the AER.[1]*

*At a time when Catholic educators were being encouraged to engage an academic mainstream that put a premium on innovative approaches to traditional questions, Fenton and Connell self-consciously rejected these standards as contrary to Catholic principles. They engaged enthusiastically in apologetics wrapped in polemics, not least on the question of the proper relationship between church and state. In the article excerpted below Father Fenton defends the church from the charge that it rejects religious liberty. But he also insists, echoing the received teaching, that it is "objectively a moral wrong" for any American "to adopt a non-Catholic religion," and he describes a pluralistic society as falling short of the ideal state, in which "the entire membership has accepted the true religion."*

A rather recent Protestant commentary upon and use of the pamphlet *Freedom of Worship,* written by the distinguished American theologian, Dr. Francis J.

---

1. *The American Catholic Who's Who 1964–65* (Grosse Point, Mich.: Walter Romig, n.d.), 75, 135. Joseph M. White, *The Diocesan Seminary in the United States: A History from the 1780s to the Present* (Notre Dame, Ind.: University of Notre Dame Press, 1989), 333, reports on the priests' output. Also see Joseph J. Farragher, S.J., review of *Father Connell Answers Moral Questions,* by Francis J. Connell, C.SS.R., *Theological Studies* 21 (1960): 312.

Connell, C.SS.R., should be a matter of some concern to the priests of this country. Dr. Connell's pamphlet appeared in the spring of 1944. Last summer two non-Catholic periodicals carried excerpts from *Freedom of Worship*. Speaking of the teachings which it has quoted from Dr. Connell's work, the August *Christian Herald* suggests a negative response to the question "Do these beliefs and principles, as heretofore stated, support the Constitution of the United States and the basic American principle of complete freedom of worship and absolute separation of Church and State — including freedom not to worship?" The July 29 issue of *Time*, introducing its notice of the *Christian Herald* article, begins by printing that section of the First Amendment to the United States Constitution which says that "Congress shall make no law respecting an establishment of religion, or prohibiting the free exercise thereof..." and then goes on to make this serious charge against American Catholics:

> Nothing about Catholicism so confuses — and often dismays — U.S. Protestants as the stand of the Church on freedom of worship. Does Catholicism support the first article of the Bill of Rights? In U.S. practice, yes; in principle, no.

That such an unwarranted and erroneous meaning could be read into a perfectly objective and accurate statement of Catholic principle must necessarily be disquieting to American Catholics. If the *Time* conclusion were correct (as it most certainly is not), then the Catholics of our country would be reduced to the category of second-class citizens, upholding out of mere expediency a basic regulation of civil law contrary to God's teaching. It would be bad enough if such an error belonged in the realm of purely speculative thought. Unfortunately, however, its implications are decidedly practical. Disseminating the false notion that accurate Catholic teaching shows American Catholics "in principle" opposed to the Bill of Rights can only serve to encourage that religious underworld which is continually engaged in badgering the Catholic Church and which can apparently be satisfied with nothing less than an out-and-out, Russian style persecution.

What *Time* and the *Christian Herald* seem to have in mind is a fear that the Catholic Church might possibly resort to coercive measures against non-Catholics in the event that the majority of American citizens should ever become members of the true Church of Jesus Christ. They claim, but, as we shall see, without any justification whatsoever, to find grounds for that fear in the Catholic principles enunciated by Dr. Connell.

Such a fear on the part of non-Catholics is a strange sort of thing. It obviously has no support in American history. Our Republic has seen many instances of extra-legal religious persecution and many powerful societies devoted to the destruction of religious liberties. In no one of these cases have American Catholics been at fault. Such social monstrosities as the Know-Nothings, the A.P.A., the Ku Klux Klan and their ilk have been composed of men who claimed the title of Protestant just as articulately and with apparently as good reason as does the writer in the *Christian Herald*. These organizations have never had anything like a Catholic counterpart. Neither have Catholics, during the long life of the Republic, ever been responsible for such outrages as the burning of the Convent in Charlestown and the mob violence which disgraced Boston and Philadelphia during the nineteenth century. It is at least remarkable to find men speaking out as defenders of the religious system which the authors of these outrages and the members of these un-American and un-Christian societies claimed to accept, pass over the manifest faults of their coreligionists and suggest that there is danger against religious liberty from the one group which has been the object of persecution....

In the light of a true understanding of Catholic teachings and of American principles, we should consider the key question asked by both the *Christian Herald* and *Time*: "Does each American have the right to choose his religion?"

(1) Every American has the *civil right* to choose his religion. By force of our Constitution, Congress is prevented from "prohibiting the free exercise" of any religion.

(2) Every American, and, for that matter, every human being, has the *moral right* to *choose* his religion, in the sense that, for a human being who enjoys the use of reason, there can be no rightful attachment to a religious body other than by way of free choice. To frustrate such a choice is, according to Catholic teaching, a moral wrong.

(3) Every American has the *civil right* to choose a religion forbidden by God. On this point, as on many others, civil law makes no attempt to enforce the divine precept. This is, according to Catholic teaching, perfectly right and proper. The state exists in order to procure and to protect the common temporal well-being of its citizens. For the achievement of this end, the state commands those actions which are manifestly necessary to its purpose, allows those things which are indifferent to it, and forbids what is manifestly destructive of or detrimental to its aim. Thus there are many acts contrary to the natural law and to the divine positive law, as, for example, sins of thought or of desire, with which civil law is not concerned.

(4) It is *objectively and morally wrong* for any American, or, for that matter for any human being, to disregard or to disobey a command issued by God Himself, when that command is directed to all men and when it is brought to the attention of mankind with adequate clarity. This is a general principle which no man who acknowledges the existence of God could bring himself to deny. No man or no group of men would be subjectively guilty of moral wrong were they to fail to act in accordance with the divine injunction because it had never come to their attention through no fault of their own. Such persons are in a state of invincible ignorance, and it is this invincible ignorance which renders activity objectively opposed to a divine command subjectively blameless as far as they are concerned.

We must remember that, objectively, a right is correlative with a law. Men have natural rights (as brute animals have not) precisely because man is empowered by the natural law to make use of terrestrial things in pursuance of supra-terrestrial destiny. Men have rights in the proper sense of the word to what has been assigned to them, to what belongs to them, according to the dictates of divine or human law.

A man has a moral right to act in conformity with the moral law. He has no right, in the strict sense of the term, to violate that law. A divine precept revealed to man constitutes a divine positive law. It would be employing the term in an utterly nugatory sense to speak of man's moral *right* to disregard or disobey such a divine precept....

The account of Our Lord's public life and teaching presented in the four Gospels stresses the fact that He insisted that acceptance of His doctrine and attachment to Him were necessary with the necessity of precept. Refusal to believe His preaching constituted a moral fault....

Hence, since there is a real and objectively manifest divine precept that all men live within the Catholic Church, it is objectively a moral wrong for any American or, for that matter, for anyone else, to adopt a non-Catholic religion. If, through no fault of his own, a person does not realize the existence of this divine command, he cannot and will not be blamed for living other than as a Catholic. If, however, a man is vincibly ignorant of the divine command, or if, *a fortiori*, he knows of its existence and refuses to obey it, his subjective attitude is morally wrong.

(5) The moral obligation to render God the worship He has chosen is corporate as well as individual. It rests on the civil society as such as well as upon the individual citizens who compose this society. The individual obligation is, however, primary. The state can satisfy its obligation in this respect only when what is for all intents and purposes its entire membership has accepted the true religion.

> Joseph C. Fenton, "The Catholic Church and the Freedom of Religion," *American Ecclesiastical Review* 115 (1944): 286–87, 298–301.

## 82. John Courtney Murray, S.J., on "the Religion of the State," 1949

*In the following essay, Fenton's chief adversary in the debate on religious freedom, Father John Courtney Murray, S.J., explains why the Catholic teaching on religious liberty requires updating — not least, because "the concrete problem that confronts us is not precisely that which the Church faced in the nineteenth century." Murray then goes on to describe different ways of interpreting "the religion of the state" in the contemporary context.*

*Father Murray's views on these questions ultimately prevailed; they are reflected in* Dignitatis Humanae, *Vatican II's Declaration on Religious Liberty (1965).*

What the foregoing exposés perhaps chiefly reveal is a common realization that the problem of religious liberty and of the relations between Church and state has once more altered in the manner of its position. The concrete problem that confronts us is not precisely that which the Church faced in the nineteenth century. The problem then was relatively simple. Its framework was the

Continental nation-state. The enemy was Liberalism — the religious, philosophical and political forms of autonomous rationalism: this enemy was acting as a solvent within nation-states traditionally Catholic. The basic categories of argument were "thesis" and "hypothesis." And the practical question was, whether this or that nation-state was in the situation of "thesis" or of "hypothesis." If the latter, a constitutional guarantee of religious freedom was the rule; if the former, the constitutional concept, "religion of the state," had to apply. And there you were.

Three factors, and their implications and consequences, have powerfully contributed to alter this problematic: first, the dechristianisation of society (not so much the fact of it, which was far advanced in the nineteenth century, but the realization of the fact); second, the emergence of the threat of the totalitarian state; third, the corresponding struggling effort to validate the right of the human person to be the center, source and end of the social order. The first two factors are of course damnably evil, but their consequences on the thinking of the Church have been good. The consciously accepted fact of the dechristianisation of society has brought a realization of the need of a spiritual effort exerted on society from the bottom up, so to speak, rather than an influence brought to bear on it from the top down, through the state and government. The nineteenth-century problem of *Kirchenpolitik* has now only a secondary importance. Moreover, there is the corresponding realization that the new effort from below, in the direction of spiritual and social change, must be carried on through the processes of freedom.

Secondly, the totalitarian threat is dispelling certain naïve illusions which Catholics are perhaps prone to cherish with regard to the whole fact and concept of "power," especially in its relations to the things of the spirit. More importantly, it has brought new clarity of meaning to the ancient principle of the freedom of the Church, in a twofold sense. There is her freedom from any sort of enclosure in the state or subordination to the purposes of the nation of which the state is the political form; there is also her freedom to enter the state, as it were; that is, her right not to have the state closed against her, either hampering her spiritual mission to men or inhibiting the repercussions that this mission, remaining always solely spiritual, necessarily has on the structures, institutions and processes of society.

Furthermore, the totalitarian threat has made it clear that the freedom of the Church is intimately linked to the freedom of the citizens; where one perishes, so does the other. It is through the freedom of the citizen that the freedom of the Church is actively and effectively defended. In turn, the freedom of the citizen finds its surest warrant in the freedom of the Church; for where the state closes itself against the Church, it likewise closes down on the freedom of the citizen. Finally, the totalitarian threat of its nature is such that it can only be met by the united effort of all men of good will; this fact gives new meaning to the problem of interconfessional relationships. The post-Reformation concept of Catholic-Protestant relations as being solely in terms of rivalry or even enmity cannot longer hold. A common Christian good has appeared, that does not indeed blur or bridge differences in religious faith, but that does make necessary a common striving for a common purpose in the temporal order; this in turn supposes positive relationships.

Thirdly, the twentieth-century experience has resulted in a sense of the significance of human personality more acute and profound than the nineteenth century knew. This is a broad phenomenon — and, if you like, a confused one too. Insofar as it is relevant here, it entails three things: first, a sensitiveness with regard to the rights of conscience; secondly, a concept of a living personal faith as the goal of the apostolate (the nominal Catholic is something of a social menace), to which is allied the notion of "Christian" society as a qualitative, not a quantitative designation; thirdly, a more exact appreciation, and likewise distrust, of the methods of constraint and coercion, in the light of fuller experience of their sociological and psychological effects. Briefly, the principle of the freedom of faith has assumed new sharpness of definition and breadth of implication.

If then the contemporary problematic of religious freedom has been significantly altered — altered, I should repeat, in part by factors that are evil in themselves but that have stimulated reflection on principles, which is very good — an important question arises. It is suggested by Leclercq when he speaks of a "deepening of the meaning of the 'thesis'"; it is more strongly suggested by Pribilla when he distinguishes what is "permanently obligatory doctrine" and what is the "theoretical echo of a passing historical situation." Both authors thus imply that we confront here a problem in the development of doctrine. In other words, we see rising in this area the same problem that is central in all other areas of theological thought today; for I take it that the central problem of today is not "faith and reason" but "faith and history." It is not so much with the essential categories of philosophy as with the existential category of time that theologians are today preoccupied.

I am inclined to think that neither of the two authors cited quite grasps the nettle where the bristles are sharpest. The primarily crucial question is simply put: Does the dogmatic concept, "the freedom of the Church," entail by necessary consequence the constitutional concept, "the religion of the state," in such wise that, where the latter concept does not obtain, an inherent right of the Church is violated and the constitutional situation can therefore be the object only of toleration, on grounds of factual necessity, the lesser evil, etc.? Or on the contrary, is this constitutional concept, as applied in the nation-state, simply a particular and contingent, historically and politically conditioned realization of the dogmatic concept, "the freedom of the Church," in such wise that, even where it does not obtain, all the inherent exigences of the freedom of the Church may still be adequately realized and the constitutional situation may be the object of approval in principle as good in itself?

It is the constitutional concept, "religion of the state," that is properly in question. Is it, or is it not, in all the elements of the content that it has exhibited in the historical era of post-Reformation Europe, a permanent and necessary part of the "thesis"? Or are perhaps some of these elements dispensable without damage to the thesis, as being the product of passing situations of political fact, accidental situations of national feeling, time-conditioned situations of religio-political necessity, etc.?

In order further to specify the question, one should distinguish the two general lines of content historically exhibited in the concept, "religion of the state." First, there is the concept of harmony between the legal order of society and the moral and canonical norms of the Church, in all the matters on which the state is competent to legislate; these matters are chiefly those which concern the structure and processes of domestic society.

In itself, this harmony is not the exigence solely of the constitutional concept, "religion of the state." It is a general exigence, valid in any political society, whatever its form, and regardless of whether its constitution embodies the concept of "religion of the state." However, in regard of this harmony one thing seems to be specific of the constitutional situation characterized by the religion-of-the-state idea, as it has been historically known. This specific thing concerns the *manner* in which this necessary harmony is to be achieved. It has been considered, namely, that it is to be achieved through the agency of a jurisdiction of the Church over the *state* itself. In other words, to the concept, "religion of the state," there has been related a particular concept of the so-called indirect power that is Bellarminian in its connotations. This was the more natural in that all the states that have exhibited this constitutional concept were states constructed on authoritarian or even dictatorial lines; and there is no doubt that the Bellarminian theory of the indirect power is the fit counterpiece to the theory and practice of centralized authoritarian government.

The only question that remains is whether either of these theories properly merits the title of "thesis." Or conversely, whether the thesis with regard to the special question *how* the harmony between the legal order of society and the religio-moral order is to be achieved and preserved, should not rather be based on another, more fundamental principle. I mean the medieval principle that the community, not the prince, is the source of law, and that the legal order is the expression of the sense of justice resident in the people. From this principle one would logically come to a concept of the indirect power (as a means of harmonizing state law with canonico-moral law) that would be rather on the lines of the school of thought of which I have elsewhere pointed to John of Paris as a representative; for in these perspectives the action of the Church would be rather on the conscience of the community than on the actual bearers of governmental authority. There is too the further question, whether the notion of a jurisdiction of the Church over the state itself, as a means for achieving harmony between the legal and religio-moral orders, could actually be made operative in a society politically organized on democratic principles (the division of powers, institutionalized political responsibility of the citizens, etc.); and if not, whether it can in any proper sense be called "thesis." I am supposing that the "thesis" is independent of political forms and therefore applicable in any of them.

The second content-elements in the constitutional concept of "religion of the state" is the more specific and crucial one. As it has historically appeared in the nation-states of post-Reformation Europe, this concept asserts that the

state itself, the organized political community does more than recognize the juridical personality of the Church as a visible religious society in her own right,
with autonomous powers and definite rights over her members; by itself this
recognition would not make the Church the religion of the *state*. The concept
also asserts that the state as such makes public profession of Catholicism as its
own one and only religion; and by consequence it asserts that no citizen may
make public profession of any other religion. In further consequences, the coercive power of the state is brought to bear to inhibit the public profession or
propaganda of other religions. This constitutional concept therefore is the legal
premise of civil intolerance in greater or less degree (there has always been —
in Spain, for instance — great argument over what "public profession" means in
the concrete).

A number of questions could be asked about this constitutional concept. For
instance, one could inquire whether it is a piece of pure constitutionalism (as,
for example, is the principle of the legal limitation of government), or perhaps
a piece of constitutional nationalism, so to speak. This would be to ask how far
it is tributary to the nationalist idea that what is *alien* to the *nation* can have no
*rights* within the *state*. Insofar as it is at all tributary to this idea it cannot claim
the name of "Catholic"; for it moves in an order of ideas essentially inferior
to the universal, supranational order of the thought of the Church. Again, one
could inquire whether it is related by a process of organic development to the
constitutionalism of the Middle Ages, and whether it can claim parentage in medieval principles of religio-political organization. Conversely, one could inquire
whether it be simply a Catholic adaptation of the territorial principle canon-
ized in the Treaty of Westphalia over the protests of Innocent X — a principle
whose parentage is definitely not medieval. (As such an adaptation it would not,
of course, be unrightful; but its rightfulness would be relative to the situation
to which it was an adaptation.)

However, the cardinal question — not indeed unrelated to the foregoing
ones — concerns, as I said, the relation between the constitutional concept, "religion of the state," and the dogmatic concept, "the freedom of the Church."
The standing of this constitutional concept within the framework of Catholic
doctrine turns on the nature of this relation, whether it is necessary and absolute, or conditioned and historical. Admittedly, this concept may be a means
to the preservation of a particular national unity or to the maintenance of the
integrity of a particular national culture; as such, however, it cannot claim the
patronage of the Church or of Catholic doctrine; for national unities and cultures do not rank as ends or values proper to the Church, nor is her doctrine
a means to them. The only proper point of reference is the freedom of the
Church, which is the single necessary end that the Church directly seeks in
her relations with political society. Consequently, only insofar as the constitutional concept, "religion of the state," is a means to this end can it claim any
doctrinal standing. The question then is, what kind of a means is it? Is it a permanently necessary means apart from which the freedom of the Church cannot
be properly secure? If so, it becomes a constitutional "ideal" by this relation to
a dogmatic "ideal," and can claim to be "thesis," as the freedom of the Church

is "thesis." If not, it sinks to the rank occupied by other constitutional institutionalizations of principle — the rank of a relative, not an absolute, a valid and valuable institution that can be defended in a context but that need not and cannot be proclaimed an "ideal."

One could suggest an analogy here. Historically speaking, as Prof. MacIver has pointed out, "the growth of democracy was the growth of parliamentary institutions," that is, responsible and representative legislative institutions wherein the medieval principle of popular consent to law and government was institutionalized. However, he goes on, "we must not assume that the free play of the public opinion *must* register itself in parliamentary forms. Historical evolution may reveal an endless train of yet undreamed-of modes of government, adaptations to changing needs and changing demands." The point of the analogy is that the dogmatic principle, "the freedom of the Church," might very well receive constitutional embodiment in institutionalized forms other than those historically implied in the concept of "religion of the state."

I do not here propose further to argue the question, but merely to insist that it is the crucial question. The dogmatic concept, "the freedom of the Church," is not of itself the premise of any kind of civil intolerance; it becomes such only through the mediating concept, "religion of the state," which is not a dogmatic but a constitutional concept. As such, it is open to discussion. And it can hardly be maintained that freedom for its discussion has been abolished by various papal approvals of it in the past. In fact, one of the purposes of free discussion would be exactly to define the bearing of these approvals. Do they canonize this constitutional concept as some sort of transtemporal, suprahistorical "ideal," beyond which there is no going, and to which there must be a return? Do they assert that the Church does not possess her inherent rightful freedom unless the state lends its coercive "arm" to a program of civil intolerance? Do they represent the mode of religio-social organization visible in post-Reformation Europe as the ultimate in the Church's adaptation of herself to the political life of humanity? In a word, have we been instructed by the Church to look beyond horizons for another return of the Bourbons, bearing with them the old "thesis," about which nothing will have been learned and nothing forgotten?

John Courtney Murray, S.J., "On Religious Freedom," *Theological Studies* 10, no. 3 (September 1949): 420–26.

## 83. The Problems with the "New Theology," 1950

*The Nouvelle Théologie ("New Theology") was a French Catholic theological movement of the 1940s "that sought to overcome the limitations of neo-Scholastic theology through a return to biblical, patristic and medieval theological sources."[1] It reintegrated theology with pastoral life, challenged the dominant Thomist-inspired exegesis of Scripture, and reexamined the development of doctrine. Despite Pope Pius XII's warning, in his 1950 encyclical Humani Generis, against the existentialist (i.e., insufficiently Thomist) orientation of the new theology, the writings of its major proponents — Yves Congar,*

---

1. *The HarperCollins Encyclopedia of Catholicism*, 922.

M.-D. Chenu, and Henri de Lubac — were profoundly influential in shaping the
theological deliberations of the Council Fathers at Vatican II.

Even before the appearance of Humani Generis, *Thomists* in the United
States (and elsewhere) were sounding the alarm against the European innovators. The Thomist, *a quarterly journal of philosophy and theology, based at the
Dominican House of Studies in Washington, D.C., and published under the auspices of the Eastern province of the Dominican friars, was launched in 1938; the
first issue appeared in April 1939. The article from which the following excerpt
was taken "was written and accepted for publication prior to the appearance
of the recent papal encyclical,* Humani Generis," *the Dominican editors of* The
Thomist *explained. "Hence, the author makes no reference to that important
document but his article gains significance in the light of the Holy Father's
words."*

The term "new theology" has, as we shall see, no very fixed content. The phrase
can mean something which all Catholic theologians worthy of the name must
reject, or it can be applied to certain tendencies which, although they may be
dangerous if carried too far, may occupy a legitimate place in Catholic theology.
One thing however is quite certain, namely that this new movement can not be
separated from what M. Maritain has called the "New Christianity," which according to him is bound to make itself felt in the present age, and which will
be characterized by an attempt to bring the doctrines of the Church into line
with the times in which we live. We might say of the new theology that it attempts to form one of the integral elements of the new christianity [*sic*]. The
partisans of this movement are preoccupied with the "man in the street" as we
know him today. He has to be won over to Christ and to the true Church, and
yet he has been brought up on the basis of a rationalistic and idealistic philosophy which has effectively sealed his mind against any approach along the old
traditional lines. Scholastic philosophy will never make any impression upon
him for the simple reason that he does not understand the terms and the concepts which it uses. The same must therefore be said of a theology which makes
use of the traditional Scholasticism for its presentation or development. That is
the real problem which confronts the theologian of today, and the whole question at issue between the new theologians and the traditional Thomist is how
it can best be solved. Confronted with this problem the partisans of the new
theology have attempted a solution, but that solution is proposed in two very
different ways which can not, by any means, receive the same criticism, as we
shall see.

Both solutions imply, even if they do not state it in so many words, the rejection of the Aristotelio-Thomistic philosophy as a fitting instrument for use
in theology and its substitution by other more modern forms of philosophical
thought. One solution has, however, gone too far, and has denied the scientific value of those deductions made from the revealed principles of the faith
with the aid of reason as an instrument. The earlier writings of Fr. Chénu and
Fr. Charlier contain a summary of this extreme solution. According to Chénu,
the source of all theology is the vital life of the Church in its members, which
can not be separated from history, the deciding factor in all theology. Thus,

strictly speaking, theology is the life of the members of the Church, rather than a series of conclusions drawn from revealed data with the aid of reason. Charlier added to this statement the conclusion that the strict theological deduction as the result of a scientific use of human reason is therefore impossible, since it would suppose that reason could attain to a true understanding of the truths of faith. Theology, as such, is therefore reduced to a simple explanation of revealed truth in terms which need not necessarily have a permanent value, but which can, and indeed should, change with time and according to the demands of circumstances. This doctrine was far too dangerous to pass unchecked, and in 1942 the Holy Office banned the writings in which it appeared.

In spite of this condemnation and the strong warning of the Holy Father in the Allocutions already mentioned, the same type of solution was proposed in a slightly more benign form in articles in Reviews and especially in some of the publications in the series, *Sources Chrétiennes* as well as in the Collection *Théologie* and *Unam Sanctam*. Once again the subtle attack on Scholasticism was evident, and it would be as well to point out at once that the focal point of this attack was not merely Thomism as such. There are different theories on certain matters pertaining to theology inside the Church and many things are open to free discussion, but up to the present all systems have attempted to base their solutions and conclusions on the solid rock of the perennial truth. It is that very foundation, wherever it may be found, which is under attack from the new theology. At the same time, the main enemy is, as always, Thomism, partly because it is the one system which has a completely coherent philosophical basis, and also because many other systems existing in the Church today are not entirely free from the taint of humanism and even of nominalism. This fact becomes very clear if we compare two articles written on the subject of the new theology, one by Fr. Garrigou-Lagrange in *Angelicum* and the other by Fr. Perego in *Ciencia y Fe*. The former sees the new theology as a dangerous innovation which strikes at the very roots of the faith itself, and which is, therefore, to be condemned. The latter, while by no means agreeing entirely with this new system, tries to lay much more emphasis on the reason for its appearance at this point in the history of civilization. The aim of the new theologians is primarily apologetic, i.e., an attempt to approach the modern mind by a direct use of modern methods, adapting for that purpose philosophical terms and concepts which are in more common use among present-day philosophers in an endeavour to break down the prejudice against Scholasticism and all that it implies. This divergence in the criticism of the new theology shows us more plainly than anything else the difficulty of obtaining any clear notion of what is really implied by this movement, a difficulty which is increased by the fact that many of those theologians who do attempt to criticise this new movement are themselves followers of systems which have departed from the clear lines of Thomistic thought.

Thus it is clear that the main contention of the partisans of this new movement is that theology, to remain alive, must move with the times. At the same time, they are very careful to repeat all the fundamental propositions of traditional theology almost as if there was no intention of making any attack against it. This is very true of such writers as Frs. de Lubac, Daniélou, Rahner and Br. de Solages, all of whom are undoubtedly at the very centre of this movement.

Their main accusation seems to be that traditional theology is out of touch with reality because it takes little or no account of modern methods and philosophical systems, and thus fails in its main object, i.e., to present to the modern world a reasonable explanation of the doctrine of Christ....Such ideas and methods must be recovered if any approach is to be made to the modern world, and they must be incorporated into theology, even if that means rejecting Aristotelianism or even Thomism as we understand it today.

The partisans of the new theology accuse the defenders of the traditional methods of being ignorant of that dramatic world, the human individual with all his anxieties and experiences, while they wander about in a world of the abstract and the speculative....

The position of the new theologians is very different from that of Aquinas. Their idea is that the theological reasoning consists in using the revealed truth in order to draw out the full latent content contained in the human truths, the contrary, in fact, of the Thomistic position. This is a logical conclusion which follows from their vitalistic attitude towards truth and especially from their statements that the theological conclusion strictly so called has little or no value. It also follows from their teaching with regard to the evolution, necessarily connected with contemporary history, through which theology must pass if it is to remain alive and to play an effective part in the modern world....

Thus the central problem which confronts us here is quite simply one of two contrary ways of considering the relation between revelation and reason. Either reason is the instrument in the development of revealed truth or the revealed truth is the instrument of reason. It is our opinion that, unless the fact which we have mentioned before of the great influence of the revealed truths on the natural truth which is used as an instrument in their full development is understood and clearly brought to light, then this fundamental error in the new theology will never be completely overcome....

The Thomist position is simple. There are certain basic lines within which we must work, and those lines will be found in the traditional doctrines of Thomism, which is no mere speculative theology and philosophy, but one which is deeply rooted in all that is best and most lasting in human experience....

From the point of view of the Thomist, then, there can be only one valid method of defence against the inroads of the new theology, and that will have to come through a revival of all that is best in the Thomist tradition. If this new movement serves as a stimulus to bring about that renaissance — and there are already obvious signs of this — then we shall have no cause to lament its appearance at this period in the history of the Church.

David L. Greenstock, "Thomism and the New Theology," *The Thomist* 13, no. 4 (October 1950): 567–68, 569–73, 591, 593.

## 84. The Social Implications Embodied in the Liturgy, 1951

*The Liturgical Movement, with its centers in Germany and the United States, was a powerful source of reform and renewal leading to the Second Vatican Council. The movement had its detractors, however, and many of the pages of its journal,* Orate Fratres *(later entitled* Worship*), were devoted to correcting misperceptions and responding to criticisms. In the following passage, a noted liturgist counters the charge that the new liturgical theology, with its emphasis on the "sociological and social implications in our sacramental system as embodied in our liturgy," was fostering a utilitarian and (typically American) activist or pragmatic approach to the sacred mysteries celebrated in the Mass.*

Catholics and Protestant Christians outside the Anglo-Saxon orbit often blame us English-speaking Catholics for being "activists." The classical case was the heresy of "Americanism" at the turn of the century. It is a common assumption of the more profound Christian critics in Latin, Slavic and Teutonic countries of the old continent, and perhaps also in Latin America and Asia, that Catholicism in the Anglo-Saxon countries (not to speak of Protestantism) has lost an element of Christianity which is best expressed by the word "contemplative" — although this term is as unfit to cover the whole complex as any other would be. There is much more involved than just contemplation itself.

It is the whole mood of cultural and civilizational optimism to which objection is taken. To these observers our "version" of Christ's religion has all but the — cross. To them we, especially we in America, seem to fall into the ancient trap of millenarianism, confusing Jesus' message of spiritual redemption with earthly prosperity, and seeing in His life, since He rose from the dead, a rewarding "success story," while forgetting that His resurrection was, though a historical fact, in a new "aion" not accessible to mortal man in his life.

Our critics feel that the optimism with which we aggressively tackle the world to make it over, is shallow and is the result of another shortcoming: a disregard for truth, for doctrine, for clarity. In their eyes we are so eager to go out and get going that we lose sight of the primacy of the "logos" over the "ethos" (to quote Guardini). And the result? The paradoxes of life, the intellectual mystery surrounding all matters of faith, is ignored, soft-pedalled; the "obscure light" becomes a very trite, banal and obvious thing, as it were a neon tube substituting for the sun.

Anglo-Saxon Christianity, even in its Catholic form, appears to all the rest of the world as entirely too practical, too efficient, too ethical a thing to be commendable. It is too fond of immediate results, of statistics, of building programs and pat answers, and too easily satisfied with solutions. Our critics fear that in centuries to come so much of the practical, Protestant ethos will have been assimilated that we will become a "do-gooding," charitable service organization, with a dogma and liturgy on a level with the weird ritual of masons and shriners and a moral code like a libertine version of Methodism or Lutheranism.

Reinhold Niebuhr somewhere stated a while ago that we live in a country where churches become sects and sects churches. By this he meant, if I understand him rightly, that even the majesty and universality of the Catholic

Church are hard to assert in our climate: for the smallest group of crackpots and fanatics not only (and justly) finds the right to speak and teach, but — because the majesty of tradition, of an integrated structure of doctrine, of well-defined laws and discipline, of cultural accomplishment count for nothing in the face of zeal and aggressiveness — is accepted without credentials as an equal, or worse, as a foreign, strange and dangerous "sect."

How long will Catholics be able to maintain their claim in this climate? Are the devices now used, often borrowed from others, like the publicity we so generously achieve, sufficient? Are we really made for competition in an atmosphere of bible-quoting puritanism? Is the claim, of having answers others do not have, sufficient? These are questions that worry the responsible leaders.

After this introduction one might come to the conclusion: if all this be so, if we need something to offset our alleged activism, our optimism so purely naturally conceived, our un-concern with the purely spiritual, then, as a part of a whole, our liturgical movement is one of the best antidotes. For what could be more anti-utilitarian than express worship of God in solemnity? What could heal us more from pelagian self-perfection, trust in human activity and achievement, than the freely given graces of the sacraments?

Yet more: why bring in sociological references which will only make it appear as if even the liturgy is being used to bolster activism? Let us restore the liturgy in its fulness to the people, as outlined by our Holy Father, and social action will flow from it quite naturally — as someone has said not long ago. If activism is our peculiar danger (and Guardini's words, written back in 1918, show that it is a very real danger even to our critics in Europe), is it wise to provide it with another source?

I think that chance must be taken. It would be utterly unrealistic not to do so. We all know of daily communicants who fail to be a witness in their circles and whose only mark of lived religion seems to be — their daily holy Communion and what it involves. They are in good faith. They are earnest. They make great sacrifices by going to Communion and by "staying in the state of grace" week after week, year after year. One cannot track down the workings of grace and their nearness to God; their transformation into members of Christ is something you can't register under microscopes or with chemico-electric waves on charts. Something is bound to happen to them and to those with whom they live, on which their daily divine repast has had a determining influence. But still: the quietism latent in their attitude, unknown to themselves, frustrates the fullest effectiveness of the holy Eucharist. In a bold image: it is like high octane gas in a broken-down one-cylinder motor.

After all, grace presupposes and perfects nature. Which means, reversed, that we are obliged to "work on nature" and do what we can to give grace a broader, deeper and more sensitive surface to tackle. And this involves not only, as activism wants us to believe, the ennobling of will and emotions, but also the broadening and deepening of our natural knowledge. Thomas à Kempis' statement, that it is better to have contrition than to be able to define it, is only good as far as it goes: to have contrition plus the most profound knowledge of true

contrition is better still! There is an objective scale of values in the realm of being which many spiritual writers disregard for the sake of pouring comfort into
the hearts of those whose invincible ignorance needs comforting.

If then there are sociological and social implications in our sacramental system as embodied in our liturgy, we should make much of them! The bride and
groom relationship of the soul and Jesus in Communion, or the aspect of divine visitation in the holy Eucharist, are certainly sublime ideals for any soul
and highly commendable. But that is not all there is to it! The Lord's Supper is
also, even primarily, a banquet and a sacrifice. That the altar rail is full of people
like myself is not just accidental, but part and parcel of the visible sign, signify-
ing a reality of this sacrament. The poor at my side must be an alarm to me. If
the colored parishioners are discriminated against, the sacrament must inflame
me. The beauty of the liturgy and its sacred order must be a thorn in my side if
at the same time the socio-economic order of my country is a mockery of the
Gospel and if Christ's friends, the poor, are ignored while the well-washed, well-
dressed, well-housed and respected are given practical preference as the "good"
Catholics.

Justice and charity cannot be excluded; the liturgy carried out to perfection, not only exteriorly, but even with the knowledge and spiritual disposition
striven after by the best liturgists, will be a tinkling cymbal in the ears of
God, unless the ones who celebrate it continue to glorify the same Lord in the
economic, social, political and cultural field....

Of course, no confusion of function is intended: housing, care of health,
interracial justice, the living wage and family subsidies are not topics of liturgical weeks. Nor is it a directly liturgical concern to decide whether "free
enterprise" can exist the Roepke-Hayek-Mises way, or whether a society compounded of social and individual ownership is the solution for our complex
social age. These are questions for the social action movement, to be solved
according to the progressively developed teaching of papal encyclicals. But a
disinterested liturgical movement, or even a mildly concerned one, would be as
worthy of suspicion as the one castigated in *Mediator Dei* as archaic. One ought
not to demand more participation for the people, more ways for the laity to
share in the conscious celebration of Christ's mysteries, unless it makes us better Christians. And this means that we have a concern, or rather, an anxiety in
our heart to see all realms of life permeated by the Savior's Spirit.

H. A. Reinhold, "A Social Leaven?" *Orate Fratres* 25 (October–November, 1951):
515–18.

## 85. John LaFarge, S.J., on Race Relations, 1956

*In their attitudes toward race relations, and toward blacks in particular, white
U.S. Catholics were adamantly segregationist well into the mid-twentieth century. The pioneers who sought to change these attitudes were social action
priests such as the Jesuits John LaFarge and William Markoe. Influenced by the
developing social doctrine of the church, they built an interracial movement*

*based on the "observe-judge-act" model of Catholic Action. In 1934 LaFarge
founded the first Catholic Interracial Council, in New York.*

*The following passage is taken from LaFarge's 1956 book looking back on
nearly thirty years of activism on behalf of interracialism with an eye to ex-
pounding both the church's teaching on race and the social measures and laws
necessary to overcome racial discrimination in U.S. society.*

In discussing the Church's position on the racial question, certain fundamental
truths should be kept in mind:

(1) All men, since they have been created by the same God, are sons of the
same eternal Father and hence enjoy the same fundamental human dignity and
rights.

(2) Jesus Christ lived, died, and rose from the dead in order to redeem
all men and confer upon them the same supernatural dignity and rights as
members of His Mystical Body.

The Church holds that fundamental human rights are not something conferred by the State or by any other human institution. They are not the result
of mere social conventions or current folkways. Basic human rights, as such,
are equal in all human beings, even though in *other* matters — personal merit,
culture, native or acquired ability — people are usually unequal. This equality
of rights derives from the essential dignity and destiny of the human being as
such, a being created by an all-wise and infinitely loving God in order to enjoy,
by his own deliberate choice, eternal happiness in union with his Creator and
origin. Hence, in the Christian concept, man's essential dignity does not arise
from anything apart from his relationship to his Creator and last end. Man does
not create his own sublime worth out of his own littleness, but enjoys it by his
very nature as a creature of God and — through the gift of divine grace — an
heir of heaven....

The Church is likewise deeply solicitous for those whose spiritual, social,
or cultural position has been retarded because they have been deprived of the
exercise of human rights. Pope Pius XII expressed this solicitude in his letter to
the American hierarchy: "We confess that we feel a special paternal affection,
which is certainly inspired by heaven, for the Negro people dwelling among
you; for in the field of religion and education we know they need special care
and comfort and are very deserving of it.... We pray fruitful success for those
whose generous zeal is devoted to their welfare."

Hence, the Catholic Church does not look upon the race problem as a mere
problem of social adjustment: how can we best figure out from experience ways
and means for people to get along together? As Chester Bowles says: "It is not a
question primarily to be solved by laws and law courts, even though these are
both useful and necessary in guaranteeing our rights. It is essentially a *moral*
problem," a question of right and wrong, of sin and justice. Since the Catholic
Church believes that men can and do sin against their Creator, and can be held
accountable for their sins, she will not excuse violations of basic rights as mere
matters of unkindness or lack of delicacy. Race prejudice, discrimination, and
compulsory racial segregation are morally sinful.

There are two approaches to Catholic teaching on racial problems: one of reason and one of faith. Reason and faith are not opposed; they complement one another. The Church respects reason and the scientific research developed by reasoning. Our natural reasoning powers are impaired, but they are not destroyed, as a consequence of the sin of our first parents. Weakened as they are by passion and greed, particularly in matters of human relations, those powers can be strengthened and rehabilitated by the grace of God. Jesus Christ, our supreme Teacher and Founder of our faith, frequently calls on ordinary human reason and good sense, in order to enforce His sublime lessons. Although His basic appeal is to the lofty motives of supernatural love, He nevertheless asks us to study and weigh the considerations that stem from ordinary human experience.

A cold, purely intellectual approach to the problems of living, suffering, and aspiring human beings is doomed to ultimate sterility. Simon-pure social science or simon-pure political science is not the effective answer. Nevertheless, genuine science — documented knowledge, armed with the techniques of modern methodology — is not only a powerful but an indispensable aid in the service of the higher charity. The divinely inspired Good Samaritan used very practical means in dealing with the wounded victim on the road to Jericho.

## The Scientific Approach

The genuinely Catholic viewpoint on race relations takes into account the body of sound, reasoned knowledge which intelligent study of this question has accumulated, particularly in the United States, over a period of nearly one hundred years. Some of the main points of this doctrine we can sum up as follows:

(1) Precisely because the racial question deeply affects our sentiments and instincts, we cannot successfully deal with it in the heat of emotion and passion. Wherever any particular issue is at stake, our first approach will be to assemble the facts. In the words of Marshal Foch, France's leader in World War I, we shall first ask: "What is it all about?" We will make a special study of the many ways by which clear reasoning can be side-tracked by various deceptive devices, such as hasty generalizations and stereotypes. Catholics, as do Protestants and Jews, deeply resent the use of these mental and rhetorical structures when applied to their own religious affiliation. Our insight into the falsity and injustice of such constructs when applied to the field of religion or nationality should alert us to their deceptiveness in the case of people of differing races.

(2) A rational approach to the race problem will expose the error of racialism: the myth of inherently superior or inferior races....

Quite apart from religious considerations, science itself also repudiates as absurd and harmful to society the idea that any group of people, by the very nature of their psycho-physical makeup is essentially superior to any other human group. Or, to express the same idea in other words, science rejects the notion of inherited racial inferiority....

### The Church Condemns Racism

As Cardinal Spellman says, there can be no doubt about Catholic teaching in this matter. In the last few decades, the exaltation of pride of race by nazis and fascists, and their contempt and scorn for "inferior races," drew stern rebuke from both Pius XI and our present Holy Father, Pius XII....

These principles are widely recognized today, even though many do not follow them in practice. Very few in this country today, and practically no one in any position of responsibility, would be willing to make public profession of a doctrine of racial superiority or of "white supremacy."

Even the politicians who have most strongly opposed the Supreme Court's decision outlawing segregation in schools have been careful to avoid any imputation that Negroes are "inferior." And the espousals of such a doctrine by Calvinist theologians in the Union of South Africa who support the dominant National Party's racial policies have evoked widespread condemnation in non-Catholic as well as Catholic circles.

Against the background of recent events in Mississippi and elsewhere, the National Council of Churches of Christ (Protestant) declared on October 5, 1955: "The National Council of Churches defends the rights and liberties of cultural, racial and religious minorities. The insecurity of one menaces the security of all. Christians must be especially sensitive to the oppression of minorities."

### The Cost of Inequality

(3) Scientific reason, however, is not content with merely exploding the "myth of race." It has accumulated a wealth of data explaining many of those human appearances which seem to lend a handle to the race theory, and that cannot be left out of consideration. Social psychology reveals many of the real causes of inequality between various racial or social groups. It shows how such inequality is the result, not of fancied racial defects, but of human factors, which normally would produce the same effects in any other people subjected to the same influences over a sufficient length of time. Poor schools and poor teaching produce backward citizens. Lack of incentive discourages any sense of vigorous social or political responsibility. People incur collective neuroses as the result of being relentlessly identified with a former subject race. An intelligent study of publicly accessible statistics will — or should — convince anyone of the heavy price we pay, as a nation, for indulging in racial prejudice.

The sheer cost to the public, for instance, of our slum areas, which are perpetuated through the pressure of racial prejudice and racial discrimination, needs to be taken into account. It is estimated as high as a billion dollars a year for the nation. The researchers of the National Urban League, in a recent study, ascertained that the slum areas of a city pay, on the average, 6 per cent of a city's taxes. But they account for 45 per cent of a city's police cost, 35 per cent of its fire cost, contribute 55 per cent of its delinquency. Somebody has to pay. The slums do not. The taxpayer *does*. For public services he pays a sum far out of proportion to what he gets out of them himself....

Proportionate, also, to the losses which slum areas inflict upon the nation would be the amount that Negroes — or other victims of job discrimination — could add to the local or the national income if they were free to seek and fill jobs commensurate with their abilities. It has been estimated, says President Eisenhower's Committee on Government contracts, that the nation's sixteen million Negroes now have an annual personal income exceeding $15,000,000,000. If equal employment opportunity were universal, billions of dollars in additional purchasing power would be created. Communities are forced to expend large sums of tax money to counteract delinquency, crime, and other social maladjustments which can be traced to discrimination in employment. Everybody pays this bill. Non-discriminatory employment reduces this bill. Companies that give employment on a basis of qualifications alone are able to hire the person with the best training and experience available for the job. They increase their labor supply. All workers gain from equal job opportunities, not only those who have been subjected to discrimination. Unions strengthen their economic position under uniform standards of pay, hiring, upgrading, promotion and lay-off for workers. A divided work force is a weak work force. Equal job opportunity improves our relations and strengthens our position among nations. Discrimination weakens the moral position of the United States in the world, gives communists an opportunity to play up racial bigotry and creates anti-American sentiment.

> John LaFarge, S.J., *The Catholic Viewpoint on Race Relations* (Garden City, N.Y.: Hanover House, 1956), 77–86.

## 86. Walter Ong, S.J., on History and the Catholic Mind, 1957

*Walter J. Ong, S.J., was "one of the most important minds of the [twentieth] century,"[1] but today his name is little known within the American Catholic community he served for decades from his perch at St. Louis University, where he held a chair in psychiatry and also taught in the English department. Ong was a scholar of Renaissance rhetoric, but his areas of expertise extended to semiotics, communications theory, sociobiology, and cultural anthropology. He wrote on topics ranging from the history of oral cultures, to Hegelian dialectic, to the gendered nature of dogmatic theology.*

*In a book written shortly before the papacy of Pope John XXIII and the Second Vatican Council, Ong anticipated the pope's and the council's turn to the historical subject, and to the events of history itself, as the arena of God's saving activity in the world. In the following passage, Father Ong urges American Catholics to become aware of their history in all its ambiguity and complexity.*

The minority complex of American Catholics has been often enough commented upon, but it is not always noted that this complex is involved not only with the status of the Church in America but with a certain historical perspective developed by American Catholics and occasioned not at all by

---

1. Mark Neilsen, "A Bridge Builder: Walter J. Ong at 80," *America*, November 21, 1992.

their minority condition in America but more simply by the fact that they are both Catholics and Americans. This double heritage of theirs generates in them a curious sense of their mission. First, Europe becomes for them, as for all Americans, a symbol of the past. Second, because this past is psychologically and geographically severed from the moving present, which to Americans is necessarily America, it becomes invested with a quiescence or even rigidity greater than most pasts ordinarily have. To an American, the past tends to be something left behind — Land's End or Cape Finisterre abandoned beyond the horizon. It loses some of its normal condition as a component of the present....

Thus far, the American Catholic is like every other American in erecting Europe into a symbol of the past and in suffering from the fact that this symbol makes the past more static for him than it does for a European. But at this point, the American Catholic comes face to face with a difficulty all his own. It is from somewhere within this past that the Faith has come. With this past, this series of spastic poses, continuity must be preserved. The resulting vision for an American Catholic can be very disquieting. He finds himself committed as a Catholic to a past whose static quality his own American situation has exaggerated for him....

He is haunted by the notion that in being older, Europe is somehow truer to the Catholic tradition than he is. Europe is the past, from which Catholicism comes, the static past — all this seems obvious but awkward, for he has no working familiarity with the static.

If it is occasionally evident to the American Catholic that Europe is not really always more static than America, if it is in European Catholic circles rather than in American that the virtues of the "historical sense" are extolled, or if it is in Europe that the new Catholic intellectual fronts form — to some extent, says the American Catholic consciousness to itself, it is natural that Europeans have something to do with activity. Theirs is a special function here. They know how to stabilize the new currents, to arrest them and thus to make them safe. The worker priests, the new liturgical efforts — these things are dangerous, and we shall wait till the Europeans have put them through the experimental stage, immobilized them like the other things we think of in connection with Europe, till the Catholics of Paris and Bordeaux and Brussels and Cologne, those suburbs of the Eternal City, have worked out what is admissible and what is not. Europeans may bristle all they want at this American way of associating them with what is immobilized. They may insist that they have no interest in stabilizing things, that they want to make the innovations *work*. But they have no choice. The Catholics of America have decided that from Europeans they will gain their assurance....

There is an obvious discrepancy between this absence of a historical sense and a mode of life which, with some éclat, is living an evolution into the future. This discrepancy has created the vague malaise in present-day American Catholicism. But the malaise is like the malaise of adolescence, full of promise, and rather likely to end in a spurt of productivity....

Kierkegaard and Heidegger are right in insisting that awareness of an acceptance of one's own personal history is necessary for maturity. This acceptance is the acceptance of the insecurity of an adult, the acceptance of the fact that the individual concrete problems which arise before me have never been settled in the history of the world, although all history brings itself to bear on my settling of them.

A kind of crisis attendant on such acceptance seems to me to be a distinctive mark of the American Catholic consciousness at the present moment. There is no doubt that this acceptance will coincide with a deepening and enriching of the Catholic consciousness in America, for acceptance of one's own history means appropriating the subject matter of that history so as to make it part of one's own inward life, which is enriched accordingly. (We speak always of the general Catholic consciousness, for there is no way to say whether one or another individual American has or has not at present a deeper Catholic consciousness than one or another individual Frenchman or German or Dutchman or Spaniard or Chinese.)

The American Catholic's budding awareness of himself in history is connected with the general increase of awareness on all sides of the place of America in history and with a growing maturity in the Church herself which marks our day. If acceptance of one's own history marks an important step in maturity, whatever her other setbacks, the Church has in this way matured more rapidly in the past few generations than in many centuries before. She has always lived in history, lived the Incarnation out of history into the present, but only with the post-Hegelian interest in history has she become reflexively aware of her mission under this aspect. This awareness involves a more complete acceptance of her own past.

Walter Ong, S.J., *Frontiers in American Catholicism* (New York: Macmillan, 1957), 4–6, 9, 16.

## 87. Gustave Weigel, S.J., on the Promise of Ecumenism, 1960

*Roman Catholicism was a relative latecomer to ecumenism, the twentieth-century movement to reunite Christians of various traditions and denominations through dialogue and study and service in common. One of the Catholic pioneers in this venture was the American Jesuit Gustave Weigel. Trained in philosophy and theological studies at Woodstock College in Maryland, he chose Plato and Augustine as his intellectual heroes, absorbed the new "transcendental Thomism" of Joseph Maréchal, and wrote a master's thesis arguing for the complementarity of Kantian and Thomistic epistemology. Favoring innate ideas over abstract metaphysical speculation, Weigel loved Thomism but rejected much of the "arid" neo-Scholasticism of his "Suarezian" professors at Woodstock. He was not much more impressed with the Gregorian University in Rome, where he studied for his doctorate until 1937, when he accepted an unexpected assignment to Chile, a country whose people he came to love. Returning to Woodstock to teach in 1948, however, Weigel adopted an ecclesiology that was "heavily hierarchical and juridical."*

*At the urging of his friend and fellow Jesuit, John Courtney Murray, Weigel undertook a series of articles on ecumenism for the journal* Theological Stud- ies *and thereby became the leading Catholic expert on American Protestant thought. In Weigel's early writings, however, "the Catholic Church's holiness and fecundity are extolled as better, existentially, than any. All others pale before it."[1]*

*Erudite, witty, and charming, Weigel was a personable representative of Ca- tholicism in the sometimes stuffy atmosphere of early ecumenical dialogue; he fostered warm personal relations with his Protestant counterparts. Yet it is a measure of the insularity of the preconciliar Church that Weigel, its official rep- resentative before the World Council of Churches, waited until the end of his life to admit that his non-Catholic brethren were somehow members of the Church of Christ, though it remained difficult for him to explain theologically how this was so.*

*How, then, did Weigel overcome an exclusivist ecclesiology in order to de- mand the relaxation of certain canons inhibiting cooperation among Christians and to encourage the Council Fathers of Vatican II to pursue ecumenical dia- logue for its own sake rather than for the (ulterior) purposes of evangelization? Patrick W. Collins, Weigel's biographer, answers: Weigel's humanity overcame his theology. One might add, however that Weigel's openness to other believ- ers — his "humanity" — was rooted in and nurtured by his distinctively Catholic worldview. In this respect Weigel's growth as an ecumenist stemmed not only from the accident of personal warmth but also from an incarnational orientation to the world that found reflections of "The Real" and "The True" even in fallen humanity and "separated brethren."*

*The following passages reflect two steps in Weigel's pursuit of ecumenical dialogue: first, the clear exposition of the self-understanding of the Catholic Church; second, the implications of this self-understanding for the methods and meaning of "Christian ecumenism."*

## 87a. How the Catholic Church Views Herself, 1961

It would be silly to ask non-Catholics to share the Catholic Church's view of herself but it would be disastrous if they were not to know it. If we are to speak to each other, we should know how each partner of the conversation appears to himself. It is antecedently thinkable that the partner in dialogue is in error in his self-evaluation but it is unthinkable that the intercourse would be fruitful if we did not take such self-evaluation into account.

The Roman Catholic Church (and therefore each Catholic to the degree in which he is assimilated into the genuine life and being of his Church) believes that this Church is exclusively the Church of Christ. By that fact she believes that she is Christ continued in space and time, with His mission to save, to teach, to judge, to comfort, to guide, to sanctify, and all this she will do be- cause Christ and Catholicism are fused into one life with Him as head and she as the body. Because she believes that His name saves and in no other name is there salvation, she conceives of herself as the saving instrument of God for

---

1. Patrick W. Collins, *Gustave Weigel, S.J.: A Pioneer of Reform* (Collegeville, Minn: Liturgical Press, 1992).

men, and in her view there is no other. She well knows that God in his soul-loving benevolence also brings men who are non-Catholics to a happy term by uncovenanted mercies. But in this saving act, such souls are attached invisibly to the visible Church. We cannot call them members, but they are truly adherents. No man can say who or how many they are, nor is that man's concern. The Roman Catholic Church must continue in the function given to her: to preach the Gospel, dispense the grace-giving sacraments, scold the slothful, protest against iniquity and sin, especially when they are at work within the Church herself. (She knows all too well that sin plays a heavy part in her own life.) If God in His love is willing to give the graces, which He entrusted to her in such a way that they are really hers, to those beyond her visible unity, there is no resentment but only joy and gratitude. In this divine act there is no contempt of the church nor a bypassing of her. God is only making up by His omnipotence for the finitude of the Church's efforts. It is God aiding His Church in her mission to save souls. But no other instrument is ordained by God to dispense grace to mankind.

This is the theory and spirit of Catholicism. It may appear utterly preposterous to a non-Catholic, but there it is. Psychologically and logically the Roman Catholic Church simply cannot conceive of any other human union as ordained by God to mediate salvation, even though individual members of such a union be in grace. Such grace is immediately given by God in favor of this individual. God can use the individual's religious union and its acts as occasions to give grace to the individual, for in non-Catholic groups there are always *vestigia ecclesiae*, vestiges of the Church, though the separated unions themselves are neither the Church nor part of it. They can be occasions for salvation but they are not ordained instruments thereof.

A council of churches not in union with the Roman Church is at the outset a misnomer from the Catholic's point of view. He considers them something less than churches. Psychologically he gags at the idea of Christian Churches which are not Roman Catholic. His intelligence tells him not to be scandalized by verbalism, but emotions defy reason....

Does this then mean that the Protestant must resign himself to the bleak picture of working ecumenically without any future encounter with his Catholic brother? I think not....

Above all, Catholic and Protestant ecumenists must develop the virtue of patience. Centuries of hostility have colored our attitudes toward each other and we cannot see simply what is simply there. Each member of the dialogue must keep on learning, keep on revising his concept and image of his partner in high talk. Misunderstandings cannot be avoided for some time to come but we must not harden the misunderstandings which the past has forced on us.

The one thing we must all remember is that the purpose of the Ecumenical Movement is conversation. Its hope is one Church, but the hope is not the humanly projected teleological goal. Hence the ecumenical obligation is to promote colloquy. To promote it we need to do more than merely be ready for it. We must with patience and forbearance overcome the difficulties which stand in the way of meeting. If my friend is embarrassed when in my house I shall hold converse with him elsewhere. The conversation is important, not the place where it is to be held.

Gustave Weigel, S.J., *Catholic Theology in Dialogue* (New York: Harper, 1961), 76–79, 82.

## 87b. How, Then, May We Proceed with Ecumenical Dialogue? 1960

For ecumenical work the Catholic can follow only one tactic. He must ask the Protestant to be converted to Catholicism. He has absolutely no other choice. Yet this invitation is not what the Protestant wants. He may courteously listen to the invitation given, but there is nothing else he can do but refuse it, unless he has already lost faith in Protestantism. From his point of view he is not being invited to ecumenical discussion but rather exposed to a proselytizing campaign. I doubt if Protestants as a rule are interested in this kind of conversation.

If I do not interpret amiss, the current Ecumenical Movement is an effort to produce or educe the *una sancta* with no prior commitment as to the final form it will take. That it might finally be the Catholic Church is not on principle excluded, but it is certainly excluded that one begin the dialogue already determined that it must. Since such are the rules of the game, I do not see how the Catholic can invite the Protestant to ecumenical encounter. The Catholic cannot play according to the rules which the Protestants have already set up, and if he doesn't, the Protestant has every right to complain that his Catholic host is not playing fair.

This holds equally for the Protestant. If the rules he has set up are such that the Catholic must collaborate on a basis which to him is irreconcilable with his being, the result will be frustrating paralysis. The lack of anterior commitment to what the *una sancta* is or will be is congenial to the Protestant principle but is a complete negation of the Catholic principle. Hence the Catholic cannot help but see in the Protestant invitation a request that he cease to be a Catholic. Of course we all understand that this is not the intention of the Protestant but it is the logical even though not the intended implication of the invitation to ecumenical meeting....

It might seem to the reader that I am cutting my own head off. I want meeting and friendly intercourse and yet I have shown that it cannot be. I do not think that such is the logical consequence of my observations. All that we have been obliged to affirm is that our coming together cannot be ecumenical as the word is understood today. It can however be what one might call para-ecumenical, i.e. action along side of but not identical with the current ecumenical enterprise. It would proceed from a different starting point and tend to a different goal.

The starting point would be that Catholics and Protestants are here as a matter of massive fact, and that neither wants to become the other. The goal, therefore, will not be that they do become one church, though this is not a negation of the hope that at some day by God's grace they will. The purpose of the continuous symposium would be to eliminate or reduce the hostilities but not the differences between the two parties. As a result they could thus live in peace and security without the constant fear of raids and inroads. The Catholic would in Christian love respect the Protestant, not simply as another man but as a Protestant. The Protestant would return this same affection. This is not a church union; it is neighborliness of love and Christian charity. The whole supposition is that there is no union, experimental or achieved, in creed, code and cult. The utter alterity of the partners in charity would be the vivid awareness of the symposiasts.

Is such action in any true sense ecumenical? In order not to identify it with ecumenical effort in its present style, I have introduced the prefix, *para*. Yet the action would have ecumenical dimensions. First of all, it would bring the members of the churches together. A union would be established; not a church union, but a union of churchmen in terms of good will and mutual respect. In matters non-ecclesiological, collaboration would be fostered and rendered fruitful.

It could also be pre-ecumenical. It could serve as a preparation of hearts and spirits for ecumenical conversation. It is hard to hold a profitable dialogue if both members are suspicious of each other. If they are friends and know each other, the talks are easy and pleasant. Understanding would be much more probable....

If Catholics and Protestants would only realize that the moment calls for a survival of faith in Christ who alone can save, they would be less prone to snipe at each other. We can easily be lulled into a narcotized sleep. In this country there is no campaign against religion and the churches....Everywhere we are told that religion is American. There is no need to sneer at the statement but there is need to ask if Americanism is our religion. One gets the impression that to be a good American you must belong to a religious congregation; it matters not which one, as long as it is one of the three socially accepted faiths: Protestantism, Catholicism, Judaism....

The ever spreading religion of Americanism is a genteel secularism. Unlike all other forms of secularism, it has not fought religion. It has done much worse; it has absorbed it. The great Christian slogans have been kept. But charity now means humanitarian giving; faith means trust in American ideals and effort. God is not our judge but our leader and helper. We do his will when we advance the American way.

This is neither Catholicism nor Protestantism. Catholics and Protestants desirous of relaxing tensions between these two groups must be wary lest they melt away the tensions by fusing both religious visions into a starry-eyed Americanism. In both groups what we need is a strong prophetic voice warning the people against the worship of Moloch.

Gustave Weigel, S.J., in Robert McAfee Brown and Gustave Weigel, *An American Dialogue: A Protestant Looks at Catholicism and a Catholic Looks at Protestantism* (Garden City, N.Y.: Doubleday, 1960), 199–200, 207–8.

## *Part 10*

# THE CONTESTED LEGACY OF VATICAN II

## Introduction

With stunning swiftness the Second Vatican Council (Vatican II) transformed the church's attitude toward the modern world. A gathering of approximately twenty-three hundred Catholic bishops from seventy-nine countries, the council opened in St. Peter's Basilica, Vatican City, on October 11, 1962, and adjourned in December 1965 after four momentous sessions that produced sixteen official documents which revolutionized Roman Catholicism.

Though various streams of reform had been flowing within the church for decades, Pope John XXIII nonetheless stunned the world by calling an ecumenical council (a council of Catholic bishops from "the whole world") that would be designed, he said, to throw open the windows of the church to the modern world. Elected pope in 1958, John convened the first session of Vatican II in 1962 and died the following summer. His short pontificate was enormously influential. The first "media pope," his joyful, avuncular presence was beamed around the world. He embraced Eastern Orthodox patriarchs and Jewish rabbis. A man manifestly of peace and goodwill, John did more to change the image of the church in the modern world than any previous pope.

The council fathers — the bishops who gathered at Vatican II and formulated its teaching — accepted Pope John's invitation "not only to guard this precious treasure [the gospel message], as if we were concerned only with antiquity, but earnestly and fearlessly to dedicate ourselves to the work our age demands of us...the Christian, Catholic and apostolic spirit of the whole world expects a leap forward...."[1]

Leap forward they did. During the course of four conciliar sessions, held each autumn from 1962 to 1965, the bishops described the church as the biblical "People of God," and they proclaimed the church's openness to and respect for human cultures. (See *Lumen Gentium*, the Dogmatic Constitution on the Church.) *Gaudium et Spes*, the Pastoral Constitution on the Church in the Modern World, recognized the legitimate autonomy of the sciences and identified the church with the social, political, and economic aspirations of all people

---

1. Quoted in R. Scott Appleby, "The Contested Legacy of Vatican II," *Notre Dame Magazine* 28, no. 2 (Summer 1999): 23–27. Parts of this introductory essay are adapted from that article.

seeking equality and opportunity for self-improvement. The council fathers affirmed the right of every person, regardless of religious affiliation, to worship God (or not) according to his or her conscience and without coercion from church or state. (See *Dignitatis Humanae*, the Declaration on Religious Liberty.) They celebrated the presence of the Spirit in other Christian churches and religions, and acknowledged the need for ecumenical and interreligious discussion and collaboration. (See *Unitatis Redintegratio*, the Decree on Ecumenism; *Nostra Aetate*, the Declaration on the Relation of the Church to Non-Christian Religions; and, *Orientalium Ecclesiarum*, the Decree on the Catholic Eastern Churches.)

Vatican II also signaled, and helped to trigger, the relocation of the church's public presence within the political sphere. Typically, the concrete expression of this identification took many forms. In 1968 the Latin American bishops meeting at Medellín, Colombia, lamented the massive poverty of the continent, and focused attention on the social and political factors responsible for the oppression of the poor. Citing Vatican II's embrace of a "new humanism," the bishops denounced the "institutionalized violence" of Latin American society, and demanded "urgent and profoundly renovating transformations" in the social structures of their countries. They urged each episcopal conference to present the church as "a catalyst in the temporal realm in an authentic attitude of service," and to support grassroots organizations for the "redress and consolidation of their rights [of the poor] and the search for justice." Finally, the bishops called for Catholics worldwide, in exercising their political and religious responsibilities, to adopt a preferential option for the poor.

Turning to the inner life of the church, the bishops asserted their identity as a college holding co-responsibility with the pope for the governance of the church. They also reclaimed the Bible as a privileged source of theological reflection, thereby welcoming through the front door those innovations in theological method and ecclesiology that had been entering through back channels carrying the "new theology" of Congar and de Lubac, Chenu and Daniélou (see the introduction to part 9). Feminist, liberationist, and other "structure-shattering" visions of Christian identity and mission appeared on the theological horizon shortly thereafter.

If the council was about *aggiornamento* ("updating"), it also embraced *ressourcement* — the retrieval of the early sources of Christian wisdom and self-understanding. The Liturgical Movement, the critical study of the Bible, and other currents of twentieth-century ecclesial reform had prepared the bishops, or the theologians advising them, to take history seriously as the arena of God's redemptive activity and thus to see the world, and the laity working daily in it, in a new and more flattering light.

The restored confidence in human agency was reflected most dramatically in the renewal of the liturgy. "Full conscious and active participation" in the Mass on the part of the faithful was the mantra, repeated over a dozen times, in *Sacrosanctum Concilium*, the council's Constitution on the Sacred Liturgy. While the ordained priesthood did receive attention in the conciliar documents, the greater excitement was generated by calls for "theologies of the laity."

The present section examines the challenging — and still ongoing — process of interpreting and applying the teaching of the council throughout the universal church and in the United States in particular. The council was pastoral in nature — concentrating, that is, on the spiritual and religious practices and attitudes appropriate to the living out of the doctrines of the church, rather than on the formal doctrines themselves. Even so, the council addressed issues fundamental to the self-understanding of the church, including its relationship to the world and its (evolving) sense of its historic mission. By its very nature, this task was controversial and fraught with tension.

The curial officials who prepared the schema, or preliminary outlines, of the conciliar documents prior to the actual arrival of most of the bishops in Rome were adamantly opposed to even the appearance of significant change in the presentation of Catholic teaching and pastoral practice. The story of the council itself was, in part, the story of the contest between these curial officials, such as Cardinal Alfredo Ottaviani, the Prefect of the Holy Office (the curial department responsible for the preservation of orthodoxy and vigilance against heresy, later re-named the Congregation for the Doctrine of the Faith) and the bishops themselves, who as a body were far more open to change.

A significant and enduring consequence of the intraecclesial battle, which featured a competition for the support of the pope (Paul VI, who succeeded John XXIII in 1963), was a certain ambivalence in the decrees and declarations of the council, mirrored in the language of the documents. This "on the one hand, on the other hand" approach stemmed from an admirable attempt to find a middle position between two extremes. Yet it introduced ambiguity into the teaching of the council and thereby opened a broad space for contesting its "true meaning" on many central points — a contest that unfolded in the U.S. church during the postconciliar period and continues to this day.

For example, the council addressed the relationship between the universal church headquartered at Rome and the thousands of local churches around the world, each rooted in its own cultural self-understanding. By speaking of "the elements of truth and grace which are found among peoples" prior to the planting of the church, *Ad Gentes Divinitus*, the Decree on the Church's Missionary Activity, reflects the general conciliar respect for cultures. But the document also underscores the church's mission to "purge [those cultural elements] of evil associations." In the church's missionary activities, the bishops explained, " ... whatever goodness is found in people's minds and hearts, or in the particular customs and cultures of peoples, far from being lost, is purified, raised to a higher level and reaches its perfection, for the glory of God, the confusion of the demon, and the happiness of humankind."[2]

Following the council, however, the liberal or progressive camp within the church, which was in the ascendancy during the council itself, emphasized the priority of local cultures and churches. "Inculturation" — the adaptation of the

---

2. *Ad Gentes Divinitus*, the Decree on the Church's Missionary Activity, in Austin Flannery, O.P., ed. *Vatican Council II: The Basic Sixteen Documents* (Northport, N.Y.: Costello Publishing Company, 1996), 454.

gospel and apostolic life to indigenous customs, rituals, and cultural values —
became the code word for the new understanding of the church's evangelical
mission. The council's respect for the integrity of cultures and the vibrant pluralism of a world church, reinforced by Pope Paul VI's internationalization of
the curia, transformed the promise of a truly globalized Catholicism into a
reality.

Few features of everyday Catholic life, from the central elements of its
preaching and worship to the most peripheral of its devotional practices, were
unaffected by the changes introduced by Vatican II. So rapid and profound were
the changes in the church's understanding of its nature and mission that less
than a decade after the Council's final session in 1965, the distinguished American theologian (now a cardinal) Avery Dulles, S.J. (see doc. 88) was able to
write *Models of the Church,* which set forth multiple possible models in part
to refute "the thesis that the church is most aptly conceived as a single, unified,
'perfect society.'" Widely read in Catholic seminaries, colleges, and chanceries,
Dulles's accessible distillation of Vatican II's basic teaching leveled severe criticism against the preconciliar model, which "Catholics today should not wish to
defend."[3] Although an institutional view of the church is "valid within limits,"
Dulles acknowledged, it had been taken to a damaging extreme, eclipsing other
dimensions — the church as "mystical body," "sacrament," "herald," and "servant" — which the council had wisely retrieved. He charged the institutional
theory of the church with stifling theological creativity and prophetic protest
against the abuse of authority.

Strikingly, Dulles accused the institutionalists of stifling theological creativity and prophetic protest against the abuse of authority. Dulles placed great
emphasis on a revolutionary turn of phrase in Article 8 of *Lumen Gentium,*
which stated that the People of God "subsists in" (rather than "is identical
with") the Roman Catholic Church. Coupled with the retrieval of biblical
images, the official recognition that God's saving presence extends beyond the
church's institutional boundaries lent support to the ecclesiology of the *mystical body,* a Pauline metaphor which encouraged Catholics to explore their
spiritual affinities with other believers, whatever their formal religious affiliation. Envisioning the church as a *sacrament* — a sign pointing beyond itself
to the encompassing, pervasive reality of Christ in society — also reinforced
the tendency to focus attention elsewhere. Finally, as a biblical people concerned with justice, Catholics were *heralds* of the gospel and *servants* of the poor
and marginalized — religious identities for which preoccupation with dogmas,
doctrines, manual-based morality, the authority of the magisterium, and other
institutional elements of the preconciliar church was irrelevant.

Or so it seemed to those many Catholics caught up in the euphoria generated by the council. For a brief, shining moment, the periodical literature of
the mid-sixties attests, Vatican II evoked a consensus that transcended the rival-
ries between "liberal" and "conservative." In part the enthusiasm for change as a
good in itself — what Notre Dame historian Jay Dolan has called the American

---

3. Avery Dulles, S.J., *Models of the Church* (New York: Image/Doubleday, 1987 [1974]), 10.

Catholic Church's "third romance with modernity" — reflected the signs of the times. The fifties and early sixties had fostered a robust confidence, particularly pronounced in the United States but also evident in Europe, in the possibilities of human agency to transform the world — to wage a successful "war on poverty," to combat racial intolerance, to foster "peace, love, and understanding" on a global scale. Although "the two Johns," the U.S. president Kennedy and the pope, had passed from the scene, hope in the durability of their legacies was high. The modern Catholic Church was effectively projecting its vital spiritual presence and moral leadership just as the world faced a "new frontier" of possibilities in science, technology, and socioeconomic development. Vatican II, it seemed, had inaugurated an era of limitless promise.[4]

The honeymoon was short-lived. As the decade unfolded, its storyline changed dramatically; subsequent events cast the assassination of the young Catholic president as an omen rather than an aberration. Race riots, Vietnam, urban blight, "the generation gap," the burgeoning drug culture, and "the new morality" turned the celebrations of the cult of progress into a prolonged wake. In this regard the council would eventually come to be seen more as the culminating moment of postwar cultural optimism, and less as the advent of a new world-transforming Christianity.

Within the American church, the year 1968 proved to be a watershed. In July, Pope Paul VI, having previously appointed a commission of bishops, theologians, and lay men and women to reconsider the church's ban on artificial means of birth control, rejected the committee's majority recommendation (leaked earlier to the press) to permit the married couple to use contraceptives to regulate the size of the family. Paul VI's encyclical, *Humanae vitae*, reaffirmed the earlier teaching that even the occasional use of artificial birth control is to be considered sinful.

The reaction, from clergy and laity alike, was stunning. Not only did Catholic couples in droves disobey the pope, priests openly dissented from the teaching (doc. 90). Theologians and clergy held news conferences to protest the encyclical; in the nation's capital, Archbishop Patrick O'Boyle suspended fifty-one priests who refused in conscience to accept its teaching. Some prominent progressive Catholics, such as St. Louis University historian James Hitchcock, embittered by the open dissent and the erosion of episcopal and papal authority it accelerated (and reflected), joined the growing ranks of conservatives who sought to exorcise "the phantom spirit of the council" (doc. 91).

Whereas 30 percent of Catholic women in the United States had admitted to using some form of birth control in 1955, a decade later the proportion had increased to 51 percent. Two years after the promulgation of *Humanae vitae*, pollsters reported that 68 percent of American Catholic women were acting in direct violation of the papal prohibition. Liberals who remained liberal

---

4. For an overview, see Jay P. Dolan, *The American Catholic Experience: A History from Colonial Times to the Present* (Notre Dame, Ind.: University of Notre Dame Press, 1992 [1985]), "A New Catholicism," 421–54.

noticed, quietly or otherwise, that the sky did not fall when millions of Catholics sidestepped an unpopular ruling of the magisterium. Almost inevitably the moderate majority in the pews, the "People of God" whom Vatican II had placed at the heart of the church, lost a measure of respect for the men in black — either for the ("authoritarian") papacy, or for the ("disobedient") clergy. In a 1982 article documenting the postconciliar drop in mass attendance, confessions, church collections, and vocations, the priest and sociologist Andrew Greeley concluded that *Humanae vitae* had canceled out the positive results of Vatican II and sent the church into a sudden and dramatic decline.[5]

Despite the turmoil over birth control, that judgment would have seemed unduly apocalyptic to most American Catholics in the seventies. But the "liberal" and "conservative" camps had begun to harden, and competing interpretations of the council constituted the dividing line between them. The literature of conservative Catholics, the ecclesiologist Joseph Komonchak notes, included complaints about the decline in traditional popular devotions, the abandonment of distinctive clerical and religious dress, the political activities of priests and nuns, the massive departures from the priesthood and religious life, the decline or dissolution of Catholic professional associations, the abandonment of Gregorian chant, and the turn to Protestant hymns or popular music.[6]

Some such sentiments were attributable to the (often lengthy) lag-time between the implementation of the reforms and the education of the priests and laity about their significance. "Suddenly we were telling the parishioners: 'You are the "People of God," obliged to participate in the eucharist and make your own moral choices,'" a Boston priest recalled. "If they asked 'Why?' we naturally relied on the old clerical authoritarianism: 'Because we say you are.'"[7]

But informed conservative opposition to extravagant interpretations of Vatican II ran deeper. Behind the apparent collapse of the unitary neo-Scholastic method and language of theology that had shaped catechism, belief, and practice for decades, the attitude of selective disregard for the authority of the magisterium, and the movement for the ordination of women, among other postconciliar developments they found unsettling, conservative polemicists perceived not only the unraveling of a distinctive Catholic subculture, but the absence of any viable, recognizably orthodox model to take its place — Dulles's 1974 "bestseller" notwithstanding.

Exacerbating the anxiety of the conservatives, some overly enthusiastic priests and nuns, as well as lay religious educators, introduced the official reforms in a manner that disparaged the preconciliar church. Unauthorized changes were occasionally presented as gospel. (Komonchak cites the example

---

5. See Andrew M. Greeley, "The Failure of Vatican II after Twenty Years," *America* 146, no. 5 (February 6, 1982): 86–89.

6. Joseph Komonchak, "Interpreting the Council: Catholic Attitudes Toward Vatican II," in Mary Jo Weaver and R. Scott Appleby, eds., *Being Right: Conservative Catholics in America* (Bloomington, Ind.: Indiana University Press, 1995), 18.

7. Personal interview with the author, 1986. See R. Scott Appleby, "Present to the People of God: The Transformation of the Roman Catholic Parish Priesthood," in Jay Dolan, R. Scott Appleby, Patricia Byrne, and Debra Campbell, *Transforming Parish Ministry: The Changing Roles of Catholic Clergy, Laity, and Women Religious* (New York: Crossroad, 1989), 58.

of a priest in the pulpit who reportedly broke a rosary in his hands, scattered the beads on the floor, and told the congregation, "You don't have to say this anymore."[8])

The conservatives were also troubled by the rise of radically innovative approaches to theology and ethics within the Catholic academy. During the same period when innovative theological works such as Mary Daly's *The Church and the Second Sex* (1968) [doc. 89], Gustavo Gutiérrez's *A Theology of Liberation* (1973), David Tracy's *The Analogical Imagination: Christian Theology and the Culture of Pluralism* (1981) [doc. 93], and Richard McBrien's postconciliar synthesis, *Catholicism* (1981), were making an impact among moderates and liberals, numerous books and articles appeared presenting an alternative view of the postconciliar church and warning that something more than "reform" was under way. Their titles featured ominous words like *dissolution, decay, apostasy,* and *crisis.*[9]

The authors of these diatribes accused Catholics in positions of authority within the church of virtually abrogating the letter of Vatican II by carrying "reforms" far beyond what was intended by the council fathers. It was not difficult to marshal evidence of this intent from the rhetoric of the theologians of *Concilium,* who launched an appeal in 1970 to go "beyond Vatican II for the sake of Vatican II," or from figures like the moral theologian Charles Curran (doc. 90), who averred that the council's documents had already become "dated on the first day after solemn promulgation." Well into the seventies, faculty members of one seminary, in New Jersey, assured the women whom they admitted into graduate theological studies (alongside the male seminarians) that it was only a matter of time before the Vatican would reward their preparations for priestly ministry by approving the ordination of women.[10]

The postconciliar period — the decades following the Second Vatican Council, through the close of the twentieth century — soon assumed its own contours. Certainly the council provided the context and foundation for many of the developments and events of the period from 1965 to 2000, but historians will be arguing about the precise nature of the relationship for many years to come. The debate within Catholicism about the status of homosexuality and the homosexual is a case in point. Vatican II did not address this topic directly and, as the gay Catholic intellectual Andrew Sullivan points out (doc. 95), *Gaudium et Spes* reaffirmed the traditional Catholic teaching on the inseparability of marriage, sexual intercourse, and procreation as its natural end. Yet Vatican II also urged Catholics to enter into sophisticated dialogue with the modern sciences, including biology, psychology, and genetics. During the last quarter of the twentieth century, Catholic ethicists began to incorporate into their thinking new findings on the origins and dynamics of human sexuality, including homosexuality.[11]

---

8. Ibid., 21.
9. Ibid., 22.
10. Appleby, "Present to the People of God," 104–5.
11. For an overview, see Jeannine Gramick and Pat Furey, eds., *The Vatican and Homosexuality* (New York: Crossroad, 1988).

Another contested arena was the role of women in the church and in society at large. A new breed of women religious, previously referred to as "nuns" or "sisters," embraced and advanced both the council's letter and spirit, citing and taking seriously passages such as the mandate of *Gaudium et Spes* that "every type of discrimination, whether based on sex, race, color, social condition, language or religion, is to be overcome and eradicated as contrary to God's intent."

Mary Luke Tobin, the superior general of the Sisters of Loretto, was one of the few women auditors at the council. As president of the Conference of Major Superiors of Women (known from 1971 as the Leadership Conference of Women Religious), she had a distinctive vantage point on, and role in, the changes most religious communities of women effected as their awareness of gender discrimination in church and society increased. In a 1986 article for *America* magazine, Tobin reflected upon these changes, including each sister's "full participation in decisions affecting her," the emergence of a generation of outstanding women theologians and biblical scholars, the push for women's ordination, and sisters' involvement in public protests against U.S. participation in the Vietnam War, the escalation of the arms race, racism, and other social justice issues. In enumerating the catalysts for these developments Tobin credited not only the conciliar documents but also the "recent psychological, sociological and philosophical insights that influenced the concept of the priority of the human person."[12]

The "outstanding women theologians and biblical scholars" included not a few "radical feminists," as the most prominent dissenters from Catholic patriarchy came to be called. Mary Daly (doc. 89) and Rosemary Radford Ruether, the author of the influential *Sexism and God Talk* (1983), took women's experience rather than the teachings of the magisterium, dogmatically defined, as the starting point for their theologies, which centered on a thoroughgoing critique of the sexist structures of the church and the distortions of the Christian message introduced by an all-male (and celibate) hierarchy and institutional leadership. Their attempt to reconstruct the social patterns, language, liturgy, and theology of the church in a way to affirm the equal dignity of women and men proved profoundly influential upon a generation of American Catholic intellectuals, and paved the way for greater radicalization, on their part, and in the work of Elisabeth Schüssler Fiorenza, Anne Carr, Elizabeth Johnson, and others.[13]

To most liberals and more than a few moderates influenced by Vatican II, the dignity and freedom of the individual was the essence of the gospel message, making personal and communal experience a primary source for theological reflection. Such assumptions seemed natural, appropriate, and fully orthodox conclusions to draw from the deliberations and documents of the council. Liberals looked everywhere for portents of radical transformation. Paul VI's

---

12. Mary Luke Tobin, "Women in the Church since Vatican II," *America* 155, no. 12 (November 1, 1986): 244.

13. Mary Jo Weaver, *New Catholic Women* (New York: Harper & Row, 1985), 167–68.

appointment of a birth control commission, despite its unhappy ending, fueled the fantasies of liberal Catholics who imagined that the episcopal "collegiality" endorsed by Vatican II would trickle down to every level of church governance, fundamentally altering and "democratizing" relations between clergy and laity. As late as 1992 a company of leading liberal American Catholic intellectuals contributed essays to a book calling for *A Democratic Catholic Church.*[14]

Other would-be Catholic revolutionaries had begun to lose hope when a second turning point for the postconciliar church occurred in the year of the nation's bicentennial, 1976. The first "Call to Action" conference, held that year in Detroit, was unlike any subsequent meeting convened under that banner. Attended by 1,340 delegates carrying more than 800,000 comments and proposals culled from "feedback sheets" produced by parish discussions in at least half the nation's dioceses, Call to Action was the culmination of an elaborate and unprecedented three-year process of consultation and collaboration at all levels of the church.

When it became painfully clear to the U.S. bishops, who had sponsored the process and the national conference, that the delegates intended to apply the conference theme — "Liberty and Justice for All" — to the internal governance of the church itself, they backed away from the process and rejected, or failed to implement, the majority of the 182 proposals submitted. These included calls for the ordination of women, the elimination of mandatory celibacy for the priesthood, the reincorporation of divorced and remarried Catholics into the full sacramental life of the church, the support of labor unions and other measures designed to enforce Catholic social teaching (i.e., "a just wage") within the church itself, the requirement that "church authorities should provide reasons for administrative and policy decisions," and a "Catholic bill of rights," including "the right to participate, in accord with each person's gift, in the life and ministry of the church." In all this the theme that stood out, Peter Steinfels contended, was "the democratic, voluntaristic character of American culture and religion, and the need for the church to evolve structures that fit it."[15]

Reviewing the recommendations approved and those ignored by the U.S. bishops, *Commonweal* judged Call to Action to be "a social justice success but a theological disappointment."[16] Liberals have said the same about the pontificate of John Paul II, the person most influential in shaping the way Vatican II is understood by the world's bishops and, ultimately, by the entire People of God. They give the pope a mixed review, for example, on ecumenism and interreligious dialogue, citing (to the good) the broad consensus that has been reached on issues that have divided Christians since the sixteenth century (e.g., the doctrine of justification, the nature of the Eucharist, the structure and theology of the ordained ministry, the exercise of authority and even the question of papal primacy, which the pope himself reopened in a challenging way in his encyclical *Ut Unum Sint*). (See docs. 92 and 94.)

14. Eugene C. Bianchi and Rosemary Radford Ruether, eds., *A Democratic Catholic Church: The Reconstruction of Roman Catholicism* (New York: Crossroad, 1992).

15. Peter Steinfels, "New Chance for the Bishops," *Commonweal* (April 1, 1977): 200.

16. "Detroit, Chicago and Rome," *Commonweal* (May 27, 1977): 324.

On the debit side, liberals complain that Rome's prohibition of women from priestly ordination inhibits additional advances in many of these areas, as well as on ethical issues involving women's rights and responsibilities (e.g., birth control, sterilization, abortion and surrogate parenthood).

With regard to interreligious dialogue, John Paul has gone further than any other pope in his appreciation of non-Christian religions, but not so far as to recognize them as salvific. Conservatives tend to be pleased by the pope's attitudes on this matter, liberals dismayed or indifferent, and the documents of Vatican II suggestive but not unambiguous as a guide for church leaders who must discern how to apply Catholic principles to the concrete pastoral and theological questions that will arise in the new millennium.[17]

Scanning the Call to Action proposals, on the other hand, one is struck by how many of them, especially those concerned with social justice, have become standard practice in the U.S. church (and elsewhere) during John Paul's long reign. The U.S. Catholic Conference and a broad range of other Catholic agencies do, indeed, work assiduously "to end all forms of discrimination, particularly in such policy areas as housing, education, neighborhood development, and job opportunities." Many if not all dioceses have established offices of peace and justice, regularly led by skilled laity who are dedicated to establishing and maintaining effective programs of education and formation in this critical area of Catholic mission and identity. Finally, the universal church under the leadership of Pope John Paul II (building on the legacy of John XXIII and Paul VI) has become perhaps the world's foremost defender of universal human rights, including the right to religious liberty.

Other "Call to Action" initiatives of 1976 have fared less well, not always for lack of good intentions. "Training in seminaries and other leadership educational centers" does include "multilingual and multicultural education," but no one is satisfied with the degree of ethnic diversity represented in the clergy or the hierarchy. Nor are the various cultural heritages of Latino/a, Asian, and African American Catholics "adequately represented within the context of prayer, worship, sacraments and various celebrations" — although it must be said that large urban, polyglot archdioceses, Los Angeles most prominent among them, have made great strides in this direction.

On matters bearing implications for the way the hierarchy governs the church, the Call to Action delegates continue to be disappointed a generation after their Vatican II–induced call to reform. "Collegiality" understood as genuine consultation and collaboration seems a faded memory or distant rumor, even to the many bishops who are uncompromisingly loyal to John Paul II. Today the American church does provide "professional training to the laity, clerics, and religious who are to be assigned to special ministries required by diocesan pastoral plans." But it is equally clear that the hierarchy appointed by John Paul II, hoping against all empirical evidence for a significant upsurge in priestly vocations, has not accepted or developed a viable theology of lay min-

---

17. Thomas P. Rausch, "The Unfinished Agenda of Vatican II," *America* (June 17, 1995): 23–27.

istry that would fully empower lay men and women, clarify their distinctive ministerial status and mission, and undergird a realistic long-term plan for their financial support.

Theologically, John Paul has attempted to lead the church away from the promise (or peril, depending on one's perspective) of pluralism — the acceptance and further deepening of the plurality of the theological methods and sources recovered, developed, celebrated, put in play, and anticipated by the (mostly) white male European theologians who shaped Vatican II. Catholic theologians teaching in American colleges and universities are more diverse than ever, however, in terms of their intellectual training, accreditation and procedures of accountability, social background, race, and gender. This tension formed the backdrop to the disagreement between some bishops and some Catholic theologians over the implementation of *Ex Corde Ecclesiae*, the pope's 1991 encyclical letter on Catholic higher education. It also might help to explain the fact that Father Dulles became severely critical of some of his liberal colleagues in the academy, whom he has publicly berated—ironically, it would seem — for their insufficient attention to the institutional contexts in which Catholic theology must be done.

## 88. Avery Dulles, S.J., on the Council's Teaching on "The Church and the World," 1967

*Rethinking the relationship between the church and an increasingly secular, modern world was perhaps the central challenge addressed by the Second Vatican Council. It was the focus of the most comprehensive documents:* Lumen Gentium *(The Dogmatic Constitution on the Church in the Modern World) and* Gaudium et Spes *(The Pastoral Constitution on the Church in the Modern World). The council fathers envisaged a two-way relationship between the church and the world, with the patterns of influence and transformation running in both directions.*

*Yet there is a tension running throughout the council documents regarding the role of the church vis-à-vis the world.* Lumen Gentium *proclaims, for example, a profound respect for the cultures of the world which, as products of human agency, bear the mark of the Creator. The church, however, is the salt and light of the world, bringing the goodness of creation to a higher plane of holiness.*

*The language of* Gaudium et Spes, *by contrast, is more searching, even diffident, regarding the church's precise contributions to human development. "Faith which shows everything in a new light and extols God's purpose...points the mind toward solutions which are fully human," the document acknowledges.*

*The council, in short, left theologians with much to debate, resolve, and reconcile. How was the church's new appreciation of the autonomy of the sciences, and of the secular world in general, to alter Catholicism's understanding of its sanctifying mission on earth? How should the respective contributions and responsibilities of the laity and the clergy be understood? Was the church destined to become one with the world, to abandon its perch "above" and "beyond" history?*

> One of the most influential American theologians to address these and other
> issues raised but not resolved by the council was the Jesuit priest and ecclesiolo-
> gist Avery Dulles, son of the prominent American statesman, John Foster Dulles.
> Father Dulles was an enthusiastic proponent of the council and embraced its
> retrieval of models and images of the church offered by scripture and apostolic
> tradition. Yet he was concerned, even in the heady years immediately following
> the council, to contain the enthusiasm and innovation within the boundaries
> set by the conciliar documents and the received teaching of the church.

We turn now to a third major area, the relations between the Church and the
world. The world, as we here understand the term, is not an additional class of
persons but the sum total of all those realities which pertain to man in his life
here below and which confront him whether he is a believer or not. Within the
life of one and the same man, if he is a Christian, the Church and the world are
simultaneously present. The polarity of these relations gives rise to many practical tensions and theoretical dilemmas which are much debated in our day. How
can we define the respective claims and spheres of the Church and the world?...

In our own day the secular tide has risen to a new high. More and more
functions which used to be considered properly religious are taken over by
government agencies or by private organizations without any definite religious affiliation. Although the churches continue to run hospitals, schools, and
charitable societies of their own, they are faced with more and stiffer secular competition in these fields. Some feel that the sacred dimension of life is
receding to the point of eventual nonexistence....

Vatican Council II took cognizance of the urgent problems posed by Christian
secularity. This was an issue which the Council simply could not dodge. In the
following pages we shall attempt to recapitulate the main conclusions set forth in
the conciliar documents, especially in the Pastoral Constitution *Gaudium et spes.*
Our first task will be to clarify the meaning of the terms "world" and "Church."

The notion of the "world" is most fully explained in the opening paragraphs
of *Gaudium et spes.* In article 2 it is described as "the whole human family
along with the sum of those realities in the midst of which the human family
lives." This world, we are then told, is "the theater of man's history, and carries with it the marks of his energies, his tragedies, and his triumphs." Fallen
into the bondage of sin, this world is nevertheless emancipated in principle by
Christ, who was crucified in order to break the stranglehold of evil, "so that
this world might be fashioned anew according to God's design and reach its
fulfillment." Since the world is involved in sin, man must approach it with
caution. In another context, therefore, the Council repeats the Apostle's warning, "Be not conformed to this world" (Rom 12:2), and immediately adds that
the world in this context means "that spirit of vanity and malice which transforms into an instrument of sin those human energies intended for the service
of God and man...." While the world is evil by reason of sin, it is also capable of redemption, and has in greater or lesser degree already been restored by
Christ.

As appears from the previous sections of this study, the term "Church" may
be understood either as organization or as community. In the former sense, it

is an institution distinct from other "worldly" institutions; it is a sacramental sign and agent of that saving unity of mankind which God intends to establish in Christ. In the second aspect, the Church is that portion of mankind which is visibly gathered into the Body of Christ and which lives by His Spirit. It stands where God wills the whole world to stand. The Church as institution prays and labors "that the entire world may become the People of God, the Body of the Lord, and Temple of the Holy Spirit...."

The Church exists, no doubt, in order to serve the world, but the service which it is required and equipped to render is a very special one. "The Church has a single intention: that God's kingdom may come, and that the salvation of the whole human race may come to pass...." Thus, before we can clarify the relation of the Church to the world, we must explain the notion of God's kingdom. Is it something to be realized in this world or in another? Is it achieved by man's labor or by God's intervention?...

Vatican II, therefore, points toward a middle path between a supernaturalism which would press the initiative of God at the expense of the proper activity of man, and a naturalism which would look upon the kingdom of heaven as a merely human achievement. This balanced position, which we have observed in the eschatological teaching of the Council, is likewise evident in its Christology, its ecclesiology, and in its doctrine concerning the states in life. We shall briefly touch upon each of these areas.

Whereas Church teaching in recent centuries has concentrated almost exclusively on Christ as Redeemer — that is, as saving man from a sinful world — the present Council goes back to the teaching of Paul, John, and the early Fathers in portraying Christ as the Lord of all things. Just as one and the same God is "Saviour and Creator, Lord of human history as well as of salvation history," ...so Christ is the crown of the order of creation as well as that of redemption....

The twofold relationship of the Church to the kingdom of God and to the city of man gives Christians a dual citizenship, both heavenly and earthly.... To some it will be given to show forth one aspect of this citizenship, to others another. The diversity of vocations and their fundamental unity of purpose are concisely explained in *Gaudium et spes.*...

As Hans Urs von Balthasar has maintained, the contrast between the lay and religious states in the Church is grounded in the twofold role of Christ as Son of Man and Son of God. Just as He fulfilled the dynamisms at work in the religious history of Israel and at the same time transcended them by a kind of dialectical negation, so the Christian life in its various forms must seek to express both the fulfillment of man's authentic aspirations and man's trustful self-surrender into the hands of a loving God. These ascending and descending aspects of ecclesial life are manifested respectively in the lay and religious states.

The special function of the laity, according to the Council documents, is to sanctify the world from within, in the manner of leaven.... 

In one passage of the chapter on the laity...*Lumen gentium* describes the function of sanctifying the world from within as a "consecration of the world."

The phrase has been criticized and is perhaps ambiguous. In the ordinary meaning of the term, as Père Chenu points out, consecration involves a withdrawal of something from the world order to devote it exclusively to God. On this definition it would make no sense to say that the world itself is consecrated. But the term is here used in a wider sense to designate a transformation of the world into the kingdom of God. The Church's work in the temporal order, insofar as it tends to lead the world toward its eschatological consummation, cannot be adequately described in the vocabulary of the secular. Just as the eternal Word of God, by His presence among men, may be said to have consecrated the world, so the Church, by sanctifying man's activity, gives the world a certain kind of sacredness.

The religious vocation, however, is more strictly related to the sacred. By its very nature it is a sign of the kingdom of God. Those who adopt a way of life according to the evangelical counsels, *Lumen gentium* declares, eloquently foretell the blessings of the resurrected state and show forth the powerful working of God's grace in this life....

The conciliar documents, however, avoid too rigid a dichotomy between the vocations of laity and clergy, or secular and religious. The opposition is in some respects more one of degree and emphasis than strictly of kind. The dimension of the sacred is to be found in the life of every Christian....

The ideal relationship between the Church and the world is, therefore, one of harmony within distinction. Until the ultimate transformation of all things, the world will retain a certain autonomy over against the Church. Created realities have a proper consistency of their own, and cannot be simply absorbed into the supernatural. We should not hope for the world to be transformed by some kind of cosmic transubstantiation into the Body of Christ. The Church and the world coexist in polar tension. Neither can get along without the other, but each retains its own nature and principles. The world will lose its way unless guided and sustained by the Church. But the Church will become ineffective unless it listens to the world. In our day, marked as it is by new and complex developments in many fields, it is particularly urgent for spokesmen of the Church to remain in close contact with specialists in the various arts and sciences....

Such a two-way dialogue may appear scandalous to those who still think in terms of the medieval hierarchical scheme, according to which the Church is related to the world simply as ruler and teacher. But in point of fact this scheme never corresponded to the true situation. The actual realization of Christianity, as Karl Rahner observes, is always "the achieved synthesis on each occasion, of the message of the gospel and the grace of Christ, on the one hand, and of the concrete situation in which the gospel has to be lived, on the other." For this reason Christianity, while it remains the same, is always different. To preach the gospel effectively, it is necessary to keep one ear open to the world. The Church cannot afford to ignore the world, any more than the world can afford to close its eyes to Christ and the Church.

Avery Dulles, S.J., *The Dimensions of the Church* (Westminster, Md.: Newman Press, 1967), 66, 70, 75–76, 80–82, 84–85.

## 89. Mary Daly and the Birth of Radical Catholic Feminism, 1968

*"When Vatican II opened new avenues of religious and liturgical experience for Catholics — especially Americans — it also tacitly encouraged them to study new theologians and to become aware of these new ideas [process thought, Rahner's work, political theology, the theology of hope, and liberation theology]," wrote the feminist theologian and religious historian Mary Jo Weaver, in her 1985 book,* New Catholic Women. *"Postconciliar theology was critical and prophetic, not dogmatic, and it is no accident that two of the most powerful feminist theologians in the Roman Catholic tradition — Elisabeth Schüssler Fiorenza and Mary Daly — are both fully conversant with the range and depth of continental theology."[1] The context also included the political realities of postwar Europe, the promise of Christian-Marxist dialogue, the political and social gains of the women's movement, the lay activism initially generated by Catholic Action and the theology of the Mystical Body, and the contributions of critical theory. "At the end of the 1960s," Weaver concludes, "it seemed tremendously exciting." Weaver quotes Mary Daly: "'It appeared that a door had opened within patriarchy which could admit an endless variety of possibilities.'"[2]*

*The Church and the Second Sex, Daly's first book, appeared in 1968 and signaled the presence of Catholic feminism as a force to be reckoned with in the academy and the church. Daly initially followed a conventional career path for a Catholic scholar, receiving her undergraduate and advanced degrees from Catholic institutions (B.A., St. Rose College, 1950; M.A., the Catholic University of America, 1952; Licentiate and doctoral degrees in theology, doctorate in philosophy, the University of Fribourg, 1961, 1963, 1965). She began teaching at Boston College in 1966. With the publication of* The Church and the Second Sex, *which led officials at Boston College to oppose the granting of tenure to Daly (a fight she won), she became a prominent critic of Catholic patriarchy and the patriarchal language that, she claimed, had hopelessly infected the Christian scriptures and church doctrine and ecclesiology (Beyond God the Father, 1973). Eventually Daly abandoned the church and what she calls "American sado-society," because she found them both to be irredeemably sexist. The following excerpt from* The Church and the Second Sex, *explores the myth of "the Eternal Woman," a cultural ideal constructed for the purpose, Daly argues, of keeping women in a position of subordination and submission to men.*

Although among the progressive Catholic theologians and writers there is an increasing trend away from the stereotypes, there has been a continual stream of Catholic works of a semi-theological nature, which are based upon the "eternal feminine" motif. Fundamentally, their authors are not at all disposed to abandon the ancient prejudices.... For the most part, these authors would keep woman on a pedestal at all costs, paralyzing her will to freedom and personhood. A classic of this brand of Catholic thinking is Gertrude von le Fort's book, *The Eternal Woman,* first published in Germany in 1934. Over one hundred thousand copies of the German original were sold, and the book was translated into French, Italian, Spanish, Portuguese, and English. Its influence

---

1. Mary Jo Weaver, *New Catholic Women* (New York: Harper & Row, 1985), 153.
2. Ibid., 154.

can be traced in a number of derivative works which perpetuate its basic fallacy, namely the confusion of "symbolic significance" with concrete, historical reality....

Such a project was doomed to be abortive, since it did not recognize the truth that man's symbolism is derived precisely from psychological, biological, historical, and social facts. Moreover, these facts are changing. Since Von le Fort and others of this school are fundamentally anti-evolutionistic as concerns women, they attempt to draw from contingent and changing situations certain "immutable" symbols and then to arrest the evolution of the situation by forcing it into the mold of these symbols drawn from past experience. This process has great attraction for a certain type of mentality (that of William James's "tender-minded" variety), which prefers easy metaphors to a critical examination of the facts of concrete experience. It is also a useful rhetorical method for those who have some psychological motivation, either conscious or unconscious, for attempting to preserve the *status quo*. Inevitably the writer is unable to stay on the high level of pure symbolism, and continually descends to the level of historical fact, making dogmatic assertions about what should or should not be the "role" of existing individuals, in order to keep them in line with the immutable symbols.

The characteristics of the Eternal Woman are opposed to those of a developing, authentic *person*, who will be unique, self-critical, self-creating, active and searching. By contrast to these authentic personal qualities, the Eternal Woman is said to have a vocation to surrender and hiddenness; hence the symbol of the veil. Self-less, she achieves not individual realization but merely generic fulfillment in motherhood, physical or spiritual (the wife is always a "mother to her husband" as well as to her children). She is said to be timeless and conservative by nature. She is shrouded in "mystery," because she is not recognized as a genuine human person. Thus, the poet Claudel in his preface to *Partage de Midi* wrote of woman that she is "someone on whose brow is inscribed the word 'mystery.'" It is, of course, the "symbol" of woman that these authors are talking about, but the symbol turns out to be normative for the individual. It is significant that the same alienating procedure is not attempted with the same degree of thoroughness for the male. There are only hints in the writings of the Eternal Woman devotees of what the Eternal Man might be. The androcentric society which engenders this type of speculation tends to see men, but not women, in personalist rather than in static, symbolic categories.

Characteristically, the "eternal feminine" school is radically opposed to female emancipation. For Von le Fort, the feminist movement had a "tragic" motivation. It was a result of the "dissonance which had come about in feminine nature." She imagines that prior to this time the home had offered the possibility of absolute fulfillment for the married woman and even for the unmarried woman. Unable to focus on the advantages of the movement, she writes of its "tragic drawbacks." For example, it is hard to get women "to do the work of domestic servants which is so rewarding and so naturally in keeping with woman's calling...."

A clue to the fears and motivations behind the opposition to emancipation can be seen in the repeated use of the term "masculinization." It is indeed characteristic of the opposition that it interprets woman's efforts to become more completely human as efforts to become masculine. Nicholas Berdyaev, for example, thought that the modern movement for the emancipation of women "seeks to lead them along masculine ways." This interpretation has been applauded by Catholic authors. Such confused thinking arises from the fact that in the past and still today many functions and activities which are quite naturally human and which have nothing specifically sexual about them have been appropriated by the males. Yet there is more involved than a mere naive confusion based on custom. This can be seen from Berdyaev's remark that the drive for emancipation is "an anti-hierarchic, a leveling movement." The opponents of emancipation have always wanted to keep the *hierarchical* form of man-woman relationship, which implies all the not all easily relinquished privileges of male headship....

Teilhard de Chardin tended to see woman as analogous to matter; man, to spirit; and matter is, of course, for the sake of spirit, which emerges from it. Subtly flattering to the male is the invariable tendency of the Eternal Woman school to describe woman strictly within the categories of virgin, bride, and mother, thus considering her strictly in terms of sexual relationship, whether in a negative or a positive sense. It would not occur to such writers to apply this reductive system to the male, compressing his whole being into the categories of "virgin, husband, and father...."

The healing of Christian antifeminism will require still other theological developments. It will be necessary that the institutionalist view of the Church — a root of many evils — be transcended. A theology which overstresses the institutional character of the Church tends to be preoccupied with defending positions held by authorities in the past and to close its eyes to present realities. It is wary of all attempts at development of doctrine, since change appears to weaken respect for authority. While the Church can certainly be considered as an institution, this should be balanced by an understanding of another side of its reality. What is needed is a more prophetic vision of the Church as a movement in the world, concerned primarily with betterment of the human condition, and seeking to cooperate with all who are striving for this goal. As this attitude develops, with its emphasis upon the work to be done rather than upon vested interests and personal and institutional prestige, women will come more into their own among the people of God. Both the Old and the New Testaments recognize that women as well as men have the gift of prophecy. As Christian theology comes to see institutional structures more in the terms of the prophetic mission of the Church, it will become evident that the exclusion of women from ministerial functions is unreasonable.

In order to create the theological atmosphere which we are seeking, it will also be necessary to develop an understanding of the Incarnation which goes beyond the regressive, sin-obsessed view of human life which colored so much of the theology of the past. Thought about this doctrine must become consonant with evolutionary awareness of modern man, welcoming and encouraging human progress on all levels as continuing the work of the Incarnation. It must encourage active personal commitment to the work of bringing about social justice and to creative work of all kinds....

As long as theology is obsessed with a conception of human nature as fallen from a state of original integrity, and considers that state to have actually existed in the past, it must be pessimistic about the present and the future. It tends to see human life chiefly in terms of reparation and expiation. As long as this is the atmosphere of theology, Christianity cannot fully recognize itself to be what theologian Karl Rahner called it: "the religion of the absolute future."

This static, sin-haunted view of human life reflects and perpetuates a negative attitude toward sexuality, matter, and "the world." In such an atmosphere antifeminism has thrived. To some theologians, "woman" came to personify all those aspects of reality which they believed should be feared, fled from, denied and despised. We have already examined some of the tirades of the Fathers against the "daughters of Eve." It is necessary to face the fact that there are warped attitudes deeply embedded in Christian thought which have continued to sustain the "daughters of Eve" theme, despite the fact that inconsistencies and absurdities should have been self-evident to reason....

We are now in a position to see that the healing of theology's built-in misogynism is related to the advancement of doctrine on many levels. Development of doctrine on one point does not normally occur independently. Advocates of progress on the women-Church issue should keep this in mind, if they hope to have deep and lasting influence. Since the roots of the disease are profound and complicated, again let us recognize that there are no instant cures. A constant effort should be made at seeing relationships, at sustaining a wide vision.

> Mary Daly, *The Church and the Second Sex* (New York: Harper and Row, 1968), 105–9, 111, 142–44, 146.

## 90. *Humanae Vitae* and the Rise of Public Theological Dissent, 1968–69

*A turning point in the history of the Catholic Church in the United States came in the aftermath of the promulgation of* Humanae Vitae, *Pope Paul VI's encyclical reaffirming the ban on artificial birth control — despite the contrary recommendation of a commission of bishops, priests, and laity he had established.*

*Among the prominent critics of the encyclical was Rev. Charles Curran, a tenured professor of moral theology at the Catholic University of America, a pontifical university chartered by the Vatican. On July 29, 1968 — the day that the encyclical was released in the United States — Curran flew to Washington and met with a group of ten theologians to study the document and devise a response. The group issued a statement which recognized the possibility of dissent from noninfallible teaching and concluded as follows: "Therefore, as Roman Catholic theologians, conscious of our duty and our limitations, we conclude that spouses may responsibly decide according to their conscience that artificial contraception in some circumstances is permissible and indeed necessary to preserve and foster the values and sacredness of marriage."*[1] *Curran was later placed under investigation by the Vatican Congregation for the Doctrine of the Faith (formerly the Holy Office); in 1986, Archbishop Hickey, the Chancellor of Catholic University, informed Curran that he was initiating the withdrawal of the canonical mission which permitted Curran to teach theology at the university. Curran was subsequently ousted from his tenured position.*

*The excerpt below is taken from Curran's initial response to* Humanae Vitae *in 1968; note his appeal to Vatican II's* Gaudium et Spes.

The Statement by Theologians takes exception to the absolute ban on artificial contraception proposed in *Humanae Vitae* primarily because of an "inadequate concept of natural law" which serves as the basis of the proposed ethical conclusion of the Encyclical....

Pope Paul's Encyclical *Humanae Vitae* explicitly employs a natural law methodology to arrive at its particular moral conclusions on the licit means of regulating births. The Encyclical admits that the teaching on marriage is a "teaching founded on natural law, illuminated and enriched by divine revelation...." The Encyclical then reaffirms that "the teaching authority of the church is competent to interpret even the natural moral law...."

The conclusions of the Encyclical receive their force, according to the Encyclical, both from the reasoning on which they are based and from the teaching authority of the Pope, which enjoys the special assistance of the Holy Spirit. In paragraph 12 the Encyclical states: "That teaching, often set forth by the magisterium, is founded upon the inseparable connection, willed by God and unable to be broken by man on his own initiative, between the two meanings of the conjugal act: the unitive meaning and the procreative meaning. Indeed, by its intimate structure, the conjugal act, while most closely uniting husband and wife, capacitates them for the generation of new lives, according to laws inscribed in the very being of man and of woman.... We believe that the men of our day are particularly capable of seizing the *deeply reasonable and human character of this fundamental principle.*" (Emphasis added.)

Though, in paragraph 28, priests are reminded "that obedience, as you know well, obliges not only because of reasons adduced, but rather because of the light of the Holy Spirit, which is given in a particular way to the pastors of the Church in order that they may illustrate the truth," nonetheless, natural law argumentation was employed in the Encyclical; and such argumentation contains certain defects.

*Failure to Admit Plurality of Natural Law Theories.* The reasoning in the Encyclical does not admit that there is a pluralism in understandings of the natural law and in the conclusions which can be derived from different natural law theories. The impression lingers in *Humanae Vitae* that the natural law is a coherent philosophical system with an agreed-upon body of content.

---

1. Charles E. Curran, Robert E. Hunt, et al., *Dissent In and For the Church: Theologians and Humanae Vitae* (New York: Sheed and Ward, 1969), 26; Charles E. Curran, *Faithful Dissent* (Kansas City, Mo.: Sheed & Ward, 1986), 17.

*Physicalism.* The notion of natural law employed in the Encyclical appears to involve a "physicalism" in identifying the moral act with the physical and biological structure of the act itself....

*Classicist World View.* The Encyclical appears to operate within the horizon of a classicist world view and does not take into consideration the more historically minded world view which is now perfectly acceptable, indeed more acceptable, to contemporary Catholic theologians....

*Rationale Excessively Deductive.* Since the Encyclical adopts a classicist world view and methodology, the natural law methodology employed in the Encyclical is excessively deductive and does not leave enough room for the inductive.

*Outdated Biological Conceptions.* The assumptions of the Encyclical seem to be based on an outdated biology. Biology in general, and the understanding of the physiology of human reproduction in particular, have changed greatly in the last century. It is quite possible that much of the earlier reasoning against contraception was based on what is now known to be inadequate....From a biological viewpoint, many acts of sexual intercourse are not truly open to procreation, since there is no ovum present. Perhaps, as one author suggests, the natural law in this matter would call for a randomness of sexual acts, a principle which would be specifically violated by rhythm....

*Single Act Analysis*...Modern biology...tells us that every act of sexual intercourse is not open to procreation. Should not the insistence be on the fact that sexual intercourse does have a relation to procreation, at least to the extent that it takes place within a procreative union? The danger exists today of many people forgetting the two inseparable meanings of marriage and sexuality, but one must also avoid the overreaction of stating that these two meanings are inseparably connected in each and every conjugal act.

*Insufficient Attention to Demographic Questions.* The Encyclical does not seem to give sufficient attention and weight to one of the most talked-about signs of the times — the question of overpopulation....

Different approaches to natural law and ethical theories currently employed in Catholic theology today would come to different conclusions on the matter of contraception. Three such perspectives could be described as: a more personalist approach, a more relational approach, and a transcendental method.

*A More Personalist Approach.* ...Personalism always sees the act in terms of the person positing the act and does not determine morality merely by an examination of the structure and finality of a given organ or faculty viewed apart from the person. The *Pastoral Constitution on the Church in the Modern World* realized that objective standards in the matter of sexual morality are "based on the nature of the human person and his acts...." Bernard Haering has shown how such a personalist approach would deny an absolute condemnation of artificial contraception.

*A More Relational Approach.* ...The natural law approach as found in the manuals of theology views nature as a principle of operation within every existing thing. Thus, man should act according to the design of God inscribed in his very nature, which is unfolded in his life and actions....Man is not a being totally programmed by the nature he has. Rather, man is characterized by openness, freedom and the challenge to make himself and his world more human in and through his many relationships. The human person is actually constituted in and through these relationships. Relationality thus characterizes man and his existence. Phenomenological and existentialist approaches view man as a being for and with others who is described in terms of intersubjectivity. A philosophy of *process* proceeds somewhat further in the direction of a more relational and historical approach to reality....

*A Transcendental Method.*...In general, transcendental method seeks to go beyond the object known to the structures of the human knowing process itself. According to Lonergan, the intrinsic objectivity of human cognitional activity is its intentionality. Lonergan's ethics is an extension of his theory of knowing. Moral value is not an intrinsic property of external acts or objects; it is an aspect of certain consciously free acts in relation to man's knowledge of the world. Man must come to examine the structures of his knowing and deciding process....Thus, Christian ethics is primarily concerned with the manner in which an authentic Christian person makes his ethical decisions and carries them out....Thus, a transcendental method would put greater stress on the knowing and deciding structures of the authentic Christian subject. Such a theory would also tend to reject the Encyclical's view of man and his generative faculties....

## Conscience as a Framework of Dissent

The penultimate paragraph of the Statement by Theologians maintains: "Therefore, as Roman Catholic theologians, conscious of our duty and our limitations, we conclude that spouses may responsibly decide according to their conscience that artificial contraception in some circumstances is permissible and indeed necessary to preserve and foster the values and sacredness of marriage."

The Statement by Theologians is not based on an unnuanced, universal moral principle that subjective conscience can be followed without moral wrong in each and every situation. In the total context, the Statement has indicated that in the matter of artificial contraception, there are sufficient reasons to reject the absolute ban on artificial contraception proposed in *Humanae Vitae*. Whether or not sufficient reasons are present in a particular case is a judgment that must ultimately be made by the conscience of the couple themselves as they try to weigh all the values involved in the situation. Such an approach to conscience is neither new nor startling for one familiar with Catholic theology; in fact, the same approach has been followed in the matter of responsible parenthood itself. The *Pastoral Constitution on the Church in the Modern World* recognizes that couples may "find themselves in circumstances where at least temporarily the size of their families should not be increased." The same Constitution affirms that "the decision concerning the number of children they will have depends on the correct judgment of the parents." Thus the Council document merely summarizes what all Catholic theologians would teach about responsible parenthood — parents do not have to bring into the world all the children they can possibly procreate but should responsibly plan their families in the light of all the values present, with the ultimate judgment in this case left to the honest decision of the couple themselves....

Catholic moral theology avoids any simplistic, absolute norm based on the rights of the individual conscience. Such an unnuanced universal norm would destroy the efforts of moral theology and Christian ethics which endeavor to point out the good, fitting and right thing to do. One cannot appeal merely to such an unnuanced moral norm to justify his actions. Some confusion apparently arises from a poor understanding of the *Declaration on Religious Liberty (Vatican II)*, but the declaration studiously avoids the technical term "freedom of conscience," probably because of the many simplistic understandings of this term....

Catholic moral theology has always tried to avoid subjectivism by holding that morality is based on reality. Today, newer epistemological theories are coming to grips with the problems of reality. Reality cannot be considered merely in terms of the objectivity of the object "out there." These newer epistemological approaches strive for a critical realism, which ultimately tries to overcome some of the simplistic, subjective-objective dichotomy of the past.

> Charles Curran, *Dissent In and For the Church* (New York: Sheed and Ward, 1969), 161–69, 189–91.

## 91. Against the Radical Catholics, 1971

*A common complaint of critics of the "radical" interpretation and implementation of the Second Vatican Council in the United States was that the radicals, or "liberals," were unrepresentative of the faithful — the people in the pews. The ordinary believing Catholic, the critics maintained, had no desire to diminish the authority of the church. The radical reformers, by contrast, were "elitists" — theologians with advanced degrees, writing for scholarly journals; the new liturgists, who were out of touch, the conservatives charged, with the everyday life of the parish; radical social action priests who rejected tradition and external authority. The conservatives delighted in pointing out that, despite the radicals' posturing against institutions, and their advocacy of the freedom of the individual, they were safely ensconced in those very institutions — colleges and universities, diocesan centers, urban ministry offices, and so on.*

*James Hitchcock, a layman and professor of history at St. Louis University, was one of the most prolific and incisive of the new breed of conservative critics — men and women who did not reject the letter of Vatican II, but who felt strongly that a number of abuses of the council were occurring under the guise of its "spirit."*

Radical Catholicism has developed from a projected antithesis between "persons" and "institutions" in which the Roman Church, representing pre-eminently the latter, is seen as basically unconcerned about people and consequently willing to inflict severe wounds on individuals who fail to conform. Many radicals proclaim their principal purpose as destroying, or at least drastically changing, the institutional Church, to allow free individuals to live as true Christians.

The obsessive concern with institutional authority which marks so much radical thought grows out of real and serious problems. But in another way the radicals' preoccupation with institutions is made necessary precisely by their lack of respect for the majority of believing persons. As reform has failed to arouse the general enthusiasm which reformers thought it deserved, and as it has failed to stimulate the deep and remarkable transformations which they expected, only a few reformers are prepared to admit their own elitist biases, the fact that where reform has failed this has often been because the reformer tried to impose changes which the masses simply did not want. Instead, in order to retain the myth that *aggiornamento* has been a great democratization of the Church, the reformer must insist that the hierarchy alone impedes change. Hence "institutions" can be blamed but not people.

The notion of "institution" which radicals employ is also a very impoverished concept. It seems to imply an Olympian, alien, authoritarian superstructure continuously imposing itself on individuals from above. On the contrary, the social sciences, as well as experience, suggest that it is extremely difficult and artificial to separate persons and institutions. There are often tensions between an individual and the institutions to which he belongs, but most often this tension is fundamentally between persons or groups of persons within the institutions, not between persons and an impersonal structure. In the Catholic Church this tension is a present roughly between progressives and conservatives, with the latter in the majority, and it is only by overlooking the personalities of the conservatives that progressives can see their problem as primarily lying with "the institution...."

This human dimension of institutions has been almost completely ignored by Catholic radicals. When Daniel Callahan wrote that the Church should totally rethink all her fundamentals, "giving no thought for the possibility of an institutional disaster; that is irrelevant where truth is at stake," he did not reflect that "institutional disaster" cannot help but include many human disasters as well — the large numbers of Catholics whose lives, in various ways, have been linked with the Church and who therefore suffer the same dislocations the institution suffers....

Since the Council, many conservatives have shown that they also possess a free faith, that as external warrant is removed from many of their values, as the authorities in fact discourage many of their beliefs, they are capable of resisting, of taking a principled stand dictated by inner conviction, even under some circumstances (as with the Catholic Traditionalist Movement) of rebelling against the hierarchy.

On the other hand, reformers also failed to sense the central importance of institutions in their own lives — what they mistook for an autonomous, free commitment often involved institutional supports which were merely more subtle than those of the masses. The great irony of so many radicals has been the fact that their anger towards the Church, and their alienation from it, seems to increase precisely as the Church becomes weaker and her oppressive powers all but disappear. They found the institution livable, if nettlesome, before it had reformed. Now, when there is almost no way in which the pope or the bishops can impose their will on independent-minded laymen, these same radicals dwell obsessively on the "repressive character" of the institution. As the priest-sociologist Andrew Greeley has suggested, many such individuals seem to need an institution which they can simultaneously hate and lean on. They demand to be treated as adults and to be freed from fatherly control, but often this freedom simply leads to deeper bitterness, uncertainty, and disorientation. For many the assault on the institution is perhaps primarily, if unconsciously, a test of the institution's solidity, and when it proves itself vulnerable the assailant himself suffers severe traumas. Many who leave the religious life, for example, seem to be prudently abandoning a sinking ship to look for a stronger institution somewhere else.

That the anti-institutionalism and anti-authoritarianism of the radicals should result finally in new forms of institution and authority should not be surprising to any but the most naïve romantics. History records the same phenomenon endlessly with respect to religious and political movements which promised to abolish tyranny and establish perfect freedom. Yet a good deal of contemporary radical thought is based on a dogma which is not even recognized as such, a highly dubious speculation which is taken as certainty — that the human race is undergoing a profound transformation which will eliminate the need for law, tradition, authority, and duty, that men of the future will live as totally spontaneous beings guided only by their own inner promptings and their concern for others and capable of freely willing and creating a world immensely superior to any yet seen. Montaigne's dictum, "He who plays the angel plays the beast," is crucially relevant here, for if this dream proves false it will result in moral and physical catastrophes of unimaginable proportions.

To some extent this dream has already been tested on a modest scale in the post-conciliar Church. Although this is still a transitional period, it has become obvious that the belief of many people that they could sustain their religious life outside the institution and traditions of the Church has proven illusory. One of the great human costs of radical reform has been the large number of individuals who have simply become cynical, disillusioned, and bitter, unable to relate any longer to the faith which they have inherited but even less able to find a new one. Some relive endlessly their psychic wars with the Church of their youth; others settle, disillusioned, into a blander and emptier life than the one they formerly knew — the ex-missionary who sells insurance, the former Christian Family Movement activist who now spends his evenings with television. This is by no means the whole story of *aggiornamento*, but it is a larger chapter than most reformers prefer to recognize....

Almost all knowledge is socially constructed, in the sense that very few individuals possess the security and courage to continue affirming ideas and apprehensions which society continuously denies, even if these apprehensions seem very real to the individual. The decline of religious faith, of a sense of the reality of God, is therefore a necessary result of the decline of the institutional Church. For the Church is a numerous, venerable, visible, and respected community of persons who publicly affirm, in a variety of ways, beliefs which in this culture are inherently improbable — God and the whole dimension of transcendence. As the institution shows itself vulnerable, as the individuals within it show themselves uncertain and groping, as many of its leaders abandon it, the beliefs and values which it has specifically affirmed become increasingly incredible. Those who are indifferent to the fate of the institution are, knowingly or unknowingly, also indifferent to the fate of religious belief, of historic Christianity. A lively sense of the transcendent — the mystical awareness which radicals sometimes oppose to the institution — is not likely to survive long in individuals if there is no public institution affirming this possibility in the face of widespread social scepticism....

If the old legalism encouraged certain states of false consciousness — salvation through rote obedience — the new "humanism" produces its own dishonesties, like spiritual and moral flabbiness masking itself as a free open-mindedness. Some radical clergy and ethicians seem unwilling to take a principled stand on any matter pertaining to personal morality; those seeking guidance are merely told to follow their own consciences. But when the conscience is confused and agonized the individual is inevitably seeking something stronger, and it is probably a mistaken liberality not to offer some kind of judgment.

The importance of traditions and institutions in the Church is intimately related to the need to extend the Christian witness over time and space. Without institutionalization — of belief, of piety, of organization, of love — the Church can never be more than an ineffective, ephemeral reality.

James Hitchcock, *The Decline and Fall of Radical Catholicism* (New York: Herder and Herder, 1971), 115–19, 129, 131.

## 92. The Real Gains in Ecumenical Dialogue, 1974

*The liberals and "radicals" fought back, charging the conservatives with attempting to undermine progress toward the implementation of conciliar reforms. Ecumenism — the dialogue toward establishing greater unity and understanding among Christians of different traditions and denominations — was an area of reform which did, in fact, move forward on the elite level, that is, among theologians and professional ecumenists. Significant gains were made, for example, in identifying and celebrating common ground between Catholics and Lutherans on justification by faith, between Catholics and Baptists on the centrality of the Bible, and between Catholics and Anglicans on matters of ecclesiology. Lumen Gentium, Vatican II's Dogmatic Constitution on the Church, acknowledged the work of the Holy Spirit in these and other Christian churches.*

*The question raised by success on the elite level was how deeply the new sensibilities and ecumenical spirit penetrated the attitudes and behaviors of ordinary Catholics, who had been raised to believe that Protestants were in grievous error and cut off from the love of God, potentially damned to hell, owing to their separation from the Roman Catholic Church. In the following excerpt, a liberal Catholic theologian reminds his readers of the progress enjoyed in ecumenical dialogues since the council, and chides those who continue to think of Protestants as standing outside the circle of the saved.*

In the earliest days of renewal and reform, teachers, writers, lecturers, and Church officials made great efforts to show the connection between the new and the old. This had the effect of diminishing the sense of fear which the changes, and predictions of change, were creating in the minds and hearts of many Catholics.

In most instances, the effort to maintain continuity with the past was both pedagogically sound and theologically responsible. Many of the changes could be regarded legitimately as a logical development of previous views.

This was not always the case, however. There were some changes in the Catholic Church's self-understanding which were achieved through leaps rather than through measured steps. The matter of ecumenism is the chief example.

In the years immediately preceding the council, we Catholics identified the Body of Christ with the Catholic Church alone.... Protestants were outside the Church because they separated themselves from the authority of the pope....

Indeed, we often accused Protestants of recognizing no authority at all, save their own private judgment which, we were quick to remind ourselves, could easily lead them into error....

Protestants could not participate in true Christian sanctity, even our sophisticated Latin textbook insisted, because they denied human freedom and held that we are justified by faith alone without works of charity....

In the worship of God, such groups are "guided more by sentiment and personal conviction than by the objective truths given to the world by Our Lord." Their founders "were not saints and generally were not holy and edifying men," and their communities "have not given saints to the world."

Their truths are "but fragments of the doctrines of the Catholic Church" and their holiness "is due to the means that the sects have salvaged from Catholic worship...."

There are many Catholics who have forgotten or were never aware of this "common teaching" regarding the Christian worth of Protestants and other non-Catholics. That is why, I should suggest, they do not fully appreciate the extraordinary advances gained at Vatican II (what I would describe as "leaps" rather than "measured steps").

On the other hand, there are still too many Catholics who refuse to admit that the council did, in fact, leap beyond these earlier views on the nature and composition of the Body of Christ. They pretend that we can operate on a business-as-usual basis.

There are some few newspapers, magazines, and newsletters operating under ostensibly Catholic sponsorship which discuss the ecumenical question as if the Decree on Ecumenism and related theological developments never even happened. Moreover, they sharply criticize any Catholic spokesman who speaks at all sympathetically of a given Protestant point of view.

Indeed, for some of these commentators the worst charge they feel they can level against a fellow Catholic is that his or her position is reductively "Protestant."

How can they understand the council's (and Pope Paul VI's!) acknowledgment that "men of both sides were to blame" for the Reformation (Decree on Ecumenism, n. 3)?...

How can they understand the council's admission that whatever the Spirit might produce outside the Catholic Church can contribute to our Church's own edification (n. 4)?

How can they understand the council's view that, while there must be unity in essentials, there is ample room for flexibility and pluralism "in the various forms of spiritual life and discipline, in the variety of liturgical rites, and even in the theological elaborations of revealed truth" (n. 4)?...

Since 1965 Catholic theologians and pastoral leaders have been in dialogue with their counterparts in the various other Christian churches: Anglican, Orthodox, Lutheran, Presbyterian, Baptist, Methodist, Disciples of Christ, and so forth.

Several of these bilateral conversations, as they are called, have produced consensus statements on topics of central ecumenical importance. While these statements are often restrained and measured in tone, they cannot obscure the major changes that have occurred in the pastoral and theological atmosphere since Vatican II.

On one controversial issue after another, the participants were able to outline significant areas of common understanding, even theological and doctrinal unity. Myths and caricatures collapsed in thundering sequence.

Contrary to the view of many Catholics that we and the various non-Catholic Christians are hopelessly divided on the question of the Eucharist, three of the dialogue groups (Anglican/Catholic, Orthodox/Catholic, and Lutheran/Catholic) claimed to have arrived at substantial agreement on the sacrificial nature of the Eucharist and on the Real Presence of Christ.

On these two issues, the Lutheran/Catholic statement concluded, "the progress has been immense. Despite all remaining differences in the ways we speak and think of the eucharistic sacrifice and our Lord's presence in his supper, we are no longer able to regard ourselves as divided in the one holy catholic and apostolic faith on these two points...."

And contrary to the views of many Catholics that we are also hopelessly divided on the question of dogma and doctrine, a very recent consensus statement emanating from the Anglican/Catholic dialogue group offers a set of principles by which our historic differences might be confronted in a more constructive and conciliatory way.

The Anglican/Catholic committee insisted that the goal of ecumenical dialogue is "not to produce statement of minimum essentials by which one Church can measure the orthodoxy of another, but to deepen, strengthen, and enrich the life of both."

The statement asserts, as a fundamental principle, that no formulation of faith can ever adequately express the mystery of God. This leads to a major practical conclusion; namely, the recognition "that Christians who are orthodox in their faith may express it in varying formulations."

The Decree on Ecumenism declared that "there can be no ecumenism worthy of the name without a change of heart." Change of heart means, of course, a kind of conversion. And conversion is never easy because it means, among other things, a repudiation of past sins.

We first have to admit those sins. There are still too many of us who cannot or will not.

Richard P. McBrien, *Has the Church Surrendered?* (Denville, N.J.: Dimension Books, 1974), 34–41.

## 93. David Tracy on Rethinking Theology within the Context of Pluralism, 1981

*Catholic theology prior to Vatican II was considered to be a rather straightforward process of searching scripture and tradition for warrants for, or evidence of, the official doctrines of the church. Theologians were, first and foremost, "church theologians." Vatican II rendered this understanding of the vocation of theology inadequate. As Father Avery Dulles wrote in his landmark postconciliar work,* Models of the Church, *church theology, owing to its almost bureaucratic allegiance to the institutional church, was lacking in creativity and originality. "A ... difficulty of the institutional model is that it raises obstacles to a creative and fruitful theology," he explained. "According to some critics it binds theology too exclusively to the defense of currently official positions, and thus diminishes critical and exploratory thinking" (44).*

*A new generation of theologians emerged in the wake of Vatican II. Disciples of the great conciliar-era theologians and philosophers such as Bernard Lonergan, Karl Rahner and Johan Baptist-Metz, they were students of history and epistemology, culture and politics. Above all they took seriously the reality of pluralism, the diversity of religious beliefs and worldviews born of different historical and cultural experiences. Our understanding of "the Christian story" and Christian symbols becomes radically transformed when we take pluralism, history, and the constructed nature of human language into account. Perhaps the most gifted American theologian of the postconciliar generation is David Tracy, a priest who spent the majority of his career teaching in a secular university, the University of Chicago, amid a richly plural student and faculty population. Tracy, a student of Lonergan, claimed that pluralism was the natural metier for Catholics, whose sacramental and analogical religious imagination opens them to the possibility of multiple perspectives on truth.*

The major aim of all systematic theology is to formulate a theological understanding of the originating religious event into a theological focal meaning. The particular focal meaning chosen for that theological understanding will prove an "essentially contested concept." More exactly, the ultimate incomprehensibility of the religious event itself as well as the inability of critical intelligence to master either situation or event will yield a recognition that all theological proposals are necessarily and intrinsically inadequate. Karl Barth spoke for all theologians when he stated "the angels will laugh when they read my theology." Any claim to final adequacy masks a manipulative spirit which does justice to neither the irreducibility of the original religious event nor the real but finite powers of critical, discursive reason. Yet a relative adequacy of a particular theology in a particular situation can be hoped for....

The ideal of conversation signals to the theologian that, even at this initial systematic moment of personal choice and interpretation leading to a formulation of the paradigmatic focal meaning for a systematics, the theologian is embedded in the history of a religious tradition expressing and communicating the event and the history of the effects of a particular cultural history now newly expressed in the contemporary situation. The choice and formulation of a focal meaning is always highly personal yet never solitary. The fact that most systematic theologies are also called "church theologies" only serves to underline the historicity of every theologian. Tradition as *traditio,* as the living reality of that event in the present, is the major concrete social, historical and theological power in every systematic theology. That religious event comes to us as the living reality of Spirit in the proclamations, manifestation and actions of an ecclesial community. The event may, of course, come more through some movement in the world than through an explicit church tradition. Yet even there it may come indirectly *as* church: as the living reality of the originating religious event in the world of history. The church as both sacrament of the Christ *and* eschatological sacrament of the world remains the primary concrete, social and theological locus of all systematic theologies.

Once a focal meaning is chosen and formulated, the rest of the journey of a systematic analogical imagination begins. For then each theologian strives — through critical interpretations of the core symbols in the full range of the Christian tradition and through critical interpretations of the realities of the contemporary situation — to find some ordered relationships for understanding the similarities-in-difference in the whole: the realities globally named God-self-world. By concentrating throughout this journey on a particular focal meaning to reinterpret both tradition and situation, each systematic theology risks its unfolding into a series of ordered relationships among the realities of God-self-world. The primary key to the order is provided by the focal meaning. At the same time, the understanding of the focal meaning itself is inevitably transformed by its exposure to the full range of the Christian symbols and the full range of questions in the situation. The reformulations of the focal meaning as the systematic theology unfolds are sometimes a clue to the relative inadequacy of the original choice. More often, the reformulations prove not negations but transformations of that focal meaning as the fuller realities of the symbol system and the further critical questions in the situation disclose themselves to the critical consciousness of the theologian. As the ordered relationships emerge in their demands upon the focal meaning, the initial insights into God-self-world provided by the initial formulation of the focal meaning are inevitably transformed. For example, a further understanding of both the biblical symbols for God and a contemporary philosophical understanding of the internal relationships among God-self-world may cause a particular theologian to shift from an understanding of the reality of God in "classically theistic" terms to a pantheistic set of concepts. As the fuller reality of a particular symbol is retrieved by some contemporary, situational rediscovery of a half-forgotten classical theme in the tradition, the focal meaning is also reformulated: as when the symbols of eschatology are released from their earlier individualism to societal, political, historical reality in order to disclose that the originating redemptive event is both always-already here yet always already not-yet here, not only to individual historicity but to history....

The reality of that Christ event is often refocused and constantly judged and corrected in contemporary christology through its concentrated focus upon the memory of Jesus of Nazareth....

What memories do we have of the actual Jesus? The memory of the one proclaimed in all the confessions and forms of expression of the New Testament, the memory lived in the discipleship of an *imitatio Christi* throughout the history of Christianity, the memory proclaimed in word and manifested in sacrament in the Christian church. Those memories — all of them — are what exist to impel every christology to attempt relative adequacy. What is that memory in the New Testament? It is the dangerous and subversive memory of Jesus — dangerous, above all, for the church which confesses it: the memory of the one who proclaimed the coming reign of God, who taught and lived the truth that God's cause will prevail for the future belongs to God; who acted with a radical love towards all — a harsh love, both judging and healing; who lived with a freedom which did not hesitate to unmask human pretensions or to take the side of the outcast. That memory is the memory of this Jewish layman, this Jesus of Nazareth, who taught and ministered, who met rejection at every step, who received the fate of crucifixion, who was raised and vindicated by God. It is the memory of this one person which freed the earliest witnesses to believe that the Crucified One lives amongst us, that Jesus *is* the Christ. The church's own memory of Jesus — a memory purified of early, late and present distortions by historical and social-scientific criticism, literary criticism and ideology critique, purified by the living praxis of discipleship and by the critical reflections of theologies — serves as the necessary focus for understanding and criticizing all christologies....

What Christians *know* historically about the "Jesus of history" they know, like everyone else, through the ever-shifting results of historical criticism. *That* Christians believe in the actual Jesus as the Christ comes to them from some present experience of the Christ event: an experience mediated by the whole community of the Christian church. What Christians believe about Jesus comes to them, above all, from the tradition witnessing to Jesus and experienced now as a fundamentally trustworthy source. *What* any particular Christian may believe or disbelieve in the traditional christological formulations produced throughout the long history of that tradition, they will ordinarily believe because of their fundamental trust in the tradition mediating that event and person, or will disbelieve as a result of some exercise of critical reason or some new experience of the Christ event in some new situation. Even the power to dissent is a power released by the freedom from and for the world disclosed in the very Christ event which the tradition mediates. History itself — for what is historical existence other than ethical life in a community and a tradition — can be trusted to sort out in the long run the truths and falsehoods for the Christian community, a community trusting in the Spirit's presence to it. The collaborative character of theology as a discipline can be trusted to sort out the theological aspects of those same realities in the short run of mutual, responsible criticism.

> David Tracy, *The Analogical Imagination: Christian Theology and the Culture of Pluralism* (New York: Crossroad, 1981), 421–23, 426–28.

## 94. The Incomplete Progress toward Ecumenism, 1988

*Not long after he authored the essay from which the excerpt below is taken, the Lutheran minister Richard John Neuhaus was received into the Roman Catholic Church and priesthood, where he became one of the leading U.S. interpreters and advocates of the pontificate of John Paul II. Neuhaus's personal journey, as he intimates below, would not have been possible without Vatican II's Decree on Ecumenism and, more generally, the Catholic Church's official embrace of the movement toward intra-Christian reconciliation. Nothing is more important to ultimate Christian reunification, Neuhaus insists, than the healing of the breach caused by the Reformation of the sixteenth century. And no communion is more crucial to that healing than the Roman Catholic Church.*

Surely no one should deny the monumental progress of ecumenism in recent decades, notably since the Second Vatican Council. The entrance of the Roman Catholic Church into the ecumenical movement of the century held, and still holds, the promise of revivifying the quest for the more visible unity of the Body of Christ. I wrote in *The Catholic Moment* that the most important "opening" initiated by the Council was not the much vaunted opening to the world but, rather, the opening to the entirety of the Church of Christ. There I spoke of Rome's "singular ecumenical calling" to take the lead in healing the breach between East and West, and the 16th-century breach between Rome and the Reformation. Some, both Roman Catholic and other, have viewed that proposition as excessively optimistic. But optimism has nothing to do with it. It is a proposition of hope and responsibility. Like every other aspect of "The Catholic Moment," it comes with no guarantees. The validity and the urgency of the ecumenical task do not depend upon our calculation of its probable success....

I would in no way suggest that all goes well on the ecumenical front. Some of our chief problems result, however, not from the abandonment of ecumenism but from its success. Hence my title, "Ecumenism Against Itself." It is a notable success of ecumenism that the wars of religion would seem to be definitively a thing of the past. With some exceptions, Christians no longer go at one another's throats, either literally or in theological polemics. Hostility has given way to mutual respect. Two decades of formal dialogue, most notably between Lutherans and Roman Catholics, have produced volume upon volume of solid theological convergence. Hopeful signs abound. In the last year, for example, the self-consciously conservative Ignatius Press published the adult catechism sponsored by the German bishops and approved by the Congregation for the Doctrine of Faith, *The Church's Confession of Faith.* That publication bears powerful testimony to the fruitfulness of the dialogue beyond the circle of academic theologians and professional ecumenists. In addition, consultations between Roman Catholic leadership and the leaders of other churches and communions have in many instances become almost routine. In a few years it will be hard to recall, if it is not already, the excitement once generated by a meeting between the Pope and the Archbishop of Canterbury or the head of the Lutheran World Federation. In sum, from parish to Pope, and at most points in between, it would seem that ecumenism is flourishing....

We should not be surprised, however, that new understandings also raise new questions. It is time to ask whether there is not a danger that the ecumenical successes now secured may lull us into a certain complacency about Christian unity. Put differently, it may be that the remarkable achievements on the way to the goal may blunt our sense of urgency about reaching the goal. The sad irony may be that the ecumenical successes now largely secured could result in making our divisions more tolerable. The increasingly pervasive spirit of understanding and good will can produce indifference to the continuing scandal of our disunity. The purpose of ecumenism is not that we be reconciled to our divisions, but that we be reconciled....

To be sure, complete and perfect communion with Christ awaits the final consummation. In the Christian life, both personal and corporate, there are many deficiencies in our communion with Christ other than the deficiency of ecclesial division. But ecclesial division is surely one such deficiency. And it is a painfully important deficiency, not least because it cripples the church's mission to be a visible sacrament of the unity of humankind. In communion — that is to say, in the eucharist — God has given a preview or proleptic sign of the genuinely new politics for the right ordering of the world. That sign is obscured by Christian disunity. Short of the end time, it seems almost certain that that sign will never be unequivocally transparent. Some divisions will endure and new divisions will occur. These considerations properly caution us against optimistic programs and schedules for ecclesial reconciliation. At the same time, they underscore the call to hopeful and determined effort in the belief that ecumenism is less a matter of prosecuting our program than it is a matter of obedience to the Spirit's leading....

Ecumenical good will in general is a virtue, but ecumenical understanding in particulars is required for ecclesial reconciliation. Constructive or positive differentiation makes ecumenism more difficult in some respects. It means that our churches must sustain quite distinct dialogues with many other churches and traditions. These dialogues do not necessarily advance in tandem. My own church, the Evangelical Lutheran Church in America, is currently sorting out its ecumenical directions. There are formal dialogues with the Orthodox, with Rome, with Anglicans, with Reformed Christians in the Calvinistic tradition, and others. There is no doubt that the relationship that is closest to...full communion is the relationship with the Anglicans. I share the view of many that the most urgent dialogue, because it is ultimately the most promising, is the dialogue with Rome. It is the most promising because the healing of the 16th-century breach between Rome and the Reformation would have the most wide-reaching and positive ramifications for Christian unity in the 21st century....

The Church of God is not yet what it is called to be. This is true in many respects, but, most pertinent to our subject, it is true in this respect: the Church of God is not visibly one, it is not at peace with itself, it is not in full communion, it is not the lucid eucharistic sign of the hoped-for unity of humankind. All these things the Church of God is called to be. We dare not despair of the church becoming what it is called to be, even when it seems an impossible possibility. Since the Council, it is evident that there is deposited in the Roman Catholic Church, and effectively at work in the Roman Catholic Church, the Spirit's impulse toward the unity to which the entire church is called. This gift is not found exclusively in the Roman Catholic Church. Indeed, were it only found there, it would inevitably be frustrated. Unity between our separated communities requires that we have in common the impulse toward unity, and what is required is given by the one Christ to his one church.

> Richard John Neuhaus, "Ecumenism Against Itself," *Theology Digest* 35, no. 4 (Winter 1988): 327–29, 331, 333.

## 95. Andrew Sullivan on Catholicism and Homosexuality, 1997

*As noted in the introduction to this section, Vatican II did not (could not) anticipate the full range of issues that Catholics would confront as a result of the new opening to the world, and to the human sciences in particular, which the council encouraged. The morality of homosexual love was one such issue. The question became prominent following the 1975 Vatican statement ("Declaration on Certain Questions Concerning Sexual Ethics"), which indicated that a homosexual orientation is not in itself a matter of choice and thus not sinful.*

*During the decade that followed, there was a great deal of ferment on the question in Catholic circles, with many American and British moral theologians indicating their willingness to reconsider the official teaching on homosexual love. (In 1985, to take just one example, the Archdiocesan Gay and Lesbian Outreach of the Archdiocese of Baltimore published* Homosexuality: A Positive Catholic Perspective. *The booklet was withdrawn from publication by the Archdiocese of Baltimore, though it was never officially repudiated.)*

*On October 31, 1986, however, the Vatican released a "Letter to the Bishops of the Catholic Church on the Pastoral Care of Homosexual Persons," signed by Cardinal Joseph Ratzinger, the Prefect of the Congregation for the Doctrine of the Faith. The letter warned that, following the promulgation of the 1975 "Declaration," some Catholics gave "an overly benign interpretation... to the homosexual condition itself, some going so far as to call it neutral, or even good." Cardinal Ratzinger noted, further, that while "the particular inclination of the homosexual person is not a sin, it is a more or less strong tendency ordered toward an intrinsic moral evil...." Special concern and pastoral attention should be directed toward homosexuals, the letter continued, "lest they be led to believe that the living out of this orientation in homosexual activity is a morally acceptable option. It is not."*

*Andrew Sullivan, a prominent Catholic intellectual who has written and spoken frequently on the challenges and dilemma of being a practicing Catholic who is also gay, offered reflections on Ratzinger's letter, some of which are found in the passage below, taken from his essay (later made into a book), "Virtually Normal."*

In a remarkable document entitled "Declaration on Certain Questions Concerning Sexual Ethics," issued by the Vatican in 1975 and released in the United States the following year, the Sacred Congregation for the Doctrine of the Faith made the following statement regarding the vexed issue of homosexuality: "A distinction is drawn, and it seems with some reason, between homosexuals whose tendency comes from a false education, from a lack of normal sexual development, from habit, from bad example, or from other similar causes, and is transitory or at least not incurable; and homosexuals who are definitively such because of some kind of innate instinct or a pathological constitution judged to be incurable."

The Church was responding, it seems, to the growing sociological and psychological evidence that, for a small minority of people, homosexuality is unchosen, is constitutive of their emotional and sexual identity, and is unalterable. In the context of a broad declaration on a whole range of sexual ethics, this statement was something of a minor digression (twice as much space was devoted to the "grave moral disorder" of masturbation); and it certainly didn't mean a liberalization of doctrine with regard to the morality of homosexual acts. "Homosexual acts are intrinsically disordered and can in no case be approved of," the declaration unequivocally affirmed.

Still, the concession complicated things somewhat. Before 1975, the modern Church had held a coherent and simple view of the morality of homosexual acts. It maintained that homosexuals as such did not exist; rather, it believed that everyone was a heterosexual and that homosexual acts were acts chosen by heterosexuals, out of depravity, curiosity, predisposition, or under the influence of bad moral guidance. Such acts were an abuse of the essential heterosexual orientation of all humanity; they were condemned because they failed to link sexual activity with a binding commitment between a man and a woman in a marriage, a marriage that was permanently open to the possibility of begetting children. Homosexual sex was condemned in exactly the same way and for exactly the same reasons as premarital heterosexual sex, adultery, or contracepted sex: it failed to provide the essential conjugal and procreative context for sexual relations.

The reasoning behind this argument rested on natural law. Natural law teaching, drawing on Aristotelian and Thomist tradition, argued that the sexual nature of man was naturally linked to both emotional fidelity and procreation so that, outside of this context, sex was essentially destructive of the potential for human flourishing: "the full sense of mutual self-giving and human procreation in the context of true love," as the encyclical *Gaudium et Spes* put it.

But suddenly, a new twist had been made to this argument. There was, it seems, *in nature,* a group of people who were "definitively" predisposed to violation of this natural law; their condition was "innate" and "incurable." Insofar as it was innate, this condition was morally neutral, since anything unchosen could not be moral or immoral; it simply *was*. But always and everywhere, the activity to which this condition led was "intrinsically disordered and [could] in no case be approved of." In other words, something in nature always and everywhere violated a vital part of the nature of human beings; something essentially blameless was always and everywhere blameworthy if acted upon.…

In one sense, then, the Church had profoundly deepened its understanding of the involuntariness of homosexuality, the need to understand it, the need to care for homosexual persons, and the dignity of people who were constitutively gay. But this was only half the story. The other half was that, simultaneously, the Church strengthened its condemnation of any and all homosexual activity. By 1986, the teachings opposed to the approval of homosexual acts were far more categorical than they had been before. Ratzinger had guided the Church into two simultaneous and opposite directions: a deeper respect for and understanding of homosexual persons, and a sterner rejection of almost anything those persons might do.…

How intelligible is the Church's theological and moral position on the blamelessness of homosexuality and the grave depravity of homosexual acts? This question is the one with which I wrestled in my early twenties, as the increasing aridity of my emotional life began to conflict with the possibility of my living a moral life. The distinction made some kind of sense in theory; but in practice, the command to love oneself as a person of human dignity yet hate the core longings that could make one emotionally whole demanded a sense of detachment or a sense of cynicism that seemed inimical to the Christian life. To deny lust was one thing; to deny love was another. And this dilemma forced me to reassess whether the doctrine made sense even in the abstract.…

Marriage is available to sterile couples or to those past child-bearing age; these couples are not prohibited from having sexual relations.

There is, I think, no rational distinction to be made, on the basis of the Church's teaching, between the position of sterile people and that of homosexual people with regard to sexual relations and sacred union. If there is nothing morally wrong, per se, with the homosexual condition or with homosexual love and self-giving, then homosexual persons are indeed analogous to those who cannot reproduce. With regard to the sterile couple, it could perhaps be argued, miracles might happen. But miracles, by definition, can happen to anyone. What the analogy to the barren suggests, of course, is that the injunction against homosexual union and commitment does not rest, at heart, on the arguments about openness to procreation, but on the Church's failure to fully absorb its own teachings about the dignity and worth of homosexual persons. It cannot yet see them as it sees sterile heterosexuals: as people who, with respect to procreation, suffer from a clear, limiting condition, but who nevertheless have a potential for real emotional and spiritual self-realization, in the heart of the Church, through the transfiguring power of the sacraments. It cannot yet see them as truly made in the image of God.

Andrew Sullivan, "Virtually Normal," in *Catholic Lives, Contemporary America,* ed. Thomas J. Ferraro (Durham, N.C.: Duke University Press, 1997), 176–78, 180–82, 184–85.

# Index